Aligning and *Balancing* *the* Standards-Based Curriculum

To Dr. David W. Champagne and Dr. James McConnell,
who inspired me as my professors, challenged me as my mentors, and willingly
collaborated in many professional endeavors over the last 30 years. This book is dedicated
to you both for your many years of friendship, inspiration, support, confidence, and good times.

Aligning and Balancing

the Standards-Based Curriculum

David A. Squires

Foreword by Fenwick W. English

CORWIN PRESS
A Sage Publications Company
Thousand Oaks, California

For information:

Corwin Press
A Sage Publications Company
2455 Teller Road
Thousand Oaks, California 91320
www.corwinpress.com

Sage Publications Ltd.
1 Oliver's Yard
55 City Road
London EC1Y 1SP
United Kingdom

Sage Publications India Pvt. Ltd.
B-42, Panchsheel Enclave
Post Box 4109
New Delhi 110 017 India

Printed in the United States of America

Library of Congress Cataloging-in-Publication Data

Squires, David A.
Aligning and balancing the standards-based curriculum / David A. Squires.
    p. cm.
Includes bibliographical references and index.
ISBN 0-7619-3962-8—ISBN 0-7619-3963-6 (pbk.)
   1. Curriculum planning—United States. 2. Education—Standards—United States.
3. Competency based education—United States. I. Title.
LB2806.15.S73 2005
375.'001—dc22

                        2004007964

04 05 06 07 10 9 8 7 6 5 4 3 2 1

Acquisitions Editor:	Faye Zucker
Editorial Assistant:	Stacy Wagner
Production Editor:	Melanie Birdsall
Copy Editor:	Elizabeth Budd
Typesetter:	C&M Digitals (P) Ltd.
Proofreader:	Mary Meagher
Indexer:	Sheila Bodell
Cover Designer:	Anthony Paular

Contents

Foreword

This is a book whose author has walked the walk, so the reader can find comfort and credibility as David Squires "talks the talk." The Squires Balanced Curriculum is what is known as a front-loaded approach to curriculum development. That is, Squires has one enter the curriculum development process by thinking about what ought to be in the curriculum first, and thinking about assessment second. This approach has a long history and tradition, not the least of which is Ralph Tyler's 1949 course syllabus at the University of Chicago, which asked curriculum developers to think about the needs of children and of society as a locus for creating goals and objectives to design learning experiences for children in classrooms. Tyler never had to worry about national and international standards, however, and current forms of assessment and accountability were not in place.

Squires has created a logical, step-by-step curriculum development process that is Web-based and that can lead not only to the creation of a platform of consensus regarding what ought to be in the curriculum, but also to a curriculum that is highly interlaced with broad-based foci of standards contingent on selection by the creating teacher.

The Squires model continues the tradition of centering on the teacher as the major defining agent within the curriculum development process, ensuring that the curriculum is not "teacher proof" but "teacher contingent." Curriculum alignment is also part and parcel of the Squires approach, within a broad band of standards selected by teachers at the outset. This model also includes continuing attention to updating the curriculum, ensuring that the curriculum "is a living document" that continually incorporates change.

In the kind of national assessment approach dominant today, a consistent, logical, and incremental curriculum model is best suited to deliver the kinds of results defined and embedded in those assessments. Questions of what is "best" are subordinated to demonstrating results within these assessment systems. Squires's approach assumes that schools and school districts will retain some forms of independence and autonomy within emerging national networks. As long as curriculum is delivered locally, this assumption remains valid. The teacher will always represent a major independent variable in curriculum delivery.

Finally, the work that Dr. Squires has done in moving the curriculum development process onto the Web has removed some of the tedium involved in crafting curriculum, making it "user-friendly" and open to the kinds of ongoing changes that make the promise of continual renewal of curriculum a reality. That in itself should ensure the reader that his or her time will be well spent in coming to understand what Squires means with the concept of Balanced Curriculum.

—Fenwick W. English
R. Wendell Eaves Distinguished Professor of Educational Leadership
School of Education, University of North Carolina at Chapel Hill

Preface

School districts face overwhelming challenges of declining resources coupled with increased expectations from state standards, high-stakes assessments, charters, vouchers, and "No Child Left Behind." A standards-based curriculum, developed by a school district's best teachers, may seem like a far-fetched solution to complex and interrelated problems. After all, curriculum does not have much of a history of making a difference. "Isn't it really just the right combination of textbooks and program initiatives along with dynamic leadership . . . if we could only get it right?"

After you read this book, you will know that creating a standards-based curriculum is the most cost-effective way to address standards, assessments, and "No Child Left Behind." This book is intended for school boards, superintendents, principals, school leaders, teachers, and university professors who are interested in addressing state standards in a comprehensive way and also in improving student achievement.

Research forms the foundation for the book's first section, which considers the following:

- Textbooks
- Standards
- State and standardized assessments
- The power of alignment

The second section of the book describes the structure used in this curriculum model (the Balanced Curriculum) and provides a unique and validated way to define the curriculum so that it is both useable and useful for teachers, principals, curriculum directors, and superintendents in their quest to help more students attain standards and higher test scores, while maintaining balance so the high-stakes assessments do not overwhelm teachers' innate good sense about what is most important.

Most of the book's third section is devoted to the use of field-tested practices in implementing, managing, and revising the curriculum to take advantage of new information from students' unit assessments, yearly assessments, and teachers' feedback so that the curriculum continues to play a central role in district and school improvement. A final chapter summarizes results from school districts and schools writing and implementing the Balanced Curriculum model.

Throughout the volume, vignettes based on experience in writing and implementing the Balanced Curriculum across the country demonstrate how teachers, administrators, and parents have conquered the challenges of the effective, but demanding, Balanced Curriculum model.

ACKNOWLEDGMENTS

Twenty years' work on a vision of curriculum playing a central role in improving district productivity happens only with significant support from a long list of people. People are listed with their position during the times we worked together; many are in other positions now. Here goes! From those who supported efforts of the Balanced Curriculum at crucial stages of its development:

- From Red Bank, New Jersey: Superintendents Dr. William DiMaio and Dr. Joan Abrams; Henry Olds, John Dorsey, and Wade Turnock, principals; Tina DeFalco and Joyce Wingerter, lead teachers; my secretary, Meg McCreesh; and the hardworking staff and teachers.

- From Far West Labs, Dr. Robert Burns and Dr. William Spady, who provided support and funding for a precursor to the Balanced Curriculum in conjunction with the Arizona State Department of Education.

- From Chicago, Vivian Loeseth of Youth Guidance, Dr. Bernie Spellman, Balanced Curriculum facilitator, participating principals and teachers.

- From Washington, DC, Dr. Marlene Guy, principal, the first school outside of Red Bank Schools to realize the potential of the Balanced Curriculum.

- From Cumberland County, VA; Harold Dodge, superintendent, Principals Janice Page, and Jim Thorton; Curriculum Director Julia Butler; Patricia Cox, curriculum specialist; Susan Absher, assistant principal, and all the talented and dedicated staff who wrote the curriculum, with special thanks to Dorothy Cosby, both principal and now curriculum director, for her vision and tenacity; and to Patricia Ceperley, from Appalachian Educational Labs (AEL), for her assistance, prodding, and dedication to the process, thanks to funding from AEL.

- From District 13 in New York City, Dr. Lester Young, superintendent; Sandra Bullock, assistant superintendent who helped me understand that it's all in the implementation; Deputy Superintendent Yvette Douglas; the many principals and teachers who worked tirelessly on behalf of students; and Cassandra Grant from the New York State Department of Education.

- For a trial run in Guilford County, North Carolina: Jeanette Gann, director of staff development; Debra Foster, principal of Western High School; Jeff German, principal of Webrourne Middle School; and Deborah Jones, principal of Hampton Elementary School; and the many teachers who wrote and implemented the curriculum.

- For a 2-year attempt in the San Francisco Bay Area: Dr. Marilyn Stepney, professor, San Francisco State University; Darcel Stockey, Oakland Public Schools; and Enomoiye Booker, in San Francisco Public Schools and the principals and teachers who worked with us under trying and difficult circumstances.

- From Newburgh, New York, Dr. Laval Wilson, superintendent; a most talented administrator, Dr. Philomena Pezzano, deputy superintendent; Mary Ann Joyce, director of curriculums; the funding miracle worker, Dr. Annette Saturnelli, in charge of funded projects; Marsha Soebel for her initial assistance in getting the project up and running in Newburgh; Olivia Henderson for constant support; and the curriculum directors, John Cafarella in science, Susan Libfeld in math, Gail Tramburillo in language arts, and Ken Mulé in social studies; for all the good will of the teachers who wrote and implemented the curriculum; and for the principals who led the charge for improvement in their schools; David Kikolar and Elaine Rosales who evaluated the Magnet Schools grant partially funding the work.

- From Parkland High School, Winston-Salem, North Carolina: Principal Harold Smith and the teachers who worked diligently to write the curriculum.

- From the Comer School Development Program at Yale University, Dr. James Comer, Founder; Dr. Edward Joyner, executive director, and all my friends who did so much to support the effort, including Dr. Valerie Maholmes, Dr. Faye Brown, Patrick Howley, Jan Stocklinski, Camille Cooper, Dr. Ann Levett-Lowe, Dr. Christine Emmons, Thomas Harbison, Sherrie Josephs, and the conscientious secretaries, Sara McIver and Etta Burke. Particular thanks goes to Michael Ben-Avie, who connected me with Corwin Press and provided editorial leadership while I was still at Yale.

- From Pontiac, Michigan: Superintendent Walter Burte, Assistant Superintendent Dr. Mildred Mason, Curriculum Directors Jesse Petway and Lorene Phillips, and the principals and teachers; and Dr. Michael Yokum for partially funding the effort through Oakland Schools.

- From Hertford County, North Carolina; Mr. DeLoatch, superintendent; J. Earl Norfleet, assistant superintendent, Patricia Hughes, director of staff development for all the support through doubts and changes in the central office; Valeria Cooper, Janet Jones, Jayne Wolfskill, and Phylis Bland for supporting the efforts in implementation; and the principals and teachers, especially the curriculum authors. Many thanks also to Sandra Jones, former assistant superintendent in Hertford, who originally sponsored and supported the project.

- From Tyler, Texas: Reba Schumacher for her tenacity in the face of great odds, Teresa Sturrock and Terri Hebert who facilitated the process with assistance from Becky Koestel, and the teachers who wrote and avidly supported the process.

- From Passaic, New Jersey: John Lockwood and John Kuca, curriculum directors in charge of reading and math, respectively, and the able and enthusiastic teachers who wrote the curriculum and the principals who saw to its implementation.

- From Englewood Cliffs, New Jersey: Philomena Pezzano, superintendent and backer in creating the Web site; Jeff Sourifman, principal and curriculum director for his tenacity and support; and the teachers who did a great job in writing and implementing the curriculum.

- For all those who led Balanced Curriculum efforts in other schools and districts, particularly, Nancy Oakley, Sandra Bullock, Dr. Lucille McEachern, Dr. Dawn Kelley, and Dr. Angelique Arrington.

- For three special friends whose support and friendship have enriched my life and whose encouragement started me writing this book: Richard Gahr, Bob Kranyik, and Kathleen Wishnick (whose dissertation in 1989 started my life in this direction).

- For colleagues at Southern Connecticut State University in the Educational Leadership Program: Dr. Brian Perkins, chair; Dr. Lystra Richardson; Dr. Bill Diffley; Dr. Katherine Magno; Dr. Henry Hein; Dr. Gladys Labas; and Dr. Peter Madonia.

- For Dick Schroth whose programming brilliance continues as the Balanced Curriculum Web site is refined, and to Jon Schroth, who, while still in high school, designed the "look and feel" of the Web site. For Vincent Oneppo, the talented graphic artist who designed the manuals customized for each site.

- For editorial assistance from Corwin: Faye Zucker and her assistant, Stacy Wagner, Elizabeth Budd for her editorial assistance, and Melanie Birdsall for assembling the book from the many separate pieces.

- My family, particularly my wife, Maureen, who suffered my absence as I worked in "the dungeon" on this book—all my love to my best friend; and my daughter, Allison, who read and critiqued some of the many drafts. Thanks for your support and inspiration.

PUBLISHER'S ACKNOWLEDGMENTS

Corwin Press extends its thanks to the following reviewers for their contributions to this work.

H. Lynn Erickson, Educational Consultant, Everett, Washington

Betty Steffy, Iowa State University, Ames, Iowa

Pearl Solomon, Professor Emeritus, St. Thomas Aquinas College, Sparkill, New York

David Champagne, Professor Emeritus, University of Pittsburgh

Michelle Barnea, Educational Consultant, Milburn, New Jersey

J. Allen Queen and the Instructional Leadership students in Admin course 6120 at the University of North Carolina, Charlotte, spring 2002

About the Author

David A. Squires is currently an associate professor working with doctoral students in the Educational Leadership Program at Southern Connecticut State University, specializing in curriculum, school reform, and organizational development. Previous employment includes the Comer School Development Program at Yale University; a stint as a central office administrator for over a decade in Red Bank, New Jersey, where student achievement improved from below to above grade level; a research specialist at Research for Better Schools in Philadelphia; a graduate research assistant in the Learning Research and Development Center at the University of Pittsburgh where he received his doctorate in curriculum and supervision with minors in language arts education and administration; and a high school English teacher in suburban Pittsburgh and inner-city Cleveland. He heads a consulting firm, ABC Education Consultants, LLC, which assists school districts to write and implement the Balanced Curriculum.

About the Balanced Curriculum Web Site

The Balanced Curriculum Web site is found at www.balancedcurriculum.com and is used to store curriculum information from participating districts. Use the buttons and blue hyperlinks available to learn more about the Balanced Curriculum process, services, results, articles, and staff at ABC Curriculum Consultants. Sample courses can be accessed by typing in DEMO as your user name and DEMO as your password. Then choose a course by clicking on "Select Course." To descend to the next level, click on any buttons or blue hyperlinks. Click on "Main Menu" to return to the home page.

Introduction

Curriculum, testing and teaching must change together to improve education. Unless all improve in concert, nothing will change.

—Steen (1989)

All children need equal access to a high-quality curriculum to attain standards. School districts' mission is to provide all children with equal access to a high-quality curriculum by marshaling resources and providing organizational structures and routines to meet these standards. The Balanced Curriculum process, a district-driven curriculum development and implementation model hosted on the World Wide Web, is a tool that facilitates this process. The symbol for the Balanced Curriculum process is a mobile. A mobile is in balance when all the pieces have a particular weight in relationship with all the others. Remove one piece, and the mobile is out of balance. Curriculum design is a similar process to designing a mobile. Each piece of the curriculum must be in appropriate alignment with the other pieces of the curriculum. Textbooks, standards, high-stakes assessments, teacher knowledge, and student development and entering competencies must be in balance so that powerful instruction results. As with a mobile, there are many ways to achieve balance in a curriculum.

Most school districts are not organized to provide for this goal. Most school districts do not have a curriculum, or have no way of ensuring that the curriculum is taught, learned, or assessed, or of managing the data gathered and used to improve students' and teachers' performance. Right now, curriculum is on the shelf, instruction is whatever the teacher wants to do, and assessment is a stressful event once a year, or once every 4 years, that teachers prepare for in their own idiosyncratic ways. Teachers continue to work hard with tools at their disposal. Not surprisingly, schools in these districts perform poorly, or improve lethargically, because no planned structure coordinates disparate efforts.

Districts need a plan for integrating curriculum, instruction, and assessment, so student performance, as defined by standards, increases in demonstrable ways. By aligning, balancing, and organizing curriculum, instruction, and assessment around existing standards, a school district can create a system to learn its way into a better future. In doing so, student achievement will also improve. The curriculum is the neglected tool of district improvement. Assisting hardworking teachers to understand, teach, and assess what is most important for students to learn is the key process to implementing a working curriculum. Every teacher making independent decisions is not democracy, but anarchy.

Picture the first-year teacher who receives the following from the principal:

- Textbooks, consisting of a student edition, a teacher edition, supplementary book of worksheets, a book of chapter tests and other assessments, and an enrichment manual
- Ancillary materials associated with the textbooks
- State standards
- National standards from professional organizations
- A class management guide for the standardized test
- Item specifications for the state tests
- Good wishes for a productive year with special attention given to raising test scores

The teacher leaves, lugging these resources piled two feet thick, and wonders how to make sense of it all when facing the class the next day. "Should I just use the 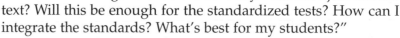 text? Will this be enough for the standardized tests? How can I integrate the standards? What's best for my students?"

Experienced teachers face the same dilemmas of balancing these competing demands. When under pressure, teachers may opt for content coverage over student mastery, leaving many students behind. Such individual teacher decisions about what to emphasize, made in isolation and with good intentions, may accelerate a school's lack of positive results.

This book outlines a plan for districts that want to ensure all children have equal access to a high-quality curriculum. These districts believe their best teachers (existing in-house expertise) can create an aligned and balanced curriculum with assessments that will quickly move the district toward higher performance. They already have the resources they need—excellent teachers who care about the development of their students and a plan for developing and implementing a powerful curriculum. The plan uses the latest Web-based technology to house the district's curriculum and assessment information so access is ensured, curriculum from other districts can inform the district's curriculum design, and a management system shows teacher's completion of the curriculum supported by vigorous staff development. The Balanced Curriculum Web site can also store student information on assessments.

The process of producing a balanced curriculum includes staff development activities whereby a representative faculty meets collaboratively, sometimes as a whole, sometimes as grade levels, or between grade levels, to arrive at consensus about what is most important to teach students (Squires, 1999). Teachers decide on the appropriate mix of their own ideas and professional expertise, perceptions of students' developmental needs, existing curriculum and instructional program, textbooks, the views of experts in the field, national standards, district and state goals and frameworks, and the content and format of standardized tests. In deciding what is most important to teach students, teachers coordinate decisions between grade levels or courses so that the school's curriculum makes sense as a whole both vertically and horizontally. They use results of unit and standardized assessments to help the school and district improve. If districts devote a majority of their staff development time to the process, completion of the writing of the Balanced Curriculum is possible in 2 months to a year.

The goal of the Balanced Curriculum is to ensure all students equal access to a high-quality curriculum. To meet the goal, it is necessary to describe what

I mean by a high-quality curriculum. Three levels—courses, units, and significant tasks—describe the curriculum. Significant tasks form the heart of the Balanced Curriculum process. Significant tasks link descriptions of complex activities with language from the standards and assessments. All teachers use the significant tasks as a basis for 60% of their instruction in each unit.

Next, the significant tasks are aligned with standards and high-stakes tests. Teacher–curriculum authors examine the results of the alignment and determine if the significant tasks are balanced. They ask whether each standard or assessment has appropriate balance within the structure of the significant tasks and modify the significant tasks accordingly. This guarantees that the curriculum is standards- and assessment-based and therefore of high quality.

After balancing the curriculum, developing the assessments follow. Teachers assess each student on each significant task, generating data by which all children's success can be judged. For each unit, students receive practice on high-stakes test formats. This ensures that students can demonstrate their knowledge using the test formats. Districts also have data to use for further curricular improvement.

Districts must create a staff development plan for implementation because all teachers will use the significant tasks described in the curriculum. Staff development and administrative support assist teachers in making a transition from a "do-your-own-thing" curriculum. Grade-level or subject-area meetings can then be used to support implementation of the significant tasks. Curriculum management through teacher record keeping on the Web ensures that administrators, teachers, and students are making progress in teaching and learning the curriculum. Teachers record significant task completions ensuring that all students receive equal access to the curriculum. High levels of implementation help ensure improved results for students (Squires & Bullock, 1999). Results of student assessment can also be captured to determine whether students are, indeed, performing to high standards.

Yearly revision captures teachers' learning in decisions about where tests and other assessments show need for improvement. To keep improving the curriculum, changing 20% of the significant tasks is necessary on a yearly basis. Experienced teacher–curriculum authors can revise a K–12 subject-area curriculum in a few days of summer work.

In development for the past 20 years, and in conjunction with the Comer School Development Program at Yale University, the Balanced Curriculum process has improved students' achievement in schools and districts around the country (see Chapter 20, "The Results So Far"), although experience indicates better success in completing the process with districtwide rather than with schoolwide implementation. Indeed, student achievement has improved in all schools or districts that both developed *and* implemented the Balanced Curriculum process. A summary of the Balanced Curriculum model follows.

1. Describe the curriculum
   - Courses
   - Units
   - Significant tasks
     - Descriptions of complex activities linked to standards and assessments
     - All teachers teach the significant tasks

2. Align and balance the curriculum
   - Standards
   - High-stakes tests
   - Textbooks

3. Assess the curriculum
   - Teachers assess each student for each significant task
   - Provide practice on high-stakes test format

4. Manage curriculum implementation
   - Introducing the curriculum
   - Teacher and student completion of significant tasks
   - Student performance on assessments of significant tasks

5. Construct staff development plans, and revise the curriculum yearly
   - Use teacher comments on significant tasks and assessments
   - Student performance on high-stakes test
   - Student performance on significant tasks
   - Revise 20% of the significant tasks each year
   - On the basis of test performance and curriculum revisions, construct staff development plans for the following year for schools and the district.

The initial chapters of the book cover tools for improvement, including textbooks, standards, standardized tests, alignment, and curriculum structure. The section concludes with a more in-depth examination of the Balanced Curriculum process.

The text continues by walking the reader through developing a curriculum that is aligned and balanced to standards, standardized tests, and curriculum-embedded tests using district-based teacher-experts. The curriculum development process is described in chapters on identifying components of a good subject-area program; developing courses, units, and timelines; deciding which standards to assign to courses; generating and validating significant tasks; aligning the curriculum; balancing the curriculum; and developing format and content assessments.

The final chapters of the book describe processes for implementing, managing, and revising the Balanced Curriculum with particular attention paid to using the Balanced Curriculum to inform school and district staff development needs, concluding with a chapter on results.

The first chapter focuses on textbooks as a tool for curriculum development and concludes that textbooks should be used as a resource for instruction, but not as a substitute for curriculum.

Section I

Curriculum Tools and Concepts

Textbooks, Standards, Alignment, and Standardized Testing

Today's curriculum authors need to understand how curriculum, instruction, and standards can work together so that students will know and be able to use important content. Chapter 1 provides one vision of how these important curricular components make sense as a whole. Curriculum authors also need to understand and capitalize on the strengths and weaknesses of textbooks, the complexity of standards, the conundrums of standardized testing, and the importance of alignment. The rest of the section provides research-based information on each of these areas so that curriculum authors and those directing curriculum development can weigh these influences to produce a balanced curriculum.

1

Curriculum, Instruction, Assessment, and Standards

I n this chapter, curriculum is defined so that readers can have a shared understanding of this key term. Next, we examine approaches to curriculum that schools use to address standards and high-stakes testing as a way to discuss the interrelationships of curriculum, instruction, assessment, and standards. I suggest why these approaches may not work over the long term and propose a model demonstrating how the balanced curriculum integrates curriculum, instruction, assessment, and standards.

CURRICULUM: WHAT IT IS AND WHAT IT IS NOT

Curriculum describes (in writing) the most important outcomes of the schooling process; thus, the curriculum is a document in which resides the district's "collected wisdom" about what is most important to teach. When reviewing book titles or chapter headings in a textbook, the titles summarize the most important concepts covered by the textbook, just as unit titles or courses in the curriculum indicate the most important ideas to be taught.

Curriculum is based on standards; as a result, curriculum and standards are linked. Curriculum specifies how standards are met. Standards are not the curriculum. Rather, standards provide a vision of the appropriate content and processes (usually for a subject area, such as mathematics) by outlining what students should know and be able to do across a range of grade levels. Curriculum is more specific than the standards. Whereas standards usually describe appropriate content and processes for a range of ages or grade levels, curriculum specifies what should happen during a shorter period of time, such as a year, quarter, or a month. Decisions about what is most important to teach and learn should be made with the standards in mind. Furthermore, a good curriculum documents the alignment process and balances the curriculum in reference to the standards.

A curriculum is the plan that focuses and guides classroom instruction and assessment. For example, if a social studies curriculum specifies a unit on World War I, teachers need to instruct on World War I and not the Great Depression or current events. Even though those topics are valuable, having a unit on World War I in the curriculum says that learning about World War I has the most value. Students, therefore, should spend time learning about World War I.

If the curriculum focuses on World War I, then the classroom assessment also needs to focus on World War I. In this way, the curriculum, the curriculum-embedded assessment, and the instruction are aligned with each other. Assessments answer the question of how much knowledge and skill are good enough to meet the standards aligned in the unit. Teachers use assessments to determine how good is good enough. Classroom assessment is inexorably linked to the curriculum.

Curriculum sequences the outcomes so they build on each other. This ensures that students have the prerequisite skills necessary for success on the next unit or grade level. Although a sequential order may not be inherent in every discipline, a curriculum can overcome problems of sequence. For example, for mathematics, automaticity in number facts is a prerequisite to fluent application of multiplication or long division algorithms. Curriculum can provide a sequential plan for instruction that specifies student memorization of number facts before going on to multiplication or division algorithms.

High-stakes tests and state standards influence curriculum design. To be fair to students, content and skills assessed on high-stakes tests need to be covered in the curriculum, requiring curriculum decisions to be aligned and balanced with these tests. In this way, the weight given to the standardized tests' content and skills is appropriate given other influences on the curriculum, such as student development. High-stakes tests are linked to the curriculum and influence its design, but they are not the only influence.

The curriculum plan is rooted in students' human development. Some view curriculum as the district's plan for student development. This expands the scope of curriculum. For example, if we know that 5th-grade students wrestle with the issue of fairness (see *Nothing's Fair in Fifth Grade* by Barth DeClements), then part of a 5th-grade curriculum might directly address this developmental task through discussions of rules or examination of literature that deals with fairness issues. When curriculum is designed to meet many different criteria, such as informing developmental tasks as well as fitting into a state-prescribed scope and sequence, the curriculum is strengthened.

Curriculum is discipline based. Subject areas (English, mathematics, social studies, science, and the arts) drive curriculum. Disciplines encapsulate different ways of seeing and knowing the world. A geologist sees a grain of sand differently from a poet. A curriculum is a plan for helping students to understand the differences in the ways various disciplines view the world.

Curriculum applies learning theory to instructional design. For example, we know from learning theory that paced practice is generally better than massed practice. So, to practice for high-stakes tests, we know that it is better to practice over a longer period of time than to practice a large amount over a shorter period of time. One-month review sessions before high-stakes testing is a misapplication of learning theory. Curriculum can help to institutionalize appropriate applications of learning theory and instructional design and provide a structure for eliminating instructional practices that do not make sense. In the Balanced Curriculum, periodic assessments give students practice on the format of high-stakes tests throughout the year, not just a month before testing.

Curriculum development and implementation is the province of the district, not the school. Schools generally do not have the capacity to develop their own curriculum, just as individual teachers find it difficult to invent a curriculum if none is provided. Furthermore, by law, districts are generally charged with developing and implementing a curriculum. When districts abdicate this responsibility, schools, students, and families suffer. In the Comprehensive School Reform Design, for example, schools could apply for money to implement one of many school reform models. In some districts, many models were adopted, leaving the district to try to manage and understand many different approaches to what is most important to teach students. This further fragmented and complicated the district's responsibility for authoring and implementing a strong curriculum.

Curriculum is not standards, tests, textbooks, or programs. Standards tell what is important for students to know and be able to do, but they don't tell a district's teachers how the standards should be met (see Chapter 3). Tests, both standardized and state developed, are not the curriculum. Tests are designed to sample a small portion of students' knowledge. From that sample of knowledge, tests are designed to support inferences about how much students know (see Chapter 4). For example, if I get the only two problems dealing with multiplication correct on a test, the testing entity assumes that I probably know how to multiply. Tests are limited by the number of concepts and applications that can be covered in a short testing period, which restricts the number of topics that can be adequately "tested" so the inferences are valid. Tests, then, contain only a small but important subset of what students need to know and be able to do. High-stakes tests are not the curriculum.

Just as tests are limited, textbooks are too broad in scope to be considered a curriculum (see Chapter 2). Textbooks, given market forces, are designed to be all things to all teachers and students. In most textbooks, complete coverage of the textbook is impossible. So teachers pick and choose what is most important for their students or what they like most. Teachers using the same text cover content differently. Generally, little coordination happens among teachers within a school, let alone coordinating what happens across a district using the same textbook series. Districts that assume the textbook is the curriculum have difficulty knowing or controlling what students learn as different teachers' decisions to cover different content in the text leaves the next year's teacher with no standard expectation of what was most important for students to know and be able to do.

Programs are not the curriculum. Generally, programs address pieces of what should be in a curriculum. Districts who rely on adopting a series of programs as a way of meeting standards or assuring high quality may underestimate the difficulty of stitching programs together in an integrated whole. For example, a handwriting program may be adopted as a way to structure and sequence instruction.

If the handwriting program requires a half-hour a day of a 2-hour language arts block, the time requirement may be too much. As a result, other parts of the language arts program, such as spelling, literature study, or phonemic awareness, might suffer as teachers make decisions to implement the handwriting program in the time period specified.

TEACHER AUTONOMY AND THE ROLE OF CURRICULUM

The dilemma for districts is to strike a balance between teacher autonomy and curriculum specificity. The diagram in Figure 1.1 indicates that teachers will have less autonomy when the curriculum is more specific. With no curriculum, teachers have complete autonomy to teach whatever they want. Conversely, a very specific curriculum that indicates what should be taught, how it should be taught, and when it should be taught leaves teachers with less autonomy.

Generally, districts have given teachers more autonomy with little curriculum guidance. High-stakes testing and standards then enter the picture. Districts try to use the high-stakes testing and standards as a basis for limiting teachers' autonomy so the appropriate content is addressed. The tool of curriculum was little used in the past; if it was used, it was constructed in such a way that it did little to limit teacher autonomy, and the curriculum atrophied. Now, districts don't see curriculum as the tool to make sure there is balance when addressing standards and high-stakes tests. District leadership may not want to be more specific about the curriculum because of the "infringement" on teacher autonomy. Yet they want the standards and high-stakes tests covered. Instead of using curriculum to decide what is most important to teach and learn, including standards and tests, districts abdicate their responsibility by saying teachers must cover what is on the test, and the rest is left up to teacher discretion.

To bring all students to high standards, districts need to examine their stance on curriculum. We know most students can learn if they are taught. Curriculum's

Figure 1.1   Teacher autonomy and curriculum specificity

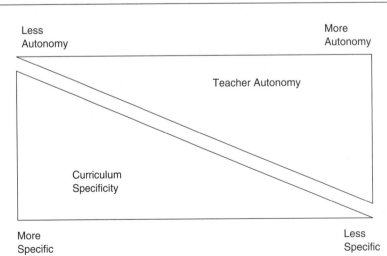

Less Autonomy

More Autonomy

Teacher Autonomy

Curriculum Specificity

More Specific

Less Specific

purpose is to help teachers understand and deliver to students what is important for students to learn, and districts need to decide what this is. Curriculum is *the* tool available to balance competing priorities. The Balanced Curriculum process provides a template for a district-developed curriculum, within which teachers have quite a bit of flexibility.

WHY IS CURRICULUM IMPORTANT?

Curriculum is the container that holds the institutional knowledge of what was the best of past instruction. The curriculum being used now is what the district has decided is the best of the past. Curriculum, viewed in this way, is a historical document.

Curriculum is also a plan for the present. The curriculum is the district's bet that the written mix of standards, content, and skills covered in the curriculum will produce better results for students. Curriculum represents the district's bet on how to improve in the future. Curriculum, while rooted in the present, takes the best of the past to make the future better.

Nothing else in the arsenal of school reform can take the place of deciding how best to structure and sequence what is most important for students to know and be able to do so that students can and will succeed. Students need equal access to high-quality instruction. The job of curriculum is to provide teachers a structure for instruction so that they can balance the often competing forces of standards, tests, textbooks, and programs. The curriculum provides the structure for management of teaching and learning as well as staff development. Without a curriculum's structure, there is chaos.

DISTRICTS' RESPONSES TO STANDARDS AND HIGH-STAKES TESTS

In this section, I examine different district responses to standards and high-stakes testing. To understand curriculum's centrality to school and district improvement, curriculum must be seen in relationship to other tools used in school, such as standards, assessments, and instruction. To understand the variety of possible relationships, typical district responses to standards and high-stakes testing are outlined. The descriptions that follow are a typology of districts' responses to standards and high-stakes tests. We identify the approaches as *Tell Them, Show Me, Test Them,* and *Keep Up the Pace.*

Tell Them

Some districts assume that if teachers have staff development on the standards and high-stakes test, then their instruction will be appropriate for covering standards. The following diagram shows that state standards influence the content of high-stakes test, which, in turn, influences instruction in classrooms. It also assumes that if teachers know the standards, the standards will be incorporated in their instruction.

State
Standards ⟶ High-Stakes Test ⟶ Instruction

One study questions the assumption that telling teachers will change behavior. The study examined the topics teachers covered in the classroom and aligned them with the topics on the standardized test (Brady, Clinton, Sweeney, Peterson, & Poynor, 1977). The range of topic coverage on the standardized test ranged from 4% to 95%. This indicates that, left to their own judgment, some teachers will cover most of the topics and some will cover very few. Teachers are not likely to change their range of coverage based on an overview of standards.

Some districts create district standards to tell teachers the standards that should be covered at particular grade levels. District standards often take the grade range of state standards (K–4, 5–8, or 9–12) and segment them into grade-level expectations. In this case, our model looks like:

District
Standards ⟶ High-Stakes Test ⟶ Standards ⟶ Instruction

Often district standards do not specify when or how during the year the standards should be taught, narrowing the playing field a little but leaving room for individual teachers to develop their own instructional strategies.

Show Me

Some districts' response to high-stakes testing and standards is to provide some staff development on the standards and then require that teachers list the standards on their lesson plans. In this way, teachers have aligned the instruction with the standards and with the high-stakes test, a derivative of the standards.

Instruction
Standards ⟶ High-Stakes Test ⟶ Lesson Plans

This guarantees that most instruction is aligned to some standards. The district, however, has no information on what is taught or whether students have grasped the concepts because the teachers and the district have no way of aggregating this alignment data. An unanswered question for this model is, "Did the teachers miss important standards?"

Test Them

Other districts decide on creating internal tests aligned with the high-stakes tests and assume that the emphasis on local testing will help teachers focus their instruction. Districts with this approach do not know how the teachers changed instruction because a management system is not in place. Another variation on this theme is to determine "exit" performances for students graduating at particular grade levels. For example, students are required to write a paper defending a point of view and present the results to an audience of those outside the school. Such an internal assessment may or may not be aligned with standards and high-stakes tests.

Standards ⟶ High-Stakes Test ⟶ Internal Assessment ⟶ Instruction

With the addition of internal assessment to the model, the district now has results of the internal assessment that gives teachers and the district feedback on how well their students do on a test similar to the high-stakes test (if there is alignment between the district test and the high-stakes test).

Show Me–Test Them

A diagram showing a combination of Show Me and Test Them strategies follows. The district created internal assessments and requires teachers to align standards to lesson plans. This exerts two forces for application of the standards and high-stakes test to instruction: the alignment of lesson plans and the assumption that another assessment in addition to the high-stakes test will focus instruction.

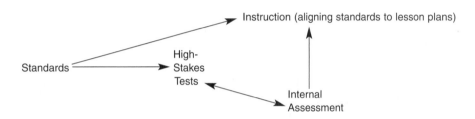

A few difficulties arise in this model. First, not all standards show up on high-stakes tests. Unless teachers know the standards tested, aligning lesson plans with standards may miss the emphasis of the high-stakes test. Second, aligning standards with lesson plans tells the standards that individual lessons address but does nothing to indicate whether, over time, some standards were left out or some were over-addressed—a matter of balance. Third, this model overemphasizes the high-stakes test by creating an internal assessment aligned with the high-stakes test. Teachers now have important pieces of data: one from the district, the other from the state, all focused on the rather narrow content of the high-stakes test. Fourth, teachers will respond to this emphasis on testing by narrowing their instruction to cover only concepts on the high-stakes test. Indeed, the district is trying to control instruction by creating emphasis on assessments. (There may be better ways to control instruction.) Fifth, as the district has no curriculum, the district does not know what is taught, or should be taught, in the classroom, except that teachers follow a certain textbook. The district is betting that by providing internal assessments and requiring that teachers align lesson plans with standards, teachers will figure out what is most important to teach.

Keep Up the Pace

Pacing guides assist teachers in making decisions on how much time should be spent on a particular area or topic. The pacing guides can tell what the topic is, give a list of standards (or objectives) that need to be covered, or show the pages in the textbook that should be covered.

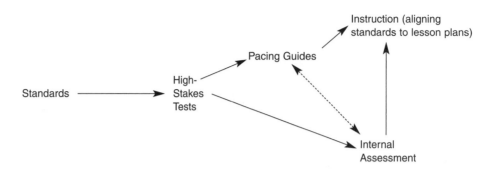

Pacing guides provide more information to teachers about what to teach and when to teach it. It is hoped that the pacing guides and the internal assessment have been aligned so that students are not required to be tested where instruction has not been provided. Pacing guides do not tell whether teachers followed them because they generally are not correlated with aligning lesson plans with standards.

All these models lack a way to know what students are learning or what has been taught because the models have no way to manage this information. Use of pacing guides may not be monitored. Alignments in lesson plans are not aggregated across time. The data from internal assessments is not in a form that can be easily used by teachers in their instructional planning. The information these systems generate is not used to further learning.

All of these models ignore curriculum as a way to help teachers and administrators understand what is most important to teach, although the pacing guide (depending on its design) approaches telling teachers the general content of what to teach and the amount of time available for a topic's instruction. Curriculum can tame the chaos of standards and high-stakes testing.

Curriculum is the lead singer, and instruction, assessment, and standards are the quartet, backed up by the management and staff development chorus. The model in Figure 1.2 incorporates ideas from the other models, but curriculum is at the center as a way to mediate high-stakes tests and state standards so that instruction produces strong results, monitored by management and supported by vigorous staff development. Curriculum's job is to decide how to incorporate the standards and high-stakes testing in the instruction and internal assessment of a school district.

Curriculum is a guide for teachers and administrators on what is most important to teach and test. Curriculum is the point at which district and state standards and high-stakes assessment are balanced with the needs of students and teachers and the materials available to teachers. Curriculum provides a cycle of conversation about what is planned for students, how well teachers deliver on that plan, and how well students achieve; it provides a structure for institutionalizing the important results of the conversation. The curriculum is the aggregate written wisdom of the district on its approach to standards and high-stakes assessment.

District and state standards and high-stakes tests create important touchstones for the curriculum. They provide parameters for teachers' decisions about what to teach and test. The curriculum is a written guide for teachers and administrators that explains how the standards should be implemented. It is action oriented and student focused.

The arrows linking curriculum to instruction and assessment are double headed, indicating that information about the curriculum informs instruction, yet instruction should also inform curriculum design. For example, the curriculum says that

Figure 1.2   Curriculum in instruction and assessment

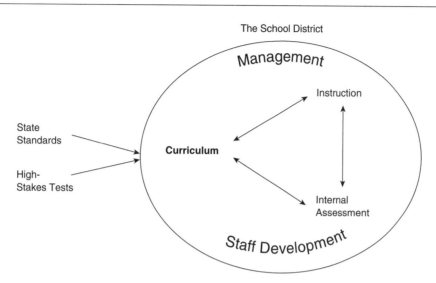

students should understand the relationship between circumference and radius and suggests a particular way this might be taught and assessed. After teaching the suggested way, teachers in turn suggest ways the technique could be improved, and thus instruction is influencing curriculum.

Assessment is also linked to instruction and curriculum. If students are taught about circumference and radius and then fail to do well on the assessment, consider the following suggestions:

- The curriculum needs to be changed (i.e., examined for appropriate prerequisite skills).
- The instructional approach may need changing so that students can perform better on the assessment.
- The assessment needs to be revised.

Which plan would work best? The conversation continues.

Management is at the top of the model because a curriculum, instruction, and assessment needs to be managed so that student and teacher effectiveness continually improves. The Balanced Curriculum structure has a built-in management system so that everyone clearly knows how he or she contributes to generating data and making improvement decisions.

Staff development suggestions will also come from the conversations about curriculum, assessment, and instruction and the management system. For example, a significant task required in the curriculum requires cooperative learning. Some teachers may be unfamiliar with cooperative learning techniques and will need to understand the processes and see them modeled. This is a staff development problem. Processes need to be in place to decide whether the school or district should provide the staff development after assessing needs. The circle indicates what the district can control; state standards, for example, are outside the district's change capability.

SUMMARY

This chapter reviewed typical approaches that districts take to standards and assessments and suggested that curriculum is a useful tool in bridging the gap between standards and assessments on one hand and instruction for students on the other. The following three chapters describe textbooks, standards, and standardized assessments to understand how they fit into a curriculum structure.

2

Textbooks

What the Research Says

Enter most classrooms, and textbooks are present. The textbook is the most successful and long-lasting innovation in education ever, and that's no small feat. Textbooks structure what is most important to teach and learn in classrooms around the world and thus serve as the surrogate or de facto curriculum for most school districts. Despite this great success, textbooks have been roundly criticized in both the popular press and academic writings. The standards movement accelerates criticism of textbooks generally because of their inability to address adequately and specifically the various standards of 49 separate state documents.

This chapter provides a brief history of textbooks, summarizes how they are written and produced by publishing houses, and what their critics see as their shortcomings. I then examine major studies of textbooks for mathematics, science, social studies and reading/language arts. This background shows that textbooks are ill suited to remain the surrogate curriculum of choice in today's environment of high-stakes testing and standards-based instruction. For the cost of adopting a textbook series, districts can better spend their money in developing and implementing their own curriculum, thus building capacity in the district to address the challenges of standards and high-stakes tests and removing the temptation to adopt the latest expensive fad designed for a quick fix.

A BRIEF HISTORY OF TEXTBOOKS

From the fifteenth to the early twentieth century, textbooks became part and parcel of a campaign for increasing literacy. At various times, secular and nonsecular institutions have controlled how literacy was taught and have used texts to control the content of instruction. Luke (1991) suggested that in Lutheran Germany, texts were controlled "to preclude theological and ideological deviation" (p. 201). This trend continued with McGuffey's Readers that "stressed allegiance to government and a learned resignation to the social and economic status quo. . . . There was a close match between the ideational content of such texts and . . . the promotion of Protestant morality, the work ethic, compliance with law, and allegiance to the nation-state" (p. 204).

Vanesky (1991) traced five periods in the development of the textbook in American society. During the colonial era, most textbooks came from Britain, thus making them expensive and unavailable to the general public. During the early national period (1780–1820) more textbooks were produced in the United States, partly because no international copyright laws existed, so popular English textbooks were copied and reproduced. At this time, textbooks were a collection of a variety of literature but had few instructions about what teachers or students should do with them. At the end of that era, commentators demanded more "child-friendly" text material.

During the pre–Civil War period, textbook publishing became a viable business. Truman, Smith and Company in Cincinnati published McGuffey's Readers and Joseph Ray's *Arithmetic,* selling more than a million copies of each and making millionaires of the company's founders. Texts still contained content with a high moral tone, more appropriate for adults than children.

After the Civil War, during the early modern period, textbook publishing rapidly expanded as more and more of the population became educated. Price cutting and bribery of school officials became common modes of doing business as competition among publishers grew more heated. Companies consolidated and combined to improve their market position and market share.

During the modern period, after World War I, high school education expanded rapidly, and so did textbooks for high school. Consolidation in the textbook publishing industry continued. At the beginning of the twentieth century, educational psychologists transformed textbooks so that the "skills of reading" were taught scientifically while de-emphasizing traditional literary and moral content. The modern basal reading series assumed the shape it has today, followed by other series in mathematics, science, and social studies. Further consolidation of the textbook industry took place in the 1980s and continues apace today.

Over this history, two important themes emerge. Content of textbooks reflects the cultural norms and themes of the time. In the early days, textbooks reflected the moral content of early Protestantism; in the modern period a reliance on educational psychology and "value-free" content enhanced the salability of textbooks to a wide range of communities. Furthermore, money could be made in the modern era by standardizing content, applying the principles of educational psychology to ensure "scientific" teaching and learning, and by de-emphasizing the moral content to appeal to an increasingly diverse population. Hence, the publishing industry came to define what was most important to teach and learn in schools through the publication of textbooks.

THE PROCESS OF PUBLISHING TEXTBOOKS

How does the publisher determine what content to include in a textbook? To bring a textbook series to market, the publishing company usually conducts a market analysis for the need for the textbook and potential sales of the new text. When the company decides to proceed, an editor chooses authors, both content specialists from academia and experienced teachers having both content and pedagogical expertise. The editor assigns the authors topics or lessons. After the authors prepare the lessons, the editor puts the lessons together and makes editorial changes for consistency. Team members generally do not meet because coordinating everyone's work falls to the publisher. As you can imagine, writing the textbook is a long and expensive process. After a draft is completed, there is generally a pilot test before the book goes into production, usually conducted with school districts that may receive a discount on the final material. Although the textbook publisher makes decisions about content, the publisher relies on an "expert network" for advice because the publisher must legitimize the chosen content. Despite this, Wong and Loveless (1991) concluded, "The review process becomes a formal exercise and fails to contribute much to improve the quality of textbooks" (p. 29).

Marketing is the last, and most important, link in the publication chain. Textbook series need to be marketed in two ways: to the 22 primarily southern and western states that have state textbook adoption committees and to individual school districts in the rest of the country through local textbook representatives.

The 22 states with state adoption committees exert a large influence on the content of the textbook series. For example, if publishers are not successful in getting their series adopted in California and Texas—states with large student populations—the economic viability of the series is in question.

Publishing companies get involved in textbooks to make money and provide a service to states and districts. A widely adopted textbook series ensures a large press run of perhaps a million copies or more. Series can be updated to maintain a current copyright at a fraction of the cost of developing the original series. Finally, the income can flow relatively evenly, with new adoptions and replacement texts making up the majority of the business. As textbook series have become more complex with elaborate teacher editions, a variety of student editions, and a wealth of ancillary material, developing a new series becomes quite expensive. Starting in the 1980s and continuing through the present, publishing companies have consolidated, leaving only a handful with the capacity and capability of developing and publishing textbooks, and decreasing the variety of textbooks and textbook series available to school districts.

The process of publishing textbooks has increased in complexity as publishers now must address 49 sets of state standards and assessments. Although some state standards overlap, there are significant differences in emphasis and specificity. Can one textbook series adequately address the 49 state standards and state assessments? (Chapter 4 examines some of the research about districts that have supplemented textbook series with other material to ensure that state standards and assessments are addressed.) When there were no standards and high-stakes assessments, one size could fit all; this is no longer the case. One size cannot fit all, and districts that want to ensure that a textbook series is in alignment with state standards and assessments will need to augment the text series with an ancillary curriculum. (Why not just develop a curriculum from scratch?) Many textbook publishers will produce evidence of complete alignment with state standards, but such an alignment may not be sufficiently in-depth to ensure that concepts are adequately covered to meet state standards; rather, the alignment may only indicate that similar topics are addressed by the series and the standards.

Nowhere in the process of producing textbook series is the series "tested" to see what results are produced. (As the consumers, the school districts drive the process;

school districts have never required publishers to validate that their products produce results. Consequently, no market pressure is exerted on textbook companies to do so.) Here's the situation: A large industry is determining the content and process of American education (with input from the network of experts and feedback from school district consumers), with no data, and no requirement for data, on whether the text series has any effect on the outcomes (such as student achievement). The textbook series is marketed to inner cities and wealthy suburbs that decide to buy the same materials, assuming it will meet their needs. (Can one textbook series meet the needs of these two diverse constituencies?)

The history and the process of developing textbook series continue to raise questions about textbooks' usefulness as a surrogate curriculum. More questions will be raised in the next section, where research on textbooks in science, mathematics, social studies, and English and language arts is explored.

TIMSS AND NAEP PROVIDE A CONTEXT FOR UNDERSTANDING TEXTBOOKS' ROLE

Before delving into the research on textbooks, particularly in math and science, understanding of U.S. performance in the Third International Mathematics and Science Study (TIMSS) and the National Assessment of Educational Progress (NAEP) is a necessary backdrop. The NAEP indicates that our national progress in science is stalled, with little improvement over the last 10 years. In mathematics, scores improved over two test administrations in the 1990s, but the most recent score declined from previous highs. The TIMSS shows our ranking in the world in mathematics and science as below or about average, depending on grade level and subject area. If widely used textbooks are the surrogate curriculum, then the lack of progress and world standing may be related to the adequacy of the textbooks.

NAEP Results for Science and Math

- Between 1996 and 2000, there was no statistically significant difference observed in the average science scores of 4th- or 8th-grade students. The average score of students in Grade 12, however, declined from 304 in 1996 to 301 in 2000 (Figure 2.1).
- In 2000, the percentage of students performing at or above Proficient—identified by NAEP as the level that all students should reach—was 29% at Grade 4, 32% at Grade 8, and 18% at Grade 12. The percentage of 8th graders at or above Proficient was higher in 2000 than in 1996. The percentage of 12th graders at or above Basic declined between 1996 and 2000.
- The 90th percentile score at Grade 8 was higher in 2000 than in 1996, indicating improvement for the highest-performing 8th graders. At Grade 12, the 50th percentile score declined between 1996 and 2000, indicating a decline in the performance of middle-performing 12th graders.

The TIMSS examined student achievement in math and science in 41 nations at five equivalent grades and provided information on the scope and content of the

Figure 2.1 Students in Grades 4 and 8 showed steady growth in mathematics achievement from 1990 to 2000. In contrast, 12th graders in 2000 scored higher than in 1990 but lower than in 1996

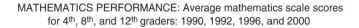

MATHEMATICS PERFORMANCE: Average mathematics scale scores for 4th, 8th, and 12th graders: 1990, 1992, 1996, and 2000

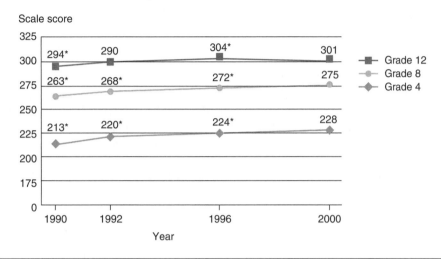

SOURCE: From *The Nation's Report Card: Mathematics 2000* (National Center for Education Statistics 2001–517, U.S. Department of Education, 2001).

NOTE: *Significantly different from 2000.

various countries' curricula. Videotapes of selected classrooms provided evidence on how the curriculum was actually taught. Finally, there were case studies of policy issues because the countries studied varied widely in their approaches. What did they find? No one is at the helm of U.S. science education. There is no helm. The vision for science education is splintered:

> Curricula [science and mathematics] are comparatively unfocused. They include far more topics than is common internationally. . . . These curricula express an intention to do something of everything and, on average, less of any one thing. . . . The general impact of these unfocused curricula in mathematics and science likely includes lower "yields" from mathematics and science education in the U.S. (Schmidt et al., 1997a, pp. 50–51)

Nonetheless, good news also comes from TIMSS. TIMSS researchers found that U.S. students at 4th and 8th grade in science scored above average when compared with students in 41 other countries. They also found that there was no significant gender gap in 8th-grade science achievement. U.S. 4th graders receive considerably more science instruction amounting to 48 more minutes per week than the international average. TIMSS also examined science education in the United States and other countries using

- State curriculum guides
- Textbooks

CONTENT OF WHAT TEACHERS TEACH

State Curriculum Guides

The TIMSS found that state curriculum guides are comparatively unfocused when compared with the curriculum guides of other countries. Because a committee usually develops curriculum guides from a state, the authors suspect that the curriculum developers would rather include a broad range of topics so as not to offend participants or potentially leave out important content. The development of the guides emphasizes inclusion of science topics while avoiding the issue of which topics are of most importance. When more topics are included, there is less time to spend teaching each of them. State curriculum guides, then, are one of the factors in having science education be "a mile wide and an inch deep." For example, the average state curriculum guide covers 50% to 75% more topics than those of the other countries studied. For the United States, state curriculum guides suggest coverage of 20 to 60 topics each year. If there are 180 days in a year, each topic would receive 3 to 9 days of instruction. This trend in the United States is in contrast to science curriculum guides in other countries, where the average number of topics covered is 25 (Schmidt et al., 1997a, p. 70).

Textbooks

The TIMSS also examined textbooks to determine the number of topics and the relative emphasis of those textbook topics in the United States compared with other participating countries. The study's authors reasoned that textbooks define the domain of implementable, day-to-day curricular possibilities. Previous studies suggest that teachers rely on textbooks to guide their decisions on what is important to teach. The study found that generally many more topics appear in U.S. science texts than in international texts.

In mathematics, coverage was also found to be "a mile wide and an inch deep" (Schmidt et al., 1997a, p. 62). In 4th and 8th grade, for example, math content includes topics emphasized in most other countries but included many additional topics as well, as illustrated in Figures 2.2 and 2.3.

Although there is a wider range of topics covered, when compared with other countries, the content of U.S. math at 8th-grade level is similar to the content of 7th-grade math in other countries. So, the United States teaches more topics than other countries, but the topics are not at as high a level of difficulty as those in other countries at the 8th-grade level. The study concluded that U.S. students have less opportunity to learn challenging mathematics. Indeed, in videotape studies of classrooms, U.S. 8th-grade teachers spent more time on whole-number operations, fractions, and decimals, whereas in Germany and Japan, lessons covered algebra and geometry.

In the United States, the officially intended curriculum is that specified by state departments of education. Thus, there are 50 sets of broad guidelines for mathematics. Even the officially intended curriculum varies widely in the United States. Textbooks, which guide a majority of the instruction in the United States, use the specifications made up by state departments as a guide to the content included. As textbooks companies want to sell their product to as many states and districts as possible, coverage of a wide variety of content is included. As the TIMSS points out, "Few states or districts closely monitor or enforce compliance with state or district standards, and U.S. teachers usually have the latitude to design the content and pace of their courses to suit their perception of their students' needs" (Schmidt et al., 1997a, p. 36).

Figure 2.2   4th-Grade Core Mathematics Topics. These topics are those that are common to 70 percent of the official curricula and textbooks of the U.S. ("U.S. core") and 70 percent of other TIMSS countries ("world core"). The "U.S. Teacher Core" are those topics reported by 70 percent of the U.S. teachers surveyed. Asterisks show emphasized topics. Even at 4th grade, U.S. curricula, textbooks, and teachers commonly include more topics than the other TIMSS countries. All except one of the "world core" topics is included by the U.S., and all three internationally emphasized topics are also emphasized in the U.S. U.S. 4th-grade mathematics includes what is common to most TIMSS countries but also enough other topics to make our curriculum "a mile wide and an inch deep"

World Core	U.S. Core	U.S. Teacher Core[a]
Whole Numbers: Meaning*	Whole Numbers: Meaning*	Whole Numbers*
Whole Numbers: Operations*	Whole Numbers: Operations*	Whole Numbers*
Whole Numbers: Properties of Operations		Whole Numbers*
Common Fractions	Common Fractions	Common Fractions
	Decimal Fractions	Decimal Fractions
		Rel. of Common and Dec. Frac.
		Prop. of Common and Dec. Frac.
		Number Theory
	Estimating Computations	Estimation and Number Sense*
Measurement Units*	Measurement Units*	Measurement Units*
Perimeter, Area, and Volume	Perimeter, Area, and Volume	Perimeter, Area, and Volume
	Meas. Estimation and Error	
	2-D Geo.: Coord. Geo.	One- and Two-Dimensional Geometry
2-D Geo.: Basics	2-D Geo.: Basics	One- and Two- Dimensional Geometry
2-D Geo.: Poly. and Circles	2-D Geo.: Poly. and Circles 3-D Geometry	One- and Two-Dimensional Geometry
	Geometric Congruence and Similarity	Geometric Congruence and Similarity
	Geometric Transformations and Symmetry	Geometric Transformations and Symmetry
	Functions, Relations, and Patterns	Functions, Relations, and Patterns
	Equations and Formulas	
	Data Representation and Statistics	Data Representation and Statistics
	Probability	Probability

SOURCE: Adapted from *A splintered vision: An investigation of U.S. science and mathematics education.* (1997). Schmidt, William H., McKnight, Curtis C., and Raizen, Senta A., Eds. Dordrecht, The Netherlands: Kluwer Academic Publishers.

NOTE: a. Some of the framework topics were aggregated together when presented to teachers and were at a different level of specificity than presented here in the world core; therefore, the numbers in this column may represent teaching of the larger category which includes the specific topic listed here.

Figure 2.3 8th-Grade Core Mathematics Topics. Common topics for 8th-grade mathematics are shown here just as they were in Figure 2.2 for 4th grade. Additionally, U.S. algebra curricular and books are separated from those not wholly on algebra. Again the U.S. contains most of the common topics in other TIMSS countries but many others as well. This is true even in books supposedly dedicated wholly to algebra. U.S. teachers report spending time on an even wider range of topics than those in official curricula and textbooks. U.S. 8th-grade mathematics is "a mile wide and an inch deep" in an even more pronounced way than 4th grade. It also suggests less "fit" to a test designed mainly to assess achievement in the "world core."

World Core	U.S. Non-Algebra Core	U.S. Algebra Core	U.S. Teacher Core[a]
			Whole Numbers: Meaning
	Whole Numbers: Operations	Whole Numbers: Operations	Whole Numbers: Operations and Properties
	Common Fractions	Common Fractions	Common Fractions
			Decimal Fractions
	Relationship of Comm. and Dec. Frac.	Relationship of Comm. and Dec. Frac.	Relationship of Comm. and Dec. Frac.
	Percentages	Percentages	Percentages
			Properties of Fractions
Integers and Their Properties	Integers and Their Properties	Integers and Their Properties	Number Sets and Concepts*
Rational Numbers and Their Properties			Number Sets and Concepts*
Exponents, Roots and Radicals			Number Sets and Concepts*
			Number Theory
	Estimating Quantity and Size		Estimation and Number Sense
	Rounding		Estimation and Number Sense
	Estimating Computations		Estimation and Number Sense
	Measurement Units		Measurement Units
Perimeter, Area, and Volume	Perimeter, Area, and Volume	Perimeter, Area, and Volume	Perimeter, Area, and Volume
	Meas. Estimation and Error		
2-D Geometry: Coordinate Geo.	2-D Geometry: Coordinate Geo.	2-D Geometry: Coordinate Geo.*	One- and Two-Dimensional Geometry
2-D Geometry: Basics	2-D Geometry: Basics	2-D Geometry: Basics	One- and Two-Dimensional Geometry
2-D Geometry: Polygons and Circles	2-D Geometry: Polygons and Circles	2-D Geometry: Polygons and Circles	One- and Two-Dimensional Geometry

World Core	U.S. Non-Algebra Core	U.S. Algebra Core	U.S. Teacher Core[a]
3-D Geometry	3-D Geometry		
	Geometric Congruence and Similarity	Geometric Congruence and Similarity	Geometric Congruence and Similarity
Geometric Transformations and Symmetry	Geometric Transformations and Symmetry	Geometric Transformations and Symmetry	
	Proportionality Concepts	Proportionality Concepts	Proportionality Concepts
Proportionality Problems			Proportionality Problems
Functions, Relations, and Patterns	Functions, Relations, and Patterns	Functions, Relations, and Patterns	
Equations and Formulas	Equations and Formulas*	Equations and Formulas*	Equations and Formulas
	Data Representation and Analysis	Data Representation and Analysis	Data Representation and Analysis
	Probability	Probability	

SOURCE: Adapted from *A splintered vision: An investigation of U.S. science and mathematics education.* (1997). Schmidt, William H., McKnight, Curtis C., and Raizen, Senta A., Eds. Dordrecht, The Netherlands: Kluwer Academic Publishers.

NOTE: a. Some of the framework topics were aggregated together when presented to teachers and were at a different level of specificity than presented here in the world core; therefore, the numbers in this column may represent teaching of the larger category which includes the specific topic listed here.

Textbooks reflect to a certain extent the state curriculum guides. Thus, if the state curriculum guides suggest covering a large number of topics, then textbooks are constructed to help schools fulfill state mandates and contain a large number of topics. So, how do teachers respond to the dilemma of both state and textbooks suggesting coverage of a large number of topics?

Teachers' Response to a Splintered Curriculum and Fragmented Textbooks

Teachers generally teach what the state curriculum guides and the textbooks suggest. The difficulty is that the large number of topics means that each topic is covered in a cursory manner. There is no depth to the curriculum. This runs counter to many recommendations to improve science education that emphasize covering fewer topics at greater depth, so that students have a chance to explore and get to know what science is about by actually "doing" science, rather than reading about and memorizing, activities used in all too many classrooms.

Teachers work hard and do what is expected. What's expected is determined in large part by what's in the curriculum guides and the textbooks. The institutional push from both state curriculum guides and textbooks is to cover more topics. Teachers may not use the textbook or the state curriculum guide exclusively, however. The study's authors indicate that teachers go about making decisions by quickly judging whether a topic is good for that grade level, teaching the topic and moving on. This process of quick decision making is called "satisficing" or making choices that are considered "good enough."

TIMSS recommends the following:

- Focus the curriculum on fewer topics.
- Provide more depth in some areas.
- Produce learning that lasts (not just surface coverage of many topics).

TIMSS OF TEXTBOOKS

TIMSS also conducted a study comparing international textbooks (Howson, 1995). The study is descriptive in nature and uses one textbook from a variety of countries from a middle-school setting. A caveat to this study needs to be kept in mind: "A single text cannot be taken as representative of all of those to be found in a particular country. . . . The texts studied provide indications—they contain messages, but they are not determinants of national characteristics or necessarily of classroom practice" (p. 13). Certainly the variety of approaches is pointed out in the study: "Nevertheless, it is somewhat disappointing that, with one exception, the books all followed the same basic pattern" (p. 11). Textbooks then have a similarity throughout the world, and, given that the textbooks are more similar than they are different, the general problems inherent in their structure, content, and organization may be near to universal. "One of the problems is that the textbooks studied fostered a limited range of learning strategies: mainly learning by listening and by practicing a restricted range of techniques in particular 'closed' situations. Learning by reading, by discussion and argument, and in an attempt to acquire the knowledge to solve a problem of one's own choosing are largely ignored. . . . The emphasis is so frequently on problem solving where the 'problem' is all too often a routine example" (p. 41). Howson (1995) also found that there is

- Little explanation of why a topic is being studied (p. 41)
- Disconnected topics tenuously linked and motivated (p. 45)
- Few hints on how to differentiate the text for use with a range of students (pp. 46–47)
- U.S. texts repeat much work from grade to grade (p. 51)

Howson went on to characterize the U.S. textbooks:

The problem of the U.S. text is readily identified. . . . Those coding the text for the main TIMSS found that it contained over three hundred units [a unit is an idea or concept]—each requiring one to three periods of class time! There is material here for three grades' work. Some is review of material covered in previous years, much is new; some reflects all that is novel in the NCTM [National Council of Teachers of Mathematics] Standards (1989), some appears very traditional. Teachers are left, with the aid of a voluminous teachers' guide, to devise a one-year course appropriate for students of very differing abilities and achievements . . . problems of selection of material are great (although advice is to be found in the accompanying guide). . . . The result is that although a study of the Japanese books provides a reasonable idea of what will be taught in their classrooms, just about anything might happen in a U.S. classroom using this particular series of texts. For the U.S. text, although not advertising this fact, is not a *course* but rather a *resource.* (pp. 28–29)

And, of course, just about anything does happen, especially when there is little guidance.

Imagine the beginning teacher who thinks the text must be taught start to finish. She or he begins the year and spends a month covering only a fraction of the textbook, but covering all the activities. Realizing that the course will never be completed at this rate, the teacher decides to speed up the instruction, spending less time on each topic but still covering the many topics addressed. Realizing halfway through the year that this strategy has little chance of succeeding, the teacher changes to a new strategy. She decides to cover only those remaining topics that she feels are important. The year ends, the students are promoted, and next year's teacher finds them unprepared for that grade level's work. Most teachers are left with little assistance in coordinating decisions on how to approach a text with three years of instructional material. Pacing guides may help but often do not specify which topics are most important. Curriculum can specify topics, amount of time, and significant tasks that all children are expected to complete, so both novice and experienced teachers know which topics and activities are most important to cover out of the three years of activities presented by the textbook.

If coverage of topics in mathematics textbooks is a mile wide and an inch deep, then many important topics may not have adequate coverage to ensure student mastery. One early study about textbooks examined the number of topics covered by standardized tests that had at least 20 practice problems in the textbook. Figure 2.4 shows that only 21% to 50% of the topics on standardized tests are covered by at least 20 problems in mathematics textbooks (Freeman et al., 1983).

Unfortunately, more recent studies of mathematics textbooks indicate continuing instructional and content coverage inadequacies.

Figure 2.4   Percentages of tested topics covered for 4th-grade mathematics covered in textbooks

Test	Textbook			
	Addison-Wesley	Holt	Houghton Mifflin	Scott Foresman
MAT (38 topics)	32	50	40	42
Stanford (72 topics)	22	22	21	22
Iowa (66 topics)	26	29	32	26
CTBS-I (53 topics)	32	32	38	36
CTBS-II (61 topics)	28	38	38	34

SOURCE: Adapted from Freeman, Kuhs, Porter, Floden, Schmidt, and Schwille (1983). Used with permission.

NOTE: Percentages are based on topics covered by at least 20 problems in a book.

MATHEMATICS AND SCIENCE TEXTBOOKS

Mathematics and science textbooks, the surrogate curriculum for most school districts, need to be examined so that teachers and administrators can understand their strengths and weaknesses. To assist in this process, this section examines a number of studies, conducted over the last 4 years, all using approximately the same framework and methodology for describing characteristics of United States textbooks in middle school math, science, algebra, and biology texts.

At its simplest level, the Project 2061 curriculum analysis procedure involves the following five steps (http://www.project2061.org/tools/textbook/matheval/appendx/appendc.htm):

- *Step 1:* Identify specific learning goals.
- *Step 2:* Review textbooks to see if they address the learning goals.
- *Step 3:* Analyze the curriculum materials for alignment between content and the selected learning goals.
- *Step 4:* Analyze the curriculum materials for alignment between instruction and the selected learning goals.
- *Step 5:* Summarize the relationship between the curriculum materials being evaluated and the selected learning goals.

In addition to its careful focus on matching content and instruction to specific learning goals, the Project 2061 procedure has other features that set it apart. For example, its emphasis on collecting explicit evidence (citing page numbers and other references) of a material's alignment with learning goals adds rigor and reliability to decisions about curriculum materials. Similarly, the procedure calls for a team approach to the analytical task, thus providing opportunities for reviewers to defend their own judgments about materials and to question those of other reviewers.

Step 1: Identify Learning Goals

For each study—middle school math and science texts, algebra texts, and biology texts—researchers selected important topics from the textbooks that also aligned with American Association of the Advancement of Science Project 2061 standards and the National Science Education Standards published by the National Research Council. All topics covered by the textbooks were not studied. The researchers assumed that how these topics were presented would be an indicator of how other topics were as well. Listed in Figure 2.5 are the topics used for the analysis of the various textbooks.

Figure 2.5 Topics used for the analysis of different textbooks

Middle School Mathematics Topics	*Middle School Science Topics*
Number concepts Number skills Geometry concepts Geometry skills Algebra graph concepts Algebra equation concepts	*Earth Science.* Key ideas focus on the changing surface of the earth and the geologic events and processes that constantly shape and reshape it. *Life Science.* Key ideas focus on matter and energy transformations in living systems, including organisms and ecosystems. *Physical Science.* Key ideas focus on basic assumptions of the kinetic molecular theory and their use in explaining thermal expansion and changes of state.
Algebra	*Biology*
Representing functions Modeling with functions Representing variable quantities Operating with symbols and equations	Molecular basis of heredity Natural selection and evolution Cell structure and functions Matter and energy transformations

Step 2: Review Textbooks to See If They Address the Learning Goals

Ten to fifteen textbooks were reviewed in each of the four evaluations. Researchers chose best-selling texts and texts that had been developed by the National Science Foundation.

Step 3: Analyze the Curriculum Materials for Alignment Between Content and the Selected Learning Goals

Figure 2.6 summarizes the alignment between the content of the textbook and the selected learning goals.

Figure 2.6 Math textbook series alignment to benchmarks

Attachment A — Most content / Partial content / Minimal content

Textbook Series	Selected Benchmarks: Number Concepts	Number Skills	Geometry Concepts	Geometry Skills	Algebra Graph Concepts	Algebra Equation Concepts
Connected Mathematics. Dale Seymour Publications,1998	Partial	Most	Partial	Most	Most	Most
Mathematics in Context. Encyclopedia Britannica Educational Corporation, 1998	Most	Most	Partial	Most	Most	Most
MathScape. Creative Publications, 1998	Partial	Most	Partial	Most	Minimal	Most
Middle Grades Math Thematics. McDougal Littell, 1999	Partial	Most	Partial	Most	Partial	Most
Mathematics Plus. Harcourt Brace & Company, 1994	Most	Most	Partial	Most	Minimal	Partial

(Continued)

Figure 2.6 (Continued)

Middle School Math. Scott Foresman—Addison Wesley, 1998	●	●	●	●	●	●
Math Advantage. Harcourt Brace & Company, 1998	○	●	○	●	●	○
Heath Passport. McDougal Littell, 1996	○	●	●	●	●	●
Heath Mathematics Connections. D.C. Heath and Company, 1996	●	●	○	●	●	●
Transition Mathematics. Scott Foresman, 1995	●	●	●	●	●	●
Mathematics: Applications and Connections. Glencoe/McGraw-Hill, 1998	●	●	●	●	○	○
Middle Grades Math. Prentice Hall, 1997	●	●	●	●	●	●

SOURCE: From *Middle Grades Mathematics Textbooks: A Benchmarks-Based Evaluation* by G. Kulm, K. Morris, and L. Grier, 1998. Washington, DC: American Association for the Advancement of Science. Retrieved from http://www.project2061.org/tools/textbook/matheval/appendx/appendc.htm. Reprinted with permission from the American Association for the Advancement of Science.

Figure 2.6 shows that *Mathematics in Context* (second from the top) has the best alignment with five of the six areas being aligned to "most content." *Math Advantage* has the weakest alignment (near the middle of the chart). Another way to view the chart is to look at one category across textbooks. For example, Geometry Concepts are rated as minimal or partial content match with the exception of one textbook. Alignment for the other textbook areas are reported in individual textbook scores and not aggregated across texts (for more details see http://www.project2061.org). Where there is weak alignment, we would expect weak results in testing.

Another way the content match was done resembles webbing of concepts. Two webs are produced; the first is what you would expect to find in the text based on the web of expert opinion; the second is the web of concepts actually explained in the text. Figures 2.7 and 2.8 are examples of two webs used for the alignment.

Figure 2.7   Cell structure and function: Ideas the reviewers looked for in the textbooks

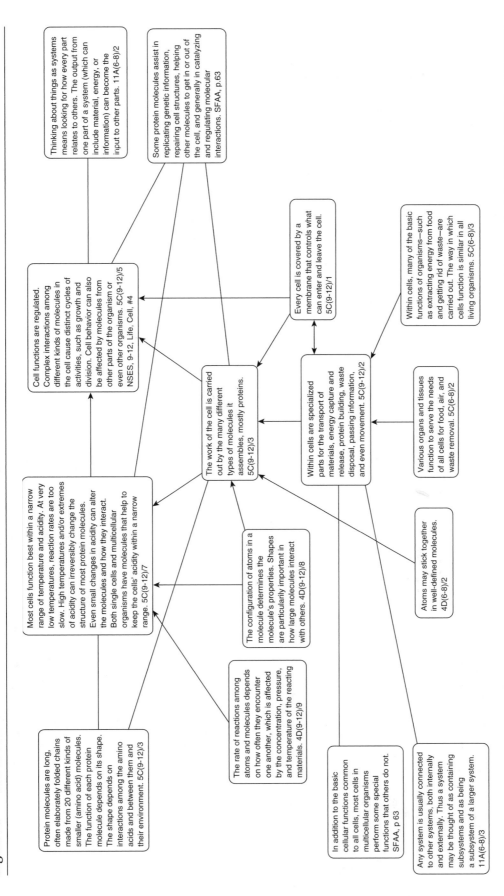

SOURCE: From the Project 2061 Web site (http://www.project2061.org/research/textbook/hsbio/cell_com.pdf). Reprinted with permission from the American Association for the Advancement of Science.

Figure 2.8 Cell structure and function: What the textbooks typically do

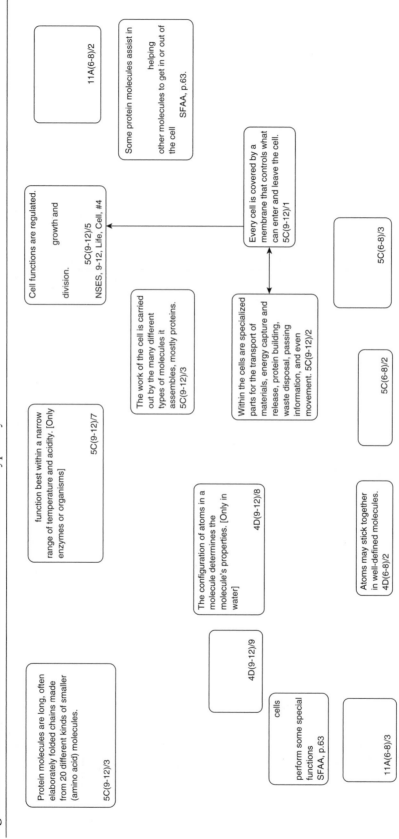

SOURCE: From the Project 2061 Web site (http://www.project2061.org/research/textbook/hsbio/cell_com.pdf). Reprinted with permission from the American Association for the Advancement of Science.

This alignment approach can be particularly powerful because Project 2061 has developed an *Atlas of Science Literacy* that is displayed in similar ways as the webbing. The atlas, a collection of 49 conceptual strand maps, shows educators how students' understanding of the ideas and skills needed to achieve science literacy might grow over time. These conceptual maps might be used as the basis for alignment of textbook to content that needs to be taught, as represented in the atlas.

Step 4: Analyze the Curriculum Materials for Alignment Between Instruction and the Selected Learning Goals

The procedure requires textbook reviewers to focus only on those textbook activities and lessons that are aligned with the identified content learning goals and to examine the specific guidance provided to help students learn that content. To evaluate the quality of instructional support, reviewers use specific criteria within each of the following categories.

Identifying a Sense of Purpose

Part of planning a coherent curriculum involves deciding on its purposes and on which learning experiences will likely contribute to achieving those purposes. Reviewers determine how effective the material is at conveying a unit purpose and a lesson purpose and justifying the sequence of activities.

Building on Student Ideas

Fostering better student understanding requires taking time to attend to the ideas they already have—both incorrect ideas and ideas that can serve as a foundation for subsequent learning. Reviewers determine how well the material specifies prerequisite knowledge, alerts teachers to commonly held student ideas, assists teachers in identifying student ideas, and addresses misconceptions.

Engaging Students. For students to appreciate the power of mathematics and science, they need to have a sense of the range and complexity of ideas and applications that mathematics and science can explain or model. Reviewers determine how well the material provides a variety of phenomena or mathematical contexts and makes them vivid to students, particularly through an appropriate number of firsthand experiences.

Developing Ideas. Science and mathematics literacy requires that students see the link between concepts and skills, see them as logical and useful, and become skillful at using them. Reviewers determine how well material justifies ideas, introduces terms and procedures, represents ideas, connects ideas, demonstrates and models procedures and applications of knowledge, and provides practice opportunities.

Promoting Student Thinking. No matter how clearly materials may present ideas, students (like all people) will devise their own meaning, which may or may not correspond to targeted learning goals. Students need to make their ideas and reasoning explicit, hold them up to scrutiny, and recast them as needed. Whether the material is effective in promoting student thinking is determined by how much the material encourages students to explain their reasoning, guides students in their interpretation and reasoning, and encourages them to think about what they've learned.

Assessing Student Progress. Assessments must address the range of knowledge and skills that students are expected to learn, as well as the kinds of applications and contexts in which such knowledge and skills are useful. Reviewers determine how well assessments align with the learning goals addressed in the material, assess students' ability to apply them, and use assessment to inform instruction.

Enhancing the Learning Environment. Providing features that enhance the use and implementation of the textbook for all students is important. Reviewers determine whether the material provides teacher content support, establishes a challenging classroom, and supports all students (Kulm, Roseman, & Treistman, 1999).

The above categories were synthesized from the research taken from Project 2061's Benchmarks (Kulm et al., 1999) and the research done for the NCTM Standards (2000). Figure 2.9 shows these categories for mathematics, although similar categories were used across middle school science, biology, and algebra.

Figure 2.9   Criteria for evaluating the quality of instructional guidance in textbooks

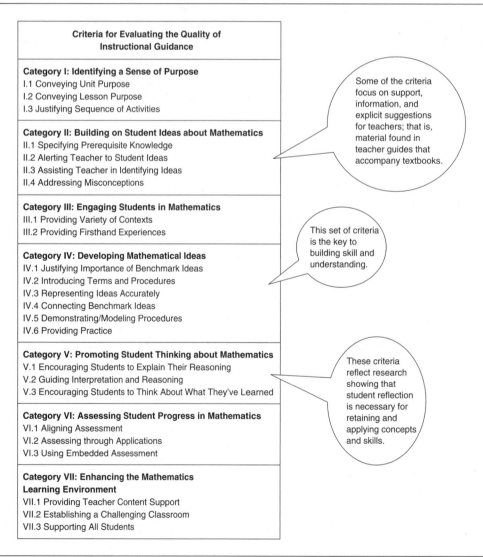

SOURCE: From the Project 2061 Web site (http://www.project2061.org/tools/textbook/matheval/part1.htm). Reprinted with permission from the American Association for the Advancement of Science.

The content for all the aligned topics were rated according to the categories just cited on a 3-point scale, with any rating over 2 points considered satisfactory.

Summaries of whether the textbooks were satisfactory or unsatisfactory were produced. Figure 2.10 shows a summary for "instructional quality" of the textbooks. The summary for instructional quality developed from averaging all the indicators of instructional quality in the figure.

Figure 2.10   Quality of middle school science texts

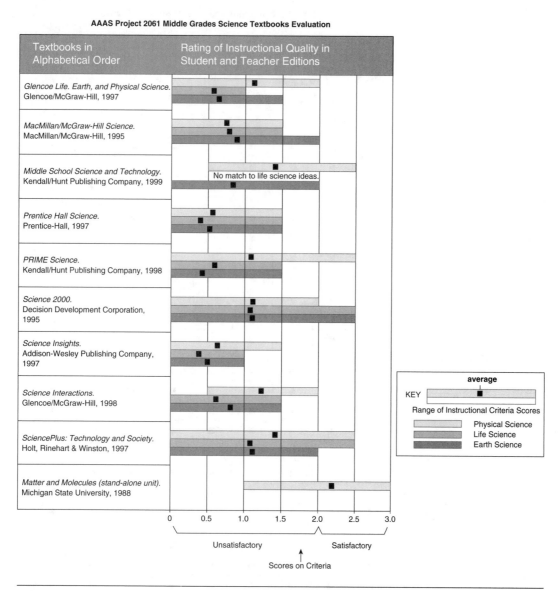

SOURCE: From the Project 2061 Web site, "Middle Grades Science Textbooks Evaluation" (http://www.project2061.org/research/textbook/mgsci/book-rating.pdf). Originally appeared in "Heavy Books, Light on Learning: AAAS Project 2061 Evaluates Middle Grades Science Textbooks" by Jo Ellen Roseman, Sofia Kesidou, Luli Stern, and Ann Caldwell, November/December 1999, *Science Books & Films*, 35. Reprinted with permission from the American Association for the Advancement of Science.

As can be seen from Figure 2.10, only one textbook in middle school science, developed by Michigan State University, was rated as satisfactory on instructional quality. All of the best-selling science textbooks received unsatisfactory ratings. Relying on textbooks as a surrogate curriculum is risky business. Next, the results of biology are examined (Figure 2.11).

All the biology textbooks evaluated had generally poor ratings. The ratings were even more negative than for the middle school science texts.

Figure 2.11 Quality of biology textbooks according to instructional categories

Average of ratings for four topics / Instructional Categories	Biology Miller-Levine Prentice Hall	Biology: A Community Context South-Western Educational Publishing	Biology: Principles & Explorations Holt, Rinehart and Winston	Biology: The Dynamics of Life Glencoe, McGraw-Hill	Biology: Visualizing Life Holt, Rinehart and Winston	BSCS Biology: A Human Approach Kendall Hunt	BSCS Biology: An Ecological Approach Kendall Hunt	Heath Biology D.C. Heath and Company	Insights in Biology Kendall Hunt	Modern Biology Holt, Rinehart and Winston
I. PROVIDING A SENSE OF PURPOSE										
Conveying unit purpose	▣	◧	■	■	■	◧	▣	■	▣	■
Conveying lesson purpose	■	▣	■	■	■	■	■	■	□	■
Justifying lesson sequence	▣	▣	▣	▣	▣	▣	▣	▣	▣	▣
II. TAKING ACCOUNT OF STUDENT IDEAS										
Attending to prerequisite knowledge and skills	■	■	■	■	■	■	■	■	■	■
Alerting teacher to commonly held student ideas	■	■	■	■	■	■	■	■	■	■
Assisting teacher in identifying own students' ideas	■	■	■	■	■	■	■	■	▣	■
Addressing commonly held ideas	■	■	■	■	■	■	■	■	■	■
III. ENGAGING STUDENTS WITH RELEVANT PHENOMENA										
Providing variety of phenomena	■	■	■	■	■	■	■	■	■	■
Providing vivid experiences	■	■	■	■	■	■	■	■	■	■
IV. DEVELOPING AND USING SCIENTIFIC IDEAS										
Introducing terms meaningfully	■	■	■	■	■	▣	■	■	□	■
Representing ideas effectively	■	■	■	■	■	■	■	■	■	■
Demonstrating use of knowledge	■	■	■	■	■	■	■	■	■	■
Providing practice	■	■	■	■	■	■	■	■	■	■
V. PROMOTING STUDENT THINKING ABOUT PHENOMENA, EXPERIENCES, AND KNOWLEDGE										
Encouraging students to explain their ideas	■	■	■	■	■	▣	■	■	■	■
Guiding student interpretation and reasoning	■	■	■	■	■	■	■	■	▣	■
Encouraging students to reflect on their own learning	■	■	■	■	■	■	■	■	■	■
VI. ASSESSING PROGRESS										
Aligning assessment to goals	■	■	■	■	■	■	■	N/A	■	■
Testing for understanding	■	■	■	■	■	■	■	N/A	■	■
Using assessment to inform instruction	■	■	■	■	■	■	■	N/A	■	■

Project 2061 Instructional Analysis of Biology Textbooks

▣ = Excellent (3); ◧ = Good (2.5–2.9); □ = Satisfactory (2–2.4); ▤ = Fair (1.5–1.9); ■ = Poor (0–1.4)

WHAT'S WRONG WITH TODAY'S MATH AND SCIENCE TEXTS?

In 1964, the Nobel Prize–winning physicist Richard Feynman reported on his experiences as an advisor to a California textbook selection committee:

> Something would look good at first and then turn out to be horrifying. . . . [the books] said things that were useless, mixed-up, ambiguous, confusing, and partially incorrect. How anybody can learn science from these books, I don't know, because it's not science. (Roseman, Kulm, & Shuttleworth, 2001)

Many of these problems remain.

Today's textbooks cover too many topics without developing any of them well. Central concepts are not covered in sufficient depth to give students a chance to truly understand them. Although many textbooks present the key ideas described in national and state standards documents, few help students learn the ideas or teachers teach them. For example, Project 2061's analysis of high school biology texts revealed the following problems:

> Research shows that essentially all students—even the best and the brightest— have predictable difficulties grasping many ideas that are covered in the text- books. Yet most books fail to take these obstacles into account in the activities and questions. For many biology concepts, the textbooks ignore or obscure the most important ideas by focusing instead on technical terms and super- fluous detail—the sorts of material that translate easily into items for multiple choice tests. (Roseman et al., 2001)

While most of the books are lavishly illustrated, these representations are rarely helpful because they are too abstract, needlessly complicated, or inadequately explained. Even though several activities are included in every chapter, students are given little guidance in interpreting the results in terms of the scientific concepts to be learned.

Did middle school mathematics and algebra textbooks fair any better? Let's examine the results. "The three top-rated textbook series had a median rating of more than 2.5 on a scale of 0–3 points for all of the 24 instructional criteria for all six benchmarks" (Project 2061 Web site; http://www.project2061.org/tools/text-book/matheval/part1b.htm). At least middle school mathematics texts scored slightly better than science. Figure 2.13 shows the instructional quality ratings of the middle school mathematics texts.

Only four textbooks scored in the satisfactory range. Isn't it strange that both the NAEP and the TIMSS show that we are doing better in mathematics than in science, yet the instructional ratings of textbooks used follows the same pattern (Figure 2.13)? The report goes on to highlight the good and bad news contained in the study.

Good News

- There are a few excellent middle-grade mathematics textbook series.
- The top two series contain both in-depth mathematics content and excellent instructional support.
- Most of the textbooks do a satisfactory job on number and geometry skills.
- A majority of textbooks do a reasonable job in the key instructional areas of engaging students and helping them develop and use mathematical ideas.

Figure 2.12   Key for instructional quality rating of middle school mathematics texts

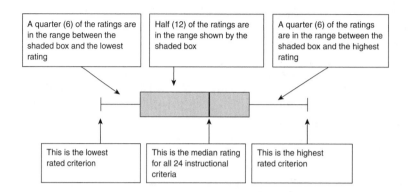

SOURCE: From the Project 2061 Web site (http://www.project2061.org/tools/textbook/matheval/part1b.htm). Reprinted with permission from the American Association for the Advancement of Science.

Figure 2.13   Instructional ratings of middle school mathematics textbooks

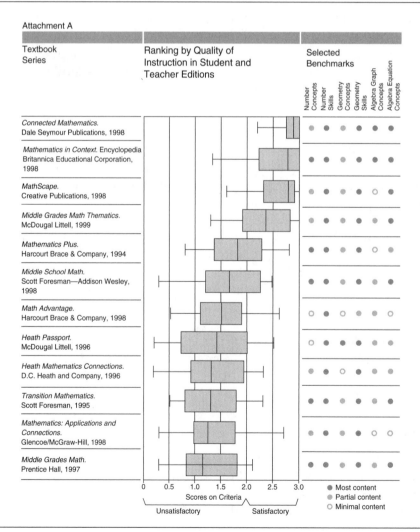

SOURCE: From the Project 2061 Web site (http://www.project2061.org/tools/textbook/matheval/overall.pdf). Reprinted with permission from the American Association for the Advancement of Science.

Bad News

- There are no popular commercial textbooks among the best rated.
- Most of the textbooks are inconsistent and often weak in their coverage of conceptual benchmarks in mathematics.
- Most of the textbooks are weak in their instructional support for students and teachers.
- Many textbooks provide little development in sophistication of mathematical ideas from Grades 6 to 8.
- A majority of textbooks are particularly unsatisfactory in providing a purpose for learning mathematics, taking account of student ideas, and promoting student thinking.

This is quite an indictment of mathematics textbooks, given the millions of dollars that school districts spend annually. Excellent textbooks are out there, however, even though they may not appear on the approved lists that some states generate outlining which books can be purchased within the state. What does this say about the criteria those states use to select textbooks?

The algebra textbooks (Figure 2.14) appear strong in their instructional ratings in the areas of Engaging Students in Mathematics and Developing Mathematical Ideas. The following texts were rated as "Textbooks With the Potential for Helping Students Learn Algebra":

- *Concepts in Algebra*, Everyday Learning
- *Contemporary Mathematics in Context*, Everyday Learning
- *Focus on Algebra*, Addison Wesley Longman
- *Interactive Mathematics Program (IMP)*, Key Curriculum Press
- *MATH Connections: A Secondary Math Core Curriculum*, It's About Time
- *Mathematics: Modeling Our World*, South-Western Educational
- *UCSMP Algebra*, Scott Foresman

Highlights of evaluation findings for algebra texts:

- All of the textbooks present algebra using a variety of contexts and give students appropriate firsthand experiences with the concepts and skills.
- Most of the textbooks do an acceptable job of developing student ideas about algebra through representing ideas, demonstrating content, and providing appropriate practice.
- No textbook does a satisfactory job of providing assessments to help teachers make instructional decisions based specifically on what their students have—or have not—learned.
- No textbook does a satisfactory job of building on students' existing ideas about algebra or helping them overcome their misconceptions or missing prerequisite knowledge. ("Algebra for All—Not With Today's Textbooks, Says AAAS," AAAS press release, April 30, 2000)

Both the studies on algebra and middle school math textbooks point out that textbook series can be evaluated not only for content but also for the likelihood that students will learn that content based on findings from the research. Such ratings

Figure 2.14 Quality of algebra textbooks according to instructional categories

AAAS Project 2061 Algebra Textbooks Evaluation

Summary of Instructional Analysis Ratings for Algebra Textbooks

Textbook Series

Instructional Categories

I. IDENTIFYING A SENSE OF PURPOSE
- Conveying Unit Purpose
- Conveying Lesson Purpose
- Justifying Sequence of Activities

II. BUILDING ON STUDENT IDEAS ABOUT MATHEMATICS
- Specifying Prerequisite Knowledge
- Alerting Teacher to Student Ideas
- Assisting Teacher in Identifying Ideas
- Addressing Misconceptions

III. ENGAGING STUDENTS IN MATHEMATICS
- Providing Variety of Contexts
- Providing Firsthand Experiences

IV. DEVELOPING MATHEMATICAL IDEAS
- Justifying Importance of Standards Ideas
- Introducing Terms and Procedures
- Representing Ideas Accurately
- Connecting Standards Ideas
- Demonstrating/Modeling Procedures
- Providing Practice

V. PROMOTING STUDENT THINKING ABOUT MATHEMATICS
- Encouraging Students to Explain Their Reasoning
- Guiding Interpretation and Reasoning
- Encouraging Students to Think about What They've Learned

VI. ASSESSING STUDENT PROGRESS IN MATHEMATICS
- Aligning Assessment
- Assessing through Applications
- Using Embedded Assessment

Textbook columns (left to right):
Algebra I: Explorations and Aplicaciones, McDougal Littell, 1998;
Algebra I: Integration, Applications, Connections, Glencoe/McGraw-Hill, 1998;
Algebra: Tools for a Changing World, Prentice Hall, 1996;
Concepts in Algebra, Everyday Learning Corporation, 1999;
Contemporary Mathematics in Context (CORE-Plus), Everyday Learning Corporation, 1998;
CORD Algebra 1, South-Western Educational Publishing, 1998;
Focus on Algebra, Addison Wesley Longman, 1998;
Integrated Mathematics: A Modeling Approach Using Technology (SIMMS), Simon & Schuster Custom Publishing, 1996–1998;
Interactive Mathematics Program (IMP), Key Curriculum Press, 1997–1999;
MATH Connections: A Secondary Math Core Curriculum, It's About Time Inc., 1998;
Mathematics: Modeling Our World (COMAP/ARISE), South-Western Educational Publishing, 1998;
UCSMP Algebra, Scott Foresman and Company, 1998

Legend: Poor: 0–1.4 Fair: 1.5–1.9 Satisfactory: 2–2.4 Good: 2.5–2.9 Excellent: 3

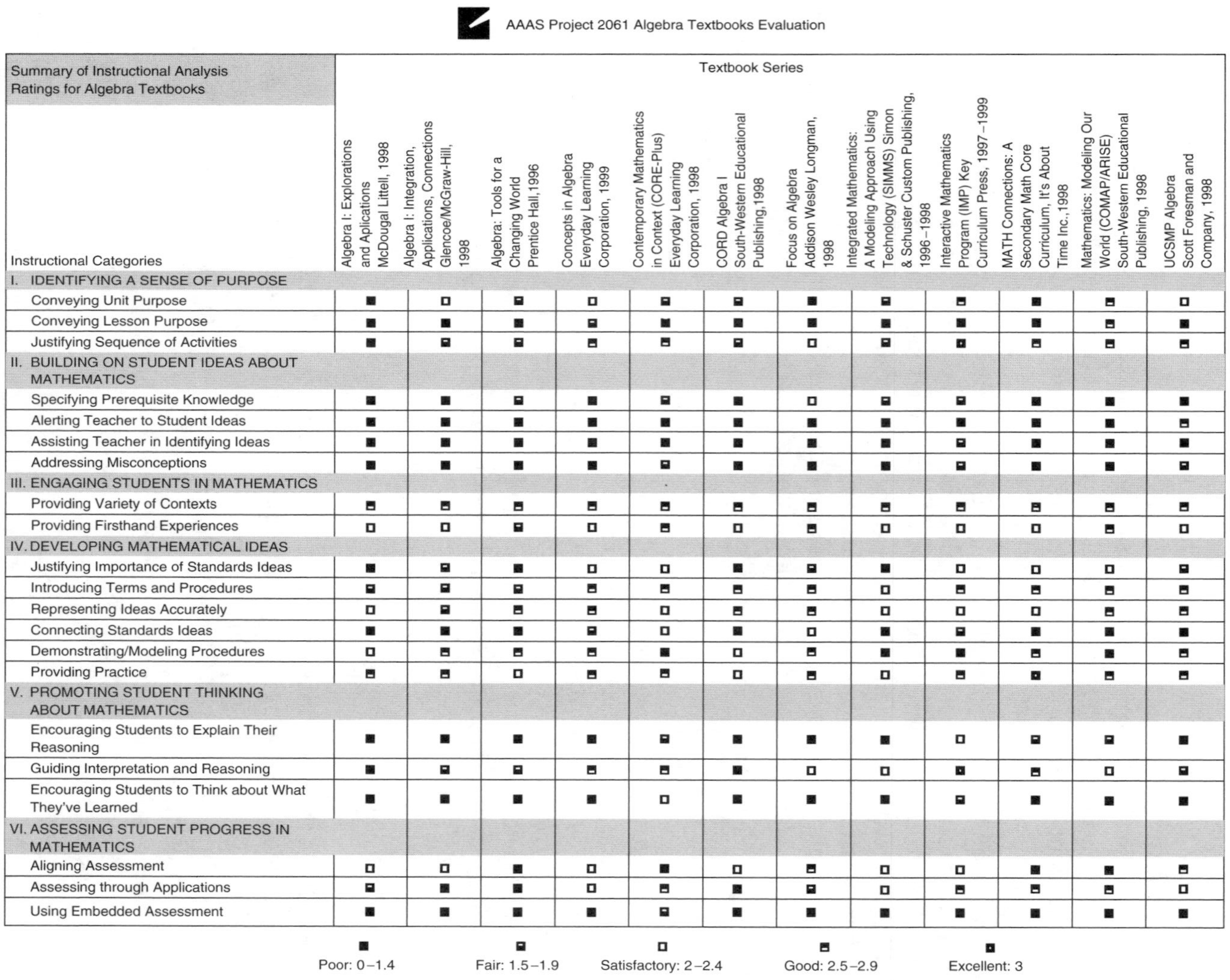

SOURCE: From the Project 2061 Web site (http://www.project2061.org/research/textbook/hsalg/ia_cover.pdf). Reprinted with permission from the American Association for the Advancement of Science.

could go a long way in giving school districts realistic ratings used to assist in choosing textbooks. Textbook publishers would change the content and presentation of their textbooks to receive a favorable rating. Businesses have adopted standards as a way to rate profitability and business practices, giving other businesses (often through a subscription) access to vital information about clients and competitors. Couldn't textbook companies and school superintendents create a similar organization for rating textbooks? Project 2061 is now opening a Center for Science Curriculum Materials in conjunction with the National Science Foundation and the American Association for the Advancement of Science to encourage the use and development of high-quality curriculum materials.

SOCIAL STUDIES TEXTBOOKS

Social studies textbooks suffer from some of the same problems of mathematics and science textbooks: they opt for coverage over depth, include incoherent statements or sequences of events that assume more background knowledge than students have, and the content is not coherent (Beck & McKeown, 1994). To illustrate this point, consider the following passage:

> *The Langurian and Pitok War.* In 1367 Marain and the settlements ended a 7-year war with the Langurian and Pitoks. As a result of this Languria was driven out of East Bacol. Marain would now rule Laman and other lands that had belonged to Languria. This brought peace to the Bacolian settlements. The settlers no longer had to fear attacks from Laman. The Bacolians were happy to be a part of Marain in 1367. Yet a dozen years later, these same people would be fighting the Marish for independence, or freedom from United Marain's rule. This was called the Freedom War of the Bacolian Revolution. A revolution changes one type of government or way of thinking and replaces it with another.

The text is difficult to understand. This is the text from a 5th-grade textbook on the French and Indian War with the agents and locations replaced by pseudonyms. In most curriculum sequences for social studies, 4th or 5th grade is the first time that U.S. history is taught. So the problems you faced with the pseudonyms would be similar to those a 5th grader with just a little knowledge of early colonial times would face with the original text. Below is the passage as it originally appeared in the text:

> *The French and Indian War.* In 1736 Britain and the colonies ended a 7-year war with the French and Indians. As a result of this war France was driven out of North America. Britain would now rule Canada and other lands that had belonged to France. This brought peace to the American colonies. The colonists no longer had to fear attacks from Canada. The Americans were happy to be a part of Britain in 1763. Yet a dozen years later, these same people would be fighting the British for independence, or freedom from Great Britain's rule. This was called the War of Independence or the American Revolution. A revolution changes one type of government or way of thinking and replaces it with another.

Marker and Mehlinger (1992) have summarized the state of the field. They pointed out that the general sequence for state-supported social studies curriculum by grade is as follows:

Grade	Topic
K	Self, school, community, home
1	Families
2	Neighborhoods
3	Communities
4	State history, geographic regions
5	U.S. history
6	World cultures, western hemisphere
7	World geography or world history
8	American history
9	Civics or world cultures
10	World history
11	American history
12	American government

Although the general sequence is usually followed, Marker and Mehlinger (1992) asserted that this sequence is based more on tradition than research. They did find, however, that the state-mandated sequence was only one of many factors that affected the curriculum. A large-scale study in the 1970s found that "despite the enormous investments by the federal government in promoting new curriculum materials and new approaches to instruction (in social studies) little had changed" (p. 834). Thus, large-scale studies have indicated that the social studies curriculum is tradition bound.

Textbooks, written by experts in the field, also influence curricular decisions. Many of the articles written about textbooks follow the format of claiming a topic's importance, reviewing the textbook to see how the topic is addressed, and concluding that more needs to be done with the topic. Topics such as minorities, sex roles, propaganda, terrorism, global interdependence, heroes and heroines, and social bias have been explored in this way. Despite the criticisms of textbooks by experts, teachers seem reasonably satisfied (Hertzberg, 1985). We know that half of all social studies teachers depend on a single text, and about 90% use no more than three textbooks (Wiley, 1977). Teachers do supplement textbooks, generally inserting locally important issues into the curriculum (Hahn, 1985).

Teachers also influence curriculum. They tend to teach what they know; hence, history remains a central focus, despite exhortations from experts to adopt an interdisciplinary approach (Farmer, 1988, p. 29). Teachers also take into account classroom management issues. For example, inquiry teaching methods are seen as more demanding of teacher time than lecture and recitation. Teachers feel the need to "cover" material through lecture, whether the material is learned or not.

State departments also have an influence on curriculum, although their influence until recently has been relatively minimal (Stake & Easley, 1978). Stodolsky (1988) found that "a look at the accountability system will frequently reveal whether a subject has high priority" (p. 4). Thus, as social studies becomes part of a state's accountability system, the importance of social studies may increase.

As academic studies have pointed to the shortcomings of social studies textbooks (see Alexander, 1960; FitzGerald, 1979; Palmer, 1967; White, 1988), the popular press has also commented (National Geographic Society, 1988; Ravitch & Finn, 1987).

One study of exceptional thoroughness is by James W. Loewen (1995) that details a study of 12 high school history textbooks and how they treated Woodrow Wilson, Helen Keller, Christopher Columbus, the first Thanksgiving, presentation of Native Americans, racism in American seen through the stories of John Brown and Abraham Lincoln, class structure and the land of opportunity, the disappearance of the recent past, and the theme of progress. To summarize, Loewen found the following:

- Textbooks handicap history by making heroes and disguising or ignoring their many faults.
- Textbooks contradict known facts and explanations for why things have happened.
- Students aren't learning the rudimentary details of American history.
- Neither passionate nor dispassionate, textbook writing lacks emotion.
- Textbooks do not provide a "causal skeleton" on which to hang facts.
- Textbooks stress the distant over the recent past.
- Textbooks give incomplete and inaccurate accounts of the past.
- Because of a textbook's size and scope, it cannot acquaint students with issues and controversies and teach the attendant skills of using logic and marshalling evidence.

Loewen (1995) suggested introducing fewer topics and examining them more thoroughly. This would enable students and teachers to examine the controversies in more depth, "do" history through assimilating primary and secondary sources, and interview diverse community members about a topic in recent local history. For each historical theme covered, Loewen proposed asking the following questions: Why was (the history) written? Whose viewpoint is presented, and whose is left out? Is the account believable? Is the account backed up by other sources? How is one supposed to feel about the history that has been presented? Consistently answering those questions, Loewen said, is the way to learn history.

A recent report by Diane Ravitch and sponsored by the Thomas B. Fordham Foundation rated social studies textbooks for U.S. history and world history. Six experts rated the world history textbooks and six other experts rated the American history textbooks according to the following criteria:

1. *Accuracy:* Is the text accurate in its presentation of facts and major historical issues?

2. *Context:* Does the text present historical events and ideas in a context that enables the reader to understand their significance?

3. *Organization:* Does the text offer a well-organized, coherent narrative that emphasizes the most important eras, cultures, events, and ideas in U.S. (or world) history?

4. *Selection of supporting material:* Does the text illustrate the most significant events, ideas, and individuals with relevant, accurate, vivid, and interesting stories?

5. *Lack of bias:* Is the text free of political or ideological bias?

6. *Historical logic:* Is the text free of presentism and moralism?

7. *Literary quality:* Does the text have a writing style that engages the reader?

8. *Use of primary sources:* Does the text make good use of well-chosen primary source documents?

9. *Historical soundness:* Does the text give adequate attention to political, social, cultural, and economic history?

10. *Democratic ideas:* Does the text give appropriate attention to the development of democratic institutions, human rights, and the rule of law?

11. *Interest level:* Are students likely to want to learn more about history as a consequence of reading this textbook?

12. *Graphics:* Do the graphics and sidebars in the text contribute to the reader's interest and understanding of history? (Ravitch, 2004, pp. 17–18)

The *Salt Lake City Tribune* picked up the report and summarized its findings, shown in Figure 2.15. Besides the ratings, Ravitch (2004) reported the following findings:

- Textbooks are not the disembodied voice of an authority whose facts and interpretations are beyond quibble (p. 63).
- The textbooks are dull and consequently will not do a good job in teaching students (p. 63).

Figure 2.15   Grading history textbooks

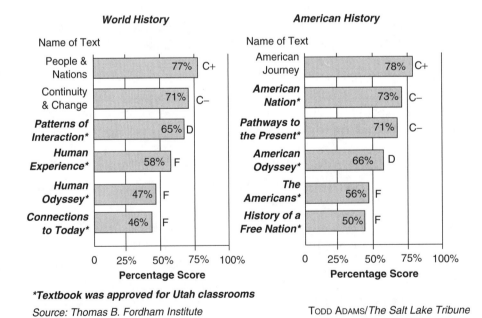

Reviewers flunk many Utah-approved history books

An independent panel, sponsored by the Thomas B. Fordham Institute, judged 12 widely used history textbooks against 12 criteria, including accuracy, clarity, writing style, lack of bias, and attention to democratic ideals. Here is how they fared (the full report is available at **www.edexcellence.net/foundation**):

Source: Thomas B. Fordham Institute

*Textbook was approved for Utah classrooms

TODD ADAMS/*The Salt Lake Tribune*

SOURCE: From "Dull texts can turn history into bedtime stories," by L. Fantin, 2004, March 25, *The Salt Lake City Tribune*. Retrieved April 2004 from http://www.sltrib.com/2004/mar/03252004/utah/ 150968.asp. Reprinted with permission.

- "The books are of identical size and heft. They are graphically gorgeous. They have beautiful multicolored images on every page. (Some actually seem to allot more space to graphics than to text.) With only relatively minor variations, all relate a similar narrative about the development of the United States or the world" (p. 64).
- Textbook authors tried to cover too much material in a small amount of space, truncating explanations of context and events (p. 64).
- World history textbooks attempt too much. There is not enough space devoted to any civilization so students remember little of what they study (pp. 64–65).

On the basis of the reviews, Ravitch (2004) recommended abolishing state textbook adoptions, reviewing textbooks by independent agencies, better educated teachers, and establishing alternative requirements to world history to reduce the scope of coverage needed (pp. 66–67).

ENGLISH AND LANGUAGE ARTS TEXTBOOKS

Many of the assumptions teachers and administrators have about how to produce good results may not be valid if the link between practice and outcomes are examined. Some professionals believe that "If I cover what's in the book, then my students will do well on the test." How a textbook is put together and how well textbooks are aligned with tests or with curriculum standards needs to be questioned to recognize the pitfalls of such assumptions.

A textbook, like any piece of curriculum, is designed with the assumption that students have certain prerequisite skills. The textbook may hit the middle of an "average" population, but, in many places, the assumptions about an "average" student population may not be valid. In large urban areas, for example, students often don't have the prerequisite skills that the text assumes. In some upper-income suburban communities, students may have reached the *Prairie Home Companion*'s goal: "all the children are above average." A balanced and aligned curriculum can help focus appropriate curriculum content for students with certain prerequisite skills.

Many teachers and administrators assume that textbooks adequately cover the topics on standardized tests; however, research in the reading and language arts suggests otherwise. Crismore (1985) and Rowe (1985) reviewed 525 studies; many compared students' progress in control groups when using only a basal reader with those in experimental groups using other instructional strategies in addition to the basal. As Figure 2.16 indicates, the experimental groups scored 24 percentile points higher than did control groups that used only the basal reader. As Harste (1989) pointed out, "The experimental group's scores represent almost a full year's growth over and above children who participated in only the regular reading program" (p. 24).

Figure 2.16   Children receiving an experimental treatment in reading instruction experienced an average gain effect of 0.70 over groups using a basal reading program

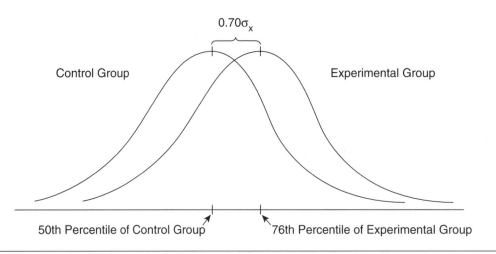

SOURCE: From *New Policy Guidelines for Reading: Connecting Research and Practice,* by J. C. Harste, 1989, Urbana, IL: National Council of Teachers of English. © 1989 by the National Council of Teachers of English. Reprinted with permission.

Indeed, the International Reading Association (IRA) published the following guideline for the use of texts in the curriculum:

> No single textbook can be geared to the needs of all students. This circumstance does not imply the need for writing new textbooks for poor readers. The existing market contains a plethora of texts which vary in their content, complexity, and cognitive expectations. New users of available texts are needed. If teachers are expert enough to present model lessons which include phrases such as prior knowledge activation, concept vocabulary development, purpose settings, development of conceptual interrelationships, and reinforcement of learning, students will have the foundation for learning from different texts in the same course. Developing the capability for using multiple texts in one class and sustaining students' strategies from these texts is a challenge to the professionalism of teachers and the ingenuity of teacher educators. (Research Department, IRA, p. 16)

Many educators and administrators assume that most teachers adequately cover the content of standardized tests during classroom instruction. Again, research suggests otherwise. Studies and research summaries (Brady et al., 1977; Squires et al., 1983) indicate that the range of content on standardized tests covered during instruction may vary from 4% to 95%. The Balanced Curriculum process can help teachers and administrators make sure that students are given a fair chance to learn concepts included on standardized tests by increasing the percentage of test topics covered.

BASAL READERS AND THE BALANCED CURRICULUM

Much of the work of balancing and aligning the curriculum will help the school understand the use and function of basal reading textbooks. Research indicates that most teachers use the teacher's guide of the basal textbook series as their primary guide for teaching reading. Indeed, a few will feel that if the textbook is covered, then students should learn how to read and comprehend. They may indicate that aligning the curriculum isn't necessary because the textbook authors have already done this when writing the books. Both administrators and teachers need to reconsider this blind faith in textbooks to understand how textbooks promote and, unfortunately, at times discourage students becoming lifelong readers and writers. By considering how basal readers, the textbooks that drive reading instruction in most schools (Anderson, Osborn, & Tierney, 1984) pose problems in the curriculum alignment process, teachers and administrators can make informed decisions. The research summarized here is contained in the book *Report Card on Basal Readers* by Goodman, Shannon, Freeman, and Murphy (1988).

If most reading instruction is driven by basal readers, then "the selection of a basal reader is tantamount to selecting the reading curriculum" (Farr, Tulley, & Powell, 1987, p. 268). Examining the characteristics of basal readers, then, is important to completing a curriculum. Although there are differences between publishers, the basal readers are more similar than different in approach and content (Goodman et al., 1987) because they are driven by market economics.

Mismatch Between Basals and Standards or Expert Approaches to Reading

Although there are other ways to think about the reading process, basal reading texts are not organized to promote them. The major orientation of most basal readers is behavioral. "A major organizing principle of basal readers is that learning to read is, more than anything else, learning words and skills for identifying words" (Goodman et al., 1987, p. 66). There is a mismatch between the philosophy of basal readers and expert opinion presented in standards or through the expert views. For example, if one holds a constructivist philosophy, the purpose of reading instruction is to assist students in making meaning and creating social situations in which the reading and writing process can be used in the pursuit of understanding. Because most textbooks have a behaviorist orientation, the emphasis is on learning words and skills for identifying words instead.

Mismatch Between Basals and Students' Prerequisite Skills

As with other textbooks, there may be a mismatch between students' prerequisite skills and the "level" of the basal. Leveling basals is often accomplished through controlling vocabulary and simplifying syntax by reducing the length and complexity of sentences. Attempts to control vocabulary often result in a loss of meaning or a story that has significant points altered as a result of substituting "easier" words for those considered more difficult. Goodman et al. (1987) noted that in many reading textbooks, "There is more concern for controlling the vocabulary than telling the story" (p. 69). This attempt to help students by controlling vocabulary may actually hinder their comprehension.

Mismatch Between Basals' Directions and Instructional Time Needed to Learn to Read

An international study of reading achievement found that in most countries "frequent readers are better readers" (Smith & Elley, 1994), particularly in early reading experiences. In balancing the curriculum, teachers will need to make sure that students read widely and frequently. Just reading the content of the basal readers will not be enough.

Following teacher instructions in the basal may actually lead to little time spent reading. For example, if the teacher's guide is followed, "only 10 to 15 percent of the instructional time will actually be spent in silent reading of cohesive texts" (Goodman et al., 1987, p. 72). If allocated time for reading is 90 minutes, only 9 to 13 minutes per day will be spent in silent reading. Is this enough for students to learn to read and develop a habit of reading? Many schools have increased silent reading time by instituting a schoolwide period when everyone at the school reads silently. Teachers and administrators need to understand that following the basal may not allow students enough time to actually engage in reading.

Mismatch of Basals' Lack of Comprehension Instruction and Students' Instructional Needs

In a classroom study of elementary teachers, "less than 1 percent of the time of thirty-nine 3rd- to 6th-grade teachers was spent on comprehension instruction" (Durkin, 1987, p. 337). In our hypothetical 90-minute time slot allocated for reading, this is a little over a minute per day. This means that a basal-based curriculum spends little time instructing students to comprehend the meaning of text. If reading comprehension scores on standardized tests are problematic, lack of reading comprehension instruction may be one place to look for improvement.

Furthermore, such comprehension questions that exist emphasize that there is "one correct answer." That's how the teacher's guide is written. Unfortunately, basal reading texts' questions generally don't have multiple answers or interpretations. "Text questions with single correct answers varied from 63% to 98%" (Goodman et al., 1987, p. 81) in a teachers' guides at a variety of grade levels. In most stories or texts, however, there is room for more than one interpretation of events. Is Little Red Riding Hood a symbol of female subjugation in a male (wolf) dominated world? Or is Little Red Riding Hood a story of childhood innocence confronting the duplicities of the adult world? Indeed, part of reading's intellectual challenge is understanding that there are many meanings and interpretations. If most of the time there is only one correct answer, this may convince students not to make interpretations or think about connections to their worlds.

Students may erroneously conclude that reading a passage is a matter of "getting the answer the teacher thinks is right" rather than examining a text for multiple meanings and viewpoints. Again, there is a mismatch between the basal curriculum and good instructional practice. "The focus of the basals is not on supporting development of the strategies for comprehending; rather it remains on the products of comprehension represented by the students' abilities to produce 'correct' answers to arbitrary questions" (Goodman et al., 1987, p. 82).

In an international study of 32 countries (Smith & Elley, 1994), an emphasis on comprehension instruction correlated positively with achievement. This finding indicates that emphasizing reading comprehension is important to improved results. Given the characteristics of basal readers, teachers will probably have to find ways to emphasize comprehension outside of the confines of teacher editions of reading textbooks.

Mismatch Between Basals' Curriculum and Formative Assessment

If comprehension is the main goal of reading, then chapter tests should focus on comprehension. Once again, there is a mismatch between the basal curriculum and the focus of formative assessments embedded in the basals. "Only 18 percent of the cumulative test questions for the level are intended to test comprehension" (Goodman et al., 1987, p. 92). Test components focus the majority of their effort on word identification and language and study skills (Goodman et al., 1987, p. 107). Although this emphasis may be consistent with a "behaviorist" view of reading, it may not reinforce the importance of reading comprehension with students and teachers.

The reliability and validity of the curriculum-embedded tests also is questioned.

There is no evidence, in their design or in their apparent development, that they [chapter tests in reading basals] meet theoretical criteria for the type of testing they represent. . . . They provide no evidence that they have evaluated pupil success, that in fact the tests are not simply arbitrary sets of questions labeled to conform to the program objective label. There is no evidence that the minimal passing scores are not simply arbitrary. (Goodman et al., 1987, p. 114)

To summarize, Goodman and colleagues stated,

At their best they [basal tests] test some of what is taught, but what is tested is not the whole of reading. They take the form of objective-referenced tests, but they do not meet the recognized criteria for design of such tests. They are, according to their own design criteria, poorly executed. We could not find justification in the tests for the claims publishers make for them, or the use of the results to make decisions about the academic lives of students. Far from being the scientific core of the basal programs the tests may well constitute their weakest components. (1987, p. 121)

Following is a list of other difficulties in the design and execution of formative testing in basal reading series.

- Right answers for the wrong reasons
- Not much to read on reading tests
- Inconsistent patterns for items within subtests

- Inconsistency between subtests of a unit or level test
- Making it hard by making it easy
- Problems with illustrations
- Uncohesive and incoherent language (Goodman et al., 1987)

SUMMARY

Despite being one of the most successful and long-lasting "innovations" in education, textbooks have some serious drawbacks. In an effort to cover all things of importance, particularly in math, science, and social studies, the instruction ends up mirroring the structure of the textbook and is a "mile wide and an inch deep." As knowledge keeps on doubling in shorter amounts of time, educators will need to realize that they can't teach everything of importance. One could argue that textbooks will fail under their own attempts to be all things to all schools, especially as the standards and testing movements impinge on local districts with high-stakes accountability schemes. The Internet has opened up and made accessible great information resources. Our problem is no longer having enough resources at our fingertips; we now have too many. The problem of the future will be how to know if information is credible and when to use it. We will no longer need facts piled jowl to jowl in a textbook to satisfy state agencies that students have access to information. What we now need is a guide (a curriculum) that can assist teachers and students through the thicket of information, giving students the tools to question information and make up their own minds. In the not-so-distant future, textbooks will become just another resource for teaching and learning, eventually fading to an arcane topic covered only in the history of education.

3

Understanding and Using National, State, and Local Frameworks and Standards

This chapter begins by defining standards and their purpose followed by a brief history of the standards movement over the last 30 years (I must be getting old). The chapter ends with an examination of the logic driving the standards movement that establishes a rationale for a curriculum aligned to standards that can guide instruction.

DEFINITION OF STANDARDS

Standards specify what students should know and be able to do within a particular subject area, such as social studies or science, and within a range of grade levels, for example, K–4, 5–8, 9–12, although some standards (Texas) are grade-level specific, and others (International Reading Association/National Council of Teachers of English [IRA/NCTE] standards for English and language arts) encompass K–12. Generally, state agencies or national professional associations develop standards through democratic and collaborative processes to reach consensus on what is most important for students to know and be able to do. A number of school districts have also generated their own standards, incorporating state or professional standards (or both). School district's efforts have often taken the state's standard and assigned particular standards to individual grade levels or have collapsed the many standards—professional association, state, state assessments, commercial assessments—into one comprehensive list (see Coyle & Pimentel, 1997; Foriska, 1998; Glatthorn, 1998; Marzano & Kendall, 1996; Reeves, 1996–1998). The Balanced Curriculum model doesn't specify that schools or school districts need to develop their own standards. Too many standards already crowd the field.

Each set of standards has a particular "slant" or "point of view." The Balanced Curriculum process uses the many standard sets already available and assumes that the slants or points of view of various standards will be sufficient, with judicious discernment of teacher-authors, to produce balance in the curriculum. Given the scarce resources of school districts, a focus on developing the curriculum is more important than developing yet another set of standards.

There are other types of standards related to education, and these can assist districts, states, and universities in building the infrastructure to deliver the content standards. For example, the National Science Education Standards (1996), in addition to content standards, have standards for teaching science, standards for professional development of science teacher, standards for constructing assessments, and standards for developing a science education system. Content standards are the focus, however, because they specify what students should know and be able to do.

A BRIEF HISTORY OF THE STANDARDS MOVEMENT

The goal in presenting a brief history of the standards movement is to highlight a few of the many strands that are interwoven in today's movement. The diagram in Figure 3.1 explains a few major events in the movement to develop standards. Along the left-hand side, three strands provide important events in the following areas: key publications, political events, and movements (Woodward, 1999).

Before 1980, the minimum competency and effective schools movements dominated the discussion on educational reform. In the minimum competency movement, states and, in some cases, districts defined the "floor" for what would be the minimum requirements for passing particular grades or for graduating from high school. State or district tests were then developed to assess whether students met the minimum competencies, thereby assuring the public that passing to the next grade level or graduating had some meaning.

The minimum competency movement established the precedent of state departments of education, as opposed to school districts, as the institutions that set requirements for passing or graduating on the basis of test results. States previously had not assumed this role but simply oversaw the funding of schools. Using large-scale testing programs, state departments of education took on the responsibility of developing and administering tests to determine whether students had met the predetermined minimum competencies. The idea was that minimum competencies could be adequately assessed using standardized instruments. Not every state participated in the minimum competency movement, but those that did gained the experience of developing tests and determining passing scores for large-scale testing programs.

The minimum competency movement provided the policy structure for the standards movement that emerged in the mid-1990s. For those states that already had the testing structure in place, developing a system to test standards was a relatively easy process. In addition, general standards were politically more "saleable" because

Figure 3.1   Diagram of the history of the standards movement

	1980	1985		1990	1995	2000
Key Publications		'83 A Nation at Risk		'89 NCTM Math Standards	'93 Science Benchmarks	'96 English Standards
					'94 Social Studies Standards	'96 National Science Ed. Standards
Political Events				'89 National Education Summit		'97 new Standards
Movements		Minimum Competency				
			Effective Schools		1994 to Present—Developing State Standards	
				Site-Based Management		

NOTE: NCTM = National Council of Teachers of Mathematics.

they not only addressed minimum competencies but also established a baseline for what all students should know and be able to do.

The effective schools movement, which began in the 1980s and is still part of the educational landscape today, also prepared the ground for the standards movement. This movement suggested that schools did control important areas and could navigate their own fates. The effective schools movement was based on research indicating that some schools serving poor and minority students were more effective than others, and effective schools shared several dimensions: a safe and orderly environment, principal leadership, parental involvement, academic emphasis, and expectations for student success (Brookover, Beady, Flood, Schweitzer, & Wisenbaker, 1979; Lezotte & Pepperl, 1999; Squires, Huitt, & Segars, 1983). The effective schools movement then prompted schools to work on areas identified by research as important for effective educational outcomes. This approach differed from the ideas of previous eras, as indicated by Coleman and colleagues' research from the 1960s: "Only a small part of variation in achievement is due to school factors. More variation is associated with the individual's background than with any other measure" (Coleman et al., 1966, p. 7). If this were so, schools couldn't do much to affect outcomes, which instead would be predetermined by students' socioeconomic status.

Partially as a result of the effective schools movement, the school—not teachers, not individual classrooms, not staff development, and not districts—became the focus of change. Research began to guide the changes that schools could make. States began paying attention to data from "school report cards," which indicated each school's results in terms of state-determined dimensions such as student achievement, attendance, and behavior; teacher demographics; and student socioeconomic characteristics. Such a process remains in effect today as states report outcomes of state testing on their standards for each school.

As the effective schools movement declined, site-based management gained popularity, leading to increased emphasis on the school as the unit of change and diminished control by the central office. The effective schools movement's emphasis on the importance of the school as the unit of change led many to adopt site-based management: If the school is the unit of change, then the school needed more power to bring about change. Schools needed to be free of district regulations because they were closest to the problems and needed control over their own destinies so that they could direct the change without hindrance from the district. Schools began to control more of their budgets, staff development time, and other resources and began to assume responsibility for developing their own instructional and curricular programs, often with little experience or preparation. The central office provided the resources and then got out of the school's way.

At the same time, schools and districts began adopting programs to do curriculum work (e.g., out of concern that students weren't developing values, they adopted programs on character education). Various programs were layered together as a way to address all of a school's needs, and curriculum became program based. The reasoning was this: Students aren't doing well in math, so the school will adopt X program, and it will address the issue. Program adoption can be politically expedient because once a need is identified, adopting a program addresses the need (whether or not it actually resolves it). Ask teachers in any school to list the programs that have been tried in the last 5 to 10 years, and they can probably list 20 to 50: DARE, Distar, Chess Clubs, Leadership Development, after-school programs, and so on. School leaders used programs to serve the function of curriculum because they didn't have the time to develop one, and they hadn't ever encountered a curriculum that actually made a difference. Program adoption became the shortcut to getting results. "Programitis" still affects many schools and districts.

Combine programitis with site-based management: individual schools adopt myriad programs; districts provide schools with resources for program adoption; many different programs are adopted in various schools, without any organizing structure from the district. The federal government exacerbates the problem by providing funding for individual schools to adopt school change models through the Comprehensive School Reform and Development Act, so districts may oversee numerous school reform models, often with competing philosophies, priorities, and demands, within a single district. Curriculum is lost in the backwaters; most schools don't have the time, expertise, or personnel to develop curriculum. Most curriculum development has had no influence on instruction, so schools and districts do not view curriculum as a viable solution because it has never worked before. Teachers make individual decisions privately on how to put all the parts and pieces together, based on a welter of uncoordinated efforts spawned by programitis. Teachers continue to decide what is most important for students to know and be able to do, but they have little guidance or coordination in doing so.

Districts and schools lament that they don't measure up to standards as determined by state assessments. Districts and schools don't see or understand that site-based management of curriculum and programitis work against better performance on state assessments. Districts have abrogated their responsibility for translating state standards and assessments into a curriculum that schools can use to address state standards and assessments. Curriculum is the missing link.

Given this explanation of the movements affecting schools today, I now use political events and key publications as a framework for understanding the standards movement. (I am indebted to Woodward's [1999] *Alignment of National and State Standards: A Report by the GED Testing Service* for the arguments used here.)

In 1983, during the Reagan administration when budget cutting for the Department of Education (DOE) was endemic (the administration even sought to eliminate the department), the secretary of education published an influential report on the state of the nation's schools; *A Nation at Risk: The Imperative for Educational Reform* (U.S. National Commission on Excellence in Education, 1983). The report cited massive documentation of U.S. school failures, suggesting that "more rigorous and measurable standards" were needed to guide reform and raise student achievement, so, in the future, our nation could continue to be a productive world leader (p. 27). At the time, states did not have standards, although the minimum competency movement had begun. Professional associations accumulated research on what students should know and be able to do but had not seen this research as a foundation for content standards for various disciplines. During this time, the call for standards was just one of many ideas for educational reform in the United States.

In 1989, the National Council of Teachers of the Mathematics (NCTM) published K–12 content standards for mathematics in its *Curriculum and Evaluation Standards for School Mathematics*. The standards delineated mathematical content at a range of grade levels. The NCTM standards provided proof that

- Standards could be developed with wide acceptance from the field
- Standards could provide a comprehensive vision of content that needed to be taught
- Standards could be based on the research evidence
- Standards could provide the basis for assessing student performance

The president and governors of the first DOE Educational Summit, held in 1989, produced the following statement: "The time has come, for the first time in U.S. history, to establish clear national performance goals, goals that will make us internationally competitive" (U.S. DOE, 1991, p. 73). That statement shows that standards emerged from a perception that the United States was no longer competitive economically with other nations of the world, especially Japan.

Over the next eight years, national professional associations, following NCTM's lead, published standards in science (1993), social studies (1994), English and language arts (1996), and then new standards (1997) for English, language arts, and mathematics. Other subject areas followed, such as health and physical education, but are not specifically mentioned here. In 2000, NCTM published a revised version of its mathematics standards. The standards from the national professional associations contributed to the development of state standards, encouraged and partially funded by the Goals 2000: Educate America Act of 1994. Currently, 49 of the 50 states have developed or are in the process of developing state content standards and state assessments of the content standards.

THE LOGIC BEHIND THE STANDARDS MOVEMENT

The logic behind using standards rests on a series of propositions, each of which needs to be true if the standards are to affect education. These propositions are now listed and analyzed as one way to understand the standards.

Propositions About Standards

- If a group can specify what students should know and be able to do,
- and if the standards are widely disseminated and accepted,
- and if the standards are used to guide instruction,
- and if the standards align with the assessments,
- and if the assessments are deemed important,
- then student outcomes (state and standardized tests and other indicators) are likely to improve.

In the following pages, each proposition is analyzed.

If a Group Can Specify What Students Should Know and Be Able to Do

Specifying what students should know and be able to do requires determining who will do the specifying. In practice, the standards specification process was broadly democratic, allowing many groups and individuals to have input on the various drafts of most standards documents. Educators participated, including teachers, state and local supervisors, college professors, scholarly organizations, chief state school officers, and teacher educators. Practitioners participated, including business leaders, policy makers, community groups, and parents. Broad public participation supported the development of most standards, defining a societal consensus of what students should know and be able to do—"Out of the Many, One." National professional associations led the way, followed by state education departments. This proposition is true.

If the Standards Are Widely Disseminated and Accepted

Sharing the development of the standards among so many groups lent support to their implementation. The federal government assisted in leading the development of standards with monetary and technical support. States helped ensure wide dissemination and acceptance of the standards as the standards became the basis for assessments and tests, often of the high-stakes variety. This proposition is also true.

If the Standards Are Used to Guide Instruction

States developed tests, and the test results were shared; in this context, the state took action as required with schools and districts. The assessments, even more than the standards on which they were based, ensured that the standards helped to guide instruction. One superintendent said, "Don't bother me with the standards, we'll just wait until the test comes out and then align what we do to the test."

The weak link in this chain of propositions is the capacity of districts and schools to use the standards to guide instruction. Standards are written at a general level, often times including multiple grade levels. The general standards statements are often too broad and unspecific to help shape instruction. One standard might apply to many lessons.

Conversely, many standards offer detailed statements—some would argue too many detailed statements—so the number of standards interferes with their effectiveness in guiding instruction. New York State, for instance, has four standards for English and language arts (which is typical for many states):

- Standard I. Language for Information and Understanding
- Standard II. Language for Literary Response and Expression
- Standard III. Language for Critical Analysis and Evaluation
- Standard IV. Language for Social Interaction

That's not too many standards, you say.
But the standards are divided into three grade-level bands:

- Elementary
- Intermediate
- Commencement

Each standard has two substandards organized around either
- Listening and reading or speaking and writing
- Listening and speaking or reading or writing

Under each substandard is a "key idea," such as, "Written communication for social interaction requires using written messages to establish, maintain, and enhance personal relationships with others."

Under the key ideas are seven to thirteen performance indicators, such as "Students produce oral and written reports on topics related to all school subjects."

After doing the math, for the four standards at the three grade-level ranges, there is a range of 36 to 37 performance indicators that apply to each grade-level range (see Figure 3.2).

The number of indicators and the grade range of the indicators are a concern as teachers try to use the standards to guide instruction. Thirty-six indicators is a lot to keep track of without any formal system to record which have been taught and learned and which have not. The textbook may take precedence over the standards because this is what teachers are familiar with. So teachers follow the sequence of the text without reference to the standards. Even if teachers reference the standards, most have no way of knowing which standards are addressed at which grade levels, so they don't know whether the scope and sequence that they have chosen dovetail with those of other teachers. Again, teachers use the textbook because it is the only way to ensure at least some coordination of the scope and sequence of the program.

Figure 3.2   New York State performance indicators for standards at the three grade levels

	Standard I	Standard II	Standard III	Standard IV	Total
Elementary	13*	10	8	6	37
Intermediate	12	10	8	6	36
Commencement	12	10	8	7	37

NOTE: *Number of performance indicators.

As mentioned in Chapter 2, curriculum is the missing link between standards and instruction. Standards may not be particularly useful in guiding instruction because they are too general, there are too many, and they generally apply to a range of grade levels. Curriculum's function is to delineate a scope and sequence for instruction aligned to appropriate standards and assessment. Without a curriculum, individual teachers cannot use the standards appropriately. Individual teachers can indeed reference their instruction to the standards through their lesson plans, but this does nothing to address whether the topic or standard has been addressed before, the students' entry-level skills (because there is no knowledge of the instruction completed during the previous years), or whether this is a topic or standard that should be addressed (is this important for students to learn?).

The standards movement will never meet its promise if districts do not embrace curriculum as the key to the puzzle of meeting standards through instruction. That's why this book exists: because curriculum is the missing link in the logic of the standards movement. If there is no curriculum to link instruction to standards, then the logic chain breaks in the middle, and the written standards will not and cannot be realized without a balanced and aligned curriculum. Without curriculum, this proposition is false.

If the Standards Align With the Assessments

Standards cover a lot of territory—what students should know and be able to do. Assessments cover a smaller territory. All standards cannot be assessed; there isn't the time or the money. For example, returning to the New York state standards, if I have 36 progress indicators, the test will not cover all of them. A progress indicator such as "Students produce oral and written reports on topics related to all school subjects" will not be tested in a standardized format on a state test because there is no practical way to determine with multiple-choice or short-answer questions whether students have produced oral and written reports in all subject areas. (Chapter 4 covers standardized testing in more depth.)

The standards that are assessed will be tested through a limited number of questions. Standards need to be assessed by more than one question to help eliminate guessing, although rarely would an individual standard be assessed by more than 10 questions because there would not be enough time to address all standards in a 2-hour testing block.

The test makers ask us to believe that if students answer the items aligned to particular standards correctly, then they have demonstrated competence in all aspects of the standard. All testing rests on an assumption that if students get an item or a series of items correct, they have learned a much larger domain of content. For example, a standard states that all students will learn their number facts. Learning number facts means addition, subtraction, multiplication, and division from 1 to 10. That's a huge number of facts. In testing whether they know the number facts, a test maker might pick five problems each for addition, subtraction, multiplication, and division. If students solve these problems, the tester maker assumes they knew *all* the number facts.

Some states do not publish test specifications, which list the domains (standards) tested, the number of items for each domain, and sample test items that show the format of the test questions. They also do not report scores so districts and schools do not know in which domains (standards) students were strong or weak, instead reporting only scores in bands, such as exemplary, proficient, and minimally proficient. Districts are asked to trust the processes of the state that the standards have been adequately assessed and that the banded scores represent what their labels say. That's why the superintendent I quoted earlier said, "I'll just wait until the test comes out to figure how to change my program." He wants to ensure that what's tested gets taught. Yet this is a smaller problem than making sure the instruction covers all the areas in the standards.

The conclusion from this discussion is that all standards are not aligned to assessments. Even when there is alignment between tests and standards, the tests are still merely samples of a domain, making it difficult to assume that passing the test represents having learned all the standards. In addition, some tests are not aligned directly to the standards, undermining public confidence in the testing process. In a district with a curriculum that includes assessments (such as the structure of the Balanced Curriculum), however, it is possible to create assessments directly linked to most, if not all, standards. Without curriculum and curriculum-embedded assessment, the alignment between standards and large-scale assessments is tenuous. Thus, the proposition about the assessments aligning with the standards is false.

If the Assessments Are Deemed Important

States have succeeded in making results on state assessments important. Some of the strategies that various states use to draw attention to the standards and the tests include publishing results in newspapers, employing sanctions or providing assistance to low-performing or declining schools and districts, linking accreditation with performance, and failing low-performing students or offering them additional assistance such as summer school or an extended school day. Districts have responded by increasing the importance of scoring well on the tests, with faculty having increasing exposure to the standards. This proposition is true.

Then Student Outcomes (State and Standardized Tests and Other Indicators) Are Likely to Improve

That's a long train of logic, and not all the rail cars are on the track, especially if a district lacks curriculum. The state has provided some "cars"—the standards and the assessments. The missing car for most districts is a curriculum that controls content, aligns with standards and high-stakes tests, and encompasses curriculum-embedded assessments that can give districts a more in-depth look at whether their students are actually meeting the standards, reducing the need to rely solely on the results of high-stakes test as a district's data source for student achievement.

SUMMARY

This chapter reviewed the history of standards and showed how standards emerged on the educational scene. The chapter also reviewed how the logic of the standards movement affects student achievement. The next chapter addresses alignment of the written, taught, and tested curriculum.

4

The Importance of Aligning Curriculum

Before delving into how the balanced curriculum is aligned, this chapter examines the concept of alignment and offers a brief history of alignment as used in education with alignment examples from the research. Next, it describes common ways that districts or schools have attempted alignment with a discussion about each plan's potential effectiveness.

THE ALIGNMENT PROBLEM: MANY STANDARDS, LIMITED INSTRUCTION

Alignment is an agreement or a match between two categories. If standards contain number concepts in math, and the curriculum contains number concepts, alignment—on one level—occurs. The categories match. The alignment presupposes that the contents of number concepts are the same for both the standards and the curriculum.

Standards can be aligned to curriculum. Standards are general; curriculum is more specific. For example, included in a writing standard is the following description: "Write on self-selected topics in a variety of literary forms." The curriculum contains a number of specific writing opportunities for students to write on self-selected topics in a variety of specific literary forms. Each writing opportunity is aligned to the standard and the curriculum, and the standards match or are in alignment. The idea of ensuring alignment means that students will have the opportunity to learn the content of the standards.

The process of alignment becomes difficult when we examine the number of documents that could be aligned and compared. Figure 4.1 has two columns that list the major areas that could be aligned or compared. Arrows beginning in the first column show that National Standards from Professional Organizations aligned to the categories in the second column. Not included are all the other possible arrows. Alignment can be a daunting task.

Figure 4.1   Alignment possibilities

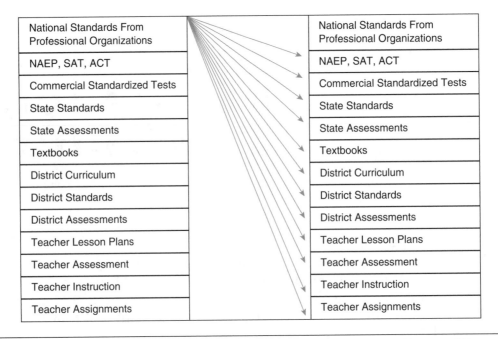

NOTE: ACT = American College Test; NAEP = National Assessment of Educational Progress; SAT = Scholastic Assessment Test

We wish national standards would align with state standards, which would in turn align with local standards. We wish national tests such as the NAEP (National Assessment of Educational Progress), SAT (Scholastic Assessment Test), and ACT (American College Test) would align with commercial standardized tests, state assessments, district, and teacher assessments. We wish that textbooks, district curriculum, and teacher lesson plans would align with teacher instruction. What we wish and what we know are different.

What we know is that for any category in the chart in Figure 4.1, district curriculum has been created in relative isolation from all other categories. Commercial tests do not reflect many state standards. State assessments are not aligned to textbooks. National professional association standards have little relationship to the NAEP, SAT, or ACT. As we work in a standards-based world, we find the tools we have to work with are not aligned. What we also know is a local district can control its curriculum, standards, assessments, lesson plans, and instruction. The district curriculum is the meeting place where all those voices of state and national entities can be brought together and district teachers—now curriculum developers—can, on the basis their professional judgment and expertise, decide what's best for students.

The advantage to the many voices from standards and local practice telling us what is important for students to know and do is that we, the curriculum authors, will decide what is actually taught during the 180 or so days that school is in session. These many voices can help inform our decisions about what is most important to teach. The problem is, we can't keep all the alignment categories in our heads at once. Curriculum provides a way that curriculum authors can make decisions about what is most important to teach and then test it—by testing their decisions and aligning curriculum to the external standards and assessments.

Webb (1997) indicated that alignment is important; teachers will place more importance on documents if alignment exists because the documents will be more useful in teaching students. Feedback from state assessments that align with standards reinforces what is taught and learned. Alignment can improve the effectiveness and efficiency of the school system by getting feedback on standards that need more work so that money and time can be allocated on the basis of need. In an aligned system, student progress is more easily mapped through large-scale assessments and district- or teacher-made assessments that parallel the larger assessments. Student results can drive professional development, textbook adoption, curriculum development, and budgeting processes.

THE HISTORY OF ALIGNMENT

This section examines how alignment came into the field of education by reviewing important ideas that have emerged over the past 50 years. This may be considered a history lesson, but this history shows the complexity of the concept of alignment and explains how others have wrestled with that complexity. To begin, I review Bloom's theory of school learning because I believe it set the conceptual stage for alignment's entrance onto the educational scene.

Bloom's Theory of School Learning

Based in part on Carroll's (1963) model of school learning, Bloom provided a theory of school learning that supports much of the design for the balanced curriculum process. Bloom wanted to "determine a small number of variables which will account for much of the variation in school learning." Bloom and colleagues selected three interdependent variables:

1. *Cognitive entry behaviors,* the extent to which the student has already learned the basic prerequisites to the learning to be accomplished;

2. *Affective entry characteristics,* the extent to which the student is (or can be) motivated to engage in the learning process; and

3. *The quality of instruction,* the extent to which the instruction to be given is appropriate to the learner. (1976, pp. 10–11)

The entry characteristics and behaviors of students, along with quality of instruction, yield three learning outcomes: level and type of achievement, the rate of learning, and affective outcomes.

Figure 4.2 Major variables in Bloom's theory of school learning

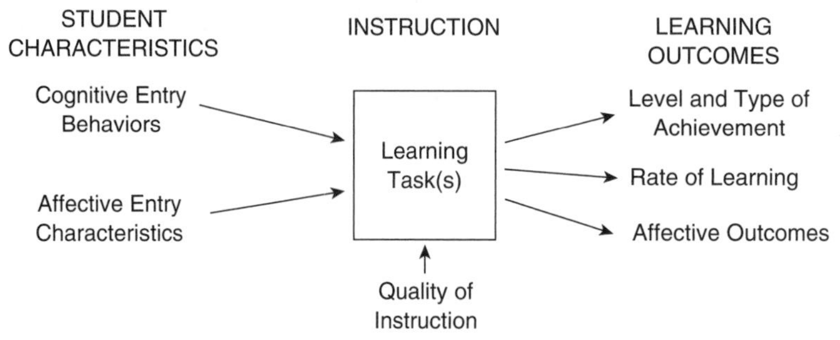

SOURCE: Bloom, B. S. (1976). *Human Characteristics and School Learning.* New York: McGraw-Hill © 1976. Used by permission of the McGraw-Hill Companies.

> Where the student entry characteristics and the quality of instruction are favorable, then all the learning outcomes will be at a high or positive level and there should be little variation in the measures of the outcomes. Where there is considerable variation among students in their entry characteristics and where the quality of instruction is not optimal for the different students, there should be great variation in the learning outcomes. (Bloom, 1976, p. 12)

Today, we still confront the problem of a wide variety of student entry characteristics, leading to a wide span of achievement. Aligning the curriculum, so eventually students' entry characteristics and prerequisite skills are more similar, is one strategy, based on research, that addresses the problem.

Bloom believed that modifications to students' prerequisites and motivations for learning are possible, as are modifications to the quality of instruction that would improve student outcomes. Specifically, if instructional quality improves, then student outcomes would improve. If student outcomes improved, then students would be better prepared cognitively and affectively for the next sequence of instructional tasks. Bloom's theory emphasized that the scope and sequence of instructional tasks—the curriculum—would make a difference in students' performances. "The quality of instruction students receive has a demonstrable effect on their achievement and learning processes over one or more learning tasks" (Bloom, 1976, p. 171).

The school district's responsibility is to develop a curriculum that specifies a sequence of learning tasks. Additionally, if students have appropriate prerequisite skills, any developmentally appropriate learning task can be learned. This implies that, although family and socioeconomic status may initially correlate with student entry behaviors and affective characteristics and determine student outcomes, the school can design curriculum that can assist students in mastering curricular tasks and thereby change student entry behaviors and affective characteristics for subsequent learning tasks over time. Indeed, in further testing of the model, Bloom (1976), Block (1971, 1974), and Block and Burns (1976) reviewed numerous studies indicating that by following a mastery learning model, it is possible to raise the achievement levels of approximately 80% of students to the high levels now reached by only 20% of students.

Curriculum is the way schools organize and sequence appropriate learning tasks and determine whether the scope and sequence of learning tasks produces results. As students improve, they have different (and better) prerequisite skills. Then the curriculum needs to change and improve so students' improved prerequisite skills can be leveraged to address a more challenging curriculum. Bloom's quality of instruction construct implies that the school controls factors that affect student outcomes—outcomes not predetermined by race, culture, or socioeconomic status.

At the time Bloom proposed his theory, the 1970s minimum competency testing movement assessed whether students could perform at minimal levels of proficiency. People who studied education also became more interested in seeing how scores could be improved and what the tests actually assessed.

Some of the first studies on alignment happened in the late 1970s. Research on differences between textbooks and standardized tests showed a lack of alignment (Freeman & Kuhs, 1980). Textbooks covered different topics with different emphasis than standardized tests offered. The emphasis and alignment of topic coverage among various standardized tests were uneven (Freeman et al., 1983). So, if a district chose one standardized test, the emphasis on what was tested would be different from that emphasized by another standardized test. Floden and colleagues (1980) also found that content of district curriculum guides did not align with district-adopted texts; teachers generally followed the textbooks, not the curriculum (Neidermeyer & Yelon, 1981).

Bloom's Theory in Practice: Red Bank, New Jersey

Could districts begin to use this emerging research to create a strong curriculum that would guide instruction and produce better results for students, as Bloom's theory suggested? Squires (1985) joined a small school district in Red Bank, New Jersey, which served mainly poor and minority students, to take charge of curriculum from the central office. The district had decided to implement Bloom's instructional model for mastery learning. Some of Bloom's ideas led to a curriculum development effort to improve achievement across grade levels and subjects.

In implementing the curriculum, courses were divided into time-bound units, with a few important learning tasks defining each unit. Curriculum committees reached consensus on district standards for each subject area that defined what was most important to teach. Research on subject areas provided one basis for inclusion in the standards. Standardized tests and textbooks formed another basis for inclusion decisions. (This was before NCTM standards or state standards had been developed.) Teachers aligned the learning tasks to the district standards to determine the adequate coverage for all standards.

The result was a curriculum matrix (Squires, 1985) in which the units and learning tasks aligned with district-set standards. Dramatic increases in achievement from below to above grade level on standardized tests reinforced Bloom's theory that if students received higher quality instruction, their prerequisite skills for the next units would be greater and they would learn more (see Chapter 20, "Results So Far," for more details). Consequently, the curriculum went through yearly revisions in which results from standardized and curriculum-embedded assessments helped determine what should be changed. Units and learning tasks were refined and, in some cases, were no longer necessary and thus deleted. For example, the 3rd grade had a long unit on addition followed by another long unit on subtraction when the curriculum was first developed. In a few years, teachers said that two long units were no longer necessary; students were entering 3rd grade with the necessary prerequisite skills. The teachers suggested combining the units and covering them in half the time. This allowed for more time to be spent on multiplication.

Cohen: Was Alignment Responsible for Bloom's Results?

Cohen's work and that of his doctoral students examined the alignment between instruction and assessments, labeling it "instructional alignment." Central to his ideas is that "Lack of excellence in American schools is not caused by ineffective teaching, but mostly by misaligning what teachers teach, what they intend to teach, and what they assess as having been taught (Cohen, 1987, p. 18.) To buttress the case, Cohen and his graduate students found that misalignment of instruction and testing caused lower aptitude students to fail, while higher aptitude students succeeded. When instruction and assessment were aligned during sample lessons, both low- and high-aptitude students scored well. When instruction aligns with assessment, large gains over a control group (instruction with no alignment) appeared across studies, with effect sizes ranging around 4 times what traditional instruction produced. This research promised better student results if instruction provided practice with test items as well as the concepts the items tested, particularly for low-aptitude students.

The next three studies showed alignment effects in actual school district settings where the curriculum or textbooks were aligned with testing (Cohen and his graduate students had conducted their research in a laboratory setting). Wishnick (1989) examined the effect of alignment between curriculum-embedded tests assessing aligned units and the standardized test in Red Bank, New Jersey (Squires, 1985). Moss-Mitchell's (1998) procedure paired the Evans-Newton, Inc. approach to curriculum alignment with a district-led approach. (Evan-Newton, Inc. provides a commercial product to assist districts and schools with curriculum development issues; see http://www.evansnewton.com/home.htm.) Both studies examined the alignment between the standardized test and curriculum materials in a large school district in Georgia. The Price-Braugh (1997) study also looked at the alignment between the state test and the instructional materials in a large district in Texas. These three studies show examples of how alignment has been used in the "real world" of school districts to improve student results within a year's time period. These studies reinforce the idea that when districts control their curriculum or materials (or both), ensuring alignment with high-stakes tests, results can be large and positive. In terms of Bloom's theory, an important indicator of quality of instruction highlighted in these studies is the degree of alignment between the curriculum or the curriculum materials and the test. Now let's examine each study in more detail.

The Wishnick Study: Alignment Is More Important Than Socioeconomic Status in Predicting Achievement

Wishnick was a student of Cohen's, whose research on instructional alignment was mentioned earlier. The purpose of Wishnick's (1989) study was as follows:

In a mastery learning curriculum, how much of the variance in norm referenced standardized achievement test (NRST) scores is explained by: (1) gender; (2) socioeconomic status (SES); (3) teacher effect; (4) scores on locally developed criterion referenced tests (CRTs) purporting to measure the same skills as what is measured on commercially published norm referenced standardized tests (NRSTs). . . . The study's purpose was to investigate the power of instructional alignment compared to the power of demographics that have usually explained significant amounts of NRST scores variance. (pp. 1, 3)

Wishnick concluded by saying, "The study compared the relative potencies of instructional methods with demographic factors" (p. 4). A preponderance of the research has established strong links between a student's socioeconomic status, teacher effect, and gender as predictors of success on NRSTs. If the curriculum and assessments are aligned, will this correlation still hold true?

From the Red Bank school district, Wishnick obtained copies of the curriculum for 4th-grade reading and math; copies of the criterion-referenced tests for each unit designed by the districts' 4th-grade teachers; logs of student scores on those criterion-referenced tests; individual student raw scores for the standardized test, along with the copy of the test and testing material; and a log of whether students were on free or reduced lunch, an indicator of poverty level.

Wishnick developed and validated an Alignment Measurement Scale (AMS) that quantified the degree of instructional alignment between the CRT and NRST item clusters. The AMS measures the alignment of the CRT (criterion-referenced test embedded in the instructional process) with the NRST given near the end of the year. Wishnick identified 17 critical features that contribute to alignment and converted these into seven subscales. Each subscale could be assigned a range of five values: 4 = *Positive Misalignment* (meaning that the CRT was more difficult than the NRST); 3 = *Perfect Alignment*; 2 = *Satisfactory Alignment*; 1 = *Poorly Aligned*; and 0 = *Misalignment* (Figure 4.3).

Each item on the scale has a particular meaning that needs to be understood by the person rating the alignment between the CRT and the NRST. The explanation that follows explains the categories:

The AMS developed and validated as part of this study identified seven alignment measurement scales: SCM (Skill Concept Match), SLM (Skill Level Match), FM (Format Match), DM (Directions Match), CM (Cue Match), EM (Enticer Match) and PCM (Performance Conditions Match). Within these seven measurement scales seventeen critical features were identified.

Skill Concept Match (SCM) and Skill Level Match (SLM) were critical features, as well as measurement scales. Format Match (FM) was divided into five critical features: FM1: Items Look Alike, FM2: Arrangement of Items, FM3: Length of Stimuli, FM4: Number of items related to stimuli, FM5: Mixture of items. Directions Match (DM) was divided into two critical features: DM1: Delivery of instructions, DM2: Format of directions. CM (Cue Match) was divided into two critical features: CM1: Type of response stimuli and CM2: Hints with the stimuli attribute. EM (Enticer Match) was divided into two critical features: EM1: Stimulus response differences and EM2: Rule application mix. PCM (Performance Conditions Match) was divided into four critical features: PCM1: Time limits, PCM2: Press to perform optimally, PCM3: Type of response sheet, and PCM4: Teacher behavior. This study measured nine critical features in determining the degree of instruction alignment between the CRT and NRST item cluster. (Wishnick, 1989)

Figure 4.3   Alignment measurement scale for aligning standardized tests to curriculum-embedded assessments

PERF 1 | PERF 2 | AMS Total

Directions: Circle the appropriate score for each item. This Likert scale assigns the following values: 4-PM Positive Misalignment; 3 = AL Perfect Alignment; 3 = S Satisfactory; 1 = P Poorly Aligned; 0 = MIS Misaligned

	PM	AL	S	P	MIS
SCM Skill Concept Match	4	3	2	1	0
SLM Skill Level Match	4	3	2	1	0
FM Format Match					
Items Look Alike	4	3	2	1	0
* Arrangement of Items	4	3	2	1	0
Length of Stimuli	4	3	2	1	0
* Number of Items (Tasks)	4	3	2	1	0
* Mixture of Items (Tasks)	4	3	2	1	0
DM Directions Match					
Delivery of Instructions	4	3	2	1	0
Format of Directions	4	3	2	1	0
Cue Match					
Types of Response Stimuli	4	3	2	1	0
Hints Within Stimuli	4	3	2	1	0
EM Enticer Match					
Stimulus Response Difference	4	3	2	1	0
* Rule Application Mix	4	3	2	1	0
PCM Performance Conditions Match					
Time Limit	4	3	2	1	0
Press to Perform	4	3	2	1	0
Response Mode	4	3	2	1	0
Teacher Behavior	4	3	2	1	0

SOURCE: Wishnick, K. T. (1989). *Relative effects on achievements scores of SES, gender, teacher effect and instructional alignment: A study of alignment's power in mastery learning.* Unpublished doctoral dissertation, University of San Francisco, CA. © 1989 K. T. Wishnick. Reprinted with permission.

NOTE: *These critical features are only measured when generating an AMS score for an entire test. Do not measure these critical features when measuring alignment of individual items.

The AMS was applied to item clusters for the CRT and the NRST. Item clusters for both were generated on the basis of concept similarity (were the concepts tested similar?) combined with the way the concepts were tested (for example, were the Predicting Outcomes items phrased positively and did they use "could" in the stem?). Item clusters from both tests were then matched, if similar, and excluded from further analysis if there were no similarities. These clusters were then rated using the AMS instrument after establishing interrater reliability and validity of the instrument. The

AMS ratings and information about students' gender and SES status and the teacher were analyzed. (The analysis is complex and beyond the scope of this chapter.)

Here are the findings (many have been directly quoted or paraphrased from the dissertation):

- Correlations between the CRT (criterion referenced test) and the NRST (norm referenced standardized test) scores of students were compared with the alignment scores on the AMS. The higher the alignment score on the AMS, the greater the correlations between the CRT and the NRST. Good alignment tends to reduce the variability of student scores. Poor alignment increases the variability in student scores.

- SES accounted for only 1% of the NRST performance variance. This means that whether a student was on free and reduced lunch had almost nothing to do with how well he or she scored on the NRST. Most research studies have found that a student's SES is predictive of how well she or he scores on a standardized test. This finding shows that aligned instruction washes out SES as a predictor of achievement.

- Gender and teacher also accounted for little of the variance in student scores. In other studies, the reverse was true. Reading scores for female students are generally higher than for male students in 4th grade. Teachers produce different results, but, in this study, the teacher assignment for a student did not matter because the chances of scoring high was approximately equal in the three classes studied.

- Taken as a whole, the higher the degree of instructional alignment between the CRT and the NRST, the less effect demographic variables—gender, SES, and teacher effect—have on NRST performance.

- The lower the degree of instructional alignment between the CRT and NRST item cluster, the higher the degree of influence of demographic variables on NRST performance.

- The alignment effect is more powerful for low achievers than for high achievers. Low achievers do better when the instructional outcomes are clear and instruction is congruent with post-instructional assessment.

- The CRT was the best predictor of scores on the NRST—better than gender, SES, or teacher effect.

- The power of instruction as measured by the CRTs accounted for 40.32% of NRST performance variance, and the alignment effect accounted for 36.72% of NRST performance variance. Taken as a whole, other variables (gender, teacher effect, and SES) accounted for 3% of NRST performance variance.

- SES is a potent factor in school performance when instruction is generated from a model of education that assumes a normal distribution of scholastic performance. When the educational model assumes that all students can demonstrate mastery, however, and when instruction is designed to cause students to perform well on competency tests, SES loses its impact on school performance. Under competency-based criterion, referenced instruction is more potent than SES.

- This study found no evidence to support previous research that suggested teachers would interact differently with these 4th-grade students. The simple correlation between teacher and total NRST performance approached zero, and the lack of teacher effect is the teacher effect in this mastery learning design.

The Moss-Mitchell Study: Alignment Predicts Outcomes Better Than Race and School Size

Whereas Wishnick's study examined results of 4th-grade reading in a small school district, Moss-Mitchell's study (1998) looked at 3rd-grade mathematics achievement in a large school district (4,000 4th graders) when aligned to the district's text. Fifty-five percent of the students were on free or reduced lunch. The study's purpose was "to examine the implication for educational administrators of effectiveness of the DeKalb County (Georgia) school system's curriculum alignment after one year of implementation" (p. 8). The Moss-Mitchell study examined the effects of curriculum alignment when analyzed by socioeconomic level, race, gender, and school size.

The district used two approaches to curriculum alignment. Four schools adopted the Evans-Newton program (Scottsdale, AZ) centering on staff development, monitoring, and managing. The other approach began with a correlation of the ITBS (Iowa Test of Basic Skills) with a math textbook. This is an example of textbook–standardized test alignment. Twenty-three percent of the text's content was not covered by the ITBS (p. 85). The district then created or selected additional curricular materials that filled in the gaps between the textbook and the test. Instructional coordinators worked with six schools to help faculty use the materials and the curriculum.

At the end of the year, students improved 6 NCEs (Normal Curve Equivalents, a scale for averaging student achievement scores), from 49 to 55 on the ITBS standardized test. "There was no statistically significant difference in the effect of curriculum alignment after one year of treatment when analyzed by socioeconomic level, race, gender or school size" (p. 96). Wishnick's and Moss-Mitchell's studies produced similar results: both showed the effects of alignment, canceling out more traditional predictors of student achievement such as SES, gender, race, and teacher effect. Two alignment measures were used in the two studies. Wishnick examined the curriculum-embedded test alignment with the standardized test. Moss-Mitchell studied the alignment of the textbook with the state mandated standardized test.

The Price-Braugh Study: Misalignment May Be Partly Due to the Content of Textbooks

The Price-Braugh study (1997) examined the effects of alignment between textbooks and the state-developed test (Texas Assessment of Academic Skills; TAAS) in Houston Independent School district for Grade 7, including 10,233 students at 35 middle schools. The textbook content was identified by TAAS descriptors. Price-Braugh then counted the number of skill- and application-level word problems for each TAAS descriptor. She then "correlated the amount of practice and explanation in the textbook for 11 target components with the percentage of students correctly answering TAAS problems on those target components" (p. 109).

Student achievement was positively correlated with all but one textbook variable. High levels of variance (over 55%) were explained by the "number of available skill-level practice items in the textbook for each target component" (p. 111); the number of pages devoted to practice problems; and the number of application-level problems included in the text. This means, for districts adopting textbooks, that the amount of practice students receive in areas that are tested has a significant effect on student achievement. Districts will want to spend the time doing their own textbook correlation to state test categories rather than relying on publisher's correlations that generally don't include the number of problems in specific areas tested.

Like Moss-Mitchell's study, Price-Braugh also confirmed the positive effect of textbook–standardized test alignment.

English: Strategies for Addressing Alignment

Fenwick English, one who has done much to focus educators' attention on alignment, is concerned with the alignment of the taught, tested, and written curriculum and has proposed numerous ways that curriculum can be developed so that it is in alignment with important outcomes (English, 1992; English & Steffy, 2001). Both books suggest ways to "backload" curriculum development to improve scores. "Alignment refers to the 'match' between the curriculum content to be taught and the test content to be used in assessing pupil learning. *Backloading* refers to the practice of establishing the match by working from the test 'back to' the curriculum. It means the test *becomes the curriculum*" (English, 1992, p. 70). Given the research just reviewed, this makes sense—particularly if used only as a stop-gap measure. By concentrating on working backward from the match between the test and curricular content, the district would ensure that important tested content is actually covered in the curriculum. Both Moss-Mitchell and Price-Braugh used a version of this methodology in their studies.

English, in his latest book, *Deep Curriculum Alignment* (English & Steffy, 2001), expanded on backloading the curriculum by listing steps to create pedagogical parallelism as the key to deep curriculum alignment. "*Pedagogical parallelism* refers to the notion that classroom teachers create an alternative but parallel environment in which their students not only learn what is on the test, but learn more" (p. 97). This is similar to Wishnick's (1989) concept of positive misalignment, where the content is more difficult than the content on the test. The steps to take in backloading for deep curriculum alignment are as follows:

- Backloading from public, randomly released test items
- Deconstructing public, randomly released test items
- Developing alternative test items
- Identifying test-item distracters
- (Constructing) test–textbook alignment
- (Determining) written curriculum–test alignment
- Going deeper: anticipate where the test is moving

Deep curriculum alignment combines two powerful forms of alignment: criterion-referenced testing to standardized (or state) testing (which is essentially achieved in the first four steps of the process) and textbook–test alignment (which is reflected in the district's written curriculum and comprises the last three steps of the process).

English (1992) cautioned that backloading is no substitute for districts developing curriculum:

Backloading should be considered an interim measure to improve test scores and not as any kind of final answer to determining what should be in a curriculum in the first place. Considering what children should know is the quintessential problem facing the schools. That always involves the frontloading approach, and it should remain dominant despite the presence of increasing "high-stakes" testing and all of the negative consequences that accrue to students, teachers, and parents with their continued use. (pp. 90–91)

Porter and Colleagues: The Reform Up Close Study Reveals a Variety of Alignment's Dimensions

Porter and colleagues, in the "Reform Up Close" work (Porter, Kirst, Osthoff, Smithson, & Schneider, 1993, 1994), studied high schools in six states, two each in large urban districts and one in a smaller suburban–rural district; the states under study represented a range of philosophies in terms of the state requirements for curricular change in math and science (e.g., increased course requirements, more emphasis on problem solving). The high schools generally required more students to take higher level courses. For example, some of the high schools eliminated general math and required all students to take Algebra I. The study reported on whether the enacted (taught) curriculum in math and science courses were "watered down" as a result of increased enrollment.

To describe the enacted (taught) curriculum across schools, Porter et al. employed a set of descriptors for math and science around topic coverage.

In the Reform Up Close study, we employed a detailed and conceptually rich set of descriptors of high school mathematics and science that were organized into three dimensions: *topic coverage, cognitive demand,* and *mode of presentation.* Each dimension consisted of a set number of discrete descriptors. *Topic coverage* consisted of 94 distinct categories for mathematics (for example, ratio, volume, expressions, and relations between operations). *Cognitive demand* included nine descriptors: memorize, understand concepts, collect data, order/compare/ estimate, perform procedures, solve routine problems, interpret data, solve novel problems, and build/revise proofs. There were seven descriptors for *modes of presentation:* exposition, pictorial models, concrete models, equations/formulas, graphical, laboratory work, and fieldwork. A content topic was defined as the intersection of *topic coverage, cognitive demand,* and *mode of presentation,* so the language permitted $94 \times 9 \times 7$ or 5,922 possible combinations for describing content. Each lesson could be described using up to five unique three-dimensional topics, yielding an extremely rich, yet systematic language for describing instructional content. This language worked well for daily teacher logs and for observation protocols. (Porter & Smithson, 2001, p. 5)

Porter and colleagues used the same three dimensions in describing daily teacher logs, teacher survey instruments of what teachers said they taught, and the "topic coverage" dimension for aligning lessons to emerging national standards. In general, the daily teacher logs, the teacher questionnaire, and the observation protocols aligned in that all descriptions were congruent with each other. Use of the matrix provided a quick way to summarize the content of lessons. Porter's approach of constructing a "taxonomy" of content topics allowed comparison across states with different standards describing math and science. Having a "universal" way to describe instruction would provide common data points for research linking instruction to achievement outcomes and internal district evaluation activities.

Porter et al. found that

content of mathematics and science courses appeared not to have been compromised by increased enrollments; and the enacted curriculum in high school mathematics and science was not at all in alignment with the curriculum reform toward higher-order thinking and problem solving for all students. (Porter et al., 1994, p. 8)

Additionally,

> We were able to demonstrate a strong, positive, and significant correlation (.49) between the content of instruction and student achievement gains. When we controlled for prior achievement, students' poverty level, and content of instruction (using an HLM [Hierarchical Linear Modeling] approach in our analysis), practically all variation in student learning gains among types of first-year high school mathematics courses was explained. (Porter et al., 1994, p. 4)

The power of alignment is demonstrated once again, but this time comparing aligned instruction to increased student outcomes.

Porter and his colleagues invented a way of describing instruction that is reliable, valid, and portable across states and correlates with student achievement. Having one valid and reliable way to describe the content of curriculum, instruction, standards and assessments takes alignment's potential to a new level. I revisit Porter and Smithson's more recent work after examining a similar approach used in describing curriculum in the Third International Math and Science Study (TIMSS).

Schmidt and Colleagues, TIMSS, and Alignment on an International Scale

The TIMSS developed a list of math and science content descriptors so that, across nations, curriculum could be described and then compared and aligned. The TIMSS found that the structure and content sequence of a country's curriculum had an effect on its outcomes when measured by the TIMSS assessments.

The TIMSS developed 10 major content categories for mathematics and 8 content categories for science; it also included two other dimensions: performance expectations and general perspectives. Under performance expectations, or how a student is expected to demonstrate knowledge, there were five categories: knowing, using routine procedures, investigating and problem solving, mathematical reasoning, and communicating. The five categories under general perspectives were attitudes, careers, participation by underrepresented groups, interest, and habits of mind.

Researchers employed the three dimensions in an analysis of textbooks and assessment activities and standards. Like the Reform Close Up study, these dimensions formed a matrix that quantitatively described the content of textbooks, assessments, and standards. The methodology, summarized by Webb (1997), follows. More complete documentation is available in Robitaille et al. (1993) and Schmidt et al. (2001).

> Trained national committees partitioned the textbooks, curriculum guides, and assessment instruments into blocks defined by changes in content or expected performance by students. The analysis scheme defined a block as a piece of text that was part of a lesson or unit devoted largely to one topic. The different forms of textbook content blocks included a narrative block, graphic block, exercise/question sets, activity blocks, and worked examples. The raters assigned each block a "signature" code determined by the different cells checked on a three-dimensional grid. More than one cell of the grid could be marked for any one block, but usually the number of cells for any one block did not exceed three. The national committees used the same grid to perform a similar analysis on the other document to be compared—an assessment instrument or curriculum guide.

The committees' analyses generated a set of content by performance expectations by perspectives matrices with filled-in cells. Circles (O) marked the block signatures produced by the curriculum guide analysis and plus signs (+) marked the block signatures produced by the assessment analysis. The proportion of cells with both a circle and plus represented the degree of match between the two documents. Cells with only one of the symbols indicated a mismatch. Easily computed measures of reliability determined the quality of the process. In sessions of 22 hours, TIMSS staff successfully trained committees in fifty countries to do this form of document analysis. (Webb, 1997, p. 12)

Marzano's Standards Compilation and the Web Site for Achieve

Marzano and Kendall, while at McREL (Midwestern Regional Educational Laboratory) and at the beginning of the standards movement, saw the need to compile the standards from states and national professional associations in one place. They then synthesized all of the standards for various subject areas into one standard for each subject area and published the data in book and CD-ROM format as *Content Knowledge: A Compendium of Standards and Benchmarks for K–12 Education* (Marzano & Kendall, 1997). Another volume is most useful to those who want to create their own district standards: *A Comprehensive Guide to Designing Standards-Based Districts, Schools And Classrooms* (Marzano & Kendall, 1996; see references cited in chap. 6 for resources on creating district standards).

Marzano then used these standards as a benchmark for comparing any state or national professional association standards and created the Achieve Web site (http://www.aligntoachieve.org) where queries for any state could be made to compare (align) one set of standards to another. Commercial applications allow test makers or textbook companies to align their tests and materials with all state standards at once. Current initiatives of the Achieve organization are as follows:

- Benchmarking standards and tests to the best, meaning aligning and analyzing the alignment of existing standards and assessments to exemplary standards and assessments
- Serving as a resource of information, analysis, and advice for state leaders through policy briefs and links to additional resources
- Helping to develop model standards, tests, and curriculum materials, starting with the Mathematics Achievement Partnership

Achieve's four criteria for alignment of assessments to standards are

1. *Content.* Does the test measure what the state standards indicate that all students should know and be able to do at a particular grade level? If not, is it because the standards are too vague to make a determination, or is it because test items measure only part of what the standards ask for?

2. *Performance.* Are students asked to demonstrate the skills the standards expect? For example, if the standards say that students will analyze the characteristics of various literary forms, does the test ask them to evaluate different literary forms, or does it merely ask students to identify one type of literature?

3. *Level of Difficulty.* Are test items easy, medium, or hard, and is the range of difficulty appropriately distributed across all the items? What makes them

difficult—the content they are assessing or another factor, such as the language of the question? Overall, is each assessment appropriately rigorous for students who have been taught to the state standards?

4. *Balance and Range.* Does the test as a whole gauge the depth and breadth of the standards and objectives outlined in state standards documents? If not, are the standards that are assessed the most important one for the grade level? Overall, do the assessments for elementary, middle, and high school focus on the most important content that all students should know?

Currently, Achieve provides alignment services for states and districts, particularly in the alignment of assessments to state standards with other services, such as standards benchmarking and augmentation analysis in which off-the-shelf tests are compared with a state's standards.

The Webb Studies: Aligning State Standards, Assessments, and Policies

Webb examined three approaches toward alignment. *Sequential development* means developing documents in sequence so that the first document, such as state standards, is aligned and used as a reference for the second document, such as curriculum frameworks or assessments. The second approach, *expert review,* utilizes experts to review the alignment between standards and assessments. The third approach, previously described in the TIMSS in Porter's work, and in Marzano's work, is to create a *common description* of curriculum and then analyze the alignment between the common descriptions and other parts of the educational system, such as standards, assessments, instruction, and instructional plans to name a few. None of these approaches had specific criteria for judging alignment; in many cases, it was a case of alignment or nonalignment. Webb's contribution is his development of five major criteria for alignment of expectations (standards) and assessments in math and science education. Additionally Webb put into perspective the complete range of alignment possibilities to include such ideas as policy elements and the use of technology, materials, and tools. Webb applied his ideas to examining the alignment between expectations (standards) and assessments for four states, using some of the criteria for alignment that he proposed.

Webb (1997) discussed the concept of alignment as follows: "Two or more system components are aligned if they are in agreement or match each other. . . . Alignment is being used to characterize the agreement or match among a set of documents or multiple components of a state or district system" (p. 3). Then Webb defined alignment: "*Alignment* is the degree to which expectations and assessments are in agreement and serve in conjunction with one another to guide the system towards students learning what they are expected to know and do" (p. 4).

Webb then developed criteria for judging alignment of content, then students, then instruction, and finally application to a system. The alignment categories are as follows:

Criteria for Alignment of Expectations and
Assessments in Mathematics and Science Education

1. *Content Focus.* System components should focus consistently on developing students' knowledge of subject matter. Consistency will be present to the extent components' logic of action and the ends achieved share the following attributes:

a. *Categorical Concurrence.* Agreement in content topics addressed.
b. *Depth-of-Knowledge Consistency.* Agreement in level of cognitive complexity of information required.
c. *Range-of-Knowledge Correspondence.* Agreement in the span of topics.
d. *Structure-of-Knowledge Comparability.* Agreement in what it means to know concepts.
e. *Balance of Representation.* Agreement in emphasis given to different content topics.
f. *Dispositional Consonance.* Agreement in attention to students' attitudes and beliefs.

2. *Articulation Across Grades and Ages.* Students' knowledge of subject matter grows over time. All system components must be rooted in a common view of how students develop and how best to help them learn at different developmental stages. This common view is based on the following attributes:
a. *Cognitive Soundness Determined by Superior Research and Understanding.* All components build on principles for sound learning programs.
b. *Cumulative Growth in Knowledge During Students' Schooling.* All components are based on a common rationale regarding progress in student learning.

3. *Equity and Fairness.* When expectations are that all students can meet high standards, aligned instruction, assessments, and resources must give every student a reasonable opportunity to demonstrate attainment of what is expected. System components that are aligned will serve the full diversity in the education system through demanding equally high learning standards of all students while fairly providing means for students to achieve and demonstrate the expected level of learning. To be equitable and fair, time is required for patterns to form in order to decipher how system components are working in concert with each other. Judging a system on the criterion of equity and fairness will require analysis over a period of time.

4. *Pedagogical Implications.* Classroom practice greatly influences what students learn. Other system components, including expectations and assessments, can and should have a strong impact on these practices and should send clear and consistent messages to teachers about appropriate pedagogy. Critical elements to be considered in judging alignment related to pedagogy include the following:
a. *Engagement of Students and Effective Classroom Practices.* Agreement among components in a range of learning activities and in what they are to attain.
b. *Use of Technology, Materials, and Tools.* Agreement among components in how and to what ends applications of technology, materials, and tools are to be included.

5. *System Applicability.* Although system components should seek to encourage high expectations for student performance, they also need to form the basis for a program that is realistic and manageable in the real world. The policy elements must be in a form that can be used by teachers and administrators in a day-to-day setting. Also, the public must feel that these elements are credible and that they are aimed at getting students to learn the mathematics and science that are important and useful in society.

For each alignment category, there are criteria for judging their adequacy. The criteria for the subcategories of Content Focus used in an alignment of four state's standards and assessments are given in Figures 4.4 through 4.7 (Webb, 1997).

Figure 4.4   Categorical concurrence criteria

Unit of Comparison	
Expectations	Content topics, subtopics, or both, identified by standards or main areas of content specified
Assessment	Topics by which results are reported (most stringent), subunits' topics of instruments, or topics of clusters of assessment activities
Scale of Agreement	
Full	A one-to-one correspondence between topics given in expectations and topics by which assessment results are reported
Acceptable	Assessments cover a sufficient number of topics in expectations so that a student judged to have acceptable knowledge on the assessments will have demonstrated some knowledge on nearly all topics in expectations
Insufficient	Important topics are excluded from assessments to the extent that students can perform acceptably on assessments and still lack understanding of important expectation topics

SOURCE: From "Determining alignment of expectations and assessments in mathematics and science education," by N. L. Webb (1997, January), *NISE Brief,* 1(2). Madison: Wisconsin Center for Education Research, National Institute for Science Education, University of Wisconsin. Reprinted with permission.

Figure 4.5   Depth of knowledge criteria

Unit of Comparison	
Expectations	Rating of most cognitively demanding expected performance for a topic and for all students as determined by number of ideas integrated, depth of reasoning required, knowledge transferred to new situations, multiple forms of representation employed, and mental effort sustained
Assessment	Rating of most cognitively demanding assessment activity for a topic and taken by all students as determined by number of ideas integrated, depth of reasoning required, knowledge transferred to new situations, multiple forms of representation employed, and mental effort sustained
Scale of Agreement	
Full	For each major topic, the most cognitively demanding expected performance for all students is comparable to the most cognitively demanding assessment activity taken by all students
Acceptable	For nearly all major topics, the most cognitively demanding expected performance for all students is comparable to or can be inferred from the most cognitively demanding assessment activity taken by all students
Insufficient	Students can be judged as performing at an acceptable level on the assessments without having to demonstrate for any topic the attainment of the most cognitively demanding expected performance for all students

SOURCE: From "Determining alignment of expectations and assessments in mathematics and science education," by N. L. Webb (1997, January), *NISE Brief,* 1(2). Madison: Wisconsin Center for Education Research, National Institute for Science Education, University of Wisconsin. Reprinted with permission.

Figure 4.6   Range of knowledge criteria

Unit of Comparison	
Expectations	All students are expected to know how to use all types or forms of major concepts or ideas within and across performance standards (e.g., graph types)
Assessment	All types or forms of major concepts or ideas included on assessments or in the specifications of the content domains are used to select assessment activities
Scale of Agreement	
Full	Students are required on assessments to demonstrate knowledge of all forms or the full range of each major concept or idea expressed in the expected performance
Acceptable	Assessment specifications account for nearly all forms or the full range of each major concept or idea expressed in the expected performance, so there is a strong likelihood that students' knowledge and use of all forms will be assessed
Insufficient	Important forms or specific cases of major concepts or ideas given in the expected performance are excluded from or ignored on assessments or their specifications

SOURCE: Adapted from "Determining alignment of expectations and assessments in mathematics and science education," by N. L. Webb (1997, January), *NISE Brief*, 1(2). Madison: Wisconsin Center for Education Research, National Institute for Science Education, University of Wisconsin. Reprinted with permission.

Figure 4.7   Balance of representation criteria

Unit of Comparison	
Expectations	Assigned importance on a scale of 100 by topic over full spectrum of performance expectations (total for all topics should be 100)
Assessment	Weight by topic or subtopics for full spectrum of assessments (weight could be determined by the proportion of activities by topic, proportion of average time allocated to do an assessment activity by topic, or according to some other rule)
Scale of Agreement	
Full	The proportion of assigned importance for topics in performance expectations is equivalent to the weight topics are given on assessments
Acceptable	Distribution of importance by topics in performance expectations nearly matches the weight of topics in assessments without major exclusions
Insufficient	Weights on assessment by topic are sufficiently different from the assigned importance in the performance expectations such that a student could be judged as meeting performance expectations without knowledge of highly emphasized topics

SOURCE: From "Determining alignment of expectations and assessments in mathematics and science education," by N. L. Webb (1997, January), *NISE Brief*, 1(2). Madison: Wisconsin Center for Education Research, National Institute for Science Education, University of Wisconsin. Reprinted with permission.

The four areas of content focus—categorical congruence, depth-of-knowledge consistency, range of knowledge correspondence, and balance of representation— were dimensions used in a study of the alignment between standards and assessments in four states. The first alignment task was to code each standard and assessment by the levels of thinking required. This allowed analysis to be done by thinking about levels by content; content was then aligned according to the four areas of content focus that follow.

Thinking Levels

1. *Recall:* Recall of a fact, information, or procedure.

2. *Skill/Concept:* Use of information, conceptual knowledge, procedures, two or more steps, and so on.

3. *Strategic Thinking:* Requires reasoning, developing a plan or sequence of steps; has some complexity; more than one possible answer; generally takes less than 10 minutes to do.

4. *Extended Thinking:* Requires an investigation; time to think and process multiple conditions of the problem or task; and more than 10 minutes to do nonroutine manipulations.

A summary of the alignment results is shown in Figure 4.8. The columns show the state, the content area, the grade where students were assessed, the number of standards, the number of objectives, the number of items in the assessment, and then the percent of standards with acceptable alignment. The findings about alignment of state standards with assessments follow.

> The analyses indicated that the standards of the four states varied in what content students were expected to know, the level of specificity at which expectations were expressed, and organization. . . . Alignment between assessments and standards varied across grade levels, content areas, and states without any discernable pattern. Assessments and standards of three of the four states satisfied the categorical concurrence criterion. This criterion, the most common conception of alignment, required the assessment and standards to include the same content topics. Alignment was found to be the weakest on the depth-of-knowledge consistency and range-of-knowledge correspondence criteria. Generally, assessment items required a lower level of knowledge and did not span the full spectrum of knowledge as expressed in the standards. However, for the knowledge and skills identified in the standards and addressed by the assessments, generally the assessment items were evenly distributed. (Webb, 1997, p. vii)

Webb (1997) shows that standards and assessments can be aligned using valid and reliable criteria and shows how the process was used in conducting an analysis of alignment on standards and assessments from four states. Districts could also use such a process as they seek to align their curriculum-embedded assessments to state standards or align the significant tasks in their curriculum to state standards of state assessments.

Figure 4.8 Summary of alignment analysis for state standards and state tests for four states in science and mathematics

State	Content Area	Grade	Standard N	Obj N	Depth-of-Knowledge Level of Objectives				Item[b] N	Students with Percent Acceptable Alignment by Criteria[a]			
					Recall %	Skill/Concept %	Strategic Thinking %	Extended Thinking %		Cat.Concurr. %	Depth %	Range %	Balance %
A	Science	3	6	61	16	61	23	0	44	67	83	33	100
		8	6	97	9	56	33	2	70	67	17	33	100
	Mathematics	3	6	94	15	45	26	13	50	67	50	0	100
		6	6	101	10	49	27	14	61	100	100	0	83
B	Mathematics	4	7	61	2	56	34	8	86	100	57	57	86
		8	7	43	0	42	42	16	86	100	71	86	71
		10	4	20	0	35	65	0	70	100	0	100	100
C	Science	4	5	60	8	72	20	0	14	und[c]	und	und	und
		8	5	86	7	77	16	0	14	und	und	und	und
	Mathematics	4	6	107	6	61	31	3	74	100	100	33	83
		8	6	105	14	42	32	12	68	83	83	0	83
D	Science	3	8	86	14	57	20	9	50	38	25	0	100
		7	8	93	11	64	22	3	49	62	50	25	100
		10	8	72	1	56	33	10	46	62	12	12	100
	Mathematics	4	10	56	0	21	41	38	54	90	40	80	90
		8	10	63	0	17	38	44	51	50	40	30	80

SOURCE: From "Determining alignment of expectations and assessments in mathematics and science education," by N. L. Webb (1997, January), *NISE Brief*, 1(2). Madison: Wisconsin Center for Education Research, National Institute for Science Education, University of Wisconsin. Reprinted with permission.

NOTE: a. Categorical Concurrence
Depth-of-Knowledge Consistency
Range-of-Knowledge Correspondence
Balance of Representation

b. Total number of assessment items

c. und – undermined because too few and only sample items were included in the analysis

The Work of Porter and Smithson: Alignment Comes of Age

Porter and Smithson (2001) continued their work on ways to describe and align instruction, standards, and assessment after their earlier efforts. They have refined their thinking, emerging with four curricula of interest: the enacted curriculum, the intended curriculum, the assessed curriculum, and the learned curriculum. We'll look at each one and then see how the enacted, intended, assessed, and learned curriculum can be aligned.

The enacted curriculum "refers to the actual curricular content that students engage in the classroom" (Porter & Smithson, 2001, p. 2). The enacted curriculum is at the heart of Porter's work. The intended curriculum, also known as curriculum standards, frameworks, or guidelines, describe the curriculum teachers are expected to deliver. The assessed curriculum represents high-stakes tests. Student achievement scores can represent the learned curriculum, although limited in their usefulness in reflecting all that is learned.

Porter & Smithson continue to use versions of their descriptors of math and science (see the "Reform Up Close" description earlier in this chapter for more information), although recently they have expanded into other subject areas. The three dimensions—topic coverage, cognitive demand, and mode of presentation—with mode of presentation category still under development didn't correlate well with other categories or with achievement gains. Added to the dimensions is the response metric, time. For example, when reporting on a topic covered, the response metric is (0) *not covered*, (1) *less than one class or lesson*, (2) *one to five classes or lessons*, and (3) *more than five classes or lessons* (p. 12). The graphic in Figure 4.9 is a pictorial representation of the four types of curriculum.

Figure 4.9   Developed and potential alignment analyses

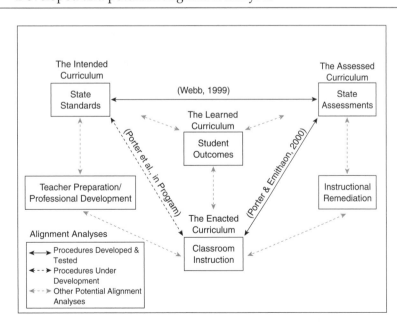

SOURCE: From *Defining, developing, and using curriculum indicators*, by A. C. Porter & J. L. Smithson, 2001 (CPRE Research Report Series RR-048). Philadelphia: Consortium for Policy Research in Education, University of Pennsylvania. Reprinted with permission.

Porter defines two approaches to alignment:

The first approach simply takes the absolute value of the difference between percent of emphasis on a topic, say, in a teacher's instruction and on a test. The index of alignment is equal to $1-((\Sigma\ |y-x\ |)/2)$ where y is the percent of time spent in instruction and x is the percent of emphasis on the test. The sum is all topics in the two-dimensional grid. The index is 1.0 for perfect alignment and zero for no alignment. This index is systematic in content in that both situations—content not covered on the test but covered in instruction *and* content not covered in instruction but covered on the test—lead to lack of alignment.

The second approach to measuring alignment is a function of the amount of instructional emphasis on topics that are tested. There are two pieces to this second index: one is the percent of instructional time spent on tested content; and the other, for topics that are tested and taught, the match in degree of emphasis in instruction and on the test.

The first index is best suited to looking at consistency among curriculum policy instruments and the degree to which content messages of the policy instruments are reflected in instruction. The second index is the stronger predictor of gains in student achievement. (Porter & Smithson, 2001, pp. 14–15)

These data can be represented pictorially. The content maps in Figure 4.10 represent the topic coverage categories by cognitive demand.

Figure 4.10   Grade 8 science alignment analysis between NAEP, state tests, and teacher reports of practice

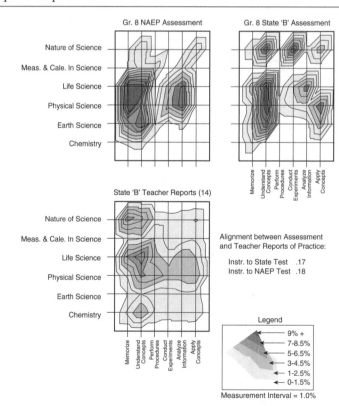

SOURCE: Porter, A. C., & Smithson J. L. (2001). *Defining, developing, and using curriculum indicators* (CPRE Research Report Series RR-048). Philadelphia: Consortium for Policy Research in Education, University of Pennsylvania.

Degree of emphasis on topics in the two space is indicated by darkness of color (for example, white indicates content receiving no emphasis). Such graphic displays assist teachers in understanding the scope of particular assessments as well as the extent to which particular content areas may be over- or underemphasized in their curriculum. We are currently developing procedures to provide similar displays of the *learned* curriculum that teachers could use in determining the content areas in which their students need most help. (Porter & Smithson, 2001, p. 16)

Such tools could be used to describe educational opportunity in schools, as an evaluation instrument in school reform, to suggest hypotheses for improving achievement, to examine the relationships between system components to determine the consistency and prescriptiveness of policy tools, to provide a baseline for monitoring change in classroom practice, to attribute student achievement gains to policy initiatives, to provide alignment measures for holding instructional content constant when examining the effects of competing pedagogical approaches, or to validate teacher reports of practice, such as in the end-of-year surveys in the Consortium for Policy Research in Education Upgrading Mathematics study that found correlations of .5 between end-of-semester teacher surveys of content taught and student achievement gains (Gamoran et al., 1997).

Summary

This rather lengthy review of alignment demonstrates the following:

- Alignment is not a unified concept. Many areas can be aligned to many others.
- There are many processes associated with alignment. At its simplest, alignment is a match between one set of written documents and another. Alignment is most useful when criteria for alignment are given and alignment procedures specified (see Webb, 1999, and Wishnick, 1989).
- Alignment can be accomplished on multiple dimensions at one time, allowing a rich database for comparisons, links with student outcomes, and possibilities for program improvement (Porter & Smithson, 2001).

The alignment octagon in Figure 4.11 offers one way to think about different areas that can be aligned.

Figure 4.11   The alignment octagon

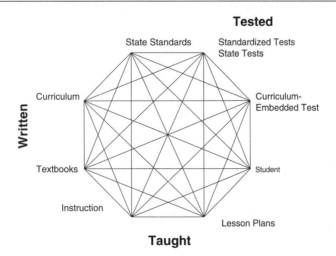

The alignment octagon shows all of the ways—tested, written, and taught—that alignment has been conducted according to the summary of the research grouped according to purpose. As school districts and states continue their alignment efforts, they can use the alignment octagon as a way to consider the possibilities for alignment and begin to strengthen their program by choosing the most powerful alignment options. The alignment octagon demonstrates that the balanced curriculum alignment process covers most of the alignment areas. Some of the options that districts currently use are reviewed in the next section.

SCHOOL DISTRICTS' ATTEMPTS AT ALIGNMENT

School districts have used many strategies in an attempt to align instruction with high-stakes tests. Unfortunately, picking out a few pieces from the alignment puzzle doesn't make the whole picture complete. This section describes some frequently used alignment strategies with a brief critique of their strengths and weaknesses.

Widely Distribute Standards and Publicly Released Versions of Assessments (Align Instruction to State Standards and Assessments)

This strategy assumes that teachers need to understand and know about standards and the publicly released versions of assessments before they can align their instruction. Many standards for a single-subject area of a grade-level band often run over four densely packed pages of text, however. For self-contained elementary teachers, that means 16 or more pages of standards that need to be used to guide instruction for each subject area. Although knowledge is a prerequisite to alignment, assuming that teachers will actually use the standards, given their length, is a faulty assumption.

Publicly released versions of high-stakes tests, especially those with-open ended questions graded through rubrics, are also lengthy because they usually have examples of student work for each rubric category, along with descriptors of the test's content and format. Often, teachers are not familiar with using rubrics as part of their evaluation. Information alone, without the necessary work by grade-level teams or by departments, is not sufficient. Widely distributing information and constructing staff development processes to ensure information use is necessary, but not sufficient, to make an impact.

Lesson Plans Linked to Standards (Aligns Lesson Plans to Standards)

The diagram in Figure 4.12 shows the alignment categories covered by aligning lesson plans to standards. From this perspective, lesson planning is a link to assignments and classroom instruction, so solid lines connect these areas in the figure. Textbooks in this case are not being aligned directly with state standards, so no line is present to indicate that relationship.

Figure 4.12   Alignment record sheet for aligning standards and lesson plans

Main Standard	Short Description	Standard Number	Standard Description	Date	Date	Date	Date	Date	Date	Total
NJ CCCS ELA 2002	3.1 Reading	78.3.1.G	Comprehension Skills and Response to Text.							
NJ CCCS ELA 2002	3.1 Reading	78.3.1.G.01	Speculate about text by generating literal and inferential questions.							
NJ CCCS ELA 2002	3.1 Reading	78.3.1.G.02	Distinguish between essential and nonessential information.							
NJ CCCS ELA 2002	3.1 Reading	78.3.1.G.03	Differentiate between fact/opinion and bias and propaganda in newspapers, periodicals, and electronic texts.							
NJ CCCS ELA 2002	3.1 Reading	78.3.1.G.04	Articulate the purposes and characteristics of different genres.							
NJ CCCS ELA 2002	3.1 Reading	78.3.1.G.05	Analyze ideas and themes found in texts.							
NJ CCCS ELA 2002	3.1 Reading	78.3.1.G.06	Compare several authors' perspectives of a historical character, setting, or event.							
NJ CCCS ELA 2002	3.1 Reading	78.3.1.G.07	Locate and analyze the elements of setting, characterization, and plot to construct understanding of how characters influence the progression and resolution of the plot.							
NJ CCCS ELA 2002	3.1 Reading	78.3.1.G.08	Read critically by identifying, analyzing, and applying knowledge of the purpose, structure, and elements of nonfiction, and provide textual evidence of understanding.							
NJ CCCS ELA 2002	3.1 Reading	78.3.1.G.09	Read critically by identifying, analyzing, and applying knowledge of the theme, structure, style, and literary elements of fiction, and provide textual evidence of understanding.							
NJ CCCS ELA 2002	3.1 Reading	78.3.1.G.10	Respond critically to text ideas and craft by using textual evidence to support interpretations.							
NJ CCCS ELA 2002	3.1 Reading	78.3.1.G.11	Locate and analyze literary techniques and elements (such as figurative language, meter, rhetorical and stylistic features, etc.) of text.							

Requiring lesson plans to be linked with standards is another way to make sure the standards are used and reviewed on a regular basis. In schools requiring standards-based lesson planning, teachers generally place the codes for the standards on their daily lesson plan. When teachers identify not only the general standard but also the substandard, or benchmark, this process will help teachers know the content of the standards and align to instruction. The difficulty is that there is no way to know, over time, whether all the standards have been met.

To solve this problem, some schools have adopted a grid that lists the standards on the left, with dates written across the top of the page. For each day, the teacher fills in the standards and substandards that are aligned to instruction. At the end of the month, the standards are summarized by adding up the addressed standards. Over a year, teachers can see the standards they have covered in their instruction. Figure 4.12 shows a truncated version of an alignment sheet for New Jersey for Grades 7 and 8 for Comprehension Skills and Response to Text standards and substandards for English and language arts. A teacher fills in the date in the small boxes at the top right and then checks the standards addressed in his or her lessons that day. At the end of a week, or a month if the chart is extended, the teacher counts the tallies and places the number in the "total" column.

The difficulty with this approach is the length of the standards (the full standards for English and language arts for New Jersey runs 10 pages in a similar chart format), and teachers may not have the patience to continue completing the chart. The greater problem, however, is that each teacher must do this individually, and, if there is no aligned and balanced curriculum, administrators must monitor individual teacher's alignment and coverage. For a typical elementary school, 10 pages times 30 teachers is a lot of paperwork. Teacher autonomy is maintained, however. Can we still justify teachers approaching standards-based instruction individual by individual if we know alignment is one factor in increasing student achievement, and alignment done right is time-consuming and tedious?

Figure 4.13   Align lessons with state standards

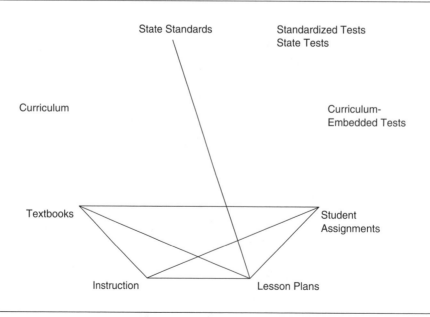

Develop District Assessments Mirroring High-Stakes Assessments (Aligns Curriculum-Embedded Assessments to High-Stakes Assessments)

By aligning district tests with state tests (Figure 4.14), few of our alignment categories are directly hit. This helps us uncover assumptions undergirding this strategy. District leaders may assume more assessment closer to home will increase the likelihood of teachers deciding to align their lesson plans and student assignments with the district tests, and hence there will be better alignment with the state tests. Indeed, this may happen, but we cannot draw lines between these categories because no procedure, process, or documentation is in place to make sure that happens, as is usually the case for districts adopting this model.

Figure 4.14   Align state tests to curriculum-embedded (local) tests

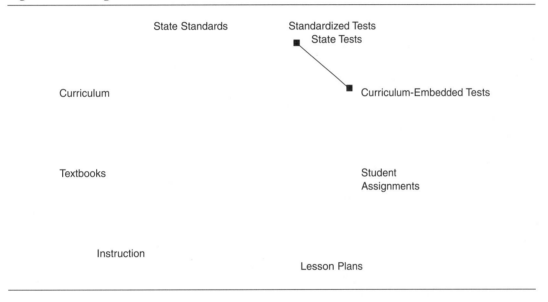

Districts know that state assessments are one influence on instruction; indeed, some view state assessments as driving instruction. Yet if state tests are administered every 4 years, then the drive may not be strong enough, some may reason. What some districts have done is to create quarterly assessments for all grade levels or courses that potentially could generate data on how students are doing along the way. These quarterly assessments may be developed by teachers or from testing software. The quality of these assessments depends on the degree of alignment. Wishnick (1989) provides the Alignment Measurement Scale, which may be useful in posing criteria that test makers may want to keep in mind when analyzing state tests and creating curriculum-embedded assessments.

Additional difficulties soon become evident. Many districts develop these quarterly assessments without first developing a curriculum, putting the cart before the horse. Without a curriculum, the district-developed assessments won't be aligned to instruction, lesson planning, or student assignments. If teachers are progressing through the year in their own idiosyncratic way, the teachers may not have taught what is on the test. If the test samples all of the domains on the state test, it is even more likely that teachers would not have covered all those domains until the end of the year. The additional problem of giving 3rd graders a test that samples all of the domains on the 4th-grade state test may not be developmentally appropriate.

Districts adopting quarterly assessments must complete a scope and sequence for what will be tested and when. In making their decisions, they are putting the cart of assessment before the horse of curriculum, and that is a horse of a different color. One of the first tasks in developing curriculum is to devise a scope and sequence chart. Why complete a scope and sequence chart for assessments before charting the scope and sequence for the curriculum?

TEXTBOOKS ALIGNED TO STANDARDS AND TESTS

Some districts figure that a combination of textbooks and high-stakes state tests drive instruction. So they align their textbooks with state standards and tests. Embedded in this strategy is the assumption that teachers will use existing textbooks as a framework for their instruction, lesson plans, and student assignments, an assumption that research on textbook use validates. The Price-Braugh (1997) and Moss-Mitchell (1998) studies are examples of this strategy. Once alignment identifies gaps, district intervention spans the gaps. I have filled in the assumptions as a broken line in Figure 4.15.

Figure 4.15   Align textbooks with state standards and assessments

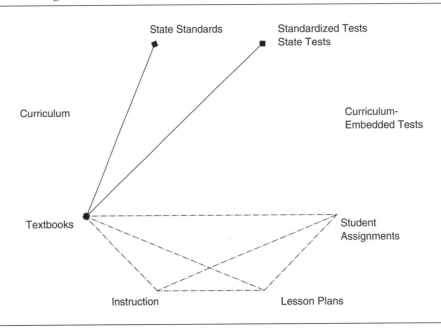

SUMMARY

A combination of strategies, if coordinated, could approach a robust alignment approach, but then so, too, could developing a good curriculum with alignments consciously coordinated among the alignment options. The purpose of this chapter has been to examine the various options for alignment. The next chapter describes more about assumptions embedded in standardized testing and about using these tests as the only measure of student achievement.

5

The Conundrum of Standardized Testing

Aconundrum is an intricate and difficult problem with only a conjectural answer (Merriam-Webster's Collegiate Dictionary, 1986). This chapter shows why standardized testing is a conundrum after describing how standardized tests are constructed and used. The chapter ends with a description of how the Balanced Curriculum process supplements results from standardized testing and some of the long-term implications of standardized testing for district curriculum and assessment development.

SUMMARY OF THE HISTORY AND PURPOSE OF STANDARDIZED TESTING

Standardized tests predate the standards movement. Standardized testing started during World War I as a way to classify and sort recruits for various positions in the U.S. Army in a standardized way so that recruits with more capability and capacity could be assigned to positions that required more capability and capacity (Madaus & Kellaghan, 1992, p. 136). Using standardized tests for individuals was seen as a way to eliminate bias endemic in other forms of selection. The science of testing could level the playing field by creating an "objective" standard used to measure accomplishments. Some who deride standardized testing today as "biased" may not realize the tests were introduced, in part, to eliminate bias.

Standardized tests for schools could help determine whether the school was completing its mission and offer a basis for comparing one school with others. Testing for schools was developed by commercial firms. The firms decided, based on expert input and an analysis of popular textbooks, what was important to test.

Multiple-choice test items were then developed to test what was most important; these exams could be machine scored, reducing the cost of testing over individual written exams. The standardized tests had standard procedures for test administration and grading but no "real" standards on which the test was based, such as the standards that represent today's consensus of the educational community.

"Real" standards began to develop with the minimum competency testing movement (see the chronology of the standards movement discussed in Chapter 3) when state departments of education began defining minimum levels of competency. From there, it was a small step to defining standards for subject areas, the basis of the standards movement today, with national professional organizations (like the National Council of Teachers of Mathematics) leading the way, followed by state departments of education defining standards applicable to schools within a state. Standardized testing has become the way that states chose to show that schools and students meet standards because it is relatively inexpensive and has the necessary validity and reliability to ensure that policy decisions based on testing are not arbitrary and capricious.

MAKING INFERENCES

According to Popham (2001), testing is an "inference making enterprise" (p. 28). From test results, we make inferences. We make inferences about individual students; for example, if a student does not receive a passing score on the test, then he or she does not pass to the next grade or graduate from high school. We are inferring that the test is able to determine who has "passed" and who has not. The first conundrum of standardized testing is determining appropriate inferences to be made from testing data.

We make inferences about schools from the data of standardized tests. For example, if a school has 3 years of declining scores, it can be "reconstituted," meaning that the existing staff and principal go to other schools, and the school reopens with new staff and administration. We infer that 3 years of declining scores is the basis for reconstituting the school.

We make inferences about districts from the data of standardized tests. For example, a district with consistently low scores is put on a state watch list. If scores do not improve, the school district can be "taken over" by the state, with the superintendent dismissed, the school board disbanded, and all administrators reapplying for their positions. In this case, we infer that consistently low scores result in a state takeover. Conversely, we also infer that satisfactory scores mean that a school district is doing its job.

As a result of in-class testing, individual teachers make decisions about moving to the next unit or reteaching skills from the current unit, based on inferences that if students didn't pass the test, they lack certain skills or concepts, and reteaching is needed. In all cases, inferences about scores lead to action.

The question is, what is the scope of inferences that are valid? For example, on the basis of the teacher's tests, if students don't do well, I might assume that students don't know the material and therefore need reteaching. I also might assume that students were lazy and knew the material but didn't perform well on the test because of their laziness. Reteaching, then, would not be appropriate.

Are the chosen inferences reasonable, based on the premises of standardized testing? Here we need to understand how standardized tests are put together to understand the premises behind the inferences we base on standardized test scores.

DEFINING THE DOMAIN OF WHAT'S TESTED

Inferences about standardized tests are based on the content that's tested. Defining the content of the standardized test leads to additional conundrums. For instance, let's assume that the domain of a standardized test is limited to memorization of whole-number facts. We want to devise a test that, if students pass, we can be reasonably assured that they know how to compute whole-numbers facts.

The domain of whole numbers is subdivided into addition, subtraction, multiplication and division. Addition and multiplication domains can be defined by any positive single digit added or multiplied by any other positive single digit. For subtraction, the domain is defined as a positive single digit number for a subtrahend, a number of 18 or less for the minuend, such that the answer is a single digit. For example,

$$18 - 9 = 9$$

is a subtraction fact from this definition, but

$$19 - 9 = 10$$

is not, because the answer is not a single digit. A division fact is a dividend that, when divided by a divisor that is a positive single digit number, yields a positive single digit number. Therefore, 81 is the dividend, 9 is the divisor, and the answer is 9. In this case, $90 \div 9$ is not a math fact. The definition of the domain is an important consideration in making inferences about scores. For example, if the domain is defined in this way, we can't make any inferences about math facts for 10s, 11s, and 12s because they are not included in the domain. Of course, some would argue that they should be included, which is another conundrum about specifying a domain—people disagree over what should be included and what should be left out.

SAMPLING THE UNIVERSE OF ITEMS IN THE DOMAIN

Testing is not only about making inferences, but making inferences based on a sample. In our math facts sample, there are 176 possible facts. For addition, the test consists of written problems such as, $1 + 1$, $1 + 2$, $2 + 1$, $1 + 3$, and so on, for a total of 176 possible problems. One alternative is to test all the facts in each domain. That would make a lengthy test, but we could confidently make the inference that if students got 100% of the test correct, then they knew their facts. Someone could also argue that children with dyslexia would have difficulties with the written test and that a better test would be an oral, timed test of all the facts, where students were read a list of facts and then wrote down the answer in a specified period of time. Another might argue that because of the length of the test, students might know their facts but not complete the test because of fatigue. Others might argue that testing in this way is unrealistic because no one ever has to complete such a task in "real" life.

For most domains, a complete testing of the domain is not possible. Sampling is the only way to go. We could randomly sample the 176 possible problems, choosing 20 each for addition, subtraction, multiplication, and division. We could also randomly sample and only choose five for each operation. The 20 problems will give us better information on which to base an inference than five problems would, but how much better? What about two problems for each operation? If students answered the 2 questions × 4 operations (eight problems) correctly, can we then infer that they know the other 168? If there was room for two fact problems on the test, would you choose an addition and division fact? Answers to such problems are indeed solved in the test development process, and all deal with how to create a sample so that we can make valid inferences that students know their math facts. Suffice it to say that standardized testing always involves sampling of a defined domain so that inferences can be made, given conditions in the testing situation.

SAMPLING DECISIONS MUST BE SECRET FOR INFERENCES ABOUT TEST RESULTS TO BE VALID

The sampling procedure and the characteristics of the items need to be held in secret to preserve the validity of the test. If I, as a teacher, knew that the test developers focused on facts involving 7s and 8s because these had proven the most difficult to answer in preliminary tests, then I might drill my kids on the 7 and 8 tables and place less emphasis on others. Students might "pass" the test, but then we couldn't infer that they knew *all* the facts from the test results that weighted the samples toward facts involving 7s and 8s because we had aligned our instruction with the test. The test developers can only preserve the validity of the tests by keeping the domain definition and the sampling strategy secret. If they publicize what is being tested, then teachers will emphasize this in instruction, invalidating the assumption that the domain has been widely and equally aligned to instruction. Chapter 4 covered the power of alignment on test results.

A superintendent once said, "Don't bother me with standards, just show me the test, and I'll make sure the kids pass." Returning to math facts, if I know how many and which kind of math facts are on the test, then I'll make sure students know all those facts so they'll pass. Yes, they will pass, but the inference that they know all their facts cannot be made on the basis of the test results. Unfortunately, this inference was the original purpose of the test. The conundrum becomes more complicated.

Test specifications must be held in secret to make valid inferences based on test results. A competing argument suggests that if a person is being tested, it is only fair to tell him or her what the test is about. The conundrum of testing is that the more the teachers and the test takers know about the test specifications, the more difficult it is to provide valid inferences from test data that students know about or are proficient in a broader domain.

LIMITED TESTING AND A LARGE NUMBER OF STANDARDS

Another conundrum of test specifications is that there are too many standards and too little time to test. We ask a lot of our standardized and state tests. In a few hours of testing, we require the tests to give us valid and reliable data about how students are doing and what they have learned about important content areas during the last 120 to 150 school days. The state standards help to specify what the important content contains for those school days. Textbooks also play a role.

Let's examine each a little further. State standards are generally specified to be applied to grade-level ranges such as K–4. State test makers will have to decide what to test out of the K–4 standards. They won't be able to test all the standards, and they have to pick the ones that are most important. Some of the standards will be difficult to test using the current testing technology of multiple-choice answers. So state test makers will choose only a subset of the standards to actually test. For example, if I am making a test for mathematics to be given at the end of 4th grade, and the seven major categories of the standards (New York) are mathematical reasoning, number and numeration, operations, modeling/multiple representation, measurement, uncertainty, and patterns/functions, then I would expect to choose items from each category for the test. Each major category has a number of subcategories. Operations have the following subcategories for Grades 5 and 6:

- 3A. Add, subtract, multiply, and divide fractions, decimals, and integers
- 3B. Use grouping symbols (parentheses) to clarify the intended order of operations
- 3C. Apply the associative, commutative, and distributive properties, and inverse and identity elements
- 3D. Demonstrate an understanding of operational algorithms (procedures for adding, subtracting, etc.)
- 3E. Develop appropriate proficiency with facts and algorithms
- 3F. Apply concepts of ratio and proportion to solve problems

If we were to test each category with one item, there would be at least six items on the mathematics tests for operations. But we couldn't say that students who got all six right knew all their number facts (3E). There aren't enough items on the test to be able to make that inference. We may be able to infer that they know operations (as defined by the standards cited earlier), but the data on which we base the inference are six questions that randomly test the domains specified by the standards (3A through 3F). Indeed, to get around this problem, many states just report a total score and determine one to four passing points as a way to get around making inferences about whether students know particular standards or substandards. For example, New York State established four categories for scoring students' achievements based on the overall test:

- *Level 4.* These students *exceed the standards* and are moving toward high performance on the Regents examination.
- *Level 3.* These students *meet the standards* and, with continued steady growth, should pass the Regents examination.

- *Level 2.* These students *need extra help* to meet the standards and pass the Regents examination.
- *Level 1.* These students have *serious academic deficiencies.*

The state department of education has no other choice but to establish cut scores. The questions then become, "Do Level 4 students actually exceed the standards? All of the standards? Some of the standards? Which standards? Can we make that inference?" In general, standardized tests provide ways to rank students but do not give information that can be used to provide information on specific curriculum topics or areas that students master or need extra help. To do so the tests would be too long and too expensive to construct and administer and score.

Popham (2001) concluded, "Standardized achievement tests should not be used to evaluate the quality of students' schooling because there are meaningful mismatches between what is tested and what is supposed to be taught, and those mismatches are often unrecognized" (p. 46).

SCORE SPREAD OF INDIVIDUAL ITEMS

To understand score spread, let's return to our test of math facts. We have arbitrarily decided on a 100-item test to determine students' competence in their math facts. If everyone got 95 out of 100 items correct on the math facts test, the score spread would be low—most students got most of the items correct. Test takers would only receive six scores: 95, 96, 97, 98, 99, or 100. Such a low score spread may be good news in that we could infer that most students knew most of their math facts. For standardized tests, however, a higher spread of scores is what test designers look for. Test designers are not looking for items that most students get correct because those items are "wasted" given the compact size of the tests. Test designers are looking for items that are difficult for those students who score low and easy for those that score high. Items that most students get right don't fit those criteria. On average, they look for items for which approximately half the examinees answering the question would get right and half would get wrong, which means it has a p value of .5. This "ideal" item has a p *value* of .5 because 50% of the examinees got the item correct and 50% of the examinees got the item incorrect. Generally, items on standardized tests have a range of p values from .4 to .6, which creates an adequate score spread for the standardized test.

How does this play into developing the content for a standardized test? Test makers will want to search for items that have a p value of .4 to .6. To return to the math facts example, the test makers know from previous test runs that most students score well on this 100-item test on math facts. They had considered putting in one item ($72 \div 9$), because 20% of the students who missed an item missed this one (a p value of .8 because 8 of 10 got the item correct). There are only so many items that they can put in their test, however, because the test lasts only an hour. A p value of .8 was too high and would not enhance the score spread of the test, so testing of math facts were left out of the comprehensive test of mathematics. What most students know will be left out of standardized tests because the p value of the items is high. Most students know their math facts, so math facts won't be tested on the standardized test. This fact of standardized test development skews the domains tested away from what most students know to what approximately half the students know (as this makes for items with appropriate p values.)

Why do we need p values or score spreads in the range of .4 to .6? The better (lower) the score spread, the more reliable the test. Reliability means consistency. When computing a test's reliability, the p value of all the test items is used. Because of the statistics involved, the lower the p values, the higher the reliability of the tests. When school districts purchase tests, they look for tests with high reliability. So the reliability is a function of score spread, and score spread is a function of p values, and items with high p values are not chosen, influencing the content of what is tested. Indeed, if the different tests for a single company were reviewed for the last 30 years, the study would show a decrease in the number of math computation questions. Could that be because most students now can compute, so that area doesn't contribute to score spread, so that area is left out of the test? For example, the New York City test for mathematics now has no computation problems included.

Popham (2001) described the cycle and his conclusions about it:

> The more important the content, the more likely teachers are to stress it. The more that teachers stress important content, the better that students will do on an item measuring that content. But the better that students do on such an item, the more likely it is that the item will disappear from the test. . . . Standardized achievement tests should not be used to evaluate the quality of students' schooling because the quest for wide score-spread tends to eliminate items covering important content that teachers have emphasized and students have mastered. (p. 48)

TESTS SERVE MULTIPLE MISSIONS

Standardized tests are perceived to meet many needs. State departments use standardized tests as a way to judge the quality of education in counties and school districts. School districts use standardized tests as a way to judge the quality of education provided by schools. Schools use standardized tests as a way to judge whether individual students and teachers are making the grade. One standardized test cannot meet all of these expectations equally well. What standardized tests do best is provide data on a large number of students at relatively low cost. Standardized tests do provide valid and reliable ways to sort students into a limited number of categories (proficient, partially proficient, etc.). Standardized tests do not do a good job of telling us what most students know and are able to do or give us information specific enough for in-depth curriculum revision and evaluation. We need to understand that standardized tests are limited, which produces conundrums for seamlessly using standardized testing as a tool for educational policy.

TESTING NARROWS THE CURRICULUM

Teachers and administrators naturally want to do well on assessments. If given information about what is on a test, teachers will naturally try to instruct students so that they will be able to do well on the test. Isn't it wrong to know what is on a test and *not* give students instruction on its content? (It is wrong, however, to give students the *exact* items that are on the test.) Tests provide one benchmark for teacher decision making on content to be taught. Textbooks, standards, and a teacher's own education may be other benchmarks used.

The higher the stakes of the test, the more teachers will try to address the test content, and the other benchmarks will be employed to a lesser degree. This narrows the content of the curriculum to ensure that what is on the test is covered in the curriculum. Tests then become a means of controlling curriculum content, especially if the stakes are high.

LACK SPECIFICS ABOUT WHAT IS TESTED INCREASES CURRICULUM COVERAGE

The specifications of the test are given using a very general description of areas tested. Generality of test specifications is necessary to maintain the validity and reliability of the test and the secrecy of the domain definition. This provides little guidance to the teachers. Teachers may then try to cover all the areas and subareas in the standards. These are also too general because they are usually written for a grade-level range. This means there is too much information covered for one grade level. Without a curriculum, teachers may try to cover all the topics, just as we saw that textbooks try to cover all the topics of the standards. Instruction then becomes "a mile wide and an inch deep." Lack of specificity in defining what's tested leads to covering more material than is actually necessary, reinforced by the textbook coverage of too many topics (see Chapter 2). Teachers cover much content in a superficial way to increase their chances of covering what is on the standardized test. Without a curriculum, they will make decisions using the information from general test specifications, standards statements, and textbooks. Generally, the results will not be positive, especially when these decisions differ across teachers if no coordinating mechanism (the curriculum) is developed.

REPORTING TEST RESULTS

Reporting test results is also a conundrum of standardized and state testing. If the results are reported very specifically, they are useful in developing and refining curriculum because we would know which children did well and which didn't on the specific item or item cluster. Remember, answering a series of test questions correctly is supposed to allow us to infer that the student has mastered a whole domain of knowledge, not just that specific area. We can reliably make that inference if we don't know ahead of time what that specific question will be. Returning to our example of knowledge of math facts, if a student answers four math fact questions correctly, then we can infer that he or she knows the other 176 math facts that weren't tested. If we specify which math facts are on the test, then teachers and administrators might say, "Just ignore the rest of the math facts but make sure everyone has memorized the four math facts everyone knows will be on the test." If everyone knows the four math facts on the test, we cannot reliably infer that they know all the rest of the 176 math facts, because students may simply memorize those four. So test scores are reported as pass and fail, or proficient or nonproficient. These scores don't tell us a lot about what exactly proficient students can do because to do so would spell out what is on the test and once teachers and students know this, they might only practice those problems, and the score of the test would no longer be valid.

Some states, such as New York, report student scores in four areas: exceed standards (Level 4), meet standards (Level 3), need extra help to meet standards (Level 2), and serious academic deficiencies (Level 1). The state tells the approximate percentage of items that will be on the test, provides sample tests, and provides a list of standards. Teachers, schools, and districts must then use this information to infer what will be tested. Parents, schools, and districts are not told how well students individually or in a group did on the item clusters. In this way, the test can maintain its validity and reliability, but little useful information for changing curriculum or the program of the school can be inferred from the test results.

ONE SCORE USED AS THE ONLY SOURCE OF INFORMATION FOR HIGH-STAKES DECISIONS

Many states' guidelines use only one test to make high-stakes decisions about the future of students, schools, administrators, and school districts. Yet the *Standards for Educational and Psychological Testing* written and published by the American Educational Research Association, the American Psychological Association, and the National Council on Measurement in Education states that

> In educational settings, a decision or characterization that will have major impact on a student should not be made on the basis of a single test score. Other relevant information should be taken into account if it will enhance the overall validity of the decision. (Standard 13.7)

When state and national legislation is revised, we hope that new legislation will conform to such standards.

WHAT TO DO

Standardized testing developed by states is not likely to go away anytime soon. The "No Child Left Behind" legislation relies heavily on the results of standardized tests to classify schools and students. There will continue to be slow, incremental improvement in scores, but the standardized test feedback loop is one of the weak links in the standards-based education movement. Not enough information gets back to districts to allow them to mold instruction so that students can succeed on these high-stakes standardized tests. Tests will continue to be administered to students because they provide statistically valid and reliable information for ranking and sorting schools and students. In a nutshell, the tests are not going away, and districts, schools, and teachers are left to deal with the conundrums of testing that they may or may not understand.

The Balanced Curriculum process provides some ways to deal with the conundrums of standardized testing. The principal flaw of standardized testing is the lack of specific information available to districts that can be used to strengthen their curricula. To create useful information for curriculum review and improvement, districts will need to develop their own assessment system capable of generating information that can be used in the curriculum improvement process.

Some districts have already begun to do this by developing quarterly assessments that mimic that format and process of the state tests. Quarterly assessments provide more data earlier than state testing—data that districts can use for improvement. Although this may improve the frequency of data, the quarterly tests may not have been aligned with the instruction that takes place during that quarter, so there is misalignment between the curriculum and the test. Assessments for each significant task provide a better way to obtain data on whether students are demonstrating competence.

The Balanced Curriculum process uses the significant tasks as a way to solve the testing conundrum by providing standard ways for teachers to assess those tasks. Because the significant tasks are aligned to both the state standards and the specifications for state assessments, alignment of instruction (the significant tasks) and assessments is robust. The 35 to 50 significant tasks for a year-long course provides a rich data source that can be mined for curricular and program improvement.

The assessment of the significant tasks can provide specific information on how well students are mastering particular standards. If all teachers of a given course are using the same significant task *and* the same assessment, then they should feel confident that, if a student passes the significant task assessment, he or she should do well on the state assessment. If that link is not established, then at least the curriculum authors can use the information to determine whether the significant task assessment was too easy or was not sufficiently rigorous. With the Balanced Curriculum, there are more handles to use in program improvement.

Once a unit, students are given a format assessment designed to provide practice on the format of the standardized tests. If there are 10 units for a particular course, there are 10 opportunities for students to practice on the format of the standardized test. Most standardized tests provide sample formats used in testing. Teachers and test authors then can use these models to design their own questions or choose questions from a commercially available item bank. In this way, students have appropriate practice with the format for demonstrating their knowledge. Because practice is spread out throughout the year, there is no need to cram for weeks on item formats just before standardized testing, saving valuable time for instruction.

SUMMARY

This chapter examined a number of conundrums built into the process of using standardized tests to assess how students are accomplishing the standards. Standardized tests provide some information to test takers, teachers, administrators, and policy makers. Standardized testing occurs outside the instructional process and is not embedded within instructional activities. The criteria embedded in standardized tests, by which students are evaluated, is often unclear to students—and frequently to teachers or administrators as well—because the test specifications are secret. Yet standardized testing does provide statistically valid and reliable data for teachers, administrators, and school board members (not to mention state legislatures and the federal government) to make decisions about schools. Our schools are caught in the middle, trying to determine what is important to teach their students. Understanding the strengths and conundrums of standardized testing allows for the design of other structures, such as curriculum and curriculum-embedded assessments, to fill the gaps that standardized tests create.

The following summarizes some of the implications of the information presented in this chapter:

1. The good news is that scores can improve on standardized tests if students get practice on the test format and content. This means that alignment to standardized test specifications and formats are critical. Most high-stakes tests do provide limited information about content and format.

2. Especially for high-stakes testing, we have an obligation to our students to make sure they have and can demonstrate knowledge as required by the standardized test format.

3. We know that tests will change as students become better at demonstrating their knowledge. Preparing for standardized tests is a never-ending cycle.

4. Curriculum is the single most direct way that school districts can ensure all students have equal access to high-quality, aligned instruction that makes sure they have access to the knowledge tested by high-stakes tests and that they have practiced on the format of those tests.

5. High-stakes tests will never tell us adequately how well students are doing on meeting standards. It's just too big a job. We will know, however, whether students are meeting standards by how they do within school districts' assessments. This means that school districts will need to demonstrate that students have accomplished the standards—not through tests but through demonstration of their knowledge. This means that districts will need to keep records of students' demonstrations of fulfilling the standards.

6. Standardized testing will be used in conjunction with portfolios to determine whether students are "passing." The tests won't have the importance it once did.

7. Accreditation agencies will begin to use portfolios (based on significant task assessments) as a way to validate their accreditation process.

8. Eventually, school districts may be rated on their portfolios, which will include a sampling of student portfolios aligned to the content of the standards. Students will use work embedded in their normal instruction to show that they have demonstrated the competencies embedded in the standards. This is one way to ensure students are meeting the standards without the drawbacks of large-scale standardized testing.

9. Standardized testing will decline in importance as this other way of demonstrating student proficiency is adopted and state agencies become more adept at writing rules and regulations to govern the process.

The next chapter examines the range of possibilities for structuring or formatting the curriculum. At first, this may appear to be a mundane issue, but we shall discover that how the curriculum is structured governs how much it can improve student achievement.

Section II

The Design of the Balanced Curriculum

In this section, the design of the Balanced Curriculum is examined. Chapter 6 introduces the reader to options for curriculum structure and the criteria for choosing one that will ensure the structured parts fit together into a curriculum that can effectively guide the delivery of instruction. It also discusses how to use data generated by the curriculum structure to improve and upgrade the curriculum on an ongoing basis. Chapters 7 through 16 provide the "nuts and bolts" of the Balanced Curriculum process with examples from the many districts that have designed curriculum using this model. These chapters also consider processes for using the Balanced Curriculum Web site to store, align, balance, and assess the curriculum. Chapters 7 through 12 show how the curriculum is described using courses, units, and significant tasks. Chapters 13 and 14 describe how the curriculum is aligned and balanced to standards and standardized testing. Chapters 15 and 16 describe how curriculum-embedded assessments are developed to address the content of the significant tasks and the format of state or standardized assessment.

6

Curriculum Structure and Criteria for a Useful and Useable Curriculum

C hapter 4 demonstrated the power of aligning curriculum, instruction, and assessment. Before investigating the structure of the Balanced Curriculum, we examine the options available for structuring or formatting a curriculum so the curriculum is useful and useable for teachers. There is no one way to format or structure a curriculum. Many districts use curriculum documents as a resource to improve instruction. Others disseminate curriculum documents because of requirements. A few use the curriculum as a plan for guiding instruction and assessment. After discussing the format options for a curriculum, I pose 10 criteria that a curriculum should meet if it is to be useful to teachers and useable by teachers and administrators. There are trade-offs in any decision about a curriculum's structure, but the Balanced Curriculum has format and structure, both useful and useable, that have produced improved student achievement. For the reader to know what the trade-offs are, this chapter introduces many of the decisions any district will have to wrestle with in designing a structure and format for curriculum.

CURRICULUM DEFINED

Curriculum is defined as a district's written plan to help guide the instruction and assessment functions of teaching. Such a plan is aligned with state standards and high-stakes or standardized assessments (or both). Curriculum focuses on what students will be able to know and do, not what teachers are supposed to cover, thereby ensuring that students enact the standards. Curriculum functions to ensure that all students have equal access to quality instruction. Curriculum provides a way for teachers to coordinate the instruction for students.

In previous chapters, the arguments put forth suggest that curriculum is the only tool available to help a district's teachers in a systematic and planned way to coordinate decisions about courses, units, and instructional activities among and between teachers. Teachers teaching the same course should address similar content in similar ways so that students have equal access to the most important content. Without coordination, teachers will emphasize what they feel is important; a personal decision, when viewed from a systemwide perspective, doesn't benefit children's development. Furthermore, instructional coordination is needed to make sure the sequence of activities build on one another and address significant outcomes of state standards. Activities presented in random order will not assist students in learning so that the standards are addressed.

Instructional units should build on skills and concepts learned in previous units. Planned units ensure that students can and will master increasingly difficult material. Without planning on the unit level, instructional activities are not likely to address all the areas specified in the standards.

Curriculum can facilitate good decision making about the sequence of courses. Does the 1st-grade math curriculum provide the prerequisite skills necessary for the 2nd-grade curriculum? Is there an appropriate sequence in middle school and high school so that all children can take algebra, the gateway into higher education?

The next section examines the options for designing a curriculum structure. Districts can use this chapter to choose their own options for curriculum structure. Resource 6A at the end of the chapter will aid districts as they work toward that purpose.

SOME OPTIONS
FOR CURRICULUM STRUCTURE

There is no standard way to put together a curriculum structure. Curriculum may be structured as a general list of grade-level expectations or as a detailed series of lesson plans. Completion of the curriculum may be required of all teachers or may simply be a suggested list of activities. Assessments may or may not be included. Provisions for monitoring and revising the curriculum may not be a part of the curriculum structure. In this section, we examine questions that districts will need to answer in designing their curriculum structure, including the following:

- What are the schedules in the schools? Are they consistent in their allocation of time?
- What is the smallest component of the curriculum?
- Will the curriculum be disciplinary or interdisciplinary?
- What will be described in the curriculum, and how will the language describing the curriculum be structured?
- Which components of the curriculum will be required, and which will be suggested?
- Will content for the standards and for objectives be aligned?
- What role will assessment play?
- How will staff development groups hammer out the curriculum?
- How will the curriculum be implemented?
- How will curriculum implementation be monitored?
- How frequently will the curriculum be revised?
- How will policy support curriculum?

These decisions need to be made before large sums of money are spent to develop the curricular documents because documents are only effective if the content is implemented. The curriculum's effectiveness rests on how each of these areas is addressed. The questions need to be considered in order because the answers to the earlier questions determine the options for those that follow.

What Are the Schedules in the Schools? Are They Consistent in Their Allocation of Time?

Schedules may seem like a strange place to start in designing curricular components. Curriculum places content within a time frame. Thus, time and content are the two structures that curriculum directs and controls. Time in schools is defined by schedules. In elementary schools, there may be a reading and mathematics block, and content for each discipline is addressed during its allotted block of time. In self-contained classrooms, the blocks are flexible. In middle and high schools, the blocks are defined as class periods. Knowing the amount of time per day, week, or month that is allocated for subject-area instruction is critical to developing curriculum because the amount of time available will determine the scope and sequence of content.

I have worked in districts in which one school has two periods for reading and language arts and other schools had only one. Different schedules demand different curriculum. In another district, the time for mathematics was increased from 30 minutes to 1 hour a day because teachers felt more time was needed so students could get enough practice to master the curriculum. Districts adopting site-based management, when specifying a district curriculum, need to assist schools in deciding the appropriate schedule that will accomplish the curricular goals. If schedules are different among schools, then districts, in accepting differing school schedules, assume that different amounts of scheduled time are needed for all students to be successful—not a practice that I would recommend. If schedules are different, a curriculum needs to be developed for each schedule. All curricula rest on scheduling considerations.

What Is the Smallest Component of the Curriculum?

Decisions need to be made about the specificity and about the smallest component of the curriculum. For example, state standards are examples of a curriculum with the smallest component usually being a grade-level range by subject area. In social studies (a subject area) standards are defined for a grade-level range: K–4, 5–8, or 9–12. In the grade-level range, there is no further delineation about time; usually a component like this is phrased as follows: "By the end of Grade 4, students will . . ." The smallest component then would be a grade-level range, such as K–4, because no further time division is mentioned. If this option is chosen, it is then up to teachers to decide what they will address, given the grade-level range. Coordination will be a problem.

Some states, such as North Carolina, have narrowed the grade-level range to single courses such as Algebra I or Grade 3 Reading/Language Arts. In this case, the component would be Algebra I and the component would read, "By the end of the Algebra I course, students will . . ."

District-level curriculum may use smaller segments of time for curriculum, dividing individual courses into units. Units are usually chunks of time shorter than a year, perhaps a few weeks or a month. If units are the component used, then the outcome statements for the units would be phrased, "By the end of this unit, students will . . ." Units may be subdivided further into lessons. Lessons are usually a teaching period in length and evolve from lesson planning by teachers. If the lesson is the smallest component, then the curriculum would be written, "By the end of this lesson, students will . . ."

The larger the component, the more latitude teachers have to make decisions about when and where to include this in their plans. The down side is, the more latitude, the more difficult it is to coordinate decisions among teachers; the less coordination, the less certain the district can be that standards are being met. The more coordination, such as a district developing daily lesson plans, the less latitude teachers have, and the more likely districts will field complaints about too much structure and not enough latitude. Curriculum is a written determination of how much latitude teachers have within a particular subject area. It determines the locus of control for decisions about what is addressed in classrooms. Standards and high-stakes testing are pushing districts to organize and control the content of what students are taught to address accountability concerns, such as No Child Left Behind. The curriculum is where this decision of teacher autonomy versus student equity is made. If individual teachers decide what is most important to teach, there will not be equity across district classrooms.

Typical district structures for curriculum are that the textbook is the de facto curriculum. Of course, the difficulty is that most textbooks contain much more information and activities than can be taught, so teachers have maximum latitude, but districts have minimum coordination.

Districts may have a curriculum, but the curriculum specifies "suggested" activities. Again, the teachers have maximum latitude, but districts have minimum coordination because the districts have no way of knowing whether the suggested activities were actually taught. Many districts have traded coordination for maximum teacher flexibility and then lament the fact that flexibility does not produce improved achievement. Improved achievement will happen, but only when the curriculum structure fosters both teacher latitude and coordination among teachers.

Will the Curriculum Be Disciplinary or Interdisciplinary?

Another decision about curriculum structure is whether there will be disciplinary-based curriculum, such as science and social studies, or some form of interdisciplinary curriculum. Crossing subject area lines in an interdisciplinary curriculum most frequently occurs in the elementary grades. An interdisciplinary curriculum might integrate science and social studies into units or lessons with content from language arts or mathematics. For example, a unit on plants might involve listening to stories about plants in reading class, integrating math into science class by involving counting and predicting in a plant experiment, and then learning in social studies how plants are used by various cultures. The decision on disciplinary or interdisciplinary curriculum will affect the schedule and what alignment categories are chosen. For example, if social studies and reading and language arts are combined in the curriculum, then the curriculum will need to be aligned to the standards of both subjects, and the schedule might indicate "Reading/Language Arts and Social Studies: 9:00 a.m. to 11:00 a.m."

Curriculum theorists debate the merits of focusing on the disciplines individually, with their unique ways of viewing the world, or focusing on the topics with a view from various perspectives. It is clear from the structure of state standards and assessments, from state requirements for certification, and from the way higher education is organized that educational institutions are systemically organized around subject areas. Schools serving pre-K and kindergarten may opt for an integrated curriculum. As grade level increases, the school's structure becomes more discipline-based (social studies schedule or classes organized by subject area). Interdisciplinary curriculum then becomes more difficult to organize, partly because of the school's discipline-based structure and partly because of teachers' discipline-based training and certification.

What Will Be Described in the Curriculum, and How Will the Language Be Structured?

Curriculum designers exercise choice about the curriculum, addressing both *what* will be taught and *how* it will be taught. Standards and accompanying benchmarks are useful in describing *what* the outcomes of courses or ranges of courses are. Objectives, such as behavioral objectives, are useful in describing the outcomes of units or lessons. Both objectives and standards focus on describing *what* the outcomes are, but, in general, they say little about *how* to enact or achieve those outcomes. Describing curriculum through objective or standard-based outcomes addresses only half of the description. The other half involves *how* the outcomes are produced.

For example, the curriculum says teachers should teach "Reading for the main idea." One teacher thinks, "The state test is coming up, and I will just drill my students on multiple-choice items about the main idea. In this way, they'll be prepared for the test." Another teacher chooses to teach the main idea by creating headlines after understanding the structure of news articles. A third decides to use the social studies book to teach children how to read for the main idea in social studies. A fourth teacher decides her students already know about main idea; she'll proceed to something more important. Although three of the four teachers address main idea, their classes do so in strikingly different ways, and with the probability of producing very different outcomes. When their students arrive at the next grade and are mixed into new classes, it is no wonder the new teacher wonders whether main idea was even addressed. Generally, curricula are designed specifying outcomes, and the teacher decides how to reach them. I address this choice in a later discussion of curriculum usefulness.

Which Components of the Curriculum Will Be Required, and Which Will Be Suggested?

Decisions about suggesting or requiring curriculum fidelity need to be made at the course, unit, and lesson plan levels, depending on the decision made in previous steps. Should reading, math, science, and social studies be suggested or required at 4th grade? This is an example of a decision made at the subject level. With districts adopting longer time periods (block scheduling) for reading and math, science and social studies in elementary and middle schools may be squeezed out of the required curriculum because of the focus on reading and math. If the subjects are "required," decisions must be made about whether units specified for subject areas are required or optional.

Many curriculum documents are constructed as suggestions for teachers. These are the suggested objectives that need to be addressed at a particular grade level or for a particular course. Implied in the word *suggested* is that the objectives are not required. Teachers can choose to focus their instruction around these objectives or choose others. Embedded in this approach is the assumption that teachers can wisely choose which objectives to incorporate and which to leave out, based on the needs of their classes.

Another common assumption is that the decisions of individual teachers will not make a difference in student learning when they are tallied across grade- or course-level ranges. Returning to the previous example of teaching the main idea, if a student had teachers two years in a row who only taught main idea through reading passages and filling in multiple-choice questions, that student would not be as likely to understand and be able to identify the main idea as one who had had instruction by teachers similar to the ones who taught main ideas through newspapers, and the one who taught main idea through learning about reading social studies texts. I argue that required curriculum is needed to ensure adequate coordination necessary to improve performance on high-stakes tests and to maintain a balance in the curriculum.

Will Content for the Standards and for Objectives Be Aligned?

Alignment means there is similar content in both the standards and the goals and objectives. Research indicates that alignment is a powerful indicator of academic achievement (see Chapter 10). Although there are many processes and procedures for aligning curriculum to standards and assessments, the preponderance of research indicates that an aligned curriculum can overcome usual predictors of student achievement such as socioeconomic status, gender, race, and teacher variables (see Wishnick, 1989).

Curriculum designers must decide how they will accomplish alignment. Many strategies exist. In some districts, teachers are required to indicate alignment when planning lessons. Although such alignment is usually not aggregated across time to

Figure 6.1   The alignment octagon

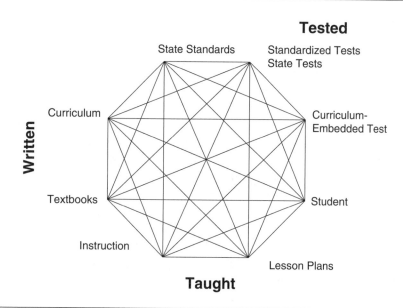

determine what is emphasized and what is left out, it does ensure that instruction addresses some of the standards and state assessment categories. Other districts align materials, either required or suggested, to state standards and assessments. Again, these alignments are not often aggregated across a course.

The alignment octagon (see Chapter 4) is one way for district curriculum designers to decide what to align. Figure 6.1 shows an example of perfect alignment; all components of the curriculum, instruction, and assessment are aligned to each other.

Districts will, out of necessity, choose something less than perfection, for example, deciding to align their textbook to state standards and assessments. In this case, the district is assuming that the textbook is powerful enough in guiding the instructional choices of teachers that the textbook needs to be aligned with the state standards and assessments. As a result, lines would only be drawn between textbooks and state standards, and textbooks and state assessments.

Other possibilities are suggested by the alignment octagon in Figure 6.1. The alignment octagon can be used by districts to chart out their alignment strategies and question the validity of their assumptions about how alignment will produce greater achievement.

What Role Will Assessment Play?

Does the curriculum include assessment? For which components of the system is assessment aimed? Will it be district- or teacher-developed? Required or suggested? Aligned to both the curriculum and the state standards or to other components? Assessments strengthen curriculum by providing feedback that students learned what was taught. This information can inform further curriculum development, assessment revision, and rules about course-taking sequences for students, as well as decisions about remedial or enrichment opportunities for students in tutoring or gifted and talented class enrollment.

Curriculum designers decide at which component level assessment takes place: the lesson, the unit, the course, or after a certain number of courses. Again, time is a factor in determining structure for assessment and may be based on previous decisions. Some districts have begun testing on a quarterly basis using state standards or frameworks as the template for the quarterly test's structure, showing that it is possible to sandwich assessment into a mixture of curriculum components (between units and courses) during the school year.

To be most effective, these assessments need to be aligned with both the curriculum and the state standards and assessments. This can be mapped on the curriculum octagon. In some districts, quarterly assessments may be aligned to state tests but not to the instruction taking place in the district. In this case, the district is attempting to coordinate the curriculum through testing. Why not coordinate the curriculum directly—that is, through the curriculum?

Assessment can be the same for all teachers of a particular course or all teachers in a particular school, or it can be left to the discretion of individual teachers to develop assessments on their own. Often this ends up to be a mix-and-match situation, with individual teachers generating unit assessments or lesson assessments, while the district or school (or both) may generate finals or quarterly assessments. Different levels in the curricular components will have different latitudes for assessment options.

How Will Staff Development Groups Hammer Out the Curriculum?

Writing the curriculum is a staff development task. Deciding who will write it, who will lead, how much time will be spent writing, and where money will come from to support the writing all are under the purview of staff development. Once the curriculum is written, staff development needs to take place to assist with the implementation. For example, one district had grade-level groups of teachers meet at their individual schools and divide the curriculum parts into three equal piles: (1) easily implemented tasks, (2) moderately difficult tasks or topics to teach, and (3) tasks or topics that would be difficult to teach. Then the groups scheduled staff development time during the year before the difficult-to-teach topics were scheduled to discuss ways to teach the topics effectively. This strategy involved the groups in solving common instructional problems. Staff development is often conducted to increase curriculum implementation.

How Will the Curriculum Be Implemented?

For a curriculum to have an effect, it must be implemented. Curriculum designers will need to consider staff development to familiarize teachers with the curriculum, ongoing support to assist teachers in planning and continuing their implementation, and further staff development to assist teachers with unfamiliar curriculum areas or strategies to assist them in preparing and implementing better instruction based on the curriculum.

Curriculum designers will need to determine the evidence they will accept as indicating that teachers have implemented the curriculum. In a suggested curriculum, it may be a teacher's lesson plans that indicate they have covered suggested content. For a curriculum with uniform assessments, good scores on the assessments may become evidence of implementation. Between implementation and evidence of implementation, there is always an assumption. In this case, the assumption is this: If a teacher implements the curriculum, the scores on the assessments (however they are structured in time) will be good.

Curriculum designers need to question assumptions in order to structure curricular systems. For example, because a teacher implements the curriculum does not necessarily support the assumption that students will score well. What about students who were absent, not paying attention, not doing their homework, not studying for tests, or goofing off in class? Curriculum designers may decide that those who complete required work should score well on the assessments. Are we then assuming that implementation is best measured at the individual or classroom level? Is evidence of implementation produced from teachers or from students?

How Will Curriculum Implementation Be Monitored?

Determining whether a curriculum is implemented requires monitoring. Who will monitor? Is it the responsibility of the principal, the assistant principal in charge of instruction, the central office, the teacher, or some combination of these? What procedure will the person follow to collect the information as discussed in the section on implementation? Monitoring is also structured by time and can take place on a daily, weekly, monthly, semester, or a yearly basis. For someone who does not comply with the monitoring requirements, consequences need to be defined. Staff development for new and existing teachers will need to be conducted so that everyone understands the information flow and a rationale for collecting the information. The collected information may need to be aggregated and sent to the central office. Procedures need to be developed to determine which stakeholders have access to the information and what they will do with the monitoring information.

How Frequently Will the Curriculum Be Revised?

Curriculum is typically revised once every 5 years or in sync with the adoption of textbooks. Yet if a district has testing data on a yearly basis, that data can only be reflected in curricular changes once every 5 years. The frequency of curriculum revision determines in part how the curriculum is used in a school system. A curriculum with only suggestions and no assessment and no monitoring requirements, revised every 7 years, may have great utility the first year but will fade into disuse as it regains its place on the shelf of a teacher's bookcase as year 6 and 7 come along. On the other hand, a curriculum that is revised annually, with accompanying staff development efforts, and is aligned to documented needs from the state test will have a better chance of surviving as a guide to instruction.

Curricular revision has budgetary implications, as teachers are generally paid for the extra work during the summer to revise the curriculum. Gathering input from staff is important if the curriculum is to reflect the knowledge staff gains through implementation. Is a unit too long or too short? Do units need to be combined? Do new state directives or district directives impact the curriculum? Curriculum revision needs to be thought about in the design stage of the curriculum, not as an afterthought.

How Will Policy Support Curriculum?

The rules and regulations around curriculum development, implementation, and revision need to be backed by sound policies. Policies need to spell out roles of the school boards, administration, teachers, parents, and community members in developing curriculum. Many of the procedures, once established, should be inserted into the policy handbook to demonstrate how the policies will be implemented. Sound policy can clarify issues, such as academic freedom and the school board's right to establish curriculum. The following is a quote from a Curriculum Management Audit, a process created by Fenwick English:

> Quality control is the fundamental element of a well-managed educational program. It is one of the major premises of local educational control within any state's educational system.
>
> The critical premise involved is that, via the will of the electorate, a local board of trustees establishes local priorities within state laws and regulations. A school district's accountability rests with the school board and the public.
>
> Through the development of an effective policy framework, a local school board provides the focus for management and accountability to be established for administrative and instructional staff members, as well as for its own responsibility. It also enables the district to assess meaningful use of student learning data as a critical factor in determining its success.
>
> Although educational program control and accountability are often shared among different components of a school district, fundamental control of, and responsibility for, a district and its operations rest with the school board and top-level management staff. (Northwest Independent School District Curriculum Management Audit, 1996)

USEFULNESS AND USABILITY AS INDICATORS OF CURRICULUM QUALITY

Designing curriculum is a matter of consciously making decisions about how the curricular elements fit together to make a coherent whole. Each component of curriculum design affects the others; these components include the schedule, decisions about whether to use disciplinary or interdisciplinary instruction, the curriculum components, the way the curriculum is described, whether the curriculum is required or suggested, the degree to which it is aligned, staff development, curriculum monitoring, curriculum revision, and curriculum policy. The staggering number of permutations and combinations may leave us throwing up our hands and adopting the curriculum format from the district down the road, with all its unexamined assumptions. How do we make a choice? This section discusses the curriculum design using the criteria of usefulness and usability. Curriculum won't help if it isn't used and useful to those making instructional decisions.

10 Criteria for Structuring a Useable and Useful Curriculum

1. Curriculum is useful and useable if it helps teachers use time to address content and pace instruction appropriately.

2. Curriculum is useable if the content is structured so that teachers know what is most important to teach and outlines how to teach that content.

3. Curriculum is useable if teachers have the flexibility to use their own creativity in planning instruction.

4. Curriculum is useful if it focuses teacher instruction on the standards.

5. Curriculum is useful if it helps teachers balance their instruction so ideas aren't over- or underemphasized.

6. Curriculum is useful if it helps teachers and administrators know that students have performed at high levels on instruction aligned with standards and assessment.

7. Curriculum is useable and useful if the results of curriculum-embedded assessments can be compared with results of state and standardized tests.

8. Curriculum is useful if it brings teachers together to collaborate on designing the curriculum and planning instruction.

9. Curriculum is useful if it has a structure for monitoring student and teacher completion of the curriculum.

10. Curriculum is useable if it is revised yearly to take into account the most recent performance on state or standardized tests (or both) and teachers' experience with the curriculum.

Resource 6B at the end of the chapter should help you to make systematic and thoughtful decisions about the structure of the curriculum for your district. I recommend tackling this task with a districtwide planning or steering committee prior to writing the curriculum. Coming to a consensus on the most appropriate design will build your capacity to implement the curriculum. The worksheet in Resource 6B provides a framework for discussing the structure of the curriculum in your district. After completing the framework, rate your design using the 10 criteria for structuring a useable and useful curriculum along with the accompanying rubrics. You can download this worksheet and criteria from the Balanced Curriculum Web site (www.balancedcurriculum.com).

SUMMARY

This chapter discussed the range of options for structuring a curriculum. In the next chapter, the structure of the Balanced Curriculum is described in detail. The components of a curriculum's structure must fit together in a powerful way so that it is both useful and useable. The Balanced Curriculum is one way to put together curriculum so that the outcome affects student achievement, and the next chapter provides an overview of the Balanced Curriculum process.

RESOURCE 6A

Framework for Deciding on the Structure of Your District's Curriculum

Directions: A committee undertaking the design of a curriculum may want to spend time filling out this questionnaire. The ordered questions should be answered in sequence. Answers to a question may change the approach suggested by previous questions. Be prepared to jump around in this sequential process and revisit previous questions as necessary.

1. For the curriculum as a whole, what are the schedule and time allocations in the schools for each subject area? Will the time allocations lead to less disparity among and between groups that are served by the schools?

What assumptions underlie your choices?

2. Will you use a disciplinary or an interdisciplinary approach?

What assumptions underlie your choices?

3. What is the smallest component of the curriculum?

Grade-level bands

Courses

Units

Significant tasks

Lessons

What assumptions underlie your choices?

4. How will the smallest component be described?

a. Will the description include *what* should students know and be able to do?

b. Will the description include *how* will they learn?

c. Give an example of a sample description.

What assumptions underlie your choices?

5. Which curriculum components are required, and which are suggested?

	Grade-Level Bands	Courses	Units	Significant Tasks	Lessons
a. Which components are required?					
b. Which components are suggested?					

What assumptions underlie your choices?

6. Alignment: What is aligned to what? Use either the curriculum octagon or the alignment chart to clarify this decision.

Alignment Chart Directions: Draw an arrow for the factors you plan to align. Example: Drawing a line between textbooks and state assessments means that you will align textbooks to state assessments. Remember, each arrow requires time and energy to complete.

Alignment Chart

National standards from professional organizations		National standards from professional organizations
NAEP, SAT, ACT		NAEP, SAT, ACT
Commercial standardized tests		Commercial standardized tests
State standards		State standards
State assessments		State assessments
Textbooks		Textbooks
District curriculum		District curriculum
District standards		District standards
District assessments		District assessments
Teacher lesson plans		Teacher lesson plans
Teacher assessment		Teacher assessment
Teacher instruction		Teacher instruction
Teacher assignments		Teacher assignments

What assumptions underlie your choices?

Fill in the alignment octagon.

Directions: Draw an arrow between what you will align in your curriculum. Remember that each line will take time and effort to complete.

Alignment Octagon

From the alignment octagon, what are the assumptions on which the lines were drawn? For example, if textbooks are aligned with state assessments, I assume that the textbook guides teachers' instruction and that the state assessments are important enough to be addressed during instruction. I also assume that aligning these two areas will be powerful enough so that students who complete the course material will be able to pass the state test. Naturally, all assumptions need to be questioned and tested.

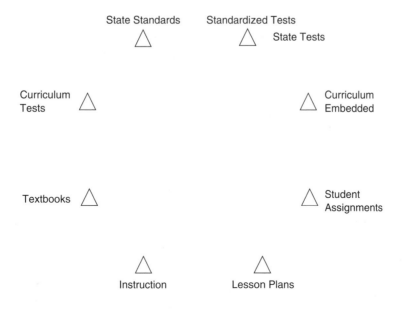

List the assumptions about your alignment strategy.

Assumption

Assumption

Assumption

Assumption

7. Will the curriculum be assessed?

a. Does the curriculum include assessment?

b. For which components of the system is assessment aimed?

c. Is assessment developed by the district or by teachers?

d. Is assessment required or suggested?

e. Is assessment aligned to both the curriculum and to the state standards or to other components?

What assumptions underlie your choices?

8. Staff Development: How will staff development groups hammer out the curriculum?

What assumptions underlie your choices?

9. How will the curriculum be implemented?

What assumptions underlie your choices?

10. Will the curriculum implementation be monitored?

a. Who will monitor?

b. Who will be monitored?

c. What evidence will monitors collect? What is the time frame?

   d. What is the procedure for collecting the evidence?

   e. What are the consequences for noncompliance?

   f. What staff development will help new and existing staff members understand the monitoring requirements?

   g. How will information be aggregated for central office administrators? Who will have access to the aggregated information, and what will they do with it?

What assumptions underlie your choices?

11. How frequently will the curriculum be revised?

   a. How often?

   b. Using what information?

What assumptions underlie your choices?

12. What is your budget for developing a curriculum?

What assumptions underlie your choices?

13. Does the board policy institutionalize the structure and process of curriculum development for your district?

What assumptions underlie your choices?

RESOURCE 6B

Rate Your Design

Directions: Now that you have put your design together using the form in Resource A, rate the design for usability and usefulness employing the following rubrics.

10 Criteria for Structuring a Useable and Useful Curriculum

1. Curriculum is useful and useable if it helps teachers use time to address content and pace instruction appropriately.

Needs Improvement	Emerging	Strong
The curriculum does not provide useful guidance about how much time to spend on curricular content.	The curriculum provides some guidance in planning time use during the school year.	The curriculum provides useful guidance in planning time use during the school year.
Teachers would not know from the curriculum if they are spending too much or too little time on a topic.	Some general guidance is provided for how much time to spend on a topic.	The curriculum can help teachers determine if they are spending too much or too little time on a topic.

2. Curriculum is useable if the content is structured so that teachers know what is most important to teach and outlines how to teach the important content.

Needs Improvement	Emerging	Strong
Neither what to teach nor how to teach it is specified in the curriculum.	What to teach is specified but how to teach it is not.	Indications of what to teach and how to teach it are included in the curriculum.

3. Curriculum is useable if teachers have the flexibility to use their own creativity in planning instruction.

Needs Improvement	Emerging	Strong
Teachers have complete flexibility because neither the curriculum content nor instructional processes are provided in the curriculum.	While the curriculum specifies content, teachers have complete flexibility in determining how the content will be taught.	The curriculum specifies both content and process but at a general level so that teachers have flexibility in planning.

4. Curriculum is useful in focusing teacher instruction on the standards.

Needs Improvement	Emerging	Strong
The curriculum is aligned with neither standards nor assessments.	The curriculum is aligned with either standards or assessments, but not both.	The curriculum is aligned to both standards and assessments.
The alignment process is not specified or shown in the curriculum document.	The alignment process was specified in the curriculum document so readers will know how the alignment process took place.	The alignment process was both specified and shown in the curriculum document. "Shown" means it is possible to make judgments about the alignment based on what is presented in the curriculum.

5. Curriculum is useful in helping teachers balance their instruction so ideas aren't over- or underemphasized.

Needs Improvement	Emerging	Strong
The curriculum gives no indication that appropriate weight was given to the standards and external assessments.	The curriculum asserts that there is an appropriate balance, but how that balance was achieved is not specified.	After alignment, the curriculum was balanced to provide appropriate coverage aligned to standards and external assessments.

6. Curriculum is useful if it helps teachers and administrators know that students have performed at high levels on instruction aligned with standards and assessment.

Needs Improvement	Emerging	Strong
Curriculum-embedded assessments are not part of the curriculum.	There is a plan to make curriculum-embedded assessments part of the curriculum.	Curriculum-embedded assessments are part of the curriculum.
Curriculum-embedded assessments are not part of the curriculum.	Teachers have access to student performance data on curriculum-embedded assessments.	Both teachers and administrators have access to student performance data on curriculum-embedded assessments.

7. Curriculum is useable and useful if the results of curriculum-embedded assessments can be compared with results of state and standardized tests.

Needs Improvement	Emerging	Strong
State scores do not give information for each standard or objective tested.	State scores do not give information for each standard or objective tested on the test. However, the district correlates scores on curriculum-embedded assessments with the scores on the tests.	The district has a way to prove that if students score high on the curriculum-embedded assessment they will also score well on the state or standardized assessment.

8. Curriculum is useful if it brings teachers together to collaborate on designing the curriculum and planning instruction.

Needs Improvement	Emerging	Strong
Only a few teachers were chosen because they were available at the time curriculum development occurred.	Curriculum development was done by a group of teachers that is not necessarily representative of all the schools in the district.	Curriculum development was done by a representative group of teachers with membership from each school in the district.
Teachers have no common planning period, so they get together infrequently to translate significant tasks into lesson plans.	Teachers have a common planning period but do not get together on grade- or course-level teams. Planning is done individually.	Teachers have common planning periods that they use to translate the significant tasks into lesson plans.

9. Curriculum is useful if it has a structure for monitoring student and teacher completion of the curriculum.

Needs Improvement	Emerging	Strong
Teachers do not report their completion of the curriculum to anyone.	Teachers report their completion of the curriculum to the principal.	Teachers report their completion of the curriculum to the principal, who in turn reports it to the central office.
Student results from curriculum-embedded tests are not gathered.	The principal gathers student results from curriculum-embedded tests on a regular basis. The results aren't used to make changes in the curriculum.	The principal gathers student results from curriculum-embedded tests on a regular basis. The results are used to provide input to curriculum authors, who update the curriculum on a yearly basis.

10. Curriculum is useable if revised yearly to take into account the most recent performance on state or standardized tests (or both) and teachers' experience with the curriculum.

Needs Improvement	Emerging	Strong
No data from testing information is used to update the curriculum. The curriculum, once written, is not updated regularly.	Data, such as item analysis from state and standardized tests, are used to update the curriculum at least every other year.	Data, such as item analysis from state and standardized tests, are used to update the curriculum on a yearly basis.
Teachers' experience with and recommendations for the curriculum are not recorded.	Teachers' experience with and recommendations for the curriculum are recorded, but the information is not used to update the curriculum.	Teachers' experience with and recommendations for the curriculum are recorded, and the information is used to update the curriculum on a yearly basis.

7

The Balanced Curriculum Process

This chapter explains the Balanced Curriculum model, which consists of five steps:

1. Describe the curriculum

2. Align and balance the curriculum

3. Assess the curriculum

4. Manage the curriculum

5. Provide staff development for the curriculum

The explanation shows how textbooks, standards, and standardized assessments are incorporated into a curriculum model that is useful, useable, and produces results.

DESCRIBE THE CURRICULUM

Everything that happens in a classroom can be described. Everything that happens to a student in school can be described. If we made a complete description of 1 hour of classroom time, we could fill an encyclopedia. Obviously, in any description, many things are left out. When creating a description, we decide what to leave out and on what to concentrate. Curriculum is a description of what should happen in a classroom and therefore includes certain things while leaving a great deal undescribed. For example, curriculum description generally concentrates on the cognitive while ignoring the affective or psychomotor, even though the cognitive is just one of the domains Bloom described in his taxonomies. Curriculum, as description, should tell what is most important in instruction so that students can demonstrate their knowledge and skills in similar ways.

The Balanced Curriculum uses three levels of description to focus on what is most important for students to learn. Each level involves smaller chunks of time:

1. Courses

2. Units

3. Significant tasks

Courses

Courses are collections of units and significant tasks that last for a year, semester, or quarter. They are the first way most schools describe what is most important. For example, in elementary schools, most students take courses in literacy, mathematics, social studies, science, and physical education.

Defining a sequence for courses assists a school district in quantifying how much time is required for students to learn certain knowledge and skills. Recently, the sequence in mathematics courses pointed out the importance of algebra as an "entry ticket" to higher education. Under Goals 2000 grants, many school districts have examined the scope and sequence of their mathematics courses to ensure that all students have access to algebra. In some cases, "below average" students take two or three semesters of algebra to gain the equivalent of a semester or year's worth that is given to more "mathematically able" students. Recently states, such as North Carolina, have taken to standardizing the content of courses so that everyone would know what passing Algebra I entailed. Ensuring that course content aligns with state requirements and professional organization recommendations is the first step in the Balanced Curriculum process. Making sure courses are consistent and build appropriate prerequisite skills for the next course is particularly important in math and science. Recent efforts to make senior year for high school students more meaningful by offering college credit for courses taken at community colleges points to the importance of courses and time. Figure 7.1 shows courses from Newburgh (New York) Enlarged City School District.

Figure 7.1 Courses from Newburgh Enlarged City School District, New York

	A Balanced Curriculum © 2000 ABC Education Consultants, LLC	Select Desired Course
		District: Newburgh Enlarged City School District	Course: Undetermined
	Help Main Menu Logout	Year: 2000-2001	Name: Dave Squires

Click on the Course Title to select the course you want to work with. Rows in Yellow represent courses you author and can edit. Rows in Blue represent courses you review and can comment on. Others can be viewed but not edited

Grade	Subject	Course Title	Start	End	Teacher	Author	Reviewer
K	English	Grade K ELA	09/01/2000	06/30/2001			
K	Mathematics	Grade K Mathematics	09/01/2000	06/30/2001			
K	Science	Grade K Science	09/12/2000	06/24/2001			
K	History & Social Sciences	Kindergarten Social Studies	09/01/2001	06/28/2002			
1	English	Grade One ELA	09/01/2000	06/30/2001			
1	Mathematics	Grade 1 Mathematics	09/01/2000	06/30/2001			
1	Science	Grade 1 Science	09/12/2000	06/24/2001			
1	History & Social Sciences	Grade One Social Studies	09/04/2001	06/25/2002			
2	English	Grade Two ELA	09/01/2000	06/30/2001			
2	Mathematics	Grade 2 Mathematics	09/01/2000	06/30/2001			
2	Science	Grade 2 Science	09/01/2000	06/30/2001			
2	History & Social Sciences	Grade 2 Social Studies	09/04/2001	06/25/2002			
3	English	Grade Three ELA	09/01/2000	06/30/2001			
3	Mathematics	Grade 3 Mathematics	09/01/2000	06/30/2001			
3	Science	Grade 3 Science	09/01/1900	06/01/1901			
3	History & Social Sciences	Grade 3 Social Studies	09/04/2001	06/25/2002			
4	English	Grade Four ELA	09/01/2000	06/30/2001			
4	Mathematics	Grade 4 Mathematics	09/01/2000	06/30/2001			
4	Science	Grade 4 Science	09/01/2000	06/30/2000			
4	History & Social Sciences	Grade 4 Social Studies	09/04/2001	06/25/2002			
5	English	Grade Five ELA	09/01/2000	06/30/2001			
5	Mathematics	Grade 5 Mathematics	09/01/2000	06/30/2001			
5	Science	Grade 5 Science	09/01/2000	06/30/2000			
5	History & Social Sciences	Grade 5 Social Studies	09/04/2001	06/25/2002			
6	English	Grade Six ELA	09/01/2000	06/30/2001			
6	Mathematics	Grade 6 Mathematics	09/01/2000	06/30/2001			
6	Science	Grade 6 Science	09/01/2000	06/30/2001			

Units

Units provide another way to organize the time and content of a course. Units are time bound in that they begin around a certain time and end at a certain time, usually with a culminating activity or a test. Major grades in a teacher's grade book or chapters in a textbook generally indicate units, and units provide teachers with a way to pace instruction through the year. They should fit into the length of time for the course. Course authors need to consider carefully how much time units take so that they do not have more units than can be taught in the time allotted for the course. How many of us actually made it into the 20th century in a U.S. history course? Making sure that all students have the opportunity to gain the knowledge from a course's units is the first and most important key in managing students' learning. Figure 7.2 and Figure 7.3 show samples of unit titles for a Grade 2 reading and language arts course and an U.S. history course for high school, respectively.

Figure 7.2   A reading and language arts course

Unit Timeline
Grade 6 Language Arts
Literacy
English
Grade 6

Englewood Cliffs Public Schools
2003–2004

Unit Title	Begin Date	End Date
Pathways	9/4/2003	10/18/2003
A Common Thread	10/21/2003	12/5/2003
With Flying Colors	12/6/2003	1/29/2004
Seek and Discover	1/30/2004	3/18/2004
Brainstorm	3/19/2004	5/7/2004
All Things Considered	5/8/2004	6/11/2004

SOURCE: Copyright © Englewood Cliffs Public Schools, Englewood Cliffs, New Jersey. Reprinted with permission.

Figure 7.3   A semester-long U.S. history course for high school students

Unit Timeline
American History
History and Social Sciences
High School

Parkland High School
Winston-Salem Forsyth County, NC
2000–2001

Unit Title	Begin Date	End Date
Colonial and Revolutionary Period	1/4/2001	1/16/2001
The New Nation	1/17/2001	1/22/2001
Nationalism and Sectionalism	1/23/2001	1/31/2001
Civil War/Reconstruction	2/2/2001	2/9/2001
Gilded Age/Turn of Century	2/12/2001	2/26/2001
International Relations/WWI	2/26/2001	3/1/2001
1920s and 1930s	3/2/2001	3/9/2001
World War II	3/19/2001	3/27/2001
Cold War and 1950s	3/28/2001	3/30/2001
Civil Rights	4/2/2001	4/4/2001
Social Change/Vietnam	4/5/2001	4/10/2001
70s/80s/to Present	4/11/2001	4/24/2001

SOURCE: Copyright © Parkland High School, Winston-Salem Forsyth County, North Carolina. Reprinted with permission.

Courses and units are two ways to describe what is most important for students to learn. The third way of describing curriculum is to tell what, specifically, will guide instruction. This is the role of significant tasks.

Significant Tasks

Significant tasks are the heart and head of the Balanced Curriculum process. Significant tasks are promises to the next grade level or course that students have performed what is described in the significant tasks. They are important activities and, at times, culminating activities for the unit. Significant tasks usually take longer than an instructional period to complete. Some significant tasks may last 2 days, others a week. The tasks are significant because they involve more than one of the skills and knowledge that are mentioned in standards. Significant tasks are complex in that they combine many skills and concepts together. Significant tasks take up approximately 60% of the time of the instructional unit. All course teachers are responsible for completing the significant tasks for the units, but there is flexibility in the way the significant tasks might be taught. Following are examples of some significant tasks designed by elementary and secondary teachers.

Figures 7.4, 7.5, and 7.6 show samples of significant tasks from Grade 2 mathematics, Grade 5 reading and language arts, and a high school chemistry course.

Figure 7.4 Significant tasks: Grade 2 mathematics

Units/Significant Tasks Grade 2 Mathematics Unit 1: Numbers, Operations, and Data		Passaic Public Schools 2002–2003 9/4/2002 10/18/2002

Significant Tasks

Skipping By Two's

Students will be given a 100 chart with 15 random numbers inserted in their appropriate spaces. Learners will:

1. Complete the chart by filling in the missing numbers.
2. Self-evaluate their completed 100 chart by comparing it to the one in the math center.
3. Skip count by two's and color appropriate number squares to 100.
4. Check their two's pattern by comparing it to the one in the math center.
5. Construct a puzzle out of their 100 chart by dissecting it into 10 pieces of various shapes and sizes.
6. Exchange their puzzle pieces with their partner and reconstruct 100 chart.
7. Record their experience in their math journal.

The Rename Game

The teacher creates a chart or bulletin board with 6 to 8 random numbers from 1-25 for display in the math center. (Note: As the year progresses this activity may be used with more difficult numbers.) The learners will be challenged to write other names for the posted numbers. For example, 25 could be 20 + 5, 26 − 1, 2 tens and 1 five, the number between 24 and 26, etc. Discuss students' responses. Set students in pairs and play Do You Know This Number, where one person poses the question, "Do you know this number − 4 tens and 5 ones?"

Numbers in the News

Students will be given newspapers, catalogs, magazines, scissors, glue and paper. Each student will be directed to cut numbers and number words from newspapers, catalogs, and magazines. Then they will be asked to categorize the words in groups such as time words, ordinal numbers, cardinal numbers, fractions, and money. Each clipping should be glued and labeled to the appropriate group. They can also put numbers in sequential order. To conclude the lesson they should describe their system for categorizing numbers in their math journal.

SOURCE: Used courtesy of the Passaic-City School District.

Figure 7.5 Significant tasks: Grade 5 reading and language arts

Units/Significant Tasks 5th Reading/LA English Grade 5 Unit: Courage	*AB/CB*	Tyler Independent School District 2001–2002 1/7/2002 2/14/2002

Significant Tasks

Call Us Courageous

   We will read or listen to a variety of texts (including those from the Internet) that depict people displaying courage (biography, myth, fable, legend, fairytale, folklore, tall tale, etc.) We will identify and infer what courage is and how the characters showed courage. We will use graphic organizers (such as Venn diagrams, T-charts, webs) to compare courageous characters across texts. We will select one character and compare him/her to ourselves using a graphic organizer. We will compose and present poems (dual bio poems, biographical poems, cinquains, lantem poems, etc.) orally or by using a multimedia presentation (such as PowerPoint, Kid-Pix, Hyperstudio, etc.) about ourselves and our courageous character. We will evaluate and respond to the student writers' views as how the poem relates to courage.

Lead The Way

   We will listen to or read biographies about historical heroes/leaders of the past and present. We will take notes to demonstrate our ability to discriminate between relevant and irrelevant information, distinguishing fact from opinion, and drawing conclusions. As part of the activity, a graphic organizer (such as Venn diagram, T-chart, table, web, etc.) can be used to take the notes. We will then write an essay to compare and contrast the qualities/characteristics of heroes from long ago to the heroes of today across time. Students could proofread other's writing and use editing and revision techniques.

SOURCE: Copyright © Tyler Independent School District. Developed by Tyler ISD Staff. Reprinted with permission.

   Significant tasks are "bets." If students receive instruction described by the significant task, results on outcome measures will improve. If not, the significant tasks need to be revised.

   Teachers use the significant tasks as the basis for their lesson planning. They may address the significant tasks in different orders, depending on the strengths and needs of the class they are teaching. Teachers may also choose to address each significant task in different ways. For example, if students have to give a speech after interviewing one another, this could be done in small groups or to the class as a whole. One school district screened prospective teachers by having them develop lesson plans from significant tasks.

   Generally, 35 to 60 significant tasks make up a yearly course, although early grades generally have more, and high school and college courses may have fewer. For a yearlong course, this means a minimum of one significant task per week.

   Significant tasks do not specify everything that should be taught, but they do specify the most important things. For example, if a student is to produce a short story, the significant task may not specify practice describing characters, but the teacher may decide to include this if the class needs it. The significant tasks do not include all prerequisite skills that build toward students' performance of a significant task.

   A significant task focuses on students' performance. It shows what students, not the teacher, will be able to do or know. Review significant tasks to ensure that they focus on student performance and learning rather than on teacher procedure. This shifts teachers thinking from concerns about material coverage to concerns about students' ability to perform the significant task. Coverage of the material is done in the service of assisting students to perform rather than having students' application

Figure 7.6   Significant tasks: high school chemistry

Units/Significant Tasks

Chemistry

Science High School

Parkland High School

Winston-Salem Forsyth County, NC

2001–2002

Unit: Safety and Measurements

1/3/2002   1/9/2002

Objectives: To learn to use the centigram balance, identify laboratory equipment, learn safety procedures as they use the equipment, name SI units for length, mass, time, volume, and density, distinguish between mass and weight, perform density calculations, transform a statement of equality to a conversion factor, distinguish between accuracy and precision, determine the number of significant figures in measurements, and convert measurements into scientific notation.

Significant Tasks

Centigram Balance Activity

   The students will identify and mass objects found at their lab station to the nearest 0.01 g.

Recovery of Sodium Bicarbonate

   Students will mass 0.50 g of sodium bicarbonate, dissolve it in water, and recover it by evaporating the water. They will calculate the percent error.

Density of Pennies

   Students will calculate the density of pennies minted before 1982 and after 1982 and account for the difference.

Thickness of a Sheet of Aluminum Foil

   The students will measure the thickness of two different pieces of aluminum foil using indirect properties.

---

of the knowledge relegated to a secondary role superceded by covering content. Having the significant tasks take up 60% of the unit's teaching time reinforces this shift. Performance supercedes coverage.

   Course content, like freeways, will fill to their capacity. We know that knowledge is exploding, but time for school has remained constant. We can talk faster in an effort to catch up, or we can carefully choose appropriate tasks that incorporate necessary disciplinary knowledge with powerful activities. We need to choose the significant tasks carefully so that they reflect standards related to a subject-area discipline.

   Significant tasks are embedded in courses associated with subject-area disciplines, such as English, mathematics, science, and the social sciences. Disciplines reflect the various, systematic ways the world can be known. Science discovers knowledge by applying the scientific method, just as literature uses stories to discover truth. Mathematics discovers knowledge by rules and proofs, but this is different from the rules of making history and confirming historical fact. Significant tasks should be constructed so that students demonstrate their knowledge of the constructs of the discipline. This means that they are learning how to think like a scientist, a historian, or an author. Teaching all the content of a discipline is impossible, but teaching how a particular discipline makes meaning of the world can be accomplished. Standards tell us about important ideas that structure different disciplines.

When students then have to apply the rules or process of discovering knowledge of a discipline to a particular situation to make sense of it, they then demonstrate their disciplinary knowledge. To illustrate, a student may be asked to describe a sunset from a scientific point of view. To do so, the student may invoke knowledge about planetary rotation, the relationship of the sun to the planets, centripetal and centrifugal force, red shift, and knowledge about optics, such as the characteristic of light shining through various densities of matter. In a literature class, the sun's description may involve thinking using metaphors and similes, a knowledge of the sun's place in mythology, the symbolic meaning of the setting sun, and images from various literary sources, such as Hemingway's *The Sun Also Rises*, or a historical illusion to the king of France. Thus, significant tasks are not just "neat activities" but are constructed with the purpose of student practice in applying disciplinary knowledge to specific situations. Interdisciplinary curriculum can follow after discipline-based curriculum is developed. Then the authors have in-depth knowledge about the various disciplines that make up the interdisciplinary curriculum. The Balanced Curriculum process is discipline based because most courses arise from an attempt to teach disciplinary knowledge, not exclusively cover content. Disciplinary knowledge links disparate subject-area content together in a coherent whole.

Significant tasks use the textbook as a resource rather than a guide. Textbooks are written with a national perspective; significant tasks are written with local and state standards in mind. Not all textbooks will adequately emphasize the standards and high-stakes test content appropriate for a particular district in a particular state employing a particular standardized test. Thus, curriculum authors need to decide whether the significant tasks in the textbook are aligned with the standards and high-stakes tests. This is of particular importance because there are more activities in textbooks and ancillary material than one teacher can use to teach a course. Thus, significant tasks help to ensure that teachers are focusing their efforts on meeting standards and scoring well on high-stakes tests rather than just covering text material. Texts can assist the teacher in meeting the prerequisite and component skills of a significant task, or facilitate extension and remediation activities. Texts can also provide instructional support necessary to complete an instructional task.

Without curriculum expectations embedded in significant tasks, many teachers may leave out important areas. Individual teachers, making individual choices about what to emphasize from the text, do not produce students with similar prerequisite skills for the next course. Exclusive reliance on individual teachers making individual choices does not culminate in skills held in common by a large number of students. For example, most 3rd-grade teachers agree that they could teach most students their multiplication facts. Yet ask the same teachers if they actually taught the multiplication facts so that most students knew them by the end of the year. Teachers may report that even though they think it was important, it was not taught to ensure student mastery.

Significant tasks also focus assessment. Curriculum authors construct significant tasks with the assessment in mind. The Balanced Curriculum model calls for each significant task to be assessed and for all students enrolled in the course to take the assessment embedded in the significant task. Significant tasks need to be described so that how they are assessed is apparent. Thus, significant tasks are the junction between instruction, curriculum, and assessment. Significant tasks describe the curriculum, focus the instruction, and help structure assessment. Significant tasks are similar to "behavioral objectives" of another era, in that they are an attempt to describe instructional tasks. Where behavioral objectives focus on rigorously defining the testing situation and the content to be tested, significant tasks focus on the activity students will accomplish linked with content from the standards.

Significant tasks form a basis for planning lessons. Teachers will need to be able to translate the description of the significant task into a series of lesson plans. The Balanced Curriculum Web site allows posting of sample lesson plans to assist in this process. The Balanced Curriculum model is flexible because there are many ways to design lessons for each significant task, and examples can be shown on the Balanced Curriculum Web site.

Significant tasks are necessary to ensure that all students have equal access to a high-quality curriculum. They structure and circumscribe teachers' choices so that students will learn the most important content and skills. Significant tasks are concrete enough to give instruction a focus but general enough to be approached in many ways. Significant tasks are time-bound, taking up about 60% of the time for the unit. This ensures that the tasks are the central focus of the unit and also allows teachers flexibility in addressing student needs. Combinations of providing prerequisites, reteaching and enrichment activities take up the other 40% of the time. Completion of significant tasks ensures that students progress to the next unit, or next grade level, with the most important prerequisite skills. Teachers at the next grade level or in another course receive students who have had a core of similar experiences guided by significant tasks. As implementation progresses, fewer comments such as the following should be heard: "I don't know what they did last year, but students just don't know how to . . ." Once the curriculum is described, the standards and tests are aligned to significant tasks and balanced using the curriculum authors' judgments.

ALIGN AND BALANCE THE CURRICULUM

Aligning the Curriculum

Alignment is a process of making sure the intentions for instruction are correlated with standards. There are many places that help to define the "intentions for instruction" such as the following:

- Standards
- High-stakes tests
- Curriculum-embedded assessments
- Texts
- Teacher expertise and background
- Teacher planning
- Administrative emphasis
- Student entry characteristics and development

Any of these areas can be aligned to any of the other areas. For example, texts can be aligned to high-stakes tests or teacher plans can be aligned to state standards. Most districts claim that they have done alignment because they have aligned two or more of these areas, knowing that alignment is important. Aligning only a few of the areas does not give a complete picture. For example, aligning teachers' lesson plans to the state test does not tell us how well the lessons are meeting the more inclusive state standards. There is a web of influences that need to be aligned.

Students do not generally learn well a subject's content and processes if they are not taught the content and processes. The goal of the Balanced Curriculum is to make sure that students are taught what is most important to learn. Learning is described with the significant tasks. Significant tasks provide the structure for aligning and balancing the curriculum. We use significant tasks because they describe the most important parts of the curriculum. Significant tasks are limited in number, making them the ideal candidate for aligning the curriculum.

The curriculum is described by the courses, units, and significant tasks. The significant tasks are the "smallest" segment of the curriculum. We chose the significant task to be the curriculum's touchstone and the basis for aligning with standards. Alignment needs to take into account the web of influences on the curriculum (Figure 7.7).

Figure 7.7   Influences on the curriculum

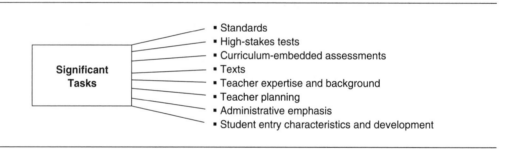

Significant tasks describe how students enact the standards; the significant task is the alignment link between the curriculum and standards.

Significant Tasks ⎯⎯⎯⎯⎯⎯⎯⎯⎯⎯▶ Standards and High-Stakes Tests

Significant tasks can be aligned to standards because the vocabulary and language of the standards are consciously embedded by curriculum authors in the description of the significant tasks. In Figure 7.8, the significant task is listed on the left. In the middle are letters. Each letter indicates a piece of the significant task that has alignment potential. On the right-hand side is an excerpt from New York State Standards. By the standards are letters that indicate alignment to the piece of the significant task. For example, B (estimating objects that are 10 times larger) is aligned with the state standards 3.MM.4.01 ("visualize, represent, and transform two- and three-dimensional shapes") and 3.MM.4.08 ("investigate both two- and three-dimensional transformations"). The curriculum authors would then determine the most important standards based on the analysis and enter the standard codes on the Balanced Curriculum Web site. For example, the curriculum authors might choose standard 3.ME.5.1 because four of the sections of the significant task are aligned to this standard.

Figure 7.8   Aligning significant tasks with standards

Significant Task *Brobdingnag's Pencil*		NY State Standards for Intermediate Math Modeling/Multiple Representation
While listening to a story that provides information about the sizes of things in the land of giants (Brobdingnag in Gulliver's Travels) students will:		3.MM.4.0 4. Students use mathematical modeling/multiple representation to provide a means of presenting, interpreting, communicating, and connecting mathematical information and relationships.
1. List as many mathematics terms as possible.	**A**	**B,F** 3.MM.4.01 visualize, represent, and transform two- and three-dimensional shapes.
2. Use the scale factor (10 times larger) to estimate and list which things in the classroom are in standard size and which things in the classroom are ten times larger.	**B**	3.MM.4.02 use maps and scale drawings to represent real objects and places
		3.MM.4.03 use the coordinate plane to explore geometric ideas.
		3.MM.4.04 represent numerical relationships in one- and two-dimensional graphs
		A 3.MM.4.05 use variables to represent relationships.
		F 3.MM.4.06 use concrete materials and diagrams to describe the operation of real world processes and systems.
		3.MM.4.07 develop and explore models that do and do not rely on chance.
		B,F 3.MM.4.08 investigate both two- and three-dimensional transformations.
		F 3.MM.4.09 use appropriate tools to construct and verify geometric relationships.
In groups, students will then select and use appropriate measurement units and tools to:		**E,F,G** 3.MM.4.10 develop procedures for basic geometric constructions.
		3.MM.4.11 build a city skyline to demonstrate skill in linear measurements, scale drawing, ratio, fractions, angles, and geometric shapes.
1. Measure each part of a given object.	**C**	**C** 3.MM.4.12 bisect an angle using a straight edge and compass.
2. Use strategies for scaling shape.	**D**	3.MM.4.13 draw a complex of geometric figures to illustrate that the intersection of a plane and a sphere is a circle or point.
3. Construct an object that will be ten times larger than the given object in all of its dimensions and characteristics (size, shape, and color).	**E** **F**	Modeling/Multiple Representation
		3.ME.5.0 5. Students use measurements in both metric and English measure to provide a major link between the abstractions of mathematics and the real world in order to describe and compare objects and data.
		B,C,D,E 3.ME.5.1 estimate, make, and use measurements in real-world situations.
		B,C,D,E 3.ME.5.2 select appropriate standard and nonstandard measurement units and tools to measure to a desired degree of accuracy.
Each group will record the steps they took to construct the object and present their final product to the class. The class will conduct a discussion on the best strategies for solving the problem.	**G**	**E,F** 3.ME.5.3 develop measurement skills and informally derive and apply formulas in direct measurement activities.
		3.ME.5.4 use statistical methods and measures of central tendencies to display, describe, and compare data.
		3.ME.5.5 explore and produce graphic representations of data using calculators/computers.
		B,C,F 3.ME.5.6 develop critical judgment for the reasonableness of measurement.
		3.ME.5.7 use box plots or stem and leaf graphs to display a set of test scores.
		3.ME.5.8 estimate and measure the surface areas of a set of gift boxes in order to determine how much wrapping paper will be required.

A report requested from the Web site shows the significant tasks and the standards and substandards that the curriculum authors chose for their alignment. The Balanced Curriculum process allows authors only limited alignment, so authors must choose two to five standards that align to the significant task. Districts can choose which standards and the number of alignments allowed. In this way, the job of aligning 35 to 40 significant tasks for a course is circumscribed.

The report in Figure 7.9 shows one significant task and the alignments at Tyler Texas Independent School District. The significant task, "It Is Your Choice," from a 5th-grade unit, is listed in the first paragraph at the top of the page. The standards are listed in the first column. Texas Assessment of Academic Skills (TAAS) Objectives are taken from the item specifications on the state test. Reading is tested in 5th grade, but writing is not tested until the 8th grade. The curriculum director decided that both 5th- and 8th-grade TAAS objectives should be included in the alignment, so the grades leading up to 8th grade are responsible for assisting in the writing process. The TEKS (Texas Essential Knowledge and Skills) are the Texas state standards. Three TEKS standards are listed in Figure 7.9: for English language arts and reading for Grade 5 (TEKS ELA & R 5), for Spanish language arts and English-as-a-second-language Grade 5 (TEKS Spanish LA & ESL 5), and TEKS technical applications Grades 3–5 (TEKS Tech App 3–5). The last standard is taken from the policy manual of the Tyler Independent School District defining expectations for graduating students.

Teachers and administrators are given copies of the report so that they can plan and monitor lessons from the significant tasks alignments. Teachers examine the alignments to help them determine what to emphasize in their lesson plans and instruction. Instruction is now aligned with standards.

Figure 7.9   Significant task aligned to full range of standards from Tyler, Texas

It Is Your Choice

After reading or listening to various texts we will analyze character(s) using graphic organizers such as webs, Fleshing It Out, etc. We will judge the logic of a character's choices. We will write skits showing how the character makes a different choice with different consequences. We will present a dramatic interpretation of our skit.

Standard	Code	Description
Bloom's Taxonomy	An	Analysis
	S	Synthesis
Developmental Pathways	E	Ethical
	S	Social
Good Components English K–12	Representing	Representing
	Speaking	Speaking
International Reading Association/ National Council of Teachers of English K–12	9	Students develop an understanding of and respect for diversity in language use, patterns, and dialects across cultures, ethnic groups, geographic regions, and social roles.
	12	Students use spoken, written, and visual language to accomplish their own purposes (e.g., for learning, enjoyment, persuasion, and the exchange of information).
TAAS Objectives Grade 5 Reading	5.10.E	Use the text's structure or progression of ideas, such as cause and effect, to recall information.

Figure 7.9 (Continued)

Standard	Code	Description
	5.11.A	Offer observations, make connections, react, speculate, interpret, and raise questions in response to texts.
	5.12.H	Analyze characters, including their traits, motivations, conflicts, points of view, relationships, and changes they undergo.
	5.12.1	Analyze story plot, setting, and problem resolution.
	5.12.C	Identify the purposes of different types of texts, such as to inform, influence, express, or entertain.
TAAS Objectives Grade 8 Writing	8.15.E	Select and use voice and style appropriate to audience and purpose.
	8.15.F	Choose the appropriate form for his/her own purpose for writing, including letters, editorials, narratives, and instructions.
	8.18.C	Revise selected drafts by deleting, combining, and rearranging text.
TAAS Objectives Grade 8 Writing	8.15.H	Produce cohesive and coherent written texts by using effective transitions, and choosing precise wording.
	8.17.C	Employ standard English usage, including subject-verb agreement, pronoun referents, and parts of speech.
TEKS ELA & R 5	5.05.C	Present dramatic interpretations of experiences, stories, poems, or plays to communicate (4–8).
	5.05.D	Use effective rate, volume, pitch, and tone for the audience and setting (4–8).
	5.11.A	Offer observations, make connections, react, speculate, interpret, and raise questions in response to texts (4–8).
	5.11.B	Interpret text ideas through such varied means as journal writing, discussion, enactment, and media (4–8).
	5.12.A	Judge the internal consistency or logic of stories and texts such as "Would this character do this?"; "Does this make sense here?" (4–5).
	5.12.H	Analyze characters, including their traits, motivations, conflicts, points of view, relationships, and changes they undergo (4–8).
	5.19.A	Generate ideas and plans for writing by using such prewriting strategies as brainstorming, graphic organizers, notes, and logs (4–8).
TEKS SPANISH LA & ESL 5	5.11.A	Offer observations, make connections, react, speculate, interpret, and raise questions in response to texts (4–8).
	5.11.B	Interpret text ideas through such varied means as journal writing, discussion, enactment, and media (4–8).
	5.12.A	Judge the internal consistency or logic of stories and texts such as "Would this character do this?"; "Does this make sense here?" (4–5).
	5.12.H	Analyze characters, including their traits, motivations, conflicts, points of view, relationships, and changes they undergo (4–8).

(Continued)

Figure 7.9 (Continued)

Standard	Code	Description
	5.12.1	Recognize and analyze story plot, setting, and problem resolution (4–8).
	5.19.A	Generate ideas and plans for writing by using such prewriting strategies as brainstorming, graphic organizers, notes, and logs (4–8).
	5.29.K	Retell, role-play, and/or visually illustrate the order of events (4–8/ESL).
TEKS Tech App 3-5	126.3.07.B	Use appropriate software to express ideas and solve problems including the use of word processing, graphics, databases, spreadsheets, simulations, and multimedia.
Tyler ISD Student Expectations	1.02	Participate in the literary, visual, and performing arts to enrich his/her daily life.
	3.01	Have a lifelong learning plan based on student's interests, aptitudes, and abilities.

SOURCE: Copyright © ABC Education Consultants, LLC.

NOTE: TAAS = Texas Assessment of Academic Skills; TEKS = Texas Essential Knowledge and Skills

Balancing the Curriculum

A curriculum may be aligned, but it is not balanced. By balance, we mean that the standards and assessments have been appropriately and adequately covered—not too much, not too little, but just right—the Goldilocks principle.

The symbol for the Balanced Curriculum process is a mobile (Figure 7.10). A mobile is in balance when all the pieces have a particular weight in relationship with all the others. Remove one piece and the mobile is out of balance. Curriculum design is a similar process to designing a mobile. Each piece of the curriculum must be in appropriate balance with the other pieces of the curriculum. As with a mobile, there are many ways to achieve balance in a curriculum. In balancing the curriculum, we are checking to see that all of the parts are balanced.

Figure 7.10   Balancing the curriculum

A Balanced Curriculum

SOURCE: Copyright © ABC Education Consultants, LLC.

Teachers' professional expertise helps to determine balance. The curriculum authors, if drawn from the best of a wise, experienced, and caring teaching staff, use their own professional judgment. By developing significant tasks, teachers are helping to determine the balance in the curriculum, one task at a time. It is the sum of the tasks, when taken together for a course or a sequence of courses, that really makes a difference, however. In one district that used the Balanced Curriculum process, teachers developed significant tasks in English and language arts and then aligned them to the Comer Developmental Pathways (Comer, Haynes, Joyner, & Ben-Avie, 1999).

One of the six pathways is ethical development. After completing the alignment, we found that few significant tasks aligned with the ethical pathway. This was surprising because one of the purposes of literature is to assist students in developing along the ethical pathway by considering characters' ethical decisions. The teacher-authors believed that ethics should be included in an English language arts curriculum but did not have any tasks aligned to the ethical pathway. The curriculum was out of balance regarding students' development and teacher beliefs. The teachers went back and revised many of the significant tasks to incorporate discussion and writing about the ethical dimensions of characters' choices.

Emphasizing a concept too much can also overbalance a curriculum. In one district, teachers were required to give students a writing assignment each week for a year. The writing assignments all had the same structure, the one "aligned" to the state standardized test. Students never had any variety in those assignments. Consequently, they may have succeeded on a particular writing task, with little practice in any other form of writing. This practice narrowed the curriculum to exactly what the test covers and denied students and teachers the full range of writing, reading, speaking, listening, and viewing opportunities.

Figures 7.11 and 7.12 provide examples of reports that curriculum authors use to balance the curriculum for Grade 5 English and language arts courses at the Tyler (Texas) Independent School District and at Hertford County (North Carolina) Public Schools, respectively.

Figure 7.11   Standards Alignment Summary report for Grade 5 English and language arts

Standards Alignments
Summary
5th Reading/LA
English
Grade 5

Tyler Independent School District
2003–2004

Standard: Bloom's Taxonomy

Subtopics

Knowledge		
K	Aligned Significant Tasks:	**4**
Comprehension		
C	Aligned Significant Tasks:	**21**
Application		
Ap	Aligned Significant Tasks:	**23**
Analysis		
An	Aligned Significant Tasks:	**13**
Synthesis		
S	Aligned Significant Tasks:	**17**
Evaluation		
E	Aligned Significant Tasks:	**7**

The report for Bloom's taxonomy indicates the number of aligned significant tasks for the Grade 5 reading and language arts course. There are 44 significant tasks for the course. Each can be aligned to two categories of Bloom's taxonomy. There are 85 alignments indicating that the authors chose to use the two alignment categories for most of the significant tasks.

Is the curriculum in balance according to the report? The report indicates a major emphasis is given to the categories of comprehension and application. Medium emphasis is given to analysis and synthesis. Light emphasis is given to evaluation and knowledge. The curriculum authors decided it was appropriate for the developmental needs of 5th graders, because comprehension and application, emphasized the most, are two processes that the 5th-grade curriculum authors felt were most important to address in 5th grade. Balancing the curriculum is a judgment call.

Figure 7.12 is the Standards Alignment Summary for the North Carolina end-of-course test for reading in Grades 3 through 8. The codes are explained in the left-hand column. Below is an excerpt from the Standards Alignment Summary report dealing with the North Carolina state reading test.

Figure 7.12 Standards Alignment Summary report for North Carolina English and language arts (ELA), Grade 5

Standards Alignments
Summary
Grade 5 Communication Skills
English
Grade 5

Hertford County Public Schools
2003–2004

Standard: North Carolina End-of-Course Test—ELA Grade 3–8

Subtopics

Use of strategies that enhance reading comprehension:			
	Number of aligned tasks		
	8	1.01	Reading to acquire information
	10	1.02	Reading to interpret information
	5	1.03	Reading to apply information
	6	1.04	Reading for critical analysis
Passage types			
	Number of aligned tasks		
	5	2.01a	Literature: Short stories
	4	2.01b	Literature: Poems
	3	2.01c	Literature: Essays
	4	2.02a	Informational Selections in Content Areas: Social Studies
	3	2.02c	Informational Selections in Content Areas: Art
Reading for various purposes			
	Number of aligned tasks		
	8	3.01	Literary experience
	7	3.02	Gaining Information
	11	3.03	Performing a Task

SOURCE: Used courtesy of the Hertford County Public Schools, North Carolina.

The Standard Alignment Summary report in Figure 7.12 shows the number of significant tasks aligned to the North Carolina Reading Assessment specifications for Grade 5. The second column contains the code for the North Carolina assessment specification. The last column tells what the code means.

Does the curriculum provide coverage of all tested categories? Yes. All categories are covered using at least three significant tasks. The authors have made a judgment that this configuration of significant tasks is in balance, despite the fact that some categories have more aligned significant tasks than others. The authors could explain this differential emphasis by referring to the number of items tested in each of the categories. Some categories may have more items; some may have fewer. For example, last year's poor results in the "Reading to Interpret Information" category showed a need to emphasize this more. During curriculum revision, the number of significant tasks aligned to this category was increased. The number of aligned significant tasks demonstrates that the curriculum authors "balanced" the curriculum so that Relationships and Outcomes had adequate coverage.

Underemphasis may also be an issue. For example, in the category "Literature: Essays," there were only three aligned significant tasks. Is this enough? The curriculum revisers need to make this decision balancing other competing demands within the curriculum, the emphasis of the state test, and the amount of time available.

Balancing the curriculum is always a matter of the curriculum authors' judgment. Curriculum authors need to look at the large amount of information given to them in the alignment reports and determine whether a balance exists. It is a challenging task for the best and brightest teachers.

ASSESS THE CURRICULUM

Internal and external assessments are aligned to significant tasks. External assessments are high-stakes state tests and standardized tests not created by the district but used by the district to provide norm-referenced data for student achievement.

Internal assessment is produced by teachers in the district, such as the quizzes, chapter tests, grading processes for papers and projects, and district assessments linked to standards. In the Balanced Curriculum process, internal assessments are generated for units and significant tasks.

In the Balanced Curriculum model, internal assessment has two complementary parts: content and format assessment. A content assessment provides teachers with a standard way to judge students' performances on significant tasks. At the end of each significant task, teachers grade students' performance on the significant task. Because all students and teachers complete the significant tasks, the content assessment is given to all students. The grading of the content assessment is therefore standardized for the teaching staff, ensuring that a performance in one class will be judged similarly to a performance in another teacher's class.

A format assessment provides practice on the format of the standardized test for the unit or the quarter. A format assessment's only function is to provide practice on standardized or state test formats; no content mastery is to be inferred from the score on format assessments. Once developed, both format and content assessments are stored on the Web site so all professional staff have access to the assessments from any computer connected to the Internet.

Results on internal assessments should predict performance on the external assessments. If students score high on the content and format assessments, the student should also score high on the external assessment. When this is true, the curriculum has been validated. The design of aligned significant tasks and assessments produce expected results.

If results of internal assessments are high and external assessments results low, then there are problems to be solved. The curriculum authors, when revising, might ask the following questions:

- Is the alignment valid? Is there a direct link between the significant task and the standard?
- Are the internal assessments—both format and content—constructed so the concepts or constructs are truly assessed? Do we need to revise the internal assessments?
- Is the topic on the external assessment important enough, given all the other pressures, to improve the alignment or the significant task associated with the alignment? If the topic is unimportant, we do not need to include the topic in the curriculum.
- Does the significant task need to be revised so it more clearly specifies what needs to be taught?
- Did most complete the significant task? If not, why not? Do we need to eliminate the significant tasks or reduce their number? Was the significant task too difficult?

The Balanced Curriculum process provides districts with both the structure and the data to begin to answer these questions in a systematic manner. Without the Balanced Curriculum, districts are left guessing and might resort to the following strategy. One district decided that the answer to poor test scores was making sure students had lots of practice on the format of the standardized test. This is backed up by research indicating that students who have practice in the formats of standardized tests generally do better than students who do not. This is only part of the equation, however, and the least important part. If format practice is all districts and schools do, their outcomes are not likely to improve significantly. Improved outcomes require more than just practicing on the format of the test.

With the Balanced Curriculum, the district would have addressed all the major factors in improving outcomes. It would have identified significant tasks that are aligned and balanced for the course. Content assessments developed from the significant tasks indicate whether students have been taught the tasks by how well the students do on the assessments. Format assessment ensures that students have spaced practice on the formats of the state and standardized tests. As a result of this structure, outcomes should improve. The following schematic summarizes why the design works:

Significant Task

Alignment + Balance + Content Assessment + Format Assessment =
Improved Outcomes

MANAGE THE CURRICULUM

Managing curriculum innovation can be informed by the research about curriculum implementation (Snyder, Bolin, & Zumwalt, 1992). The chapters on managing implementation examine this research in more depth. For now, I highlight one finding about managing implementation: "We found that with clear, direct leadership from building and central office administrators, training by a credible person in the use of practice that was known to be effective, and continued support and assistance, teachers tried the new practice, mastered it, saw results with their students and developed a strong sense of ownership" (Crandall, 1983, p. 7). Leadership, staff development, and ongoing support appeared to be three essential ingredients of getting an innovation off the ground. Following is a range of tasks for school and district leaders to assist them in managing the curriculum.

Leadership: Process Leadership

The Balanced Curriculum process is directed through a planning team consisting of representative teachers, principals, central office administrators, and parent team leaders. The planning team meets to develop a long-range plan for curriculum development and implementation and to develop a purpose statement that summarizes the goals of the Balanced Curriculum process. They meet at least quarterly to review problems and progress, modify existing plans, and report back to their constituent groups. In this way, all stakeholders are represented and have input into the process. An existing curriculum council might be used as a leadership team.

Research suggests that "Life and death of an innovation depends on the unique configuration of social, historical, political and ideological factors that make up the school and its social, community context" (Snyder et al., 1992, p. 416). The school and district culture often present problems for program implementation. To address this, the team's second function is to reflect on the culture of the school and district and anticipate ways to use that culture to enhance curriculum implementation.

Leadership: Building-Based Leadership

The planning team needs to keep building leadership (building principals, staff developers, lead teachers) informed before the construction and implementation of curriculum. Principals are important because their support of the Balanced Curriculum will determine the quality of implementation (Huberman, 1983; Huberman & Miles, 1984; Squires & Bullock, 1999). Principals need to be convinced about the rationale for the Balanced Curriculum and their role in helping to implement the curriculum.

Ongoing Support: Building-Based Staff Development

A staff development plan for building and utilizing a team ensures that responsibility spreads to the leadership of the school while building the necessary resources to help teachers learn the curriculum and support their continued implementation.

Many building-based staff development plans include groups of teachers by grade level or course who examine the curriculum and determine the significant tasks that can be easily implemented and those they might require assistance.

Ongoing Support: Districtwide Staff Development

The planning team, and district leadership in general, will need to determine how the curriculum might influence its role and how to use that role to increase implementation of the curriculum. For example, a central office leader in charge of funded projects devised ways to use Title I dollars to support curriculum implementation. A bilingual director helped specify the staff development that clarified the role of the bilingual teachers and regular teachers in meeting the needs of bilingual students within the Balanced Curriculum.

Ongoing Support: District Leadership

District leaders also may want to determine which significant tasks need to be supported by districtwide staff development. For example, after developing a mathematics curriculum, teachers needed specific assistance in using Cuisenaire rods, which were required in significant tasks at a number of grade levels. District staff created after-school staff development "courses" on Cuisenaire rods and their use in the mathematics curriculum.

Ongoing Support: School Leadership

Principals and school leadership teams can also design staff development opportunities for their school or for individual grade levels or courses within the schools. One school leadership team proposed a school retreat focused around cooperative learning because many cooperative learning significant tasks were included in the curriculum. One district saw the need to redefine roles of school staff developers so they were more focused on instructional support. The district provided monthly staff development opportunities that assisted the staff developers in adopting this new role.

Introduction of the Curriculum

The planning team will need to develop strategies for introducing and implementing the curriculum. Generally, a list of different roles or audiences needing information about the Balanced Curriculum is generated. Then the planning team examines existing opportunities to strengthen implementation, such as principals' meetings with central office staff or cross-district grade level or course meetings.

Logging Completions on the Web Site

The planning team also develops strategies for introducing administration, faculty, staff, and parents to the Balanced Curriculum Web site. Faculty can log completed units on the Web site, principals can receive reports on the progress of their school in implementing the curriculum, and district administrators can see progress across schools. In this way, records are kept for all students and their teachers, who have equal access to a high-quality curriculum, making the principals' management of the curriculum evident.

Figure 7.13 is a summary report of one teacher's completion of the science curriculum's significant tasks. The teacher has completed all of the significant tasks in the first three units of the course: Earth, Seasons and Weather, and Matter. If the report were completed at the beginning of February, the teacher would not have completed the unit on Energy and so might have been behind. This report can be replicated using multiple teachers in multiple courses in multiple schools.

Figure 7.13   Teacher completion report summary

School/Course/Teacher
Significant Task Completion Summary
Carson Valley

Test District
2003–2004

Significant Tasks in Units Ending Through 06/30/2004

Grade 1 Science		Completed	
Cafarella, John		**33%**	**7 of 21**
Earth	12/22/2003	100%	2 of 2
Seasons and Weather	6/22/2004	100%	3 of 3
Matter	2/4/2004	100%	2 of 2
Energy	2/4/2004	0%	0 of 3
Balance and Motion	3/16/2004	0%	0 of 3
Living and Nonliving	3/29/2004	0%	0 of 2
Ecology	5/4/2004	0%	0 of 2
Plants and Animals	6/1/2004	0%	0 of 2
Good Health, Healthy Habits and Safety	6/22/2004	0%	0 of 2
Total For Grade 1 Science		**33%**	**7 of 21**

The report in Figure 7.14 is a detailed version of the same report, only the report lists the significant task titles and when they were logged on the Web site as being complete. This report also can be replicated for multiple teachers teaching multiple courses at multiple schools.

In conclusion, managing curriculum involves teams reflecting on district and school culture and the nature of the curriculum, and then figuring out ways to assist the district and school manage the inevitable problems and difficulties that arise.

Figure 7.14   Teacher completion report with details

School/Course/Teacher
Significant Task Completion Detail
Carson Valley

Test District
2003–2004

Significant Tasks in Units Ending Through 06/30/2004

Grade 1 Science		*Completed*
Cafarella, John		**33%, 7 of 21**
Earth	*12/22/2003*	*100%, 2 of 2*
As the World Turns		4/21/2001
Earth on a Plate		3/14/2001
Seasons and Weather	*6/22/2004*	*100%, 3 of 3*
Environmental Investigations		3/14/2001
Monthly Weather Graph		3/14/2001
Sequencing Seasons		3/20/2001
Matter	*2/4/2004*	*100%, 2 of 2*
Liquid, Solid, Gas		3/18/2001
States of Matter		1/3/2001
Energy	*2/4/2004*	*0%, 0 of 3*
I'm Melting		
Sun Pictures		
I'm Shocked		
Balance and Motion	*3/16/2004*	*0%, 0 of 3*
Balance		
Spinners		
Rollers		
Living and Non-Living	*3/29/2004*	*0%, 0 of 2*
Living and Non-living		
Things		
Scavenger Hunt		
Ecology	*5/4/2004*	*0%, 0 of 2*
How Does Your Garbage Grow?		
Then and Now		
Plants and Animals	*6/1/2004*	*0%, 0 of 2*
At Home On Earth		
Food Chain		

Revising the Balanced Curriculum

Curriculum is the school district's best bet about how to improve student outcomes. Once a year, the district needs to examine the data and see what improvements should be made. We suggest making changes to 10% to 20% of the significant tasks within the curriculum. If a course has 35 significant tasks, then we would suggest a target of changing 3 to 8 of the 35 significant tasks. As with all guidelines, some courses might require more and some less.

What data does a district look at when examining the curriculum, grade level by grade level and course by course?

Comments

Using the Web site, teachers can log in comments for each unit and each significant task. Figure 7.15 is a sample from Web site with comments about a significant task.

Figure 7.15 Significant task comments

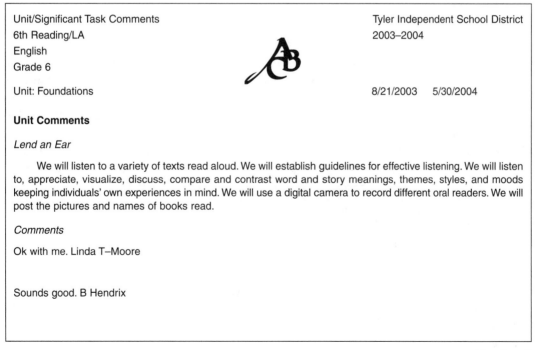

(Continued)

Figure 7.15 (Continued)

A good variety. Karen Parrish

I like the digital camera, posting the pictures, etc. Mary New

This does sound lika good exercise. MC

Sounds good to me. GPaschall

This sounds good but I didn't know digital cameras could record sound. I think if you don't have access to a digital camera, a polaroid camera or reg. camera would be okay too. JBrown making their own visuals will help them remember too. Butler, Tucker, Hooker

I'm not real sure why it would be important to take pictures of oral readers. I think the digital camera use is great but maybe to photograph different student products and then produce a power point presentation. E. Raid Hubbard

This sounds good. I like the idea of using the digital camera. Keeping students' individual experiences gives each student the opportunity to participate in the activities. T. Wallace–Dogan

Keeping in mind an individual's own experiences would allow each student to participate is a great idea. T. Lyons - Dogan

SOURCE: Copyright © Tyler Independent School District (ISD). Developed by Tyler ISD Staff. Reprinted with permission.

Comments can be used for revisions. The curriculum authors will need to make decisions about how much weight to give the comments and which comments should receive attention. For example, in the first year of the process, many comments are usually registered about the significant tasks taking longer than the 60% of time allotted in the Balanced Curriculum design. The authors know that during the second year of the curriculum implementation, these comments are less frequent because teachers have become more proficient at teaching the significant tasks and adjusting the significant tasks to their students. But the authors also know that some significant tasks did take longer than envisioned. The authors will balance their decision making between competing demands.

Test Data

State and standardized testing also provides valuable information. Usually the tests have an item analysis that accompanies the test results. The item analysis (Figure 7.16) links the results to the curriculum because the curriculum has been aligned and balanced according to categories in the test's item analysis.

Figure 7.16 Item analysis. Significant task alignment report for one significant task, with alignments to the state test

---

English
Full Text Grade 4   2003–2004
Unit: Reflection–Unit 1   9/2/2003   10/16/2004

Comprehension

Students will read and discuss a variety of literary genre taken from unit text and/or supplemental materials. Through guided reading and use of graphic organizers, they will read literally, inferentially, and critically. Through oral discussion, use of charts, and some practice/reteach/challenge workbook pages, students will recall details, make inferences, identify and explain conventions of print/figurative language, use context clues, identify central idea and supporting details, and write a personal response to a critical thinking question. Students will proofread for final corrections and edit for appropriate syntax, spelling, grammar, and usage.

Standard	Code	Description
NJ Language Arts Literacy ESPAK-4	WA4	Analyzing/Critiquing Text: forming of opinions.
	WK6	Knowledge: audiences and purposes for writing.
	WK7	Knowledge: that critical reflection and analysis contribute to the writing experience.
	WS2	Skills: engage in the full process of writing.
	RK5	Knowledge: that authors and readers have purposes.

SOURCE: Copyright © Englewood Cliffs Public Schools, Englewood Cliffs, New Jersey. Reprinted with permission.

If test results indicate that many students had difficulty producing a written document that explains how to do something, then the authors will review the significant tasks alignments to see how many significant tasks align to explanatory essays. The authors must then decide how to answer the following questions:

- Were enough significant tasks addressing this category?
- Were the alignments justified? Were the links between the significant tasks and the tests strong?
- Do we need more significant tasks to address this category?
- Are students receiving the appropriate prerequisite skills in previous grade levels? Do changes need to be made in other courses leading up to this course?
- Is there enough practice so that students can demonstrate mastery in the course?
- Is the sequence of the significant tasks addressing this category strong, requiring students to build their abilities in sequences that make sense?

Answers to such questions require the good judgment of the curriculum authors. Although the data are there, the answers to such questions will depend on the talent of the authors.

Completion Information

For the aligned tasks, did teachers complete the tasks with their students? This question asks whether students had access to this segment of the curriculum. Research suggests that if students do not cover particular content, then they are not apt to learn it. Providing coverage is a goal of the Balanced Curriculum. Asking teachers to indicate whether they completed a significant task is a way to gather data about whether students did, indeed, have access to the curriculum's content.

Perhaps the low scores in explanatory essays were due to the fact that many students hadn't completed that significant task in the curriculum. The Web site allows authors to gather the information for their course, determine whether this is a problem, and make suggestions for curriculum revision or staff development.

Data From Format and Content Assessments

Schools may keep samples of student work on significant task assessments that address explanatory essays. These work samples may yield insight into students' difficulty on the test. If available, authors will want to examine the work samples for clues on how to revise the curriculum.

Curriculum Authors' Experience and Opinions

All of the above data give authors a general direction in which to proceed but can be interpreted in many ways. Recruiting the best, most caring, and brightest teachers to do revision is important because their judgments and decisions will effect the design of the curriculum for the next year. The authors' decisions are based on the available data and on their experiences. There are many ways to improve explanatory essays; the authors need to choose the ones that they think will be best for most teachers and students. The authors are the bridge between the past year and the future. They are in charge of using the data to invent a better future. In doing so, the revisers capture the best curriculum for the next year.

Realigning and Rebalancing the Curriculum

After decisions are made about changing significant tasks, based on available data, the authors need to realign the significant tasks that changed and check to ensure that the curriculum is balanced. Authors follow the same process they did when creating the curriculum; however, the process will proceed at a quicker pace because only a portion of the curriculum has changed.

Modifying Assessments and Attachments

For each changed significant task, there needs to be a change in the content assessment to indicate how the modified significant task will be assessed. The new assessments replace the old assessment on the Web site. Districts that show exemplars or anchor papers of students' work for a significant task will need to develop strategies for collecting new exemplars and posting them on the Web site as attachments. Some districts also post sample lesson plans for significant tasks in the attachment column. These, too, will need to be revised.

PROVIDE STAFF DEVELOPMENT FOR THE CURRICULUM

The Balanced Curriculum is a staff development tool that can help districts improve on a number of fronts. The curriculum authors learn firsthand about curriculum scope and sequence, alignment, balance, and assessing the curriculum. The process challenges the best and the brightest.

Implementing the curriculum is also a staff development activity. Principals and teachers may need to learn about new aspects of their jobs. Principals learn about monitoring the curriculum implementation and structuring staff development activities that will assist the school's teachers in their curriculum implementation. Teachers may be challenged by some of the significant tasks, providing an opportunity to master different instructional processes. District personnel need to assess where support will be needed to ensure implementation. Support may come in the form of in-service on instructional techniques, providing role-playing opportunities for principals assisting reluctant staff to implement more fully, or developing accountability structures for principals and their monitoring of the curriculum implementation.

Analysis of test results so that they are translated into curriculum changes will continue to challenge the curriculum authors as they revise. Principals and school teams can use test results to determine areas of instruction in the curriculum where they fell below the district average. School improvement plans can then be written with these areas of staff development in mind.

Grade- or course-level meetings provide another staff development venue. Teachers of the same course meet together to share plans about approaching the significant tasks of the next unit, reflect on student work from the previous unit, make comments about the significant tasks as a group on the Web site, and read the comments of others. New teachers will be more swiftly incorporated into a culture that values teaching if they participate in such meetings.

Staff development flows from the content, scope, and sequence of the curriculum. The curriculum is the skeleton; staff development is the musculature that make the curriculum work.

SUMMARY

This chapter has described the framework for the Balanced Curriculum process and showed how it uses textbooks, standards, and standardized tests to align curriculum with instruction and assessment. The next chapters are devoted to a more in-depth look at the process of writing and producing the curriculum using staff from the district's schools.

8

Setting Up
the Curriculum
Writing Process

T his chapter discusses the role of the planning team, the point person, the superintendent, recruitment of curriculum authors, the role of principals, and different models for the curriculum writing process.

THE PLANNING TEAM, SUPERINTENDENT, AND POINT PERSON

The role of the planning team is to develop plans for writing and implementing the curriculum. The number of people and their roles may change over the course of writing and implementing the curriculum. Initially, the planning team might include a district's curriculum person(s), the central office personnel responsible for special education and bilingual education (because they will be using and perhaps modifying the curriculum to serve special needs students), a technology coordinator (to assist with teachers' and administrators' use of the Balanced Curriculum Web site), a representative teacher and principal (to provide suggestions and input from those perspectives), and the business manager or funded projects representative (to provide input about funding for teachers' pay for curriculum writing). The superintendent is an ex officio member of the committee and may lead the committee until a plan is completed.

The planning team's initial activities include the following:

- Participating in an overview of the Balanced Curriculum process
- Developing a purpose statement to guide the work
- Confirming and developing an understanding of roles and connections among roles within the district, and between the district and consultants
- Deciding on standards and assessments for alignment of the curriculum
- Reviewing district policy for curriculum and the document "A Process for Aligning the Written, Taught, and Tested Curricula" to determine whether the Balanced Curriculum process is a good match for fulfilling district mandates
- Making plans to inform schools about the Balanced Curriculum process
- Learning about the Balanced Curriculum Web site
- Making plans to inform other stakeholders about the process
- Developing a long-range schedule for writing and implementing the curriculum
- Looking to establish common planning periods for grade- or course-level teachers so that the planning periods can be partially used for implementation
- Identifying possible curriculum writing sites and dates
- Establishing a teacher recruitment strategy that will result in the best, brightest, and most caring teachers accepting the role as curriculum authors.

The purpose statement, generally no more than one page in length, sets out the goals and objectives of the process in broad terms.

Newburgh Enlarged City School District Balanced Curriculum Project Purpose Statement

1. To improve student opportunity and achievement:
   Align and balance curriculum, instruction, and assessment for all students at all levels in all subjects, beginning with English Language Arts (K–12). The ELA curriculum will be aligned with NYS Learning Standards and Assessments, and the National Council of Teachers of English/International Reading Association (NCTE/IRA) English Language Arts Standards.

2. The Newburgh Enlarged City School District and the Newburgh Enlarged City School District Board of Education will:
   Adopt, implement, and work for continuous improvement of the process of aligning and balancing the curriculum.

3. The Curriculum Alignment Project will:
   - Build the capacity to improve student opportunity and achievement;
   - Produce documents that
     a. Describe the curriculum (with units and significant tasks)
     b. Indicate alignment and balance of units with the NYS Learning Standards and standardized assessments
     c. Contain the internal unit assessment that are aligned with the units
   - Implement and institutionalize the process and the aligned and balanced curriculum

4. The Curriculum Alignment Project will:
   Partner students, parents, and community members to create an awareness of the Learning Standards and their value, and the importance of an aligned and balanced curriculum.

A "point person" is appointed with the agreement of the superintendent to head the process and keep it on track. The point person:

- Might be the superintendent, deputy or associate superintendent, or the director of curriculum
- Takes district and school concerns to the consultants and consultant concerns to the district planning team or the schools for resolution
- Is in charge of the project's direction, timing, and scope
- Is known by school teams, the planning team, the technology team, and the superintendent and is available to assist with problems as they arise
- Will be able to direct and coordinate the efforts of principals and the various teams
- Will be available to the consultants
- Should review the proposal in depth and for each item, and write down the amount of time the person estimates will be needed to arrange or supervise each task
- Needs to decide if he or she can reasonably expect to satisfactorily accomplish the supervision of this project, given their other duties
- May need to use the planning team to help with the project's tasks
- Will become a lightning rod for the anxieties, concerns, and frustrations of project participants, other teachers, and other administrators whose daily lives are affected by the project

The effectiveness of the curriculum development effort rests on the ability of the point person to organize, coordinate, monitor, and problem solve with the wide range of personnel around the tasks listed in this proposal.

The Balanced Curriculum process produces results only if the balanced and aligned curriculum is actually taught and assessed. There are many bumps down this road. The district needs to decide whether it is willing to weather the storm and move the project to completion with the point person as leader.

THE SUPERINTENDENT

Districts do better in writing and implementing the curriculum if the superintendent has a visible role in bringing the process to the district and marshals support for writing and implementing among the various constituencies, such as the school board, the teacher's union or association, and community groups, to name a few. When the principal is actively involved in both curriculum writing and implementation, the process proceeds more smoothly. Difficulties always arise when a superintendent leaves the district before the process is complete. The superintendent and the point person need to collaborate on a strategy to make sure the project continues if the superintendent leaves. Given that the average tenure of a superintendent is less than 3 years and the Balanced Curriculum process for all subject areas may take 3 to 5 years, having a succession strategy makes sense.

Successful superintendents visibly support the project during curriculum writing and the beginning stages of implementation. As the writing and implementation of successive subjects and grade levels continues, less time is required. The superintendent and the point person will need to develop strategies for institutionalizing the process. This may require rewriting curriculum policies, including curriculum implementation in professional improvement plans of principals and teachers and including curriculum maintenance in the district's staff development plans. Adequately funding curriculum maintenance requires line items in district budgets, with vigorous defense of the curriculum line by the superintendent. (See Chapter 19 for more suggestions by a superintendent on the superintendent's role.)

RECRUITMENT OF CURRICULUM AUTHORS

Warm bodies do not write good curriculum. The best teachers who care deeply about students, who have at least a few years of experience, and who are comfortable expressing themselves in writing, make the best curriculum authors.

The Balanced Curriculum process is different from other processes. The significant tasks will be taught and assessed by all teachers teaching the course. The authors have the responsibility for crafting significant tasks that can be used as the basis for lesson planning for the rest of the staff. Maturity is needed to make decisions that are right for students, not just fulfilling personal agendas. The significant tasks will be used as the basis for future staff development at both the school and district level. Significant tasks that are too difficult will result in teachers giving up teaching the curriculum. Significant tasks that are too easy may reduce the curriculum's credibility. Significant tasks that are challenging—for both teachers and students—are the best.

Curriculum authors need to be respected by their colleagues because their professional credibility will go a long way toward assisting those who are uneasy. Curriculum authors need to be able to stand up to criticism, both in the give-and-take of an author group developing significant tasks and in the warp and woof of implementation. This is not summer work for everyone. This is a mission for the talented, ennobled few. The quality of the curriculum rests on the shoulders of the curriculum authors.

THE ROLE OF PRINCIPALS

Principals know teachers best and are usually in the best position to assist in the recruiting effort. Our research suggests that principals who have the most curriculum authors have the fewest problems with implementation. Curriculum authors, after the curriculum is written, become advocates for the process. They have thought through the implications and often have perceptive ideas about the best way to conduct implementation at a given grade level or for course-level teachers.

Principals can also support the curriculum authors by providing them with recognition and commendations. One principal, during the curriculum writing process, took all the teachers from his school to lunch once a week, partially to check on how the process was going but also to thank the teachers for the hard work they were contributing.

VARIOUS MODELS FOR THE CURRICULUM WRITING PROCESS

Over the period of developing this process, many models for curriculum writing have been tried. The one that works best is concentrated time during the summer (usually during a 2-week period, when the curriculum's units, significant tasks, alignments, and balancing can be completed). The advantages of this are that no substitute teachers are necessary, participants do not worry about what is happening to students in their absence, there is sufficient time to complete a curriculum that can begin implementation in the fall, and there are no stops and starts that require the group to reassemble and revisit topics from a previous meeting.

Other models include hiring substitutes to release teachers to write curriculum. The advantage of this model is that it can be done within the school day and school year, and teachers can be assigned rather than "volunteering" for summer duty. The disadvantages include that teachers are pulled out of classrooms and away from students and instruction, that hiring substitute teachers adds to the expense of the process, and that teachers find their minds are in two places at once.

Some districts use a mix-and-match approach. The planning team organizes all teachers during an in-service day to define unit titles, unit introductions, and pacing guides for the units as a prelude to the curriculum authors working during the summer. This model allows everyone to have input into the curriculum and to experience a little of what its development is all about. The difficulty is that many people are needed to facilitate such a process.

Other districts use a more incremental approach. The authors develop unit titles, unit introductions, and pacing guides and then post these on the curriculum Web site. During district in-service, a school's faculty meetings, or teacher planning time, teachers go on the Web site and comment on whether there is a way to improve this work. Then the curriculum authors meet, retrieve and review the Web site comments, and make adjustments where warranted. For the next increment, authors record some significant tasks on the Web site, and teachers again review the significant task and make comments. The incremental approach allows everyone to comment on the strengths and needs as the curriculum is developed so there is more buy-in when the curriculum is completed.

Mapping the curriculum (Jacobs, 1997) can be used as a precursor to developing consensus on unit titles and pacing guides by asking all staff members to "map" how they proceed through their course. The maps can be used by curriculum authors to suggest unit titles and pacing guides based on the most common way that teachers generally proceed through the curriculum. Significant tasks can be generated from important projects or culminating activities that teachers are already using.

Many districts already have outlined units and established objectives for them. In this case, the Balanced Curriculum process builds on existing curriculum documents, adding the missing pieces. Some districts have developed grade-level "standards" from their state's K–4, 5–8, or 9–12 standard documents. These can also be used as part of the Balanced Curriculum process.

Two patterns emerge from planning with districts. First, the district determines how and when curriculum writing occurs, based on what makes sense from a district's history, its culture, and its personnel. Second, the Balanced Curriculum process seeks to move as quickly and expeditiously as possible by using as much of what already exists as possible, so that the wheel does not need to be reinvented.

SUMMARY

This chapter has been devoted to setting up the curriculum writing process with an eye toward implementation. A writing process that doesn't consider implementation is doomed to failure. The goal of any curriculum is to be implemented in the schools and classrooms of a district, and curriculum writing is the beginning of curriculum implementation.

9

Defining the
Components of
a Good Program

Whom teacher-authors meet to develop curriculum, one of the first activities they consider is defining components of a good program in their particular subject area. This assists them in the process of bringing their own standards to surface and serves as a basis for establishing coverage priorities during curriculum writing. This chapter describes how Jamil, a secondary English teacher, and Constance, a primary school science teacher, use the Balanced Curriculum process to help consolidate and define components of a good program in their subject areas. This process helps surface teachers own "internal standards." Using the two teachers as examples, the chapter shows how a teacher's beliefs influence curriculum design.

JAMIL

Jamil, an energetic teacher, well liked by his students, is now in his 4th year teaching and part of the curriculum design team for 9th-grade reading and language arts. After the overview of the Balanced Curriculum process, the presenter asked each team to divide into pairs and describe the components of a good reading and language arts program.

No one had ever asked this before. In college Jamil had studied American, British, and African-American literature; wrote the requisite number of essays; dabbled in Japanese literature in translation; and wrote the required senior paper. After an introductory speech class, he became interested in acting and tried out for a small part in one of the many college productions, an experience that gave him a taste for directing, scenery design, and the complex process of putting on a play. A short stint writing a column in the college paper taught him the power of the press because he received a great deal of feedback on a controversial article. Of course, he took the teaching methods course in English, but the course had focused on various techniques, many that he had used since becoming a teacher. Stating the components of a good reading and language arts program, however, was not something he had ever taken time to do.

The presenter asked the authors to spend a few minutes thinking about the question, "What are the components of a good English and language arts program?" Jamil figured he was a smart guy and started jotting down a few ideas.

Reading. What do I want my students to do when reading? Understand what they are reading, whatever that may be. So that would include fiction and nonfiction, plays and poetry, screenplays, newspapers, textbooks, and trade books. In fiction (I concentrate about 80% of my class time on fiction), I'd like them to be able to get "inside" the characters and anticipate what they would do while understanding their motivations.

Writing. My students write almost every day and turn in something to me at least once a week. We concentrate on using the writing process, focusing on different areas for each assignment. Good writing is good thinking. Good writing promotes good thinking; that involves logic and reasoning. [It occurred to me that most of my student-assigned writing was "nonfiction," in contrast to what the kids read—mostly fiction. An odd paradox that I let pass for the moment.] Editing, grammar, and usage, three inescapable areas, were a focus of many editing groups.

Speaking and Listening. Of course, there are classroom discussions about character's motivations, the correctness of their actions, and heated arguments among the kids when they finally let down their guard. I try to jam a speech or two a year into the crowded schedule. The text has a few excerpts from plays, and sometimes the kids form teams to act them out in class—a taste of what I had done in college.

Television and the Internet have some impact on Jamil's English class. Research papers, advertising, and accessing information on the World Wide Web are all skills that students use at one time or another for his class.

Jamil looked at the list and realized that he taught using reading to reinforce writing through exercises that involved speaking and listening. The categories overlapped.

"Another few minutes," the presenter said.

What about the state tests that students would be required to pass in 10th grade? Over the past few years, as the importance of state testing for 10th graders increased, he learned more about the content of the test. Now, a few times a year, Jamil's students practiced writing a persuasive essay from a prompt. Of course, that was only one of many writing assignments that covered descriptive and expository writing. The testing program changed Jamil's view of the importance of persuasive writing.

Jamil felt a welter of confusion because his neat list didn't look tidy anymore. Things started to creep from category to category. Aren't speaking and writing similar processes because both involve the production of language? Should they be together? Aren't television shows another venue for drama? Given that most of his students watched 2 to 3 hours of TV a night, shouldn't he be spending more time on that medium? What should be cut? Perhaps it's not possible to do it all—if only it was clear what was most important.

CONSTANCE

Constance, a 2nd-grade teacher in a self-contained classroom, loves her children and wants school to be a nurturing place where they can grow and develop. She became involved as a science curriculum author for the Balanced Curriculum process after 10 years of teaching; for her, this was a way to find out more about science and offer what she could in the way of ideas.

Recently, science had received little attention in her district because everyone was concentrating on reading and math for the state tests. At one point, Constance's principal said he didn't care whether teachers got around to science because it was more important to bring up reading and math scores. So Constance completed only the science activities she enjoyed doing and didn't attempt to cover all the assignments in the science book. Constance figured science was important enough to teach, despite what the principal said. In the fall, students collected leaves and made a book out of their pressed leaf collection. They went to the pumpkin farm and watched and talked about the animals. Dinosaurs took time in the winter. In the spring, children grew bean seedlings under different conditions. Near summer, they went on a walking tour to a park nearby and talked about how plants grew.

Constance said, "I think children need to be introduced to science in a way that makes it fun and engaging. So I don't use a science book but work with kids around hands-on activities. I remember about my 4th year teaching, I went to a 1-week, intensive, hands-on science workshop. Many of the activities that I do in my classroom came from ideas they gave us in the workshop.

"When the presenter at the Balanced Curriculum workshop asked, 'What are the components of a good science program?', I was brought up short; I never really had thought about it. Kids should enjoy science. It shouldn't be boring or difficult. Science should be activity based with lots of opportunities for hands-on experiences. I use science as a way to help kids go more in-depth with their abilities to describe and to see similarities and differences. For example, when we collect and press leaves, we have to organize their leaf book in some way. I ask them, 'Which of the leaves goes together?' Some sort by shape, others by color, still others with some combination scheme.

"A good science program deals with nature. We do activities around leaves, visit the farm and collect pumpkins, study dinosaurs (the kids' favorite), grow beans in the spring, and conduct nature walks. This pulls us out of the classroom and into the real world.

"I did have a science and mathematics methods course way back in the dark ages when I was in college, but I don't really remember much except things need to be hands-on for both math and science. Being an elementary education major, I was only required to take one science and one math course in college.

"The sharing we've done so far in the Balanced Curriculum workshop has helped me realize that there are many other things I could do in science class that might actually help my students in math and reading."

COMMENTARY

The Balanced Curriculum process begins by surfacing teachers' understandings of the components of a good subject-area course. Jamil and Constance shared their understandings of what was most important to them. These ideas can be built on, challenged, and enriched as Jamil and Constance discuss their ideas with their author teams and review national professional standards, state standards, and test specifications. Obviously, Constance has a rudimentary understanding of important science concepts, whereas Jamil evidences more sophistication.

The teacher-authors control the curriculum development process from the beginning. Their internal standards guide selection of units and significant tasks. Yes, the state "imposes" standards and tests, and there is little to be done about the state's role. The teacher-authors, however, use their experience and expertise to determine how those standards will be addressed in the units and significant tasks. Teachers base their curriculum decisions partially on their own internal standards and what their experience and training suggests. Jamil and Constance are at very different points in their understanding. Constance has little knowledge or understanding of science and the major ideas underpinning the discipline of science. Jamil, on the other hand, has a much more sophisticated understanding of English and language arts. Understanding what individual authors value in a particular subject area and then finding a consensus among the course authors is valued in the Balanced Curriculum process. Curriculum writing teams use this information as an important basis to ensure that the significant tasks are aligned to their personal standards. For curriculum to have power, it must harness the beliefs of the teachers who create it.

We are not the victims of the state, the standards, or the test. We have control. We will exert control in the service of our students learning in developmentally appropriate ways through defining a curriculum. The curriculum will encompass our own personal standards.

The next section examines the idea of the teacher's personal standards and the influence those standards might have on the curriculum development process. The issues to be examined are as follows:

- Teachers hold personal standards both tacitly (internally and unconscious) and explicitly (conscious and able to be expressed verbally).
- Teachers act on both their tacit and explicit standards in choosing what and how to teach. Both tacit and explicit standards influence what will be taught and how it will be taught.
- Making tacit standards and beliefs explicit is part of the staff development process of curriculum development.
- Personal standards can come more into alignment with professional and state standards once personal standards are known and discussed.

Teachers Hold Personal Standards Both Tacitly (Internally and Unconscious) and Explicitly (Conscious and Able to Be Expressed Verbally)

The curriculum development process requires that teachers' tacit (internal and unexpressed) standards be made explicit (held consciously and expressed verbally). Both Jamil and Constance have explicit standards. For example, Jamil groups his ideas into categories of reading, writing, and speaking and listening. Constance's ideas haven't developed that far, but she states that science should be "hands-on" and "activity based." Both teachers have expressed standards (beliefs) that they hold about their subject matter. These beliefs influence the curriculum.

Jamil also implies some tacit standards in his description. For example, "It occurred to me that most of my student-assigned writing was 'nonfiction' in contrast to what the kids read—mostly fiction." Jamil realized a contradiction in his own practice that is just beginning to surface on a conscious level. Implied in the contradiction is Jamil's emerging (from tacit to explicit) notion that fiction might be better understood if students wrote fiction instead of nonfiction because then they would learn more about fiction through "writing fiction."

When Constance states, "I use science as a way to help kids go more in-depth with their abilities to describe and to see similarities and differences," her tacit belief may be that science as a process encompasses a unique way of understanding the world that uses "rules" different from those of other subject areas. She is not able to state her standards about the scientific process, but it is tacitly covered in her statement.

Teachers Act on Both Their Tacit and Explicit Standards in Choosing What and How to Teach. Their Standards, Both Tacit and Explicit, Influence What Will Be Taught and How It Will Be Taught

Jamil believes that writing is linked with students' thinking and their use of logic and reasoning. Jamil states, "Good writing promotes good thinking; that involves logic and reasoning." If Jamil believes this, we would expect his writing lessons also to involve instruction about logic and reasoning. Making the case, the structure of arguments, and what constitutes good evidence are all topics that one would expect to be taught as part of Jamil's understanding of the writing process.

Constance's belief in hands-on science is confirmed in her description of her science activities for the year: leaf collections, a visit to a pumpkin farm, studying dinosaurs, growing bean seedlings, and taking nature walks. Her standards, although not encompassing many standards from state or national lists, still influence the content and process she uses in teaching science.

The personal standards that Jamil and Constance use emerge from the unexamined part of their professional repertoire as they verbally seek reasons and rationale for why this content or that significant task needs to be learned by most students. Curriculum development will assist Jamil and Constance in understanding their subject areas in more depth.

Making Tacit Personal Standards and Beliefs Explicit Is Part of the Staff Development Process of Curriculum Development

Jamil, when examining the components of a good reading and language arts program, started to uncover a discrepancy in his practice. A formerly tacit standard became explicit. "It occurred to me that most of my student-assigned writing was 'nonfiction' in contrast to what the kids read—mostly fiction." Because Jamil defined the components of a good reading and language arts program, he started to make some of his tacit ideas explicit.

As Jamil shares these ideas with others, he will also uncover more tacit standards and begin to test them with the others in his author group. Although he has found an emerging belief in teaching fiction through writing fiction, he will also need to convince other team members. In posing the rationale for teaching fiction through the writing of fiction, he tests his (now explicit) ideas against others. These conversations are an important part of the curriculum development process because the teachers must test their ideas (their standards) against those of other team members.

Constance, in dialogue with other authors on her grade level, will learn more about scientific structures and processes. Through conversation about what is most important, her ideas about science should help children to develop "their abilities to describe and to see similarities and differences." This may expand to include ideas about science as inquiry: asking questions, planning and conducting investigations, and using data to construct a reasonable explanation (National Science Education Standards, 1996, p. 122). In this way, her tacit beliefs are expanded and elaborated, becoming conscious so that they can be used to develop the curriculum's significant tasks.

Personal Standards Can Come More Into Alignment With Professional and State Standards Once Personal Standards Are Known and Discussed

Jamil's author group will share their standards with each other and reach for consensus among the authors, where possible. This assists the group in surfacing problems of approach before they start writing significant tasks. Constance uses others' ideas to refine her notion of what is most important to teach in science.

In surfacing the standards of the author group, they are also preparing for their exploration of state and national professional standards. Author groups generally find that the standards they hold are similar to those of the state or national professional organization. By first uncovering personal standards, discussions take place that confirm the professional expertise of the authors and set the stage for state standards.

Constance, in moving from thinking about science as a tool for helping students with description and noting similarities and differences, adopts ideas about "scientific inquiry" from the national standards. When Constance designs her significant tasks, she will not simply focus on noting similarities and differences but also will use the full range of inquiry skills suggested by the national standards: asking questions, planning and conducting investigations, and using data to construct a reasonable explanation.

Jamil, when examining his state standards, finds that he has not included a major category for language arts—viewing—as one of five domains: reading, writing, speaking, listening, and viewing. Although Jamil understands the importance of viewing (he knows his students watch 2 to 3 hours of television daily), raising it to the level of reading and writing may not have occurred to him. If viewing is one of five domains, then shouldn't one fifth of the significant tasks include viewing activities? Or are some of the domains more important than others? Jamil and others in his author group will wrestle with such questions as a way to shape the group's understanding of what is most important to teach.

SUMMARY

Curriculum development happens when a group of teachers share what they think is most important about the subject area as a way to help make tacit knowledge explicit, and explicit knowledge shared. Control is vested in the author group who has examined and shared their personal standards to further their understanding of what is most important for students to know and be able to do. Understanding personal standards provides the foundation for working through and understanding state and national standards. The Balanced Curriculum process helps to uncover hidden beliefs and provides a basis of comparison with state and national standards so author groups can make informed decisions about what is most important for teachers to teach and students to learn.

10

Reviewing Standards, Sequencing Courses, Describing Units, and Delineating Unit Timelines

The previous chapter contained a discussion of teacher's tacit and explicit standards and the importance of developing curriculum with teacher's own standards in mind. This chapter addresses putting together the skeleton of the curriculum by reviewing state and national standards, sequencing courses (how to order content across courses), checking on consistency of schedules across schools to ensure all students have comparable time to learn the curriculum, and sequencing units within courses.

REVIEWING STANDARDS

Curriculum authors review the state and national standards that apply to their subject areas, revisiting and revising their personal and corporate definitions of the components of a good program for a particular subject area. The Balanced Curriculum process uses both state and national standards to demonstrate to curriculum authors that each standard "set" has a particular point of view and that these viewpoints may differ. By including multiple standard sets, the process of developing the curriculum will include diverse (and sometimes conflicting) points of view. The curriculum authors can use this diversity to help clarify their decisions about what is most important to know and be able to do. State and national standards tend to be lengthy and involved, so the following shortcuts help curriculum authors examine the standards comprehensively, yet quickly. (For a discussion of standards, please review Chapter 3.)

• Curriculum authors examine the standards, marking each with a green, yellow, or red magic marker. Green indicates standards that are emphasized in instruction by the curriculum authors. Yellow indicates that the authors are unsure whether the standards are emphasized. Red indicates standards that are not addressed in instruction. The author group then discusses and writes down implications for designing units and significant tasks.

• Curriculum authors compare the outline they generated in deciding the components of a good program to the general outline provided by the standards, noting similarities and differences. From the similarities and differences, the curriculum authors discuss the implications for emphasis in designing their units or significant tasks.

• Curriculum authors choose a standard (or standard group) that they believe should be emphasized or choose a standard (or a standard group) that they know is not emphasized. The author group then brainstorms tentative significant tasks that would address these areas. This activity assists the authors in seeing how the standards can be translated into significant tasks that shape the curriculum.

• Curriculum authors compare the state standards to the national standards and examine the similarities and differences. For reading and language arts, they would compare the International Reading Association/National Council of Teachers of English (IRA/NCTE) standards to state standards. The national standards in this case are 12 statements that should encompass the K–12 curriculum. State standards are always more specific than the IRA/NCTE standards. Which standard set provides the best guidance when thinking about courses, units, and significant tasks? Many subjects encompass the subject of social studies. Should the National Social Studies standards be used, or should the authors employ specific standards related to geography, economics, and history?

• Curriculum authors rank the general headings of the state and national standards according to which ones they think are most important for students to know and use. After ranking the standards, curriculum authors discuss the implications for designing courses, units, and significant tasks. Curriculum authors may want to come to a consensus about the percentage of coverage each major category deserves.

• Curriculum authors examine state and national resource material and Web sites and bring back to the author group examples of significant tasks that address the standards in ways that are appropriate for students at that grade or course level. This helps authors to understand that many wonderful "significant tasks" have already been developed and the authors will not have to construct all the significant tasks from scratch. Authors may also want to examine how these suggested "significant tasks" address or align to multiple standards at the state and national level.

Once curriculum authors are familiar with national and state standards, they are ready to consider sequencing courses, developing units, and delineating timelines.

SEQUENCING COURSES

Determining courses and course sequences is the first step in the Balanced Curriculum process. Courses structure time and content in a curriculum. Courses usually begin and end on certain dates. Courses usually contain a certain amount of classes or class time and out-of-class time.

Course-taking sequences affect students' future in education. Students in elementary school generally take a prescribed list of courses, such as reading, mathematics, science, and social studies. As students move from middle school to high school, they have more choice and more requirements for the courses taken. Course-taking sequences—Mathematics 9 in 9th grade, algebra in 10th grade, geometry in 11th grade, no math in 12th grade—often determine eligibility for further education. Following this course sequence, the student may not be accepted to a college major of science or mathematics or may need to take additional math courses in college, without credit, to pursue math and science because more math courses are usually required for college entrance in a math or science major.

Preparing for curriculum development means determining the sequence of courses and the courses' prerequisites. For example, in a high school district, students taking algebra in 8th grade *and* passing an entrance exam were permitted to continue with Geometry Honors in 9th grade. Only those taking Geometry Honors in 9th grade would be eligible for Algebra II Honors in 10th grade. Only those taking Algebra II Honors in 10th grade were eligible for Trigonometry Honors in 11th. Only those taking Trigonometry Honors in 11th grade were eligible for calculus in 12th. So, by either not taking algebra in 8th grade or failing the entrance exam, students would not be eligible to take calculus in 12th grade. Some competitive colleges look favorably on those who have taken and passed calculus; not taking this sequence of courses effectively excluded students from calculus and from those colleges.

A way to summarize course-taking sequences is with bar and whisker charts (Figure 10.1). The bars consist of the courses in a sequence; the whiskers are the options students have in moving from one course to another.

Figure 10.1   Charting course-taking sequences: bar and whisker charts

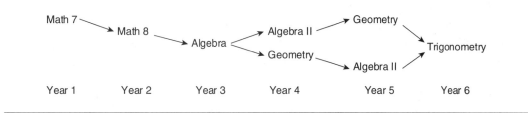

Figure 10.1 shows Math 7 as a prerequisite for Math 8 and the course sequence if followed through to trigonometry, which would take 6 years.

When designing a sequence, assumptions about prerequisites need to be examined. "We've always done it that way" is not good enough. A small committee of middle and high school math teachers may want to get together and review the course-taking sequences in math. For example, one assumption is that Math 7 is a prerequisite to Math 8. If that assumption isn't justified, then the following course-taking sequence may need to be changed. Perhaps students could go from Math 7 directly to algebra. In that way, more students could complete calculus after trigonometry. This in turn may lead to a discussion about the necessary prerequisite skills and abilities needed for success in algebra. The committee may want to take a look at the data they have about students who did well in 1st-year algebra versus those who did not. What are the similarities and differences? What do the data suggest we need to do to strengthen the math program before students start taking algebra?

Try the following exercise as a way to see if the sequence on a particular topic is appropriate.

1. Obtain two math textbooks at contiguous grade levels.

2. Choose a mathematics topic that is likely to be covered by both texts (division in 4th and 5th grade) or pick a standard from the state standard list.

3. Look in the table of contents or the index for the topics related to the standard.

4. Review each of the topics and make note of sample problems presented in the text.

5. Compare the sample problems from the two grade levels. Determine the amount of overlap.

One way to look at assumptions is through an examination of textbooks at contiguous grade levels or courses. Examining the table of contents to the 7th- and 8th-grade math series and comparing content covered is one way to determine whether the content is different. What content is repeated from the previous year? What content is new? Another way to compare course content is by examining the unit tests and comparing the content and the difficulty of the items. The Third International Mathematics and Science Study (Schmidt et al., 1997a) shows that in the United States, content presented in 8th grade is often a repeat of 7th-grade mathematics. In fact, the content at many grade levels is often repeated at successive grade levels, partly because texts must be aligned to many states' standards, forcing coverage of many topics during a year. This means that students have no in-depth instruction because they must "cover" many different topics during the year (see Chapter 5 for more information on characteristics of textbooks in various subject areas).

If the curriculum team decides that repetition exists, then could the assumptions be changed? Could students passing Grade 7 math move into algebra? This brings more conversations about what are the prerequisite skills for algebra and are they addressed satisfactorily in Grade 7 math? If not, could the course content be changed represented by the bar and whisker chart in Figure 10.2?

By reviewing course assumptions, the curriculum team can eliminate, consolidate, or change course sequences or content. At an elementary school level, think about what would happen if most of the students came to a grade level with mastery of mathematics facts? Would the mathematics course take as long to teach?

Figure 10.2 Bar and whisker charts: Math 7 as a prerequisite to algebra instead of Math 8

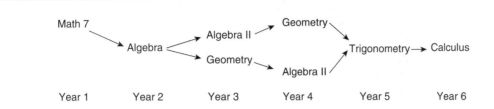

What topics deserve more time to cover? What additional topics could be covered in the time given? Courses remain powerful tools for deciding how time is spent on instruction.

The sequence of courses in one subject area affects the course-taking sequences in other areas. If Algebra I is a prerequisite course for taking chemistry and if trigonometry was a prerequisites for physics, and if Algebra I is offered in 8th grade, then 9th graders could be eligible to take chemistry, and 12th graders could take physics using their trigonometry skills to solve vector problems. See Figure 10.3 for a bar and whisker graph for this course-taking path. This scenario assumes that physics is taught using trigonometry and chemistry is taught using algebra. Year 5, or junior year, might then be the time for students taking many science courses to take the Chemistry II or Advanced Placement Biology if Biology I was given in Year 2, or 8th grade. Continuing the assumption testing, is geometry really a prerequisite for trigonometry? If not, trigonometry could also be offered in Year 4, allowing physics to be offered in Years 5 and 6.

Course structures, course-taking sequences, and prerequisites are equity issues. In most course structures, there is bias built in because assumptions have not been adequately examined. The design of the course structures will affect who remains in school and who drops out. The test of an improving school system is to examine course-taking patterns, particularly in the high school, and determine whether more students are taking more courses at a more difficult level than the year before. Educational leaders know that if the patterns are similar from year to year, inequity is present. Course sequences should expand educational opportunity, not delimit it.

Educational leaders can set goals, such as "we would like to increase the number of students taking 3 or more years of mathematics by 10% in 3 years." If there are

Figure 10.3 Bar and whisker graph for both math and science

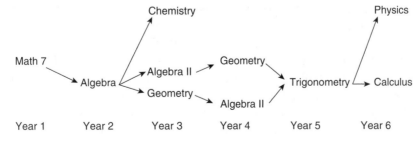

250 students in a graduating class, to reach the goal will require another period of mathematics in 3 years; this raises questions of how the staff will be sure that enough students are able to qualify for higher levels of study and how teachers and administrators can help students see the advantage of further study in mathematics. Do we need to change prerequisites and requirements for existing courses? Do we need to assign better teachers to courses to improve the outcomes? Do we need to provide staff development around topics in beginning courses with which students have difficulty? All of these questions can be answered in ways that encourage a school to meet a challenging goal.

Districts have the responsibility to ensure that students have appropriate, similar, and adequate amounts of time to spend on each subject area. Usually in middle and high schools this isn't a problem because student requirements are the same, and the same amount of time is devoted to particular subjects across schools. In some districts with a history of site-based management, however, schools may have constructed their schedules differently. For example, in a district where site-based management had become entrenched, one school had 45 minutes per day of language arts, whereas all the rest of the schools in the district were scheduling double that time, or 90 minutes a day. After the district wrote the curriculum assuming a 90-minute block per day, the school with only 45 minutes a day complained that it was too much. And it was, given their schedule.

For elementary schools, the curriculum leadership in the district needs to ensure consistency across the district in the amount of time allocated to various subject areas. Some districts with low math scores decide to increase the time allocated for math from 30 minutes to an hour per day, reasoning that increasing allocated time will allow for more content mastery, which will produce better understanding, which will produce better scores. If the amount of time required is not specified, individual schools will make individual decisions, ensuring that students won't have an equitable chance at completing the curriculum. Equity begins with consistent time spent on various subject areas. Districts, not individual schools, need to make the call on how much time is spent on each area of the curriculum.

DESCRIBING UNITS

Once courses are sequenced and expectations for time use developed, units and dates need to be specified. This serves two curricular functions: (1) a pacing guide specifying the approximate amount of time each unit should take and (2) a consensus outline or "map" of important topics or concept areas. Like courses, units have beginning and ending dates and are time bound. The beginning and ending dates for units act as a pacing guide for the teaching staff by giving approximate dates when units should begin and end—useful information when teachers are planning. The pacing guide should not be seen as rigid, but if, for example, every unit takes a week more than what is recommended, students will not complete all units by the end of the year.

Units might be outlined or mapped around chapters in a textbook, a class, an individual project, or a subject-area theme—or a combination of these. Usually teachers record a significant grade in the grade book at the end of a unit. Each unit has a title. Teachers use unit titles to communicate with one another about the content of instruction. Units are a way to "map" important curriculum content within units (Jacobs, 1997). Unlike the curriculum-mapping process outlined by Jacobs, this

Figure 10.4   Unit titles from the Balanced Curriculum Web site

Unit Timeline
Grade 3 Language Arts
English
Grade 3

Passaic Public Schools
2003–2004

Unit Title	Begin Date	End Date
Finding My Place	9/10/2003	10/19/2003
The Whole Wide World	10/22/2003	12/7/2003
Getting The Job Done	12/10/2003	1/25/2004
From Past to Present	1/25/2004	3/1/2004
Are We There Yet?	3/4/2004	4/26/2004
Imagination Kids	4/29/2004	5/31/2004

SOURCE: Used courtesy of the Passaic Public School District.

mapping process is driven through exploring consensus at the beginning of the curriculum development process about what is most important to teach and for all students to learn. Curriculum mapping explores what is most important to teach but does so beginning from individual teachers' perspectives or maps, using those maps to work through to a consensus. The Balanced Curriculum process is faster because it is easier to get stakeholders to agree on unit titles at the beginning, instead of each individual spelling out how he or she approaches particular courses and the skills in those courses. The Jacobs' mapping process could also be used to generate unit titles, however. Figure 10.4 provides a list of unit titles.

The first rule for units is that the time needed to teach all the units can't exceed the time allocated for the course. Teachers can't run out of the teaching year before they run out of units to teach. Courses need to be designed so that they are doable. If most teachers don't cover all the chapters in the textbook, then the units should only reflect how many chapters are actually covered, or the curriculum authors need to decide which chapters contain the most important material. I remember American History courses in which we didn't make it to World War I, although we spent months studying the exploration of America and the colonial period. Curriculum authors are directed not to put too much in; this is not the ideal curriculum but the real curriculum. (See Chapter 4 for a discussion of textbook's contents.)

Research strongly suggests that students' prerequisite skills influence instruction. Bloom (1976) reviewed research that highlights the importance of attending to students' prior learning. As much as 80% of the variance in posttest scores may be accounted for by pretest scores alone. Similarly, Bracht and Hopkins (1972) found that about two thirds of the variance in 11th-grade achievement could be predicted from 3rd-grade achievement. The knowledge the student brings to the learning situation, then, has a strong effect on how well the student performs on subsequent measures of student learning. Unless low-scoring students are given instruction that takes into account what they currently know and can do, their pattern of achievement in unlikely to change.

If everything cannot be contained in the curriculum, then the curriculum authors need to decide what is most important and what is less important. Most teachers make these decisions privately, skipping over lessons in the textbook or not covering particular topics. Often these decisions are made "on the fly." These decisions have large consequences: When students go to the next grade or course, each has a different set of prerequisite skills because their previous teachers decided what to leave in and what to leave out.

Students move onto the next course or grade level and are assigned to different classes. The teachers of the new classes then aren't sure of what was taught at the previous level. The less coordination and consensus there is about what is taught, the greater the variability in students' prerequisite skills. The greater the variability in students' prerequisite skills, the more pressure teachers experience in designing instruction to meet a wide variety of prerequisite skills. If many students don't have expected prerequisite skills, then teachers will not be able to teach everything in the curriculum well because time will be spent "catching students up." They will make independent decisions about what to leave in or take out. The cycle starts anew.

Curriculum is a way to break the cycle by the curriculum authors deciding which units must be taught and learned. Curriculum development is an opportunity to make these decisions deliberately rather than "on the fly." For example, if students haven't mastered addition and subtraction facts by 3rd grade, the 3rd-grade teachers are at a disadvantage when beginning multiplication. This means that either the 3rd-grade curriculum authors need to plan time for a unit to make sure students master the facts in 3rd grade, or convince the 2nd-grade curriculum authors that mastery of facts is important enough to include in the 2nd-grade curriculum. Such cross-grade-level discussions will continue throughout the curriculum-development process.

UNIT INTRODUCTIONS

The curriculum authors summarize the content and standards in unit introductions. Developing unit introductions serves a number of purposes:

- Curriculum authors reach consensus about the most important content to cover in the unit by discussing what is most important to capture in the introduction.
- When writing introductions, curriculum authors deal with sequencing the units throughout the year so that the units build on one another.
- Curriculum authors ensure the content can be covered in the time allocated for the unit.
- Curriculum authors use the unit introductions to check and make sure that units address important standards.
- The sequence of the curriculum can be checked across grade levels or course sequences to ensure that important prerequisite skills provide the foundation for the next course or unit.
- Many of the significant tasks will come from the introduction, providing preplanning around designing significant tasks. The content of the introductions provides the content addressed by significant tasks.

The district and schools design the format for the unit introductions. Some districts require a lengthy introduction, such as the one in Figure 10.5. This has the advantage that much of what is included in the unit is planned ahead of time.

Figure 10.5 Lengthy unit introduction

Unit Timeline with Introduction Southern Connecticut State University
Physics Dumais 03A   2003–2004
Science
High School

Unit Title	Begin Date	End Date

Estimation   9/3/2003   9/13/2003

The skills of estimation and approximation will be explored through exercises requiring students to investigate orders of magnitude and make appoopriate judgments of size and amount. Students will gather and synthesize information concerning a problem such as determining the amount of water flushed each day by a large city or the number of auto repair technicians in a state. Since direct, exact methods for determining such quantities are frequently unavailable or reasonable, students will need to recognize and analyze alternative explanations and models.

Kinematics in One Dimension   9/16/2003   10/4/2003

Students will use the basic measures of kinematics—displacement, velocity, acceleration, and time—along with conceptual, numerical, and graphical methods to solve problems involving the linear motion of objects. Students will need to interpret the results of experimentation using statistical reasoning and use technology and mathematics to improve investigations and communications through the use of the calculator based laboratory equipment.

Kinematics in Two or Three Dimensions   10/7/2003   10/25/2003

Students will add, subtract, and resolve vectors using graphical and numerical methods. Students will apply their vector addition/resolution skills to solve relative velocity, projectile motion, and other two- or three-dimensional problems. Students will have to formulate and revise scientific explanations and models using logic and evidence as they apply knowledge developed in the previous section (Kinematics in One Dimension) to this one.

Force & Dynamics   10/28/2003   11/15/2003

After developing a historical perspective of the development of the concept of force through the past two thousand years, students will apply Newton's three laws to dynamics problems. They will produce free body force diagrams for static and dynamic situations involving tension, weight, normal force, friction (kinetic and static), and other forces. The laws of motion will then be used to calculate precisely the effects of forces on the motion of objects. The magnitude of the change in motion of objects will be calculated using the relationship $F = ma$, which is independent of the nature of the force.

Circular Motion & Gravitation   11/18/2003   12/3/2003

Students will apply Newton's laws to situations involving horizontal circular motion, vertical circular motion, banked circular motion, and nonuniform circular motion. Students will explore the Law of Universal Gravitation as it applies to previous problems, satellite motion, and Kepler's Laws. Experimentation with gravity will be done to show that the strength of the gravitational attractive force between two masses is proportional to the masses and inversely proportional to the square of the distance between them.

Work & Energy   12/4/2003   12/24/2003

Students will amend their problem-solving strategies to include the conservation of energy. The concepts of work, kinetic energy, potential energy, conservative forces, and power will be used to solve new problems and to solve old problems more efficiently. Through experimentation with systems in which energy is nearly conserved, students will explain how interactions between various energy forms and matter can produce physical changes in a system and will also classify various forms of energy as either kinetic or potential.

(Continued)

Figure 10.5 (Continued)

| Linear Momentum | 1/2/2004 | 1/17/2004 |

Students will explore collisions, incorporating momentum, impulse, conservation of momentum, and the conservation of energy. Systems of particles and their momenta will be investigated through the concept of center of mass. One-dimensional and two-dimensional collisions on a collision table and air track will be investigated and the results of the experimentation will be interpreted using statistical reasoning.

| Rotational Dynamics | 1/21/2004 | 2/7/2004 |

Students will use the rotational equations of motion and the rotational equivalents of Newton's Laws to calculate the rotational inertia of objects and to determine the subsequent motion of systems of objects. The relationships between linear and angular variables will be explored and applied to situations involving rotation and translation (i.e. rolling). Students will design an experiment to determine the relationship between mass arrangement with respect to a central axis and the corresponding distribution of translational and rotational kinetic energies. In addition, the laws of motion will be used to calculate precisely the effects of forces (and torques) on the motion of objects. Students will investigate the conservation of angular momentum and its relation to angular precession, culminating in the formulation and revision of scientific explanations and models using logic and evidence for a counterintuitive physical situation.

| Translational & Rotational Equilibrium UBD | 2/10/2004 | 2/14/2004 |

Static equilibrium (Latin for "equal forces" or "balance") is achieved when two conditions are met. The sum of the forces on an object in every direction must be equal to zero, and the sum of the torques on an object (calculated about any axis) must also be zero. A body in static equilibrium, if left undisturbed, will undergo no translational or rotational acceleration since the sum of all the forces and the sum of all the torques acting on it are zero. How is static equilibrium established? What is the acceleration (translation and rotational) of an object in equilibrium? What is the sum of the forces and the sum of the torques on an object in static equilibrium? What keeps things from falling over? How is it that tightrope walkers keep from falling? Why do travel mugs have wide bottoms? Why do wrestlers get lower in their stance before they engage? How is it that many Roman arches have stood for thousands of years? How does a "deadman" keep a retaining wall from falling over? Students will develop the concepts necessary to explore answers and explanations to these questions.

Translational and rotational dynamics are sufficient tools to independently analyze the motion of bodies or systems of bodies, but, alone, they are not enough to determine the forces and torques that act on systems in equilibrium. Students will bring together the translational and rotational concepts to solve equilibrium problems, determining forces and torques that act on simple systems. Students will design and conduct a scientific investigation to explore the stability of different structures and will be expected to interpret the results of experimentation using statistical reasoning. A historical perspective on the stability of early Roman architecture will be presented and investigated through model building.

| Fluids—Statics & Dynamic | 2/24/2004 | 3/13/2004 |

The study of fluids applies to all actions and motions in the air and the water that surround us. A comprehensive history of the development of the theories of Bernoulli, Pascal, and Archimedes will be presented, and then students will incorporate the concepts of pressure (atmospheric and gauge), Pascal's Principle, buoyancy, continuity, and Bernoulli's Principle in solving static and dynamic fluid problems. Through the use of calculator based laboratory equipment, students will use technology and mathematics to improve investigations. Through the use of "low-tech" equipment, students will develop methods for performing such tasks as "filling a water balloon in the wild."

| Electric Charge & Electric Field | 3/14/2004 | 3/31/2004 |

The electric force is a universal force that exists between any two charged objects. Opposite charges attract while like charges repel. The strength of the force is proportional to the charges and, as with gravitation, inversely proportional to the square of the distance between them. Students will mathematically and experimentally determine the electric fields produced by various charge distributions and explore the interaction of those fields with moving and stationary point charges. Students will design and conduct a scientific investigations to show that, between any two charged particles, electric force is vastly greater than the gravitational force. Through a historical perspective of mechanical and electric forces, students will revise scientific explanations regarding most observable forces such as those exerted by a coiled spring or friction, which may be traced to electric forces acting between atoms and molecules.

Electric Potential & Capacitance   4/1/2004   **4/25/2004**

Students will use electric potential to determine the electric field surrounding various arrangements of charged objects. Students will use the previously developed concept of work to solve problems involving capacitance and stored energy in electric devices. Students will design and modify an experiment to calculate the electric field and the stored energy in a particular charge distribution. Results from the laboratory experiment will then be used to formulate theories about the Earth's electric field.

Electric Currents   4/28/2004   **5/7/2004**

In some materials, such as metals, electrons flow easily, whereas in insulating materials, such as glass, they can hardly flow at all. Semiconducting materials have intermediate behavior. At low temperatures some materials become superconductors and offer no resistance to the flow of electrons. Students will use the concepts of voltage, current, resistance, and resistivity to determine the power consumption of electric circuits. Additionally, investigations of low temperature superconducting materials will be done, and students will revise scientific explanations and models of conductivity using logic and evidence.

DC Circuits   5/8/2004   **5/23/2004**

Students will analyze multiloop circuits, determining numerically and experimentally branch currents and voltages. EMF's, resistors, and capacitors will be used independently and in RC (time-varying) circuits. Using experimental setups incorporating the aforementioned components, students will observe, measure and represent mathematically the changes in the various energy forms taking place during the physical and chemical transformation of substances.

Magnetism   5/27/2004   **6/11/2004**

Students will use the concepts of diamagnetism, paramagnetism, ferromagnetism, and electromagnetism to describe the magnetic fields associated with natural and man-made phenomena including, but not limited to, bar magnets, current carrying wires, the Hall Effect, mass spectrometers, solenoids, and electromagnets. Investigations of the inverse square nature of the magnetic force will be designed and performed by students, and associations between this force and the forces of gravitation and electricity will be explored.

Electromagnetic Induction   6/12/2004   **6/22/2004**

Electricity and magnetism are two aspects of a single electromagnetic force. Moving electric charges produce magnetic forces, and moving magnets produce electric forces. Students will develop the concept of magnetic flux and apply it to electromagnetic situations including, but not limited to, moving conductors in magnetic fields, generators, eddy currents, and transformers. Through the actual design and construction of an electromagnetic motor/generator, students will explore the foundations of electromagnetism. Students will be encouraged to demonstrate inquiring attitudes, open-mindedness and curiosity as they attempt to produce the fastest running motor from the same base set of materials.

SOURCE: Copyright © Charles S. Dumais. Used with permission.

Other districts require focus questions or essential questions (see Figure 10.6; Wiggins & McTighe, 1998). The focus or essential question provides both teachers and students with a path into the unit. For example, students might begin a unit by discussing what they already know and are able to do around the focus question. Students and the teacher can decide how they want to go about learning more about the focus questions. The teacher may want to return to the focus questions periodically throughout the unit to assess the progress of student understanding.

Some districts require more structure for their introductions. Figure 10.7 shows one with a short unit overview that lists important skills (standards from the state), a description of some of the unit's activities, and products that will result from the unit's completion. Listing the products provides the beginning for thinking about significant tasks and assessments because each product described by a significant task needs to be assessed.

Figure 10.6   Unit introduction with essential questions

Unit Timeline with Introduction
Grade 9 English Harkins 03B

English

Grade 9

Unit Title: *Julius Caesar* and *Antigone*

Southern Connecticut State University
2003–2004

	Begin Date	End Date
	1/3/2004	2/2/2004

Introduction

    This six-week unit will focus on the elements of drama. Students will read *Julius Caesar,* by William Shakespeare and *Antigone,* by Sophocles. They will evaluate the use of literary devices, dramatic irony, stage direction, setting, characters, plot, climax, conflict, etc. They will interact with each other through the delivering of lines and the discussion of performing. Students will examine the feelings, thoughts, and behaviors of these characters in relationship to the thematic ideas discussed throughout the year. They will also gain exposure to writing drama by adding scenes to existing plays and creating their own original storyline. When they read *Julius Caesar,* they will also write journal entries in the voice of a character to explain that character's motivations, ideas, and beliefs.

Essential Questions

    a.   What makes someone a good leader?
    b.   Is ambition a positive or negative attribute?
    c.   Should a leader be given a chance to ruin a nation before others punish him/her for it?

    a.   Is loyalty to country or friend more important and honorable?
    b.   Can acts of violence ever be seen as honorable?
    c.   What is the link between honor and patriotism?

    a.   How does jealousy affect people's behavior?
    b.   Can jealousy be overcome by decency?
    c.   Do people convince themselves that their acts are necessary to avoid the issue of their envy?

Enduring Understanding

    1.   Julius Caesar was killed because other politicians felt his ambition would destroy Rome.
    2.   Many times patriots need to choose between friend and country in time of conflict.
    3.   Jealousy fuels some people to act ruthless by masking their motivations in acts of vigilance.

SOURCE: Copyright © Melissa Harkins. Used with permission.

Figure 10.7   Unit introduction with subareas

Mathematics

Grade 4

Unit Title

1. Numbers and Operations Chapters 1-4

		2002–2003
	Begin Date	End Date
	9/4/2002	9/27/2002

Learners will be able to:

- Add and subtract up to 4-digit numbers without regrouping
- Identify place value up to 1,000,000
- Compare and order numbers through millions
- Round to given place value thru hundred thousands
- Round to estimate sums and differences
- Add and subtract up to 4-digit numbers with regrouping
- Develop algebraic expressions with variables
- Solve problems: use the five-step process, identify key information, write or rewrite a word problem

SOURCE: Used courtesy of the Passaic Public School District.

UNITS AS PROMISES

Curriculum is about accountability. Curriculum is the promise made by professionals about how students will demonstrate competence on standards. Developing units and the conversations about what is most important to teach is the first step in figuring out what teachers of a particular course or grade level are promising their students, each other, next year's teachers, and parents.

Unit titles and introductions are promises to students that each will have access to the knowledge and skills contained in the units, regardless of who the student's teacher is. Particularly with students in poverty, assuring equal access to a body of knowledge and skills is important because they may not receive such information from other sources.

Teachers on the same grade level or course use the curriculum as a promise to each other that the most important knowledge is covered and learned. As each teacher gives the same assessments to understand how well students did on significant tasks, teachers will know if they are delivering on their promises.

This year's teachers promise next year's teachers that most students will have the needed and necessary prerequisite skills. Time required for review and reteaching can then be reduced, allowing more time for grade- or course-level content.

Teachers can promise parents that their children will complete course- or grade-level requirements that will assist their children in the future. Teachers can promise parents an understandable curriculum summarized by unit introductions.

AUTHOR AND PLANNING TEAM ACTIVITIES IN DEVELOPING COURSE SEQUENCES AND UNITS

Members of the author teams are grouped by course or grade level. The planning team structures the activities of the author teams. The planning team's tasks to be shared with curriculum authors include the following:

- Developing course sequences
- Validating course sequences
- Developing units (titles, pacing guides, and introductions)
- Sharing with the previous course or grade level
- Sharing with the next course or grade level
- Validating decisions about units across courses or grade levels

Listen as Fred and Freeda, assistant superintendents of two different districts, tell how their districts structured these activities through their planning teams.

Fred: When our planning team confronted how to begin, we decided that a small cadre of instructional leaders should be involved in developing and validating course sequences. So we decided to invite the high school department chair and an experienced teacher from the high school department who had had the opportunity to teach most of the courses in the subject area. The chair of the guidance department also received an invitation. Two middle school teachers with experience at multiple grade levels received invitations, along with four teachers from the elementary school with experience teaching different grade levels. We called these folks the Sequence Task Force.

The Planning Team reasoned that a small number of members would make the discussions and decisions easier, and then everybody would give input on the recommendations of the Sequence Task Force at grade-level or faculty meetings. That input then validated the recommendations of the few.

Freeda: Our planning team decided we needed to spend more time on the sequencing because our district had not had those conversations on a districtwide basis in a long time. Our four middle schools hadn't talked to each other about the content of courses; our high school had made small changes in course content and sequence, and there was a confusing welter of course-taking options and prerequisites that needed to be addressed.

We developed a two-phase approach, beginning with representatives of the middle schools coming together to agree on course sequences at the middle school level. We found that to define course sequences, we needed to sketch out the units and introductions for the courses as a way to understand enough of the specifics of each course.

Once we achieved clarity over the course sequence at the middle school level, we then moved on to the high school. We had more teachers involved than you did, Fred. We started out with the math department, but soon brought in science as the course-taking sequence interacted. Math prerequisites do influence the content of science courses. Because science involves lab time, science course-taking patterns influenced areas such as physical education from a scheduling point of view. Eventually, we involved all departments at the high school, including guidance counselors, because small changes made for big consequences in unexpected places. For example, we found that the lunch schedule (10:30–12:30) was being driven by the schedule of part-time cafeteria workers who only worked from 9:30 to 12:30. We moved their working hours to 10:30 to 1:30 and then could have lunch for students at a more reasonable time. By doing this we found it easier to schedule because we had bigger blocks of time available in the morning.

Fred: Our conversations sound easier. When we adopted block scheduling, we reviewed some of the course sequences and tried to simplify a complex system at the high school.

We set ourselves the goal of increasing student participation in upper-level courses while decreasing participation in "lower-level" courses. The teacher leadership in the district, after reviewing the work of the Sequence Task Force, felt that we could make courses more demanding for students.

Freeda: Our process in the high school led to the same conclusion. We then investigated the scheduling across the district to ensure equity in exposure to various subject areas.

Fred: When we reviewed the amount of time for each subject across the schools in the district, I was pleased to see a general consensus among the schools. Many schools had decreased the time available for science and social studies to spend more time on literacy and numeracy. When we discussed this with schools that hadn't taken that step yet, all schools decided it was a good idea. We were then able to come to a consensus across the district. The superintendent headed up that discussion at a principals' meeting. Then the principals took the recommendation back to their staffs for comments. After reviewing various schools' comments, the principals and superintendent adopted the schedule.

Freeda: Our examination of the schedules was initiated through the central office but then taken to the site-based leadership team at each school. The site-based teams reviewed the recommendation and made comments, which were then distributed via the central office staff. The comments revealed what things needed to be changed, and the site-based teams then adopted the modified proposal.

Fred: The process ate up a lot of time, but it is worth it now because kids are getting equal access, time wise, to each subject area.

SUMMARY

This chapter discussed standards, the function of units, timelines, and unit introductions as a vehicle to build consensus around what is most important to teach students. Consistent time allocations across the district are necessary to ensure equal curriculum access as well. The next chapter examines other standards-based areas that might inform the choice of units and significant tasks.

11

Other Standards
for Alignment
and Balance

Available standards from states and national professional organizations can be used to improve the balance in a curriculum. This chapter gives a synopsis of some other standards and suggests ways those standards have been used to improve curricular balance.

THINKING AND
REASONING STANDARDS

How standards are defined indicates what is most important. Most would agree that an important outcome of education is the ability to think and reason across a wide variety of subjects. Some argue that thinking and reasoning is more important than subject-area knowledge because the ability to think and reason in new settings about new problems will be more in demand as our society becomes more complex and diverse. If this is so, then curriculum should be developed to incorporate thinking and reasoning. Choosing standards by which to align and balance the curriculum is a decision about how to frame the importance of thinking and reasoning. Different standards are configured in different ways to address thinking and reasoning.

Marzano and Kendall (1996) defined three approaches to thinking and reasoning standards. The first is to separate thinking and reasoning standards from content-area standards. The advantage to this approach is that the thinking and reasoning standards are explicit, so they can help to focus curriculum, instruction, and assessment. For example, Marzano and Kendall (1996) identified the following as "good representations of the thinking and reasoning skills and abilities found in the national documents" (p. 38):

1. Understands and applies basic principles of presenting an argument

2. Understands and applies basic principles of logic and reasoning

3. Effectively uses mental processes that are based on identifying similarities and dissimilarities (compares, contrasts, classifies)

4. Understands and applies basic principles of hypothesis testing and scientific inquiry

5. Applies basic troubleshooting and problem-solving techniques

6. Applies decision-making techniques.

Wiggins and McTighe (1998) gave six facets of "understanding":

1. Can *explain:* provide thorough, supported, and justifiable accounts of phenomena, facts, and data

2. Can *interpret:* tell meaningful stories; offer apt translations; provide a revealing historical or personal dimension to ideas and events; make it personal or accessible through images, anecdotes, analogies, and models

3. Can *apply:* effectively use and adapt what we know in diverse contexts

4. Have *perspective:* see and hear point of view through critical eyes and ears; see the big picture

5. Can *empathize:* find value in what others might consider odd, alien, or implausible; perceive sensitively on the basis of prior direct experience

6. Have *self-knowledge:* perceive the personal style, prejudices, projections, and habits of mind that both shape and impede our own understanding; we are aware of what we do not understand and why understanding is so hard

When developing and aligning significant tasks, curriculum authors consult and use the list of thinking and reasoning standards to enhance the scope of the significant task, explicitly incorporating the standards into the significant task. The difficulty of a separate list of thinking and reasoning standards is an artificial separation of thinking and reasoning from specific subject-area content. In real life, thinking and reasoning are always used with subject-area content as a focus. Furthermore, the meaning of the thinking and reasoning standards is dictated in part by the subject-area context. For example, problem solving in mathematics may have different rules than problem solving in social studies. A consensus has yet to emerge on whether such thinking and reasoning standards are actually transferable across subject areas.

A second approach is to list thinking and reasoning standards as part of subject-area standards. For example, the National Council of Teachers of Mathematics standards list the following thinking and reasoning standards as part of its mathematics standards:

- Problem Solving
- Reasoning and Proof
- Communication
- Connections
- Representation

These thinking and reasoning standards are grounded in the subject area of mathematics and use mathematical references. The difficulty is that not all the thinking and reasoning standards are subject-area specific. For example, the Problem Solving Standard for Grades 3–5, "Apply and adapt a variety of appropriate strategies to solve problems," is general enough to apply not only to mathematics but to other subject areas as well.

The third approach is to subsume thinking and reasoning standards in benchmarks or performance tasks without explicitly highlighting the standards. For example, from the National Geography Standards (National Geographic Society et al., 1994),

A student is able to *evaluate the characteristics of places and regions from a variety of points of view, as exemplified by being able to* assess a place or region from the points of view of various types of people—a homeless person, a business person, a taxi driver, a police officer, or a tourist.

Assessing a place from various points of view involves comparison and contrast, synthesis and analysis—all parts of thinking and reasoning skills. The thinking and reasoning skills are embedded in the task, however, and are not explicitly stated as thinking and reasoning skills. The disadvantage of this approach is that thinking and reasoning skills are not explicitly formulated or highlighted, leaving to chance whether these skills will focus instruction and assessment. The advantage is that the skills are embedded in benchmarks so that teachers will not have to worry about another set of standards to address.

Decisions about which standards to align are not automatically made based on the state standards. Simply choosing the state standards may miss the opportunity to address thinking and reasoning standards appropriately. The district's curriculum steering committee will need to decide how to address thinking and reasoning standards and then choose standards that put the appropriate emphasis on thinking and reasoning.

LIFELONG LEARNING STANDARDS, WORKPLACE STANDARDS, AND TECHNOLOGY STANDARDS

Education doesn't stop when we leave school. Are we getting the tools and attitudes we need to keep learning on the job, in our personal relationships, and through our communities? Lifelong learning standards or workplace standards describe what is needed and necessary to be a contributing member of society. Standards of this type are based on research. See, for example, *What Work Requires of Schools: A SCANS Report for America 2000* (Secretary's Commission on Achieving Necessary Skills, 1991) and *Workplace Basics: The Essential Skills Employers Want* (Carnevale, Gainer, & Meltzer, 1990). Marzano and Kendall (1996, p. 41) found the following "Standards for Life Skills" present in many of the standards documents they examined.

Working With Others

1. Contributes to the overall effort of a group
2. Uses conflict-resolution techniques
3. Works well with diverse individuals and in diverse situations
4. Displays effective interpersonal communication skills
5. Demonstrates leadership skills

Self-Regulation

1. Sets and manages goals
2. Performs self-appraisal
3. Considers risks
4. Demonstrates perseverance
5. Maintains a healthy self-concept
6. Restrains impulsivity

Life Work

1. Makes effective use of basic tools
2. Understands the characteristics and use of basic computer hardware, software, and operating systems.
3. Uses basic word processing, spreadsheet, database, and communication programs
4. Manages money effectively
5. Pursues specific jobs
6. Makes general preparations for entering the workforce
7. Makes effective use of basic life skills
8. Displays reliability and a basic work ethic
9. Operates effectively within organizations

Such lists are helpful is designing and assessing significant tasks.

States may have standards that are intended to cross subject matter lines to ensure that students are employable after graduation. New Jersey's Cross-Content Workplace Readiness Standards follow. In New Jersey, all subject areas align to both the content and the Workplace Readiness Standards.

New Jersey Cross-Content Workplace Readiness Standards

Career Planning and Workplace Readiness Skills

Information, Technology, and Other Tools

Critical Thinking, Decision Making, and Problem Solving

Self-Management Skills

Safety Principles

Michigan produced a different list divided into grade-level bands; following are the major headings across grade levels.

Michigan Career and Employability Skills

Applied Academic Skills

Career Planning

Developing and Presenting Information

Problem Solving

Personal Management

Organizational Skills

Teamwork

Negotiation Skills

Understanding Systems and Using Technology

Using Employability Skills

Some states have separate standards for technology. This means that the states consider technology to be important enough to have developed discrete standards for it rather than simply combining them with other workplace standards. Because technology can be used throughout the curriculum, the curriculum steering committee may want to apply technology standards as part of the design of all subject areas. For example, in Tyler, Texas, the school district decided to align content area standards and the technology standards that follow for each course.

Texas Essential Knowledge and Skills (TEKS) for Technical Application

1. Demonstrate knowledge and appropriate use of hardware components, software programs, and their connections

2. Use data input skills appropriate to the task

3. Comply with the laws and examine the issues regarding the use of technology in society

4. Use a variety of strategies to acquire information from electronic resources, with appropriate supervision

5. Acquire electronic information in a variety of formats, with appropriate supervision

6. Evaluate the acquired electronic information

7. Use appropriate computer-based productivity tools to create and modify solutions to problems

8. Use research skills and electronic communication, with appropriate supervision, to create new knowledge

9. Use technology application to facilitate evaluation of work, both process and product

10. Format digital information for appropriate and effective communication

11. Deliver the product electronically in a variety of media, with appropriate supervision

12. Use technology applications to facilitate evaluation of communication, both process and product

From the lists, notice the similarities and differences. Choosing a particular list will direct teachers and curriculum authors toward designing significant tasks and curriculum-embedded assessments to demonstrate that students are addressing areas defined by the standards. For example, teachers from Texas using the TEKS for Technology Application may include many more opportunities to use technology that teachers in New Jersey using the Workplace Readiness Standards because the Texas standards are more specific.

DISTRICT-BASED STANDARDS

Larger districts sometimes specify their own standards for particular grade levels, usually derived from state standards documents in which grade-level ranges are present (i.e., K–4, 5–8, 9–12). For example, a district might specify standards for kindergarten, Grade 1, Grade 2, and so on from the K–4 standards in the state documents. Grade-level standards assist the curriculum authors with scope and sequence issues between grade levels. For example, a state-level standard indicates that by 4th-grade students will master basic arithmetic facts. District grade-level standards indicate that addition and subtraction facts to 10 will be part of the 1st-grade standards, and multiplication facts will be part of the 3rd-grade standards. The Balanced Curriculum framework and Web site can handle these individual situations by including the district standards right along with the state and national standards.

Districts may also have expectations for what their graduates will be able to do. These statements can also be incorporated in the Balanced Curriculum process and Web site as a way to focus instruction and assessment around exit competencies. For example, in devising their reading and language arts curriculum, Tyler, Texas, used the Tyler Independent School District Student Expectations (which follow) as one of their alignment categories.

Tyler Independent School District Student Expectations

Be Academically Prepared for Postsecondary Education and the Workforce

- Have the knowledge in mathematics, science, social studies, English, and other languages
- Participate in the literary, visual, and performing arts to enrich his or her daily life
- Have technology applications proficiency
- Demonstrate personal health habits

Be Responsible Citizens

- Understand the value and rewards of work
- Contribute to community and/or school service organizations
- Make and evaluate decisions based on ethical principles and respect of the law
- Understand and appreciate the benefits of democratic government and free enterprise

Have an Individualized Postsecondary Education and Lifelong Learning Plan

- Have a lifelong learning plan based on students' interests, aptitudes, and abilities
- Have a lifelong learning plan that is realistic, informed, and reasoned with continuous guidance and planning.

When students in Tyler read fables, for example, one of the significant tasks requires them to evaluate the decisions made by characters in the fable on the basis of whether the character made an appropriate (ethical) decision. This aligns with the third standard under "Be Responsible Citizens."

LEARNING STYLES

The Hertford County, North Carolina, school district felt that, in designing and aligning significant tasks, it was important to take a wide range of learning styles into consideration. Thus, each significant task was aligned with one of the following learning styles descriptors:

Auditory learning style

Hands-on learning style

Lecture learning style

One-on-one learning style

Small group learning style

Visual learning style

After aligning their significant tasks to the descriptors, stakeholders in this district could determine for each course whether there was an appropriate balance of the different learning styles. When an imbalance was found, significant tasks could be changed so the curriculum reflected balance. The Balanced Curriculum process and Web site can accommodate unique district, county, and state requirements.

STANDARDS FOR ENGLISH-AS-A-SECOND-LANGUAGE (ESL) STUDENTS

Across the country, many districts have experienced a growing ESL or bilingual program population. Aligning to state or national ESL standards ensures that the curriculum will meet their needs. States such as Texas and New Jersey have also adopted state standards for this population. Districts with large ESL populations may want to consider developing and aligning the district's curriculum to these standards. Again, state or national standards can be placed on the Web site to customize it for district needs. Following are the categories included across grade-level ranges for the nation.

Teaching English to Speakers of Other Languages (TESOL) and ESL Standards

- To use English to communicate in social settings

  Students will use English to participate in social interactions
  Students will interact in, through, and with spoken and written English

- To use English to achieve academically in all content areas
- To use English in socially and culturally appropriate ways

Both the standard English curriculum and the ESL or bilingual curriculum could be aligned to these standards.

COMER'S DEVELOPMENTAL PATHWAYS

A criteria for a good curriculum is developmental appropriateness. Does the curriculum help students by providing them with developmentally appropriate experiences? Does the curriculum take into account the full range of developmental tasks for a particular age? The Balanced Curriculum process matured as part of the Comer School Development Program at Yale University. Underlying the Comer Process for School Development is the idea that schools exist to foster student development. Schools aren't simply places where reading, writing, and arithmetic are taught; their primary mission is to develop the total student. As standards-based education focuses on subject-area content standards, developmental issues may not be addressed or even noticed in the curriculum development process. High-stakes testing reinforces the emphasis on content-driven instruction, at times to the exclusion of students' developmental needs. For example, one district eliminated recess for kindergarteners so they could have more time-on-task for reading and math.

To help heighten teachers' awareness and use of developmental knowledge, Comer proposed six developmental pathways (see Maholmes's and Corbin's chapters in *Child by Child* (Comer, Haynes, Joyner, & Ben-Avie, 1999):

- Cognitive
- Language
- Social
- Psychological
- Physical
- Ethical

Some districts decide to use Comer's Developmental Pathways as a way to help the curriculum authors think about the range of development that should be addressed in the curriculum. For example, in one district we worked with (District 13 in Brooklyn, New York) to develop a reading and language arts curriculum, we found, after aligning the significant tasks to the developmental pathways, very few alignments to the ethical pathway. Teachers discussed some of the reasons: They were hesitant to mention ethics because this was associated with judging whether something was right or wrong; they didn't feel it was their place to make those judgments; and they felt uncomfortable discussing right and wrong because their students came from various backgrounds and what was right for some was not for others.

We discussed the stories that they read and noted that each story involved a conflict that was resolved a particular way because of the character's decision and what they felt was the best way through the conflict—an ethical decision. Eventually, the teachers realized that all the stories dealt with ethical issues and that discussion of these issues was important and appropriate for children's understanding of themselves and others. When approached from that point of view, the teachers saw a way to bring the discussion of ethical issues into the curriculum. The curriculum authors then went back and revised the significant tasks to highlight the ethical dimensions of the stories. Without the job of balancing the curriculum by taking into consideration students' ethical development needs, such a discussion and discovery of teaching tendencies would not have taken place.

ASSESSMENTS

Just as there are many kinds of standards, so there are also many kinds of assessments. States usually require students to take state-designed assessments. No Child Left Behind will increase the number of assessments students take. Most assessments have content specifications that tell, in a general way, what the test will cover and provide samples of items or testing procedures used. The content of assessments summarized by publicly available content specifications should be part of the alignment and balancing process as well. With the flexibility of the Web site, it is possible to incorporate a wide range of content specifications for assessments for whatever test the district is using. District- and state-mandated assessments provide another lens with which to focus the curriculum development process.

DECIDING ON AND USING OTHER STANDARDS TO DEVELOP A BALANCED CURRICULUM

State standards and assessments form the core of the process of developing, aligning, and balancing the curriculum. Other standards exist, however, that illuminate different dimensions of schooling besides those centered in a content-driven perspective. The Balanced Curriculum steering committee, the committee that guides and plans for curriculum development and implementation, needs to decide the standards that will be used to determine balance in the curriculum. Too many standards may mean a diffused focus; too few may mean overreliance on a single viewpoint. The team understands that the Balanced Curriculum process is a way to help teachers assimilate the standards so that the external standards become internalized in the design of significant tasks and the process of aligning and balancing the curriculum to the standards. The process allows districts to customize their alignment so that the curriculum is stretched appropriately without breaking the patience of the authors.

During an overview session, a teacher asked, "How can you design significant tasks without understanding what the standards say? Does that mean we must know all the standards that we will align to before we begin?"

This is a chicken-and-egg problem (which came first?). The fact is that it is impossible to have in-depth knowledge of all the standards. Standards are often long documents, densely packed with ideas that are difficult to read and comprehend because they have so many implications for curriculum design.

So we begin in the middle, after reviewing a few of the most important standards and learning how to design significant tasks. The two processes of understanding the standards and developing the significant tasks feed off of one another. Teachers learn the standards through the development of significant tasks. As a significant task is developed, standards documents are used as a resource. Looking at the standards might suggest another way to approach a significant task. When completing alignment, the curriculum authors must examine the match between the significant task and the standard, providing another opportunity to internalize more of the standards. When balancing the curriculum, curriculum authors must decide whether areas they think are most important have received appropriate emphasis across significant tasks. When the curriculum authors develop assessments, authors again reexamine the standards to provide clues about what is most important to assess.

SUMMARY

This chapter examined the process of aligning the significant tasks to a wide variety of standards and assessments. Choosing the standards helps to specify the scope and range of the curriculum; the use of a variety of standards was explored in this chapter. The next chapter explains how the significant tasks are generated and validated.

12

Generating
and Validating
Significant Tasks

Significant tasks are the heart of the Balanced Curriculum process. Significant tasks are where the rubber of the standards meets the road of student outcomes. Using significant tasks to describe a curriculum is a departure from traditional curriculum practices. Many traditional curriculum models rely on "objectives" to describe what is to be taught. The teacher's job is to use the objective and create instruction that will fulfill the objective. The teacher's role is to decide how the objective will be taught. For example, Teacher 1 might fulfill the objective of "finding the main idea" by having students complete a series of worksheets on which they practice finding the main idea. Teacher 2 decides to fulfill the objective of finding the main idea by examining newspaper stories and inventing headlines for the articles. Both teachers have "covered" the objective of main idea, but the instructional methods differ, and so, most likely, will the outcomes. Most teachers would readily agree that Teacher 2's way of teaching main idea exemplifies best practice. Significant tasks provide a way to institutionalize best practices across a district's classrooms.

Traditional curriculum (the list of objectives for teachers to teach) specifies only the objectives, not the teaching process. The traditional curriculum model does not provide enough specificity to ensure consistent student outcomes because each teacher decides how to teach each objective. If teachers make their decisions in isolation, students may have covered the objective but learned the objective in very different ways. Students have different prerequisite skills when moving to the next grade level.

Returning to the example, Teacher 1's students may have learned about picking the best answer from the four given; Teacher 2's students may have learned about the structure of a news article (the first sentence of the article contains the most important information) and learned about creating headlines (brief statement containing a subject and an active verb). Teacher 2's students created headlines, whereas Teacher 1's students made the best choice out of four. Student learning is very different even though both addressed the objective of the main idea. To remedy this flaw in traditional curriculum design, significant tasks are used that encompass an objective and the instructional process that leads to an assessable student product.

To create a powerful curriculum, the objectives for instruction must be reconnected to the instructional process so that adequate prerequisite skills can be built for succeeding units and courses. Significant tasks include both standard objectives (the what) and the instructional process (the how).

Standard Objectives + Instructional Process = Significant Task

This chapter examines the characteristics of significant tasks by viewing a few models in various subject areas. Next, Ms. Creighton demonstrates how a significant task is used as a structure for lesson planning, with comments on the thought processes Ms. Creighton used. Emily and Ricardo, two curriculum authors, then discuss the process of developing significant tasks. Finally, a rubric is used for validating significant tasks for adequacy, with examples given. The following major ideas listed provide the outline for the chapter:

- Significant tasks, summarized by a paragraph, define for teachers the most important student outcomes for the unit.
- Significant tasks are designed by the curriculum authors to take up about 60% of instructional time.
- Thirty-five to fifty significant tasks adequately define the major student outcomes for the course.
- All teachers are required to complete the significant tasks for assigned courses.
- Teachers use their skill and expertise to devise many plans for accomplishing the significant task, but the focus of their instruction is the significant task.
- Significant tasks link the language from the standards with a series of important instructional activities. Significant tasks specify the content of instruction using the language of important standards.
- Significant tasks are complex, combining many standards-based objectives in a student-performance- or student-generated product. Significant tasks show what students will be able to do, not what the teacher does.
- Significant tasks provide the structure for assessment.
- Significant tasks provide a basis for lesson planning by summarizing 3 to 10 days' worth of instruction in the paragraph describing the significant task.

SIGNIFICANT TASKS:
A BASIS FOR LESSON PLANNING

Significant Tasks, Summarized by a Paragraph, Define for Teachers the Most Important Student Outcomes for the Unit

---

Sample Significant Task

After reading the selection "Cleaning Up America's Air" on pages 604–608 [in the district adopted text], students will use a variety of reference materials such as newspapers, magazines, the Internet, or other resources to find out more about electric cars and compare and contrast them with gas-powered cars.

1. Students then choose a graphic organizer to compare and contrast their findings. They must write their findings on a poster board to display.

2. Students will write a clarification paper in which they give reasons to support the benefits of driving either an electricity- or a gas-powered car.

This significant task contains two activities linked through examination of the characteristics of electricity- and gasoline-powered cars. The first activity is about organizing a compare-and-contrast exercise on a piece of nonfiction to be reported with a student-selected graphic organizer. The second activity is a "clarification" paper in which benefits of driving an electricity-powered car are explored. Important student outcomes for the significant task are the graphic organizer to be displayed to the class and a clarification paper giving reasons to support the benefits of driving an electric vehicle. The curriculum authors assume that students have had experience in using graphic organizers or they wouldn't have asked students to select an appropriate organizer for the activity. (When taking a significant task out of the course's and unit's context, we can't tell if an assumption like this is correct.)

The curriculum authors may have considered other activities for the significant task. For example, students could have prepared a speech to explain their poster, or students could discuss in small groups the benefits of driving electricity-powered cars. They didn't choose these activities, however, because they felt that the most important way, at this point in the year, was for students to display their compare-and-contrast graphic organizer and write the benefits paper.

By giving all students access to the same significant tasks, the district is ensuring equal access to a high-quality curriculum. All students (and all teachers) for a particular course will have an opportunity to complete the requirements of the significant task. Coordination of instruction through the use of significant tasks ensures that students will have the necessary prerequisite skills for the next unit, course, or grade level.

Consider what would happen if there was not a focus on the significant task—how content will be taught and assessed. What if the significant task specified only that "Teachers will use graphic organizers, practice compare and contrast, and work on reasoning to support an argument."

Individual teachers then would decide what tasks would be appropriate. In Classroom A, Mrs. Smith decided that she will only use a Venn diagram because she really doesn't like these fancy, new schemes to produce a "traditional" outline.

Mrs. Smith further decides that she will have students practice compare and contrast by making lists with the headings "Same" and "Different" but does not think writing these lists up into paragraph form is really necessary (it's a lot of work to grade 125 student papers). Mrs. Smith decides to skip the reasoning stuff completely because students this young really shouldn't be required to learn about reasoning; that can be done later (and Mrs. Smith isn't sure what good reasoning is or how to teach it at this grade level).

Mr. Jansky, in Classroom B, uses a very different approach. He has used various graphic organizers throughout the year and asks students to choose an appropriate one to compare and contrast in a variety of situations. He has had students translate a number of graphic organizers into three-paragraph compositions. They have chosen the ones they thought were best and edited, in editing groups, the papers to turn in. Mr. Jansky used the papers students turned in as examples of how students used reasoning in a persuasive essay. After class and editing group feedback on the reasoning used in the papers, students had an opportunity to rewrite the papers again and received input on those papers from Mr. Jansky using "reasoning" rubrics.

Without significant tasks, Mrs. Smith and Mr. Jansky can interpret the standards statements in very different ways with very different student products and performances. Mr. Jansky has numerous drafts of reasoning papers, whereas Mrs. Smith has compare-and-contrast lists. Both are valid ways to interpret the standards but do not give students the consistency of skills and experience needed across classrooms. A teacher next year who receives half of Mr. Jansky's students and half of Mrs. Smith's students will find some of those students better prepared than others to use reasoning and write comparison essays. Next year's teacher, after assessing where the students are, decides to start in the middle, so half the students are reviewing much of what they learned previously. Multiply this across a student's tenure in public school to see why this approach to instruction is inadequate, particularly with students from poor families.

Administratively, the system has not guaranteed children equal access to high-quality, coordinated instruction. This is the professionals' problem to fix, not a problem with students. Only when we can coordinate instruction around the standards (using tools such as significant tasks) will we have a world-class education system. Standards give us a general outline of what students should know and be able to do. Standards do not specifically indicate how instruction should be planned. Significant tasks combine the general standard with an instructional activity for students leading to a student product or performance. Standards provide the starting place, not the end of the road. Curriculum is the lynchpin for providing students with equal access to high-quality, coordinated instruction.

Significant Tasks Are Designed by the Curriculum Authors to Take Up About 60% of Instructional Time

Figure 12.1 shows a significant task list written for a district with a large bilingual population that recently adopted a textbook. The prerequisite skills for this significant task are in Lesson 2.4 for the regular program and in Lesson 3.1 for the bilingual math textbook. The significant task is used in conjunction with the material provided in the textbook. This significant task, including the prerequisite lessons, and the three other significant tasks in the unit are designed to take up about 60% of the unit's instructional time. A worksheet is provided via the Balanced Curriculum Web site; teachers print out the worksheet from the Web site and duplicate a set for their class to use in completing the activity.

Figure 12.1 A significant task list written for a district with a large bilingual population

---

Mathematics Grade 4   2002–2003

Unit 1 Task 2 String It Up/Estimate Sums & Differences

- Materials: string, index cards, worksheet
- Students will develop an understanding of estimation through addition and subtraction of *4-digit numbers.*
- Teacher tapes a long string along the middle of the chalkboard. Label 3,000 at one end and 4,000 at the other end. Tape an index card labeled 3,500 in the middle of the string.
- Each student will write on their own index card a number that is between 3,000 and 4,000.
- One at a time, students will place themselves within the string line to the position that corresponds to their number on their index card. As they show where their number would be on the line, they will say their number to the class.
- Students will round their index card number to the thousand, hundred, and ten place values and share their answers with a partner.
- Partners will use their original index card numbers to create an estimated addition problem using their two numbers as addends.
- Partners will round these addends to find a sum.
- Partners will use their same index card numbers to create an estimated subtraction problem.
- Partners will round these numbers to find the difference.
- Students will record answers on teacher-made worksheet.

SOURCE: Used courtesy of the Passaic Public School District.

During the other 40% of the time, teachers can fill in missing prerequisite skills, hold review sessions, provide students with extra practice for those who didn't understand the first time through, extend the lesson for those who mastered the content quickly, or provide additional enrichment activities that complement the unit's goal.

Generally, teachers are willing to focus on the significant tasks because they have enough "wiggle room" to address individual and small group needs. Beginning teachers, lateral-entry teachers, or teachers new to the grade level may need more than the 60% time allotment for their students to complete the significant task satisfactorily.

Thirty-Five to Fifty Significant Tasks Adequately Define the Major Student Outcomes for the Course

As a significant task takes more than a few days instructional time, the duration of the significant tasks and the length of the course limit the number of significant tasks. Most school years have 36 weeks, so 35 significant tasks would be sequenced about once per week. Using 50 significant tasks, one would need to be taught about every 3 days.

The number of state standards also influences the number of significant tasks. If state standards contain many items, more significant tasks may be needed to cover all the standards. Generally, 35 to 50 significant tasks provide enough alignment possibilities for most of the existing standard sets.

All Teachers Are Required to Complete the Significant Tasks for Assigned Courses

To ensure that all students have access to high-quality instruction, all teachers are required to teach their students the significant tasks. Curriculum authors, when designing the significant tasks, choose the best tasks that fit into the instructional sequence that meet appropriate standards. The best, brightest, and most caring teachers—the curriculum authors—know what is most important and come to a consensus on the best way to teach important ideas. The authors must sift through a wide range of instructional sequences to determine which they think will be the most powerful. The best of what is known in a district is "institutionalized" in the curriculum.

Across districts adopting the Balanced Curriculum model, this rule—all teachers are required to complete the significant task—causes the most difficulty. Some teachers now don't have time to cover content that was covered in previous years. For example, in one district, "The Family" unit had been taught in kindergarten and 1st, 2nd, and 3rd grades, with a culminating activity of having students make a family album. The curriculum authors decided that such a sequence provided too much redundancy, and they limited the family unit to kindergarten and 1st grade, with each grade having different significant tasks. The curriculum authors used the additional time available in 2nd and 3rd grade to address other important social studies' topics. Understandably, some 2nd- and 3rd-grade teachers were upset by the changes. School administrators and staff developers assisted in helping the disgruntled teachers to understand the curriculum authors' logic. The district moved from a "do your own thing" curriculum to a more rationale scope and sequence. As states specify course content, there is less room for teacher autonomy in deciding what is most important to teach. An assumption on which the Balanced Curriculum process is based is that a coordinated scope and sequence of instruction is better than an uncoordinated one.

Teachers Use Their Skill and Expertise to Devise Many Plans to Accomplish the Significant Task, but the Focus of Their Instruction Is the Significant Task

Figure 12.2 shows the first social studies unit for Grade 7. The three significant tasks in the units could be planned and sequenced in many ways. Figure 12.3 shows three possible sequences of using the time devoted to teaching the social studies unit. The hash marks represent days. The bars represent the three significant tasks. In the first example, the three significant tasks are taken in order. The teacher begins by providing an introduction to the unit and some review, spending a day or two making sure students have all the necessary prerequisite skills. On Day 3, she begins her first significant task. The significant task lasts a few days. The same pattern is repeated for the second and third significant tasks. This might be the pattern where the last significant task is dependent on the first two.

In Figure 12.3, the three significant tasks are clustered at the end of the unit, and the teacher has decided to do them in reverse order. The teacher uses the time at the beginning of the unit to prepare for the three tasks. This might be the pattern if the three significant tasks are not dependent on each other. In the third example, the second significant task is begun, but not completed until after the teacher has provided some intervening instruction. This might occur, for example, when a teacher assumes that students have the prerequisite skills but, once into the activity, finds out that this is not the case. Another scenario would be if the teacher wanted to start with the significant task but knew students could not complete it without further instruction. In this case, by focusing on the first significant task, the teacher provides students with a taste of what the task would be, but more instruction is needed to get there.

Figure 12.2 First social studies unit for Grade 7

History & Social Sciences Grade 7   2002–2003
Unit: Unit 1: Global Heritage of the American People Prior to 1500

                                                             9/4/2002   10/31/2002

Significant Tasks

Map Skills

Students will review and refine the following skills using the overhead projector, hand-outs, and classroom models:

- Globe, types of maps such as political, physical, population, economic, and natural resource
- Directions: cardinal and intermediate
- Major landforms: continents and hemispheres
- Bodies of water: oceans, lakes, and rivers
- Latitude and longitude
- Parts of a map: title, scale, key, grid, and compass rose
- Tracing routes
- Measuring distances

Once the students have become familiar with the major characteristics of maps, they will make a map that traces their bus route to school from their home. The map must include:

- Their home
- Their school
- The Hudson River
- Compass rose
- Key which interprets the symbols used
- Labeled roads
- At least 5 landmarks passed on their morning journey such as NFA, Newbargh Mall
- Washington's Headquarters, the Balmville Tree, Wal-Mart, the YMCA, and the 6 corners

Skills Covered

- Map skills

Iroquois Culture

After reading and discussing the Iroquois Creation Story, students will demonstrate an understanding of the Iroquois Civilization of the Atlantic Coast of North America by analyzing various pictorial, graphic, and text-based documents and answering the questions that follow each document. Then, the students will construct a well-written thematic essay which includes a topic sentence, supporting paragraphs, and a conclusion by explaining and synthesizing the information provided in the documents and their knowledge of social studies.

Skills Covered

- Analyzing written, geographic documents
- Focus on literacy
- Organizing a thematically based essay that includes introduction with the main idea, several paragraphs explaining the main idea using evidence from the documents, and a conclusion

Native American Culture Study

After learning about the various Native American cultures in the Americas, students will demonstrate an understanding of their social and economic characteristics such as customs, traditions, child-rearing practices, gender roles, foods, and religious and spiritual beliefs by creating a moral using physical and human characteristics from one of the Native American cultures studied. In their morals, students should include religion, food, clothing, climate, housing, language, locate, government, and whether the culture was matrilineal or patrilineal. This could be an individual or group project.

Skills Covered

- Organize collected information
- Draw inferences
- Classifying and categorizing dates

SOURCE: Used courtesy of the Newburgh Enlarged City School District.

Figure 12.3 Units and organization of significant tasks

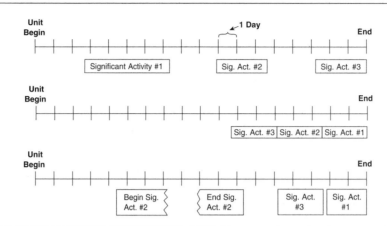

SOURCE: Copyright © ABC Education Consultants, LLC.

Significant Tasks Link the Language From the Standards With a Series of Important Instructional Activities. Significant Tasks Specify the Content of Instruction Using the Language of Important Standards

Figure 12.4 is a sample significant task and a list of standards (from New Jersey) on writing. Because the task is mainly about writing an argument, the New Jersey standards listed in the figure apply. Words in the standards are also used in the significant task, providing a direct curriculum link from instruction to the standards.

Significant tasks, a part of the curriculum, are the link between standards and instruction. Standards specify what students need to know and be able to do in a general sense; the significant tasks use the language of the standards for the significant task in a course or unit, thereby anchoring the standards within a time frame and within an instructional sequence. More will be said about linking standards with significant tasks when the curriculum is aligned and balanced.

Figure 12.4 Sample significant task aligned to a list of standards on writing

Sample Significant Task. After reading the selection "Cleaning Up America's Air" on pages 604–608 [in the district-adopted text], students will use a *variety of reference materials* such as newspapers, magazines, the Internet, or other articles to find out more about electric cars and compare and contrast them with gas-powered cars.

1. Then they should *choose* a graphic organizer to compare and contrast their findings. They must write their findings on a poster board to *display*.

2. Students will write a clarification paper in which they *give reasons* to *support* the benefits of driving an electric-powered car versus a gas-powered car.

Writing Forms, Audiences, and Purposes (exploring a variety of forms)

Gather, select, and organize the most effective information appropriate to a topic, task, and audience.

Choose an appropriate organizing strategy such as cause/effect, pro and con, parody, etc, to effectively present a topic, point of view, or argument.

When writing persuasive essays, present evidence, examples, and justification to support arguments.

Demonstrate writing clarity and supportive evidence when answering open-ended and essay questions across the curriculum.

Use a variety of primary and secondary sources to understand the value of each when writing a research report.

Significant Tasks Are Complex, Combining Many Standards-Based Objectives Together in a Student Performance or Student-Generated Product. Significant Tasks Show What Students Will Be Able to Do, Not What the Teacher Does

In Figure 12.4, note how the complex significant task encompasses five of the New Jersey Standards on writing. Most states have so many standards that it is not possible to address the standards one at a time. The significant tasks combine many standards around one complex significant task, ensuring that all standards can be covered by the end of the year.

Note also that the significant task summarizes what products they will produce to demonstrate that they have addressed the standards. The teacher's job is to help students reach the standards by assisting them in performing the requirements of the significant task. Thus, the significant task is performance based for students, relying heavily on what they can demonstrate through the significant task.

Significant Tasks Provide the Structure for Assessment

Read the sample significant task in Figure 12.5 and use it to construct an assessment. Applicable standards are listed under the significant task.

This significant task requires two types of products:

1. Three marketing brochures from different geographic regions

2. A paper describing a significant pattern across the three colonies

The products provide structure for assessing student work. The description of the brochures includes content that should be covered (history of the colony, economic activities, etc.); when assessing students' work, teachers may use this list as a criterion for grading the paper. A rubric might be developed to show the adequacy of each area's description.

Significant tasks can also focus assessment on process—how well did students use their editing groups to make their papers better? The editing groups, rating themselves against pre-established criteria, might be one way to do this. Or the teacher may give each group a grade on group process based on how well the papers from the group turned out.

Figure 12.5 Sample significant task for high school American History based on North Carolina standards

Students will work in pairs to develop 3 brochures that will market a colony from each of the three geographic regions. Brochures will describe why the colony was founded; significant people and various racial, ethnic and religious groups; history of the colony; economic activities; social and political life, geographic factors (climate, soil etc.); pictures and original captions. Students will then individually write a paper showing a significant pattern across the three colonies that they discovered while writing the brochures. After producing an outline of the paper, students will use editing groups to refine their ideas. The final draft will also be submitted to editing groups before being given to the teacher for grading.

Applicable North Carolina Standards

- Describe how geographic diversity influenced economic, social, and political life in colonial North America.
- Describe the contributions of various racial, ethnic, and religious groups including African-Americans and Native Americans to the development of a new culture.
- Trace the development of religious liberty and toleration in the new nation.

When designing significant tasks, curriculum authors ultimately use their descriptions to design assessments from the significant task descriptions. (More complete explanation of the assessment process is given in Chapters 15 and 16.)

Significant Tasks Provide a Basis for Lesson Planning by Summarizing 3 to 10 Days' Worth of Instruction

Figure 12.6 demonstrates a significant task from the Middle School Science Curriculum from Newburgh, New York. At the time the curriculum was developed, Newburgh moved to a hands-on science approach. They felt their teachers would benefit from an expanded format for the significant tasks by giving more detail and context than in previous examples of significant tasks.

Figure 12.6   Sample expanded significant task for middle school science (Newburgh, New York)

Significant Task Summary

Students will compare and contrast different forms of living organisms, from one-celled creatures to humans. Students will grasp the concept that living things are similar in construction, yet differ in complexity. Then, using a Venn diagram, students will cite similarities and differences.

What Is the Science?

Living things are similar to each other yet different from nonliving things. The cell is a basic unit of structure and function of living things (cell theory). For all living things, life activities are accomplished at the cellular level. Human beings are an interactive organization of cells, tissues, organs, systems.

Materials: Diagrams of one-celled animal, plant, animal and plant pictures

Vocabulary: Cell, cell wall, stem, root, cortex, phloem, organ, system, nucleus, tissue

Time: Three to four 40-minute periods

Doing the Investigation

- Display pictures of plants, animals and one-celled animals. Have students bring in as many pictures of plants and animals and one-celled animals as possible.
- Have students, using prior knowledge, hypothesize on the differences they see or know concerning the animals in the pictures.
- Have students sort the pictures into categories. Orally discuss the categories they chose and the rationale behind those choices.
- Create Venn diagrams to show the similarities and differences among and between the different categories.
- Use the Venn diagram to summarize in writing the similarities and differences.

Possible Solutions

Living things share the following traits:

- Organisms are made up of cells: one to trillions
- Organisms use water and food, and they produce waste
- Organisms reproduce
- Organisms grow and develop
- Organisms respond
- Organisms adapt to their environment

New York State Science Standards Addressed

Living things are both similar to and different from each other and nonliving things.

- Compare and contrast the parts of plants, animals, and one-celled organisms.
- Conduct a survey of the school grounds and develop appropriate classification keys to group plants and animals by shared characteristics.

SOURCE: Used courtesy of the Newburgh Enlarged City School District.

EXAMPLE OF LESSON PLANNING WITH SIGNIFICANT TASKS

The following section describes a teacher using a significant task to plan a lesson. The teacher, Ms. Creighton, has been teaching middle school science for a number of years. This is the first year of curriculum implementation in science. Previously she had used the district-provided textbook to structure her course. Headers for the discussion provide readers a structure for examining significant tasks and translating them into lesson plans.

Examine, Understand, and Segment the Significant Task

Ms. Creighton: When I first looked at the significant task (see Figure 12.6), it appeared straightforward enough. What students had to do were sort pictures, then learn from sorting the pictures what the similarities and differences were among and between the various groups using a Venn diagram. Then they would write a brief summary of their findings. The textbook had a chapter on characteristics of living things that I will rely on for backup information.

Set Priorities for Instruction

Ms. Creighton: My priorities for instruction are really set out in the significant task summary: "Students will grasp the concept that living things are similar in construction, yet differ in complexity." I started to do a web to figure out the supporting concepts I would need to cover with the students. Some of the concepts I wanted to cover are under the "Possible Solutions" section of the significant task.

Living things share the following traits:

- Organisms are made up of cells—one cell to trillions of them
- Organisms use water and food, and they produce waste
- Organisms reproduce
- Organisms grow and develop
- Organisms respond
- Organisms adapt to their environment

I started to have some difficulties with the significant task because the possible solutions, such as reproduce, grow and develop, and respond (listed in the Possible Solutions section of the significant task), were all functions that living things have in common. If I were given pictures of animals and cells as a student, however, I would probably classify them in terms of size, shape, coloring, and wouldn't even think about the functions.

How do I get students to think about functions of living things?

One way would be to begin by showing a cell after we had read about cellular functions and then show a picture of an elephant; I could then ask how the two are similar. (Because there are few physical similarities in color or shape between an elephant and a cell, the students would have to begin discussing functions.) Then we could list the similarities, bring in pictures of dissimilar living things, and go through the same search for similarities. When we start to see the patterns beginning to emerge through the one-on-one comparisons, we can put all the pairs students brought in to class into the mixture and see if this changes anything. (It wouldn't because we were looking for similarities of living things.)

Examine Alternatives and Begin Sequencing Activities

Ms. Creighton: I wasn't sure whether I should use this as an introductory or a culminating activity. I could probably keep coming back to the comparisons because we kept learning more about life functions, especially as we were working toward the Venn diagram and its summary. So I thought the week could be sequenced by reading and discussing about the life functions of a cell through the chapter in the textbook. Then they'll need to apply the information that they learned in comparing a cell to the elephant. I'll review what a Venn diagram is at this point and use it in our discussion about the similarities and differences between an elephant and a cell.

Homework will consist of the students bringing in odd pairs of living things. The next day, the students could report on their pair's similarities. We construct another Venn diagram in class for each student's pair. The next day, we share our Venn diagrams while keeping notes on the similarities and differences in the Venn diagrams, but especially the similarities (because these will be the life functions). For homework students can begin drafting a paper about similarities and differences in life functions that we'll work on the next day in class with small groups. A final paper will be due the next day. This sounds like a plan.

Think About Assessments

Ms. Creighton: Now that I've done this work, I decide to look at the assessment that the curriculum authors from our district posted on the Balanced Curriculum Web site. (Of course, I realize that I probably should have looked at the assessment first to clarify how I should focus my instruction.) The assessment provides a rubric to use in grading the paper. In addition, I can add my own points for class participation. The attachments section of the Web site highlights copies of student work graded by the rubric, giving me a clear idea of what constituted acceptable work. My plan will help students produce good papers, especially if I use the anchor papers from the Web site as models for students.

Confirm Alignments

Ms. Creighton: My instruction is definitely aligned to the significant task. After checking the New York State Standards, we didn't make a survey of the school grounds for plants and animals, but we did compare and contrast living things, the second part of the standard.

Make Comments for Improvements

Ms. Creighton: I will place a comment on the Web site stating that a survey of the school grounds could be included in the significant task, increasing the alignment to state standards. If my lesson plans work out well, I will also e-mail them to the science supervisor, who may post the lesson plans on the Web site so others can see how another teacher approached the significant task.

Reflections on the Teacher's Thought Processes During Lesson Planning

Ms. Creighton used the significant task as the focus for her lesson planning. The significant task provided structure: a Venn diagram about living things and an essay about the similarities and differences. Despite the detail in the significant task, Ms. Creighton unearthed the possibility that students would compare form and not function, influencing her choice about how to structure the comparison of living things. Her lesson design avoided student misunderstanding. She examined a few ways to sequence the task but appeared certain about the instructional sequence once she had figured out how to focus students on functions of living things. In thinking about the assessment, she would use the provided assessment but add grades for areas, such as participation, that she deemed important. She confirmed the alignments for the significant task as a way to check that her instruction did, indeed, cover important standards. Finally, she used the Web site to comment on the significant task. (Comments like Ms. Creighton's allow good tasks to become better and clearer.)

The significant task actually saved Ms. Creighton time because it highlighted "functions of living things" as an important topic and showed a way to cover it. Ms. Creighton did not have to decide this was important or determine how to cover all the topics in the textbook.

AUTHOR GROUPS CREATE SIGNIFICANT TASKS

Author groups create significant tasks for a course, although individuals can create significant tasks as well. The idea is to capture the best the district has to offer from either individuals or groups of teachers. Authors begin discussing significant tasks when deciding on the scope and sequence of unit titles. They then gather and refine more ideas for significant tasks when formulating the introduction to the unit or examining resource materials from the state. If author groups keep notes, these may provide a starting point to identify the most important and timely significant tasks to place within the curriculum.

Teachers who have had experience in teaching, who are caring about their students, and who know their subject area well make good curriculum authors. Let's listen in as Ricardo and Emily, two curriculum authors, discuss their thought processes when developing significant tasks.

Ricardo: Our group took a while to figure out how to determine the significant tasks. Some of the group wanted to look at the standards, see what they required, and then write significant tasks to address the standards.

Emily: I remember I was one of the authors who disagreed with that approach. I said, "If we have a textbook, we should use it because we know most of the teachers of our course will be using the textbook." There are some great significant tasks in the textbook.

As a matter of fact, there are so many ideas in the textbook and teacher's edition that we could turn into significant tasks, we really didn't need to look further.

Ricardo: Emily, you were very persuasive on that point. But as we talked further, I realized that there are things that I do that are great significant tasks but aren't necessarily in the textbook because they just came out of my head.

Emily: And as the discussion continued, I realized that I got a bunch of great ideas from the Internet. Even the state education department Web site has some great ideas.

Ricardo: As we continued talking, it became clear that we needed to develop the strongest significant tasks, and it really didn't matter whether we made them up, got them from the textbook or Web sites, or derived them from the state standards.

Emily: That was great experience for me because I got to hear all the other curriculum authors' ideas about activities that would make great significant tasks.

Ricardo: Once we decided that it didn't matter where the significant tasks came from, we had the problem of figuring out how to organize ourselves to get the job done. At first, we all stuck together. Emily, do you remember it took us a couple of hours to talk through the first significant task?

Emily: By that time, I needed a break. The next few significant tasks went much more smoothly and quickly. We got in a groove. I started to see the patterns in other authors' thinking about significant tasks. I started to trust that they would do a good job, even if I wasn't around to put in my two cents' worth.

Ricardo: That was when we decided to work in pairs, with each pair taking a unit, and developing the significant tasks for that unit.

Emily and Ricardo did make a good team in writing significant tasks because they understood that significant tasks could come from a variety of sources. The most important thing authors can do out of a welter of possibilities is choose the significant tasks that they believe have the best chance in helping students perform to high standards.

BOTTOM-UP OR TOP-DOWN PLANNING?

Chicken-and-egg problems are alive and well. Do authors start with their good ideas first and incorporate the standards second—the bottom-up approach? Or do authors begin with the standards and let the content of the standards suggest good ideas for significant tasks—the top-down approach? Author groups should try out various ways of generating significant tasks so that they understand the different thought processes involved in the top-down and bottom-up approaches. Groups should spend some time discussing the process of creating significant tasks. Author groups may experience conflicts if they have different approaches to developing significant tasks.

The steps for creating significant tasks using the bottom-up approach are outlined in the following pages.

STEPS FOR CREATING SIGNIFICANT TASKS: THE BOTTOM-UP APPROACH (DEFINE TASKS AND THEN REFER TO STANDARDS)

1. *Locate* tasks within a unit.
2. *Describe* possible unit activities, including how students will demonstrate their learning.
3. *Chunk* activities into tasks.
4. *Describe* the most important activity in each chunk.
5. *Add or modify* an objective to incorporate language from the standards
6. *Validate* the significant task with five questions for quality control.
7. *Visualize* the assessment

1. *Locate* Tasks Within a Unit

This is easy. Authors already have a list of unit titles that the grade or subject teachers agreed on.

2. *Describe* Unit Activities, Including How Students Will Demonstrate Their Learning

Let's listen as two 9th-grade teachers from Texas, Don and Belinda, converse about how they approach a unit on writing a speech using a bottom-up approach.

Belinda: Don, you and I decided to develop our significant task using the bottom-up approach to our speech unit.

Don: I generally start out the speech unit by listening to short excerpts of some speeches. Then the students and I discuss what we liked about each of the speeches. The Net has some great Web sites where speeches can be downloaded. I also have some video clips of speeches from famous people in history or people in the news today making short speeches.

Belinda: I start by showing students a script of a speech and having them read it over. Then we take a look at how a number of people have completed the same speech.

Don: The next thing we talk about is presentation techniques. This includes the use of the voice and also the way the text is organized. We ask the students to use the parts of speeches to identify how various presentation techniques are used. Then students make a list of presentation techniques that they would like to use in their speeches.

Belinda: I do that later. Before I look at presentation techniques, we brainstorm some topics on which they would like to make a speech.

Don: That's usually the last thing I do. I don't want to close out their options too soon.

Belinda: I find if students have a topic, then they can spend time on actually organizing and polishing their speech. I guess we differ on sequence here.

Don: But I know both of us concentrate on the organization of the speech. We talk about what makes a good beginning, how to choose relevant examples, and how to sequence and structure the argument.

Belinda: Right. And during those discussions we generate criteria that we will use to evaluate the speeches when they are given in class. In that way, when students are organizing for their speech, they know what is expected. I generally turn those criteria into rubrics that everyone in the class uses to evaluate the speeches.

Don: I use small writing groups of three or four students who help each other through the stages of writing and delivering the speech. I know that you have used writing groups throughout the year, so this process won't be foreign to any of our students.

Belinda: In the past, we have taped the speeches, and kids receive their own video-tape so they can do a self-evaluation using the same rubrics the class uses. Do you think this is too much pressure?

Don: No. I help out by videotaping myself at some point during the unit. Then we use the videotape to practice applying the rubrics. Students have a great time joking about the inevitable mess-ups I make. It also gives us time to discuss how to make this activity safe so that students can take some risks. We generate rules for discussing the tapes in the class and in the small writing groups.

Belinda: Anything else that's super important that we want to include in the unit?

Don: I'm sure there are lots of "variations on the theme," but I think we have mentioned all the important activities.

Commentary

Don and Belinda agreed to do a unit on giving a speech. Each approached the unit in different ways. Yet common significant tasks emerged. Indeed, there may be too many good ideas in this unit for the amount of time available. Don and Belinda placed their good ideas on the table, without arguing about which one was best. In this way, they opened a space for dialogue and reflection. When Don and Belinda had the discussion, they went ahead and listed many ideas without the interruption of having to judge whether the ideas were good or not so good. Consequently, many good ideas surfaced. Now they have to bring more order to the ideas by chunking the activities into tasks.

3. Chunking Activities Into Tasks

After more discussion, Don and Belinda made an outline of the activities they would both cover during the unit. The outline included as many of the activities that they thought could reasonably fit into the unit's time frame.

Don and Belinda's Outline of Activities

1. Use tapes of actual speeches and discuss with students what they liked and didn't like about the speeches.

2. Examine a few speech scripts and see how different people, including some students, delivered them.

3. Brainstorm topics for student speeches.

4. Identify techniques for organization of speeches.

5. Identify techniques for delivery of speeches.

6. Generate criteria for evaluating delivery and organization of speeches.

7. Use small writing groups to provide feedback to students.

8. Set rules for delivering feedback on speeches the students give.

9. Students become familiar with using rubrics to evaluate speeches.

10. Use videotape to encourage student self-evaluation.

From this list of ideas, Don and Belinda then chunked or grouped the activities that went together. They thought about what made instructional sense from a student's viewpoint and from the experience of other teachers who would also be teaching the units. In their discussion, they narrowed down the possibilities so that they had what they considered the best summary of the many activities in the unit.

Don and Belinda discussed the 10 proposed activities to see if they could chunk the activities into two to five segments. They came up with the following:

- Develop criteria for good speeches through viewing, listening, and reflecting on a number of speech models with particular attention to organization and delivery of speeches.
- Work in small groups to assist others in crafting the organization and delivery for a speech.
- Evaluate speeches through rubrics developed by the class.

4. Describe the Most Important Activity in Each Chunk

Don and Belinda came to understand that their focus in the speech unit was to assist students in developing and applying criteria for good speeches. They felt that if students understood the criteria for good speeches, then, as they went through their life and had to deliver and listen to speeches, they would have an adequate framework to do this effectively. Therefore, each significant task concentrated on developing and using the criteria for good speeches. Once they understood that this was their focus, they strengthened the second significant task in the unit:

Work in small groups to assist others in crafting a speech's organization and delivery using the criteria developed for the organization and delivery of speeches.

5. Add or Modify an Objective to Incorporate Language From the Standards

To help add standards-based language to these activities, Don and Belinda looked at the Texas Essential Knowledge and Skills (TEKS), the Texas standards. Don and Belinda went through and underlined all the words from the standards that they wanted to incorporate in their significant tasks. Next, they figured out ways to incorporate the ideas from the standards into their significant tasks. Figure 12.7 shows the pieces of the standards Don and Belinda incorporated into their significant tasks.

Figure 12.7 Standards aligned to significant tasks.

Texas Essential Knowledge and Skills

8.2 Listening/speaking/critical listening. The student listens <u>critically to analyze</u> and evaluate a speaker's message(s):

    A. interpret speakers' messages (both verbal and nonverbal), purposes, and perspectives (4–8);

    B. analyze a speaker's <u>persuasive techniques and credibility</u> (7–8);

    C. distinguish between the speaker's opinion and verifiable fact (4–8);

    D. monitor his or her understanding of the spoken message and seek clarification as needed (4–8);

    E. <u>compare his or her own perception of a spoken message with the perception of others</u> (6–8); and

    F. <u>evaluate</u> a spoken message in terms of its content, <u>credibility, and delivery</u> (6–8).

Develop criteria for good speeches through viewing, listening <u>critically, analyzing</u> and reflecting on a number of speech modes with particular attention to the organization, <u>persuasive techniques, speaker's credibility</u> and delivery of speeches. <u>This whole-class activity will allow students to compare their own perception of a spoken message with the perceptions of others</u>.

---

6. Validate the Significant Task Using Five Questions for Quality Control

The authors checked to see if they could answer "yes" to five questions to validate the significant task:

1. Does the significant task include an activity that can guide instruction?

2. Does the significant task include language from the standards?

3. Is the significant task description complex yet doable for most students?

4. If students successfully complete this significant task, will they understand the ideas, concepts, processes, and procedures from the standards embedded within the significant task?

5. Will the significant tasks in the unit take (consume) 60% of the unit's allocated time?

More explanation about validating significant tasks occurs later in the chapter.

7. Visualize the Assessment

Significant tasks link instruction and assessment because each significant task is assessed. Authors determine whether the significant task is specific enough to yield an assessment. Using the significant tasks from the speech unit, Don and Belinda decided that the assessment for the first task would be the list of written criteria that the class arrived at after listening to speeches. The student who receives group help can evaluate the second task. The student will fill out a feedback form about what the group did that was most helpful to him or her in crafting a speech. The teacher keeps a record to make sure everyone completed that form because the group would help everyone at some point during the unit. The last significant task can be evaluated by giving students credit for filling out the rubrics for the speeches given in class. Students who give supporting comments would receive higher marks. All the significant tasks are specific enough to support assessments.

Speech Unit Significant Tasks

- Develop criteria for good speeches through viewing, listening critically, analyzing, and reflecting on a number of speech modes, with particular attention to the organization, persuasive techniques, speaker's credibility, and delivery of speeches. This whole-class activity will allow students to compare their own perception of a spoken message with the perceptions of others.
- Work in small groups to assist others in crafting a speech's organization and delivery.
- Evaluate speeches through rubrics developed by the class.

STEPS FOR CREATING SIGNIFICANT TASKS: THE TOP-DOWN APPROACH (GENERATE SIGNIFICANT TASKS BY REFERRING TO STANDARDS FIRST)

The top-down approach to creating significant tasks uses the standards as a springboard for generating possible activities. Significant tasks created in this way emphasize the alignment of the standards with the significant task. Some authors prefer to begin with the standards because the significant tasks will eventually need to be aligned with the standards. Other authors prefer to start with a robust activity that is familiar and then determine how the standards are addressed.

1. *Locate* task within a unit.

2. *Examine* standards to determine possible activities.

3. *Describe* possible unit activities, including how students will demonstrate their learning.

4. *Chunk* activities into tasks.

5. *Describe* the most important activity in each chunk.

6. *Validate* the significant task with five questions for quality control.

7. *Visualize* the assessment.

Because I have already identified the speech unit (Step 1), we now skip to Step 2 in the top-down approach. Don and Belinda examine the standards first to generate the significant tasks for the speech unit. A more complete list of the Texas Essential Knowledge and Skills is provided in Figure 12.8 as a reference. This is not the complete list but only the standards that pertain to speeches.

2. *Examine* Standards to Determine Possible Activities

Don: Beginning with the standards helps me to consider the full range of the standards before I figure out what the activity should be.

Belinda: That's our first challenge—figuring out which standards to emphasize, then designing significant tasks to address those important standards.

Figure 12.8 Using Texas Essential Knowledge and Skills (TEKS) to generate significant tasks

---

8.2. Listening/speaking/critical listening. DB The student listens critically to analyze and evaluate a speaker's message(s).

DB A. Interpret speakers' messages (both verbal and nonverbal), purposes, and perspectives (4-8);

B B. Analyze a speaker's persuasive techniques and credibility (7-8);

C. Distinguish between the speaker's opinion and verifiable fact (4-8);

D. Monitor his/her own understanding of the spoken message and seek clarification as needed (4-8);

DB E. Compare his/her own perception of a spoken message with the perception of others (6-8); and

DB F. Evaluate a spoken message in terms of its content, credibility, and delivery (6-8).

8.5. Listening/speaking/audiences. The student speaks clearly and appropriately to different audiences for different purposes and occasions. The student is expected to:

D A. Adapt spoken language such as word choice, diction, and usage to the audience, purpose, and occasion (4-8);

B. Demonstrate effective communications skills that reflect such demands as interviewing, reporting, requesting, and providing information (4-8);

C. Present dramatic interpretations of experiences, stories, poems, or plays to communicate (4-8);

DB D. Generate criteria to evaluate his/her own oral presentations and the presentations of others (6-8);

DB E. Use effective rate, volume, pitch, and tone for the audience and setting (4-8); and

D F. Clarify and support spoken ideas with evidence, elaborations, and examples (4-8).

8.24. Viewing/representing/production. The student produces visual images, messages, and meanings that communicate with others. The student is expected to:

B A. Select, organize, or produce visuals to complement and extend meanings (4-8);

B. Produce communications using technology or appropriate media such as developing a class newspaper, multimedia reports, or video reports (4-8); and

DB C. Assess how language, medium, and presentation contribute to the message (6-8).

Don: Let's both read through the standards and put our initials next to the ones we feel are most important in this unit.

Belinda: Good idea. (Don places a D by the standards that are important for him, and Belinda places a B next to the standards that are important to her.)

Don: I see we almost agree on which standards to emphasize. As I read through the standards, I started seeing students giving speeches and then evaluating how they did on the speeches that they just presented. That was one of the reasons I thought 8.5A and 8.5F were important in giving speeches; students would need to adapt their language to the speech topic and support spoken ideas with evidence.

Belinda: I chose 8.2B for the same reason, because I would like to have the class analyze a speaker's techniques. I suppose we could review a series of speeches, perhaps from famous speeches in history, and discuss the techniques used. Then the students could practice applying some of those techniques to their speeches.

Don: Great idea! Models usually help students get the picture. So if 8.2B is important, then we will be focusing on a "persuasive" speech. Perhaps we should do something around persuading people to buy something.

Belinda: Or we could identify issues, either from concerns out there in the school—like the proposal for shorter lunch periods—and use that for our topic.

Don: That would work except that I don't want to sit and listen to 25 speeches on why we should or should not have shortened lunch periods.

Belinda: Do we need to give the students persuasive topics at all?

Don: Good question. We could have them figure out their own topic for a speech. Then there would be sure to be a variety, although that would take more time.

Belinda: So we have a persuasive speech; students will generate their own topics. I noticed we also agreed on 8.2E and F, focusing on comparing student perceptions of speeches and evaluating speeches. Those seem to go hand in hand. 8.5D and E centers on generating criteria for evaluating their own presentations. Now that's something important. We're trying to get students to know "intuitively" what makes up a good persuasive speech.

Don: Maybe that's where we use the models. Perhaps we could use the models to help generate criteria for good persuasive speeches with the students.

Belinda: That means we will need to cover persuasive techniques used in speeches. Then we'll need the models of the ones that we decide to emphasize.

Don: If we videotaped the speeches, we would have student models for next year. That might be fun.

Belinda: Of course, time is a factor. Do you think videotaping speeches would take that much longer?

Don: If we videotape, students will want to see the videotape, so that has the potential to take twice as long. And everyone would see each speech twice. Another alternative would be to have the individual student take the evaluations and feedback that they got from applying our criteria to the speech and review that feedback on the basis of what they saw on the videotape. Then they could respond to the responses.

Belinda: I just don't know if we'll have time to do that. And how would students respond to the feedback?

Don: Tell whether they agree with it or not, then cite examples from the videotape. Then the class and we, as teachers, wouldn't have to watch a speech twice. This would also cover more of the standards in 8.24 because students would need to view their speech.

Belinda: I'm not sure how to use 8.24C that asks the students to assess how the language, medium, and presentation contribute to the message.

Don: Perhaps that should be one that we don't specifically address, even though we both thought it was important.

3. Describe Possible Unit Activities Including How Students Will Demonstrate Their Learning

Belinda: To summarize, we've decided on a persuasive speech as the focus for this unit. We'll use models of persuasive speeches to develop criteria for good persuasive speeches. Students will choose their own topics and then plan their speech so that the criteria are met. Then students will present their persuasive speech to the class while being videotaped. The audience will give the speech-maker feedback using the criteria for good speeches. The speechmaker will then take the video home and determine whether the class's feedback was accurate. The student will then write a short response to the feedback citing examples from the videotape.

Don: That sounds great. Now we need to "chunk" the list of activities into significant tasks making sure we incorporate the language from the standards we've agreed to address. (After more discussion, Don and Belinda came up with the following list of significant tasks.)

4. Chunk Activities Into Tasks

1. Listen and analyze models of persuasive speeches.

2. Choose topics for speeches.

3. Outline speeches and check against class-generated criteria.

4. Give speech and receive feedback.

5. Review video of speech to determine accuracy of feedback.

5. Describe the Most Important Activity in Each Chunk

a. Students will listen to and analyze models of persuasive speeches to develop criteria for good persuasive speeches that take into account evaluating the content, credibility, persuasive techniques, and delivery of the speech.

b. In small "author" groups, students will brainstorm and help each other choose topics for their persuasive speech.

c. Students will then help each other construct an outline of the speech that will meet the criteria the class generated.

d. Students will present their persuasive speech to the class while being video-taped. The audience will give the speechmaker feedback using the criteria for good speeches.

e. The speechmaker will take the video home and determine whether the classes feedback was accurate. The student will then write a short response to the feedback citing examples from the videotape.

6. Validate the Significant Task With Five Questions for Quality Control

This time, we demonstrate how the significant tasks meet the criteria for quality control or we discuss changing the significant tasks so they meet the criteria for quality control.

Does the Significant Task Include an Activity That Can Guide Instruction?

Following are the most important activities listed in each example:

a. Develop criteria for good speeches

b. Choose topics for the speeches

c. Construct a speech outline

d. Present speech to class. Receive feedback.

e. View videotape and feedback for accuracy. Write a short response to the feedback.

Note that the activities in the significant task are what students should know and be able to do, not what teachers will do.

Does the Significant Task Include Language From the Standards?

a. "Evaluating content, credibility, persuasive techniques and delivery of the speech," TEKS 8.2B and F. "[G]enerate criteria to evaluate presentations," TEKS 8.5D.

b. Necessary to do but does not address any listed standards. This significant task could be linked to TEKS 8.2E: "monitor understanding and seek clarification if needed," and the link could be established by changing the significant task to the following: In small "author" groups, students will brainstorm and help each other choose topics for their persuasive speech, while monitoring their understanding and seeking clarification if needed." Not all significant tasks will have direct links to the standards, although most will.

c. Students will need to check the outline of their speech against the criteria generated by the class: "generate criteria to evaluate presentations," TEKS 8.5D.

d. When giving the speech, students will be judged on criteria generated by the class: "generate criteria to evaluate presentations," TEKS 8.5D.

e. When viewing the video at home, the class criteria will be employed: "generate criteria to evaluate presentations," TEKS 8.5D.

A validator might question whether the significant task employs standard 8.5D *too much*. Should other standards in speaking and listening be incorporated more than they are?

Is the Significant Task Description Complex Yet Doable for Most Students?

a. The central focus of this significant task is applying class-generated criteria to speeches. This presupposes that the class-generated criteria are robust. If the criteria were weak, then applying weak criteria to speeches wouldn't help students improve. Designing the criteria as a whole group ensures that the teacher will be able to guide the class to generate good criteria. Because the teacher is in control of the activity, this appears to be a reasonable assumption. The significant task is complex yet doable.

b. For a validator to agree that this is complex yet doable depends on what experiences students have had with author groups and the process of brainstorming. A validator might want to look at previous units to ensure that students had enough practice in author groups so that this task would be doable without consuming a lot of time.

c. Again, the validator would need to consider whether students had experience with constructing outlines in author groups. The validator might review previous units to determine whether outlines had been introduced, whether adequate practice on making outlines was included in previous units, and whether students had practice helping each other on writing outlines or working on outlines in author groups.

d. Don and Belinda discussed the amount of time videotaping the class would consume. The validator might question whether teachers had access to videotaping equipment, whether they knew how to use the equipment, and whether they had practice using the equipment. Answers to such questions contribute to whether the significant task is doable.

e. The validator might question whether all students have access to videotape machines at home or outside of school. The task is doable if the access problem can be solved.

Complexity. Complexity was not discussed in applying the criteria. Each task is complex in that they address the upper levels of Bloom's taxonomy: analysis, synthesis, and evaluation. As students apply the criteria for good speeches over and over again for each member of the class and for themselves, they start to internalize the "standards" for good speeches.

If Students Successfully Complete This Significant Task, Will They Understand the Ideas, Concepts, Processes, and Procedures From the Standards Embedded Within the Significant Task?

To complete the significant task on speeches, students will have made and presented a speech, developed criteria for good speeches, and applied those criteria while developing their own speech and listening and evaluating others' speeches. Based on the amount of practice students will get in applying the criteria, they will understand what is involved in making a persuasive speech.

Will the Significant Tasks in the Unit
Take (Consume) 60% of the Unit's Allocated Time?

Both Don and Belinda, in formulating the significant task, expressed concern about the amount of time needed to complete all the significant tasks. The validator provides an additional check to determine whether enough time has been allocated for the unit.

7. Visualize the Assessment

Each of the significant tasks is centered on the student demonstrating important parts of creating a persuasive speech. Student-centered significant tasks lend themselves to assessment because the student creates a product or performance that is the focus of the assessment.

a. Class-generated criteria for speeches.

b. Individuals choose speech topics with help of author groups.

c. Individuals outline their speeches with help from author groups and tell how the speech will meet the criteria.

d. The speech is presented to the class (a performance), and the members of the class apply the criteria.

e. The speechmaker applies the criteria to the videotape of the speech and checks to see that the classes perceptions were accurate. This could be evaluated in the speechmaker's short response to the feedback.

The checklist in Figure 12.9 is one way validators can provide feedback to authors.

Figure 12.9   Validator's checklist for significant tasks

Grade/Course _____ Unit Code _____ Date of Validation _____ Validator _____

	Activity 1	Activity 2	Activity 3	Activity 4	Activity 5
1. Does the description include an activity that can guide instruction?	Y N	Y N	Y N	Y N	Y N
2. Does the description include an objective that can guide instruction?	Y N	Y N	Y N	Y N	Y N
3. Is the description complex yet doable?	H M L	H M L	H M L	H M L	H M L
4. If students successfully complete this activity, will they understand the ideas, concepts, processes and procedures?	H M L	H M L	H M L	H M L	H M L

NOTE: Y = yes; N = no; H = high; M = medium; L = low.

Commentary

Developing the activities from the standards ensures that the activities actually reflect the standards. Don and Belinda agreed on most of the important standards and could see where the ones important to the other might fit. The standards led them to focus on a persuasive speech. The significant tasks also emerged differently from the bottom-up example. The videotaping of the speech ensures that standard 8.24 becomes much more important than for the bottom-up model. So using the top-down process may ensure more coverage of the standards. The bottom-up process emphasizes teachers knowledge and experience. Which is best? Author teams will generate ways of collaborating that work best for them. There are many roads to a single destination.

SUMMARY

This chapter focused on significant tasks with an explanation of what they are and offered two scenarios of how to construct significant tasks. Curriculum validators use five questions to ensure the quality of significant tasks. The next chapter provides background on aligning the curriculum. Using that discussion, the chapter describes how the balanced curriculum process uses alignment to continue to focus the curriculum on important standards and assessments.

13

Aligning the Balanced Curriculum With Standards and Assessments

I n this chapter, dimensions of alignment for the Balanced Curriculum process is shown using the alignment octagon introduced in Chapter 4. Rules for aligning the curriculum are given and illustrated using sample significant tasks.

In many schools, textbook adoption is the main tool used to control the content of the curriculum. Adopting a textbook is assumed to structure the content and sequence of instruction, student assignments, and lesson planning, assuming the textbook is used by most teachers as the primary tool for instruction. The Balanced Curriculum rests on a different assumption.

In the Balanced Curriculum process, significant tasks, not textbooks, focus the curriculum and alignment efforts. In the Balanced Curriculum process, significant tasks directly align with student assignments because significant tasks are written as an expression of what students know and are able to do. Student assignments in turn form the foundation for lesson planning because the significant tasks represent 60% of the time available for a particular course or subject area.

Individual teachers sequence the significant task into lessons so that the significant task is aligned with lesson plans. Principals will need to check lesson plans to determine whether they support student completion of the significant tasks.

The significant tasks align to lesson plans that then direct teacher instruction and student assignments. The sum of the student assignments results in the completion of the significant task. Thus, the significant task is aligned to instruction, lesson plans, and student assignments, although the teacher has flexibility in deciding, based on the

Figure 13.1   Alignments of balanced curriculum to instructional components

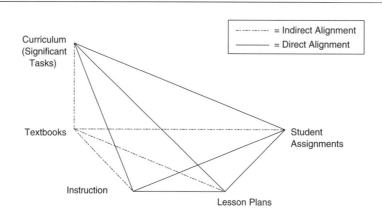

unique characteristics of the class, how to sequence the instruction, the lesson plans, and student assignments so that the significant task is completed successfully by all students.

The relationship of the significant task to the textbook is not as connected or aligned. The significant task may or may not require use of the textbook. The text-book is meant to be used as a resource for the teacher. The significant tasks, not the textbook, form the basis for sequencing instruction. Where necessary, the significant task may reference material or projects based in the textbook. Generally in the Balanced Curriculum process, there is little concern about "covering" the textbook because the textbook probably doesn't cover everything in the standards and state or standardized assessments. The written curriculum (the significant tasks), then, is aligned to the taught curriculum, as is shown in Figure 13.1.

Significant tasks are also aligned to curriculum-embedded assessment because each significant task requires a content assessment (Figure 13.2) that assesses how students demonstrated their knowledge of the content required in the significant task.

Figure 13.2   Alignments of balanced curriculum with instruction and curriculum-embedded assessments

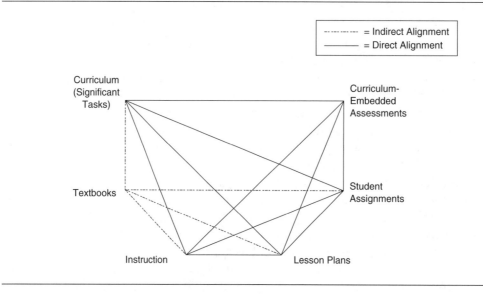

Curriculum-embedded assessments are directly aligned to student assignments, lesson plans, and instruction because they assess the culmination or performance of the significant task that teachers and students have been working toward completing.

Next let's examine how significant tasks are aligned to standards and standardized and state tests (Figure 13.3). Each significant task is aligned directly to state standards and then again to standardized tests or state tests (or both). The Balanced Curriculum is not concerned with alignment between state standards and testing (although this is important). Rather, by aligning to both the standards and the item specifications for the tests, alignment is achieved. Many curriculum authors decide to place more emphasis on the alignment to the tests because this accountability measure is widely publicized. This, then, becomes a matter of balance to be discussed in the next chapter.

Figure 13.3 Alignment of significant tasks to state standards, standardized tests, and state tests in the Balanced Curriculum process

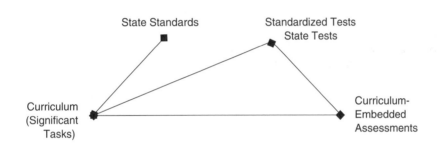

ALIGNMENT OF SIGNIFICANT TASKS TO STATE STANDARDS, STANDARDIZED TESTS, AND STATE TESTS IN THE BALANCED CURRICULUM PROCESS

Curriculum-embedded assessments that happen once every unit provide students with practice of the format and content of the standardized or state test. This is called a format assessment. The format assessment uses a version of Wishnick's Alignment Measurement Scale (1989) to ensure that students have practice with all of the formats of the standardized and state test. See Chapter 5 for an explanation.

State standards and standardized and state tests have an indirect alignment with instruction, lesson plans, and student assignments because significant tasks are the lynchpin of alignment (Figure 13.3). Putting the complete alignment of the Balanced Curriculum together produces the graphic in Figure 13.4.

Figure 13.4 Alignment model for the Balanced Curriculum process

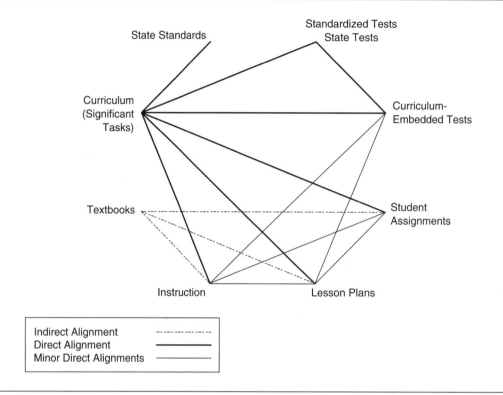

The significant tasks of the curriculum have direct alignment with instruction, including lesson plans and student assignments, assessments, and standards. The significant tasks align to important parts of the standards, forming a coherent whole representing a goal for instruction, lesson plans, and student assignments. Significant tasks de-emphasize the textbook by using the text as a resource for significant tasks that govern instruction. Curriculum-embedded tests are aligned to both significant task (content assessment) and the formats of the state and standardized test (format assessment). State, standardized, and curriculum-embedded assessments are aligned, but assessments don't have an overarching emphasis reflecting the notion that curriculum drives assessments, not the other way around. Not all possible alignments are covered, but the important ones are included in the Balanced Curriculum model.

ALIGNING THE BALANCED CURRICULUM

Alignment can take many forms, use a variety of criteria to determine the degree of alignment, and align to many aspects of the written, taught, and tested curriculum.

Many districts claim to have completed alignment, but questions need to be raised about what exactly this means. The Balanced Curriculum process uses significant tasks as the focus of curriculum and consequently as the focus for alignment. Sample significant tasks are provided in the box that follows.

Units/Significant Tasks
2003–2004
Science High School
Southern Connecticut State University
Physics Dumais 03A

Unit: Kinematics in One Dimension

Students will use the basic measures of kinematics—displacement, velocity, acceleration, and time—along with conceptual, numerical, and graphical methods to solve problems involving the linear motion of objects. Students will need to interpret the results of experimentation using statistical reasoning and use technology and mathematics to improve investigations and communications through the use of the calculator-based laboratory equipment.

Significant Tasks

Displacement, Speed, and Velocity

We will identify and utilize the basic definitions of descriptors of the motion of objects. We will differentiate between the magnitudes of displacement and velocity and their corresponding directions. Data will be collected and analyzed for systems that are designed to demonstrate uniform (constant velocity) motion.

The data will be statistically interpreted, and a written scientific report will be produced to communicate the process and the results logically. Using calculator-based laboratory equipment, we will identify and reproduce graphical representations of linear motion involving constant velocity.

Acceleration

We will define acceleration and establish its relationship to the change in velocity of an object moving in one-dimensional motion. We will differentiate between the magnitude of acceleration and its corresponding direction. Data will be collected and analyzed for systems that are designed to demonstrate uniform (constant acceleration) motion. The data will be statistically interpreted, and a written scientific report will be produced to communicate the process and the results logically. Using calculator-based laboratory equipment, we will identify and reproduce graphical representations of linear motion involving constant acceleration. In our investigation of constant acceleration, we will examine the specific case of the acceleration due to gravity by experimentally determining the acceleration of a falling object. This will be accomplished through calculations made from the measurement of the object's position as a function of time. The concept of change and the constancy of the direction of the acceleration due to gravity will be examined by analyzing the data produced by an object rolling up and down an inclined plane.

SOURCE: Used with permission by Charles Dumais.

We define the curriculum for all students by curriculum authors choosing significant tasks. When these tasks are performed well by students, we assume that students have mastered a portion of the curriculum. We use the significant tasks because we assume that all students do not have access to a high-quality curriculum.

Remember what happened to you as a new teacher, receiving a huge stack of material and being left on your own to decide what was most important to teach? Curriculum is there to help focus teachers on the most significant tasks in the curriculum.

If teachers are encouraged to do their own thing, students will have a wide variety of experiences, some aligned to important standards and outcomes, some not. When they move to the next grade or course, the group will have a mix of prerequisite skills, making instruction for the new teacher more difficult than if most entered the grade having similar instructional experiences. We know that our best teachers have developed significant tasks over a number of years that produce good results. In defining the curriculum, we start the alignment process by narrowing how we define instruction; we define instruction by significant tasks that occupy about 60% of the unit's instructional time, the tasks the best teachers feel most students can master. The curriculum is then thin with a limited number (35 to 50) of significant tasks for a year-long course.

The significant task describes a task or activity that all students will accomplish. The activities link with an objective—a description of what the task accomplishes. The objective provides the link to align the significant tasks with the standards and assessments. Standards and assessments are usually described with statements about the general learning that should take place. For example, a standard might read, "Gather and interpret information from such forms as charts, graphs, maps, and diagrams." This tells *what* the task should accomplish, just as the objective part of the significant task tells what the task should accomplish. The standard or assessment usually does not tell *how* that task should be accomplished, however; the task or activity does that. Obviously, the task could be accomplished in many ways. The significant task provides one powerful way that most children demonstrate their understanding of the standard or assessment. Thus, the objective is the link between the significant task and the standard and assessment (Figure 13.5).

Alignment is the process of linking a significant task with the standards or assessment. The activity describes what all students should do; the objective provides the link to the standard or assessment.

Figure 13.5 Significant task links activities and objectives to standards and assessments

SOURCE: Copyright © ABC Education Consultants, LLC.

When we developed significant tasks, we developed the most important activities that would take up about 60% of our teaching time. Simply developing the significant tasks did not tell us whether the curriculum aligns with important standards and assessments, or whether the curriculum was in balance. Developing the significant tasks alone was not enough to ensure a balanced and aligned curriculum.

When we described the significant tasks, we established the link between the instruction and the assessments or standards. The objectives are the link we use for alignment. The standards and the assessments are written in the language of objectives. Thus, both the significant tasks and the standards and assessments are using the same language. This allows alignment to take place.

From reviewing the important standards and assessments for your school or district, you know that there are

- Hundreds of standards and assessments objectives
- 35 to 50 significant tasks

Therefore, each of the significant tasks will need to be aligned with and carry the weight of a number of standards and assessments (Figure 13.6). Like a pinball, one significant task will target and "light up" many standards.

Figure 13.6 The pinball principle: One significant task "lights" many standards

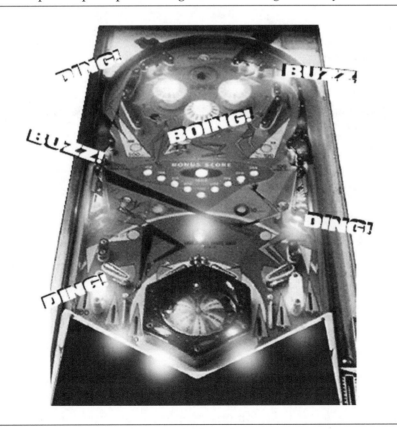

Alignment is a tedious chore; each significant task is aligned to the state standards, national professional standards, characteristics of good programs in particular subject areas, state assessments, standardized assessments, and other areas of importance such as the Comer developmental pathways and Bloom's taxonomy. The number of significant tasks is limited, in part because the alignment task would be larger if there were more significant tasks.

SETTING UP COURSES TO ALIGN WITH STANDARDS ON THE WEB SITE

Once a system administrator user is registered on the Balanced Curriculum Web site, they will start to define courses. Part of the course definition process is to assign standards to the course. A Texas school district would align its courses to the TEKS (Texas Essential Knowledge and Skills), the state's standards for the appropriate subject and grade level. (Chapters 5, 6, and 8 explain the standards available on the Web site.) Curriculum authors then review the applicable standards and write the significant tasks. After validating the significant tasks, the curriculum authors are ready for the alignment process (Figure 13.7).

Figure 13.7   Assigning standards to a course on the Web site

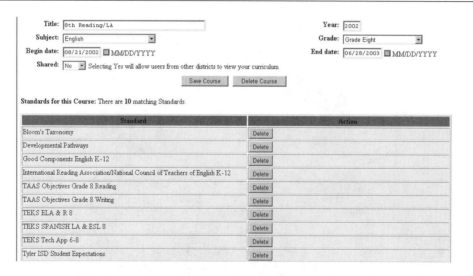

Most teachers, as experts in their subject matter, can align a significant task to a great many standards. For example, for the significant task shown next, most of the following standards in Figure 13.8 might apply.

"We will gather information to support our ideas about saving the environment and cite examples from famous people's lives, from news articles, from fiction or nonfiction books, or from television by taking notes and preparing a paper about our idea."

The case has been made that this significant task aligns to all of New York's Intermediate Listening and Reading Standards (Figure 13.8). Indeed, most significant tasks will align to many standards. If most standards apply to most significant tasks, however, then the strength and utility of aligning the curriculum is diminished. If all activities can align to most standards, then we don't really have a way of knowing what is of most importance.

To improve the utility of the alignment process, alignment to standards is limited to what the curriculum authors feel are the most important standards. For example, curriculum authors are generally limited to five alignments for each major standard. For all of the New York English and language arts standards, only five alignments for each significant task are allowed.

Figure 13.8   New York Intermediate Listening and Reading Standards for Grades 5–8

Grade 5	2000–2001

NY ELA Standard 1 Intermediate

Listening and Reading

I1-LRc	Interpret and analyze information from graphs, charts, diagrams, and electronic databases intended for a general audience.
I1A	Listening and reading to acquire information and understanding involves collecting data, facts, and ideas.
I1B	Listening and reading to acquire information and understanding involves discovering relationships, concepts, and generalizations.
I1C	Listening and reading to acquire information and understanding involves using knowledge from oral, written, and electronic sources.
I1-LR-1	Produce a summary of the information about a famous person found in a biography, encyclopedia, and textbook.
I1-LR-2	Use facts and data from news articles and television reports in an oral report on a current event.
I1-LR-3	Compile a bibliography of sources that are used in a research project.
I1-LR-4	Take notes that record the main ideas and most significant supporting details of lecture or speech.
I1-LRa	Interpret and analyze information from textbooks and nonfiction books for young adults.
I1-LRb	Interpret and analyze information from reference materials, audio and media presentations and oral interviews.
I1-LRd	Compare and synthesize information from different sources.
I1-LRe	Use a wide variety of strategies for selecting, organizing, and categorizing information.
I1-LRf	Distinguish between relevant and irrelevant information.
I1-LRg	Distinguish between fact and opinion.
I1-LRh	Relate new information to prior knowledge and experience.
I1-LRi	Understand and use the text features that make information accessible and usable, such as format, sequence, level of diction, and relevance of details.

When the alignments are summarized, we must use our professional expertise to make decisions about the standards that capture the essence of each significant task. To assist us in exercising our professional expertise, three rules guide decisions:

1. Link vocabulary

2. Limit assumptions

3. Limit alignments

Link Vocabulary

A significant task aligns to a standard only if the significant task's vocabulary is the same as the vocabulary of the standard. The vocabulary must be linked. If a link that should be there is not, change the significant task. For example, in the significant task that follows (Figure 13.9), the main "vocabulary" is underlined with numbers in parentheses to indicate the possibility of alignment. An alignment arrow points from the significant task to the standard. A discussion about each possible alignment is included in Figure 13.9.

Limit Assumptions

If the vocabulary is not the same, do not assume alignments. Most significant tasks can be aligned to most standards when many assumptions are made. Don't make those assumptions.

Point 7 from the Figure 13.9 shows that producing a paper is not the same as "Understanding and using text features," even though we might *assume* that we would pay attention to text features if we produced a paper. We may want to pay attention to text features because we feel this is an important idea to emphasize, and this would change the significant task. Making the alignment specific and detailed by limiting assumptions helps to strengthen the significant task.

Limit Alignments

Choose only the alignments that are most important. Generally, a significant task may be aligned with numerous standards. The alignments are limited to make the task more manageable and also to ensure the choosing of important standards for each significant task. In the example in Figure 13.9, we are limited to three alignments for the standards listed. We need to decide the most important of the seven possible alignments we generated. We already have rejected aligning 1, 6 and 7 (unless we make changes to the significant task), leaving 2, 3, 4, and 5. News articles and television are in the same standard statement, leaving us with three alignments to standard statements: I1-LR-1, I1-LR-2, I1-LRa. In this case, producing a paper and taking notes from an oral discussion was felt to be more important than the other three standards that had been chosen. The significant task was then reworded (Figure 13.10).

Figure 13.9 Linking vocabulary to help align to state standards

"We will gather information (1) to support our ideas about saving the environment and *cite examples from famous people' lives* (2), *from fiction or nonfiction* books (3), *from news articles* (4), or *from television* (5) by *taking notes* (6) and *preparing a paper* (7) about our idea."

NY ELA Standard 1 Intermediate

Listening and Reading

I1-LRC Interpret and analyze (information) from graphs, charts, diagrams, and electronic data bases intended for a general audience.

I1A Listening and reading to acquire information and understanding involves collecting data facts, and ideas.

I1B Listening and reading to acquire information and understanding involves discovering relationships, concepts, and generalizations.

I1C Listening and reading to acquire information and understanding involves using knowledge from oral, written, and electronic sources.

I1-LR-1 Produce a summary of the information about a (famous person) found in a biography, encyclopedia, and textbook.

I1-LR-2 Use facts and data from (news articles) and (television) reports in an oral report on a current event.

I1-LR-3 Compile a bibliography of sources that are used in a research project.

I1-LR-4 (Take notes) that record the main ideas and most significant supporting details of lecture or speech.

I1-LRa Interpret and analyze information from textbooks and (nonfiction) books for young adults.

I1-LRb Interpret and analyze information from reference materials, audio and media presentations and oral interviews.

I1-LRd Compare and synthesize information from different sources.

I1-LRe Use a wide variety of strategies for selecting, organizing, and categorizing information.

I1-LRf Distinguish between relevant and irrelevant information.

I1-LRg Distinguish between fact and opinion.

I1-LRh Relate new information to prior knowledge and experience.

I1-LRi (Understand and use the text features) that make information accessible and usable, such as format, sequence, level of diction, and relevance of details.

1. "Gather information" is only partially aligned with "Interpret and analyze information" from the standards. Gathering information is not interpreting or analyzing information. So a match would not be considered unless the significant task was reworded to include "interpret and analyze information."

2. "Famous people" in the activity matches "Famous people" in the standard. This is a good alignment.

3. "Fiction and nonfiction books" alignment to "nonfiction books" is a good alignment because the vocabulary (at least for "nonfiction") is the same. The authors may want to consider whether they can get information they need from fiction or whether to include textbooks as another source for information.

(Continued)

Figure 13.9 (Continued)

4. and 5. "News articles" and "television" is a good alignment because the vocabulary is the same for the significant task and the standard. This information is supposed to be used in an oral report, however. Curriculum authors will need to decide whether they want to add an oral report component to the significant task.

6. "Taking notes" is in both the significant task and the standard. The standard, however, states that information needs to come from a lecture or speech. Here, even though the vocabulary is the same, no alignment is possible unless the significant task is changed to include speeches. This is the second time an oral report or speech was mentioned. The standards emphasize gathering information from speeches a number of times. Through the alignment, the curriculum authors have discovered a pattern in the standards that they may not have realized from their initial reading.

7. "Understand and use text features" might be aligned to "prepare a paper" in the significant task. To prepare a paper, a student needs to demonstrate understanding and use of text features. The activity did not specify that this would be part of the paper preparation process, however. It would not be part of the instruction because it was not specified in the significant task. No alignment exists. We could change the significant task to incorporate the use of text features in writing the report.

Figure 13.10 Initial and revised significant tasks after limiting alignment

Initial Significant Task

"We will gather information to support our ideas about saving the environment and cite examples from famous people's lives, from news articles, from fiction or nonfiction books, or from television by taking notes and preparing a paper about our idea."

Revised Significant Task

"We will gather and analyze information to support our ideas about saving the environment and cite examples from famous people's lives, from news articles, from fiction or nonfiction books, or from television by taking notes on classroom discussions and preparing a paper about our idea that utilizes textual features to help make an argument. An appendix to the paper will tell what textual features the author used to highlight the argument."

Commentary

Alignment can deepen authors' thinking about their significant tasks. As they compare their significant tasks to the standards, they will include more standard-based vocabulary, thus increasing the alignment to standards. Authors will also make decisions about what is most important in the alignment, helping them to focus the significant tasks to make them more manageable and more teachable. Authors can add to the significant tasks and change them, but adding components to significant tasks may mean lengthening the time needed to complete the significant task. Curriculum authors must balance these difficult trade-offs.

Authors will need to use their professional judgment about adding components to keep within the 60% rule—remember, significant tasks are to take up approximately 60% of a unit's time. This helps authors grapple with designing tasks that are both aligned to the most important standards and doable within the context of the unit.

ALIGNMENT PROCESS

When the significant tasks are complete, authors return to the Balanced Curriculum Web site and print out a codebook with all the standards and their codes assigned to the course. A sample is given in Figure 13.11 for New York English Language Arts Intermediate Standards for Listening and Speaking.

Figure 13.11 Excerpt of codebook for New York English Language Arts Intermediate Standards for Listening and Speaking

Standard Codes for Course Grade 5 ELA		*AB C*	English Grade 5	Newburgh Newburgh, NY 2000–2001

NY ELA Standard 4 Intermediate

Listening and Speaking	
14A	Oral communication in formal and informal settings require the ability to talk with people of different ages, genders, and cultures.
14B	Oral communication in formal and informal settings required to adapt presentations to different audiences.
14C	Oral communication in formal and informal settings required to reflect on how talk varies in different situations.
14-LS-1	Act as hosts for open house at school.
14-LS-2	Participate in small group discussion in class.
14-LS-3	Give morning announcement over the public address system.
14-LS-4	Participate in school assemblies and club meetings.
14-LSa	Listen attentively to others and build on others' ideas in conversations with peers and adults.
14-LSb	Express ideas and concerns clearly and respectfully in conversations and group discussions.
14-LSc	Learn some words and expressions in another language to communicate with a peer or adults who speaks the language.
14-LSd	Use verbal and nonverbal skills to improve communication with others.
Reading and Writing	
14D	Written communication for social interaction requires using written messages to establish, maintain, and enhance personal relationships with others.

SOURCE: Used courtesy of the Newburgh Enlarged City School District, New York.

Authors use the codebook to pick out the appropriate codes and transfer them to the Alignment Worksheet. This sheet has spaces for the number of alignment codes that will be placed on the Web site. Figure 13.12 is a sample code sheet for North Carolina American History Course.

Authors fill in the unit and significant task title. Then they fill in the standard codes for the five standards listed: Bloom's Taxonomy, Developmental Pathways (see Chapter 5 for an explanation of this), the publicly released North Carolina End-of-Course Test specifications, the North Carolina Social Studies Standards, and the standards from the National Council on Social Studies, Grades 9–12.

The alignment worksheet is then used to enter codes on the Web site. To do this, authors navigate to the alignment page shown in Figure 13.13. The codes will appear in the pull down box (Arrow 1). Highlight the appropriate code (Arrow 2). When the desired code is shown in blue, users click on "Add New Alignment" at the bottom

Figure 13.12 Sample alignment worksheet for North Carolina American history course

Alignment Worksheet
American History   High School   Parkland High School
                                                                         Winston-Salem
History & Social Sciences   Forsyth County, NC
                                                                         2000–2001

Directions: Fill in the codes from "Standard Codes for Course" report

Unit: _____

Significant Task: _____

Bloom's Taxonomy _____ _____

Developmental Pathways _____ _____

North Carolina End-of-Course Tests—U.S. History (revised 1995) _____ _____

NC Social Studies 9–12: U.S. History (revised 1995) _____ _____ _____ _____

National Council on Social Studies 9–12 _____ _____

SOURCE: Copyright © Parkland High School, Winston-Salem Forsyth County, North Carolina. Reprinted with permission.

Figure 13.13 Alignment page from ABC Web site

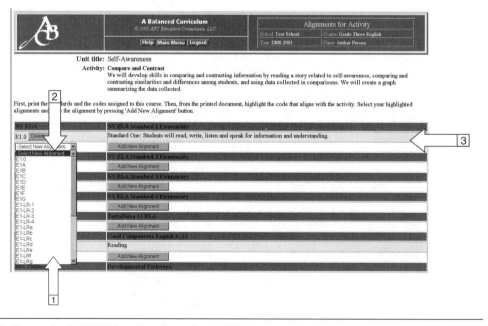

SOURCE: Copyright © ABC Education Consultants, LLC.

of the screen. The alignment will appear on the screen in orange. The code is listed in the box at left. The text of the standard is automatically inserted and shown on the right (Arrow 3). Alignment codes for all significant tasks for a course can be entered in a few hours.

Once alignment is completed, reports can be printed from the Balanced Curriculum Web site to show the alignment. Figure 13.14 is for 6th-grade mathematics from Passaic, New Jersey. Standards include Bloom's taxonomy, Developmental Pathways, the National Council of Teachers of Mathematics standards for Grades 6

Figure 13.14 Grade 6 mathematics alignment report for one significant task

Tip to Tip (Significant Task)

In small groups, learners will practice the strategy of predicting and testing to determine how many learners it will take to reach across the classroom with their arms out and fingertips touching:

Learners will estimate a reasonable response and then record their measurement guesses into a table, using inches and then converting into feet and yards. They will also explain their reasoning behind the estimate.

Learners will determine the actual number of students needed to span the classroom by counting the actual students.

Learners will construct a table to compare and analyze estimates with actual measurements.

Standard	Code	Description
Bloom's Taxonomy	S	Synthesis
	E	Evaluation
Developmental Pathways	P	Physical
	S	Social
NCTM 6-8	68.01.3.00	Compute fluently and make reasonable estimates
	68.06.1.00	Build new mathematical knowledge through problem solving
	68.06.2.00	Solve problems that arise in mathematics and in other contexts
NCTM 6-8	68.06.3.00	Apply and adapt a variety of appropriate strategies to solve problems
	68.07.2.00	Make and investigate mathematical conjectures
NJ Core Curriculum Content—Math—Grade 6	N.C	Estimation
	G.D	Units of measurement
	G.D.05	Use measurements and estimates to describe and compare phenomena
	G.E.05	Develop informal ways of approximating the measures of familiar objects (e.g., use a grid to approximate the area of the bottom of one's foot)
	DA.C.01a	Organized lists, charts, tree diagrams, tables
NJ Cross-Content Workplace Readiness	3.13	Select and apply appropriate solutions to problem-solving and decision-making situations
	4.02	Work cooperatively with others to accomplish a task
NJ Math GEPA 5–8	I.A	Make appropriate estimations and approximations
	III.D	Use iterative patterns and processes to describe real-world situations and solve problems

NOTE: GEPA = Grade Eight Proficiency Assessment; NCTM = National Council of Teachers of Mathematics through 8, the New Jersey Core Curriculum Content Standards for Math for Grade 6, New Jersey Cross-Content Workplace Readiness Standards, and the publicly released standards for the New Jersey math assessment (Grade Eight Proficiency Assessment) given in Grade 8. (All the standards for Grade 8 math assessment will not to be aligned in Grade 6, but the report does show the standards that are addressed in the Grade 6 mathematics' curriculum.)

Authors use this report to check their work. Once authors sign off on the alignment, an alignment validation takes place. Someone from another course or grade level, or a curriculum administrator, checks the alignment to determine whether the categories chosen align with the significant task.

When publishing the curriculum, many districts have found that this is the most useful report for teachers. Grade- or course-level teachers can use this report when planning their instruction because many of the core skills are listed in the alignments. Teachers want to make sure their lessons cover all of the component skills listed in the standards. This increases alignment's effectiveness as teachers make sure to teach and students to learn both the significant tasks and the associated standards.

SUMMARY

This chapter used the alignment octagon as a way to show how the Balanced Curriculum demonstrates alignment between curriculum, instruction, and assessment, demonstrating alignment's importance in meeting standard-based demands. The chapter then reviewed the process for aligning significant tasks. The next chapter describes how to use the alignment results to balance the curriculum.

14

Balancing the
Aligned Curriculum

During alignment, curriculum authors matched significant tasks to standards and standardized assessments. In examining the details of alignment, the big picture of whether the alignments are in balance is often missed. Balancing the curriculum is a way of taking a look at the big picture and determining whether there is appropriate emphasis on all categories of the standards—a professional judgment that curriculum authors will make. Authors wrestle with questions such as the following:

- Is there enough emphasis on standards that are tested?
- Are we ignoring important ideas from the standards because of the emphasis on the test?
- Does this grade level or course provide adequate emphasis on the prerequisite skills needed at the next grade level or course?
- Is the balance consistent with my own vision of what is most important to teach in this subject area?

THE ROLE OF PERSONAL PROFESSIONAL STANDARDS IN THE PROCESS OF BALANCING THE CURRICULUM

Experienced teachers use their own personal professional standards as a screen for selecting and sequencing significant tasks. For example, if I value group work in the classroom because I believe that the ideas and opinions of others enrich reading and writing, then I am likely to include many significant tasks involving groups in my curriculum. If I include too many group activities, however, I may be slighting other important areas, such as reading or writing independently (which may be how students must complete high-stakes tests). The Balanced Curriculum process asks teachers to talk about and decide how to balance their values with the values sanctioned by the state in standards and assessments as well as values developed by professional organizations and encompassed in their standards.

In the process of developing significant tasks, participants exhibit more understanding about what they value and why and understand values inherent in the standards and assessments. They can articulate with more precision and confidence what they believe should drive instruction. They determine a scope and sequence of significant tasks from a shared understanding of each other's values and the standards and assessments. (See Chapter 8 for more discussion of the use of personal standards in the curriculum development process.)

Balance cannot be "objectively" determined. Think of mobiles—those art objects, balanced so they appear to float on air, yet take one part away and the mobile becomes unstable, collapsing into a jumble (Figure 14.1). A curriculum is like a mobile; it is the weight we give each significant task and the way each significant task is balanced to keep the "whole" afloat. We might also think of balance in a painting, a piece of pottery, a musical composition, a poem, or a sculpture. All have as part of their design concepts the idea of balance. Take one section away, and the work no longer feels whole. The other pieces are out of balance.

Figure 14.1   Balance: A mobile's perspective

SOURCE: Copyright © ABC Education Consultants, LLC.

Conversely, when making a mobile, the whole often balances when the right piece is placed in the right spot; what hung limply now springs to life. Thus, the work we do in balancing the curriculum is more akin to art or literary criticism than it is to a scientific experiment.

My wife is a calligrapher, and I have been to a few of her classes. Each week beginning students bring in their practice sheets filled with letters mimicking a particular style. She asks students to post their work around the room and then pick out the letter they made the best and tell why they liked it. Through conversation, students learn about form, weight, and structure of the letters; their emerging internal standards become public as they explain the letter they did the best. Advanced students do the same with their compositions made with letters.

We are somewhere between novices and experts in designing curriculum for our students. The conversations about balance are a way to deepen understanding of the dynamics of developing a sequence of significant tasks. Determining balance and adequacy is a matter of professional judgment grounded in personal professional beliefs (see Figure 14.2).

Figure 14.2 Balancing professional values, standards, and curriculum

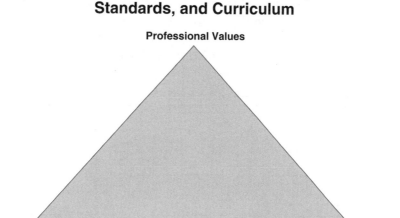

THE BALANCING PROCESS

To begin the balancing process, the curriculum authors use an exercise to examine personal professional beliefs. The authors rank the major standard categories from most to least important, reflecting their professional values. Figure 14.3 is an example of an author of an English and language arts curriculum ranking the Developmental Pathways from the Comer School Development Program at Yale University (Comer et al., 1999; see also Chapter 11 of this volume). The language pathway is most important for this teacher, who ranked it first; the physical pathway is the least important, ranked sixth.

Figure 14.3 Developmental priorities for author groups

Author Group's Priority for Comer's Developmental Pathways

Standard: Comer's Developmental Pathways

Subtopics:	Rank
Cognitive	2
Ethical	4
Language	1
Physical	6
Psychological	3
Social	5

Authors complete this ranking for each standard area, including state standards and state assessments. Then they compare their rankings with others in their group, coming to a consensus about the rankings. These conversations are rich because there is no right answer. In ranking the standard's subtopics, an approximate value is established.

The authors' ranking can then be compared with a report generated from the Balanced Curriculum Web site that shows how many significant tasks were aligned with the standard's subtopics, such as the one in Figure 14.4.

Figure 14.4   Number of significant tasks aligned with a standard's subtopics

Standards Alignments
Summary
Grade 6 ELA

Standard: Developmental Pathways

Subtopics

Cognitive C	Aligned Activities:	9
Ethical E	Aligned Activities:	1
Language L	Aligned Activities:	13
Physical P	Aligned Activities:	1
Psychological Ps	Aligned Activities:	2
Social S	Aligned Activities:	8

The report in Figure 14.4 shows that the language pathway has 13 aligned significant tasks, whereas the ethical pathway has only has one. Figure 14.5 summarizes the ranks from the teachers and the ranks from the Standards Alignment Summary report. Language is ranked number 1 by the teachers and is also aligned to the most significant tasks.

Figure 14.5   Comparing authors' ranking of standards with the standard alignment summary

	Authors' Ranks	Rank From Standards Alignment Summary
Cognitive	2	2
Ethical	4	6
Language	1	1
Physical	6	5
Psychological	3	4
Social	5	3

When the author group examined the Standards Alignment Summary Report for Developmental Pathways, this is what they found. The language and cognitive categories aligned to the most aligned significant tasks (Alignments 9 and 13, respectively, ranked first and second). Only two significant tasks aligned to the psychological pathway, however, and only one significant task aligned to the ethical pathway. Yet these were ranked third and fourth according to the author group's rankings. The social pathway had eight alignments to significant tasks yet was ranked as fifth in the authors' priorities. The number of significant tasks aligned to each substandard for Comer's developmental pathways were not aligned to the author group's rankings. The author group decided to emphasize the ethical and psychological pathways more and place less emphasis on the social pathway. What does this mean? The author group needs to change some significant tasks.

The author group decided to decrease the emphasis on the social pathway and increase the emphasis on the psychological and ethical pathways. To do this, they examine the significant tasks that are aligned to the social pathway and changed the significant task. Figure 14.6 shows the original significant task.

Figure 14.6   Original significant task

Unit Title: Survival and Heroes

Significant Task: Research for readers' theater. We will research and paraphrase information about a nonfiction hero using at least three sources (e.g., books, articles, etc.). We will synthesize the information gathered and write a three- to five-minute script in the first person, readers' theater style. (In readers' theater style, a student dresses in character while reading the script.) We will perform the script for the class.

Developmental Pathway Alignments: Language and Social

Goal: Decrease social pathway; increase ethical and psychological pathways

---

SOURCE: Copyright © ABC Education Consultants, LLC.

The author group took the significant task and decided on possible changes that could be made with the goal of decreasing the emphasis on the social pathway and increasing the emphasis on the ethical and psychological pathways.

The social pathway alignment is indicated because the readers' theater is social in nature and therefore an appropriate alignment. The author group wants to align the significant task more to the ethical and psychological pathways. So the author groups reexamine the significant task to see whether those pathways could be included. One person in the author group suggests that the subject of a nonfiction biography discusses an ethical dilemma encountered in life; the script could be centered on the person's thinking about the ethical dilemma. Others in the group agree that this is a good idea.

The significant task was modified to include this idea. As the significant task changed, the alignment changed as well. The group felt the changes strengthened the significant task by the inclusion of the ethical pathway. They also felt that the ethical pathway was now a stronger component and so deserved the alignment; the social pathway had been de-emphasized and did not deserve an alignment because of its decreased importance. The revised significant task appears in Figure 14.7.

Figure 14.7   Revised significant task after rebalancing the curriculum

---

Unit Title: Survival and Heroes

Significant Task: Research for readers' theater. We will research and paraphrase information about a nonfiction hero using at least three sources (e.g., books, articles, etc.). We will identify a number of <u>ethical dilemmas</u> faced by the character. We will synthesize the information gathered about the character and the <u>ethical dilemma</u> and write a three- to five-minute script in the first person, readers' theater style. (In readers' theater style, a student dresses in character while reading the script.) We will perform the script for the class. The <u>students will identify</u> <u>the dilemma and discuss what they would do in the same situation</u>.

SOURCE: Copyright © ABC Education Consultants, LLC.

BALANCING THE CURRICULUM WITH REFERENCE TO PREVIOUS TEST RESULTS

Another way to help create a more powerful curriculum is to pay particular attention to the balance of the curriculum compared with the latest results from state or standardized tests, while maintaining balance for other standards. Usually these tests come with a district or school item analysis. Authors will want to examine the item analysis and determine the strengths and needs from this. An author group can use the item analysis report to determine which areas should be emphasized in balancing the curriculum. Areas in which the district scored poorly probably deserve more emphasis to balance the curriculum. If the district scored well, the area might be de-emphasized.

For example, the ranking standards report in Figure 14.8 shows the categories from the Connecticut tests in Editing and Revising. The author group examined the item analysis from the most recent testing and found that students did not do well in the area of Composing/Revising: Content, Organization, and Tone. So they ranked this area number 1. Students had done well in the areas of Capitalization, Punctuation, and Usage, so these areas received a low ranking. Areas needing moderate emphasis were Revision—Revision and Syntax—Word Choice. The author group then decided to concentrate on emphasizing "Content, Organization, and Tone."

Next, the author group ran the Standard Alignments Summary report (Figure 14.9) to determine the emphasis of the curriculum on the area of "Content, Organization and Tone." The report shows the number of significant tasks aligned to this area and to each of the subareas for "Composing/Revising: Content, Organization, and Tone," such as "Topic Sentence."

Once the strengths and needs are identified, authors run the Standard Alignments With Significant Task Title report, which shows the aligned significant tasks for each standard with the unit title. For example, CAPT 1.1 is aligned with the

Figure 14.8   Ranking standards report according to test results

English
Grade 9
Standard: CAPT Grade 10 Editing and Revising   2003–2004

Directions: Rank order the subtopics, giving the most important topic a ranking of one, the next most important topic a ranking of two, etc. Put the ranks on the line to the left of each subtopic

Rank	Subtopics
1	Composing/Revising: Content, Organization and Tone
2	Composing/Revising: Revision—Syntax
3	Composing/Revising: Revision—Word Choice
4	Editing: Capitalization
6	Editing: Punctuation
7	Editing: Usage
5	Editing: Spelling

SOURCE: Copyright © Melissa Harkins. Used with permission.

Figure 14.9   Standard alignments summary for priority area identified from test results

English
Grade 9   2003–2004

Standard: CAPT Grade 10 Editing and Revising

Subtopics

Composing/Revising: Content, Organization and Tone

4	CAPT 1.1	Topic sentence
3	CAPT 1.2	Supporting detail
4	CAPT 1.3	Extraneous material
1	CAPT 1.4	Chronological/logical order
1	CAPT 1.5	Tone
2	CAPT 1.6	Redundancy of ideas

SOURCE: Copyright © Melissa Harkins. Used with permission.

Figure 14.10 Standard alignments detail with significant task title

English

Grade 9   2003–2004

Standard: CAPT Grade 10 Editing and Revising

Composing/Revising: Content, Organization and Tone

Unit Title	*Significant Task Title*
CAPT 1.1 Topic Sentence	
Search For Self	Balanced Person
Survival	Physical/Mental Survival
Power	Power Structures
CAPT	CAPT Prep
CAPT 1.2 Supportive Detail	
Search For Self	Records of Daily Life
Short Story	Unified Effect
Betrayal	Poster Project
CAPT 1.3 Extraneous Material	
Conviction	Vocabulary Skills
Power	Conformity vs. Nonconformity
Power	Peer Editing
Poetry	Writing Poetry
CAPT 1.4 Chronological Order	
Survival	Physical/Mental Survival
CAPT 1.5 Tone	
Search For Self	Portfolio Project
CAPT 1.6 Redundancy of Ideas	
Survival	Night
Betrayal	Linking Ideas

SOURCE: Copyright © Melissa Harkins. Used with permission.

Search for Self unit and three significant tasks in that unit titled "Portfolio Project," "Balanced Person," and "Records of Daily Life" (see Figure 14.10).

A few patterns may emerge.

Strengths

Areas of test strength are aligned with many significant tasks. The authors will question whether the high scores are due to the amount of emphasis in the significant tasks. For example, the area CAPT 1.3 about "Extraneous material" has the most emphasis because it is aligned with four significant tasks. Is the area overemphasized, considering that CAPT 1.4 "Chronological order," has only one significant task? Could "Redundancy of Ideas" be de-emphasized without hurting the scores? Authors will then decide whether there are too many significant tasks or just the right amount in the areas of test strength.

Needs

Areas of test weakness are aligned with too few significant tasks. This may continue the pattern of low achievement in the weak area if changes aren't made. For example, only one significant task is aligned to the areas of "Tone" and "Chronological order" (see Figure 14.10). In this case, the authors will want to review other significant tasks unaligned to this weak area and revise some of those tasks to include student practice with "Tone" and "Chronological order" to increase the curricular emphasis.

REVIEWER'S ROLE

The curriculum reviewers play an important role. Their first job is to understand the curriculum and how it is put together to be both balanced and adequate. The purpose of reviewing the balance and adequacy of the curriculum is to confirm the design as balanced and adequate through a conversation between the curriculum author group and someone outside the curriculum writing process, whom we call the reviewer. The reviewer checks the alignment to make sure there is linking vocabulary. The reviewer may suggest to members of the author group that they more closely link the vocabulary of the significant task with the vocabulary of the standards.

The reviewer's second role is to understand how the curriculum authors made decisions about balancing the curriculum. The author group familiarizes the reviewer with the Ranking Standards report, showing the results of the author group's ranking of the standard's major categories. Then the reviewer checks the Standard Alignment Summary report to see if the authors' views of importance (Ranking Standards report) are consistent with the alignment of the curriculum (Standard Alignment Summary report).

SUMMARY

This chapter discussed the idea of balance in the curriculum. Curriculum authors need to determine their professional standards and beliefs as one basis for determining curricular balance. Standards and standardized tests also provide touchstones for determining whether the curriculum is in balance. Specific processes for balancing the curriculum were also enumerated. The next chapter discusses the role of assessments in the Balanced Curriculum process, criteria for judging good assessments, and a process for creating the content assessments, one for each significant task. The content assessments provide a way for students to demonstrate their achievement of the aligned standards in a significant task. The content assessment also provides teachers with a standard way of judging students' achievements across the district and provides schools and districts with "real time" data on students' accomplishments on the significant tasks.

15

Constructing Content Assessments

This chapter begins with a discussion of how assessment reinforces the Balanced Curriculum process, proceeds to a discussion of characteristics of good assessments, demonstrates how a content assessment is developed, and provides a model of a completed content assessment with a rubric to ensure high quality.

THE ROLE OF ASSESSMENT IN THE BALANCED CURRICULUM

A curriculum defines what is most important for students to know and be able to do. It should incorporate teachers' ideas, blended with the ideas from standards and the content tested on state or standardized tests. Significant tasks describe what is most important for students to learn. The significant tasks provide the basis for aligning and balancing the curriculum to fulfill requirements of standards and tests. Teachers use the significant tasks as the basis for approximately 60% of their instruction, making sure the taught curriculum is aligned with the intended curriculum. To complete the package, the curriculum must also encompass curriculum-embedded assessment so that teachers and students can judge whether students have adequately demonstrated proficiency with the aligned standards. The assessment chapter (Chapter 5) demonstrates that state tests are too small to demonstrate proficiency adequately in all the standards. Curriculum-embedded assessment is the only way to know students are proficient on areas specified by the standards.

Curriculum-embedded assessment also provides an "early warning" system; proficiency with significant tasks should predict passing on state or standardized tests. So rather than wait for the state or standardized test results, district administrators should be confident that students are demonstrating proficiency on the standards as instruction progresses (see Wishnick, 1989, for research confirming this point). Using only standardized assessments is like having a bank account with lots of activity but checking the account's balance only once a year. You may be rich. Or you may be out of cash. Reconciling your account (assessing after each unit) is a way to help keep track of progress.

Two types of assessments are incorporated into the Balanced Curriculum process:

1. Content Assessments that assess students' proficiency on the significant tasks

2. Format Assessments that provide students practice on the format of the standardized test once during each unit

Content and format assessments are separated because they provide two distinct functions. The format of the standardized test is generally not a "natural" way for students to demonstrate their knowledge. The format of standardized tests is limited because of the demands placed on them to be valid, reliable, and to cover much content in a relatively brief period of time. As test companies know, it is difficult to develop items that adequately, validly, and reliably combine a particular testing format with subject-area content. (See Chapter 5 for a more complete discussion of standardized tests.) So we do not attempt to do so in the Balanced Curriculum. What we do know is that students need practice on the formats of standardized tests so that they can demonstrate their knowledge in the specialized way required to obtain good scores. The format assessment provides students with that format practice once during each unit of instruction. (Chapter 16 summarizes the process of developing format assessments.)

Content assessments are linked to significant tasks. Indeed, the significant task description should specify what needs to be assessed. The significant task is already aligned to standards and tests, so by using the significant task description as the basis for assessment, alignment between curriculum-embedded tests and the standards and standardized test is ensured. Figure 15.1 shows the alignment between the written, taught, and tested curriculum, encompassing curriculum-embedded assessments, standards, and state and standardized tests.

Figure 15.1   Alignment between the written, taught, and tested curriculum.

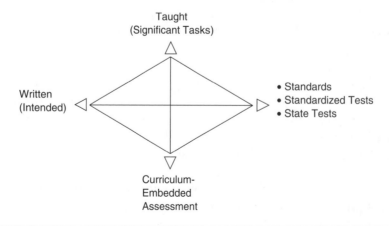

CRITERIA FOR GOOD ASSESSMENTS

Before delving into developing the content assessments, a discussion about criteria for good assessments is in order because the assessments developed in the Balanced Curriculum process need to be developed to

- Confirm teachers' intuitive judgments
- Have face validity (i.e., most would accept that this is a good way to have students demonstrate their knowledge)
- Are aligned to significant tasks
- Are authentic
- Require little additional time (away from instruction)
- Confirm students' understanding of standardized test format
- Align with subject-area standards
- Provide a platform for student and teacher reflection
- Provide public models and criteria for acceptable performances

Good Assessment Confirms Teachers' Intuitive Judgments

Assessments confirm teachers' professional judgment about whether students can understand, apply, and evaluate what they have learned. Most teachers, if they spend 2 or 3 weeks on a particular unit and if they review their students' work regularly, have a good idea whether students actually know the content. The function of a content assessment is to confirm the teachers' professional judgment with more "objective" information. If the unit assessment shows that a student passed when all the other evidence the teacher has shows that the student should fail, then there is probably something wrong with the unit assessment, not the teacher. Thus, there needs to be a dialogue between a teacher's intuitive sense about students' understanding and the results of a demonstration of that understanding—the content assessment. This exchange is an important component of alignment.

Good Assessment Has Face Validity

Face validity means that most teachers or parents would accept the assessment as a good way to have students display or apply their knowledge. We assume that the significant tasks have high face validity because the tasks' authors thought that they represented the most important ideas in the significant tasks. On the other hand, paper-and-pencil tests may not have high face validity. Think about how many paper-and-pencil tests there are in the world of work—very few. By basing assessment within the context of important instructional activities, face validity is usually ensured.

Good Assessment Is Aligned to Significant Tasks

Assessment needs to arise from the curriculum's significant tasks. This ensures that students are assessed on applying their knowledge and understandings, rather than only assessing their knowledge and understandings on a paper-and-pencil test. This also ensures consistency within a course or grade level.

Good Assessment Is Authentic

Assessment is authentic (rather than artificial) because it is derived from the instructional process. Many significant tasks involve projects or applying concepts within complex frameworks. Some significant tasks involve groups. Some significant tasks involve students in their own self-assessment. All of these make the assessment process authentic.

Good Assessment Requires Little Additional Time (Away From Instruction)

If assessment is done within the context of instruction (as defined by the significant tasks), little additional time is needed for assessment. For example, if students produce editorials on key issues in the school and the assessment is an evaluation of the editorial, then no additional time is needed away from instruction. Students have more time to learn.

Good Assessment Confirms Facility With Format

A good assessment should confirm a student's facility with standardized tests formats. These formats, as demonstrated in Chapter 5, are, at times, tricky. Within instruction, students have a few opportunities to practice demonstrating their knowledge in ways similar to the standardized test format. A format assessment meets this need. A curriculum assessment program is out of balance if it only contains items in multiple-choice format.

Good Assessment Aligns With Subject-Area Standards

The significant tasks are already aligned with the subject-area standards. If the assessment is based on these standards, then the assessment process itself will help to reinforce the standards. By relying on the standards, we help to maintain a balance in the curriculum and assessment process.

Good Assessment Provides a Platform for Student and Teacher Reflection

What did we want to do during class? How well did we do it? What did we learn that can be applied the next time? Good assessment involves both students and teachers in answering these questions. Students alone, students and teachers together, teachers alone and together—all should use the results of assessments to consider how the instructional experience could be modified and improved. Good classroom assessment brings this mind-set to bear on students' learning and teachers' instructional improvement.

Good Assessment Provides Public Models and Criteria for Acceptable Performances

Good assessment requires that models of performances are available and accessible for teachers and students. If students are writing a paragraph, then models of acceptable and unacceptable paragraphs should be available so that students can see how the final product looks. Having models is only half the battle, however.

Criteria for acceptable performance also need to be included so that students and teachers know and can identify key characteristics. If students are learning to write a paragraph, they will need to see models of good topic sentences and know why those topic sentences are good. This helps to eliminate guessing on the students' part and fuzzy thinking on the teachers' part. More important, when models and criteria are public, the teacher's job is to help a student meet the criteria; the student and the teacher are on the same "side." The teacher can say to students, "Here's the final product we're working toward, and my job is to help you be as successful as possible. Help me to help you." This changes the power relationships between teachers and students, who can now be on the same team, collaborating to improve student performance to meet publicly stated and held criteria.

Fortunately, we do not have to start at the beginning. The significant tasks are the foundation of the assessment process and represent the teacher's definition of what is most important in the curriculum. We know there is curricular balance for the significant tasks because the teachers have aligned them with the standards and standardized tests. Thus, we have already defined and aligned the most important curricular aspects to assess. The characteristics of significant tasks are that they

- Summarize the most important skills and content in the unit
- Represent a consensus by grade-level or course teachers on what all students should demonstrate
- Encapsulate a grade-level or course promise to the next grade level or course
- Allow students to demonstrate their knowledge and skills in complex ways
- Show alignment with important content standards
- Show alignment with standardized test content

The aligned significant tasks are the skeleton on which we will build the body of a complete curriculum-embedded assessment system. The significant task usually requires a performance; thus, the assessment is performance-based. Students have to perform or demonstrate what they know when they complete a significant task. Their performance on the significant task confirms that they deeply understand the aligned content. For example, the significant task tells what students will be able to do. "After reading *Clifford Goes to the Circus*, we will summarize and sequence the story by discussing the order of events in the story and summarize our discussion by drawing pictures of each event and putting those pictures in order." The student performance is drawing and ordering pictures. The assessment authors would create rubrics so that teachers will know, as a group, the criteria for good performance on this significant task. This is the heart of developing content assessments based on the significant tasks.

DESIGNING CONTENT ASSESSMENTS

An assessment system cannot assess everything that students learn. Most assessment systems have a process for picking out the most important things to test. Assessment designers rely on the assumption that if they choose a sample of the most important student learning to assess, then students will, most likely, have a good grasp on the less important aspects of the curriculum. The key is picking out what is most important to assess. To do this, the significant task is divided into chunks that provide assessment opportunities. Then the assessment authors choose the most important chunks or assessment opportunities to focus their assessments.

To illustrate the process, the following is a significant task for a friendship unit in 3rd grade that has been chunked to show assessment opportunities. Each assessment opportunity is segmented by a "/":

a. Students will read stories from the grade-level story list on friendship/The class will

b. collectively generate/

c. revise/

d. and refine a list of characteristics about friendship/

e. *Individuals in the class will write personal stories about how they have lived these characteristics in their own friendships/

f. and share these with one classmate/

g. Students will set writing goals for their story/

h. *Students will assess how well they met their goals/

i. Students will practice using the list of friendship characteristics in searching for the stories' main idea/

Nine chunks were identified. Some chunks are more important than others. The author group highlighted with an asterisk the chunks (e and h) deemed most important in assessing this significant task. Debates often arise between assessment authors on the most important chunks. For example, for this significant task, one of the authors thought that "i" should be assessed, as identifying the main idea was important for the testing. Another author countered that writing, not reading, was the focus here and that main idea had been practiced extensively in the previous significant tasks. Authors, after discussion, generally can come to a consensus.

After deciding to focus on "e" and "h," the authors' next step is to decide a way to assess the important chunks so as not to take time away from instruction. For "e," authors decided to assess whether the students used the friendship characteristics in their stories. They also decided to focus on subject-verb agreement and topic sentences because these were important issues at this time of the year. The authors decided that rubrics would be a good strategy to use for assessing subject-verb agreement, topic sentences, and use of friendship characteristics in their story. For the use of friendship characteristics, they came up with the rubric in Figure 15.2.

Figure 15.2   Sample rubric for topic sentences

Unsatisfactory	Needs Improvement	Satisfactory	Good	
No topic sentence is evident in the paragraph.	There is the beginning of a topic sentence, but it needs to include specifically one of the friendship characteristics discussed in class.	The topic sentence states the friendship characteristic, but it is simply stated with no creativity involved.	The topic sentence states the friendship characteristic in a creative or unusual fashion.	⊲ A ⊲ B

NOTE: Arrow A: Categories have been established. Arrow B: For each category, criteria are listed. The criteria are specific and descriptive enough that teachers across the district will make similar judgments.

Good rubrics contain categories such as satisfactory and good, or 1, 2, 3. Stating the categories is not sufficient; they must also contain criteria that are specific and descriptive enough that all teachers grading student work will make similar judgments. This is both the most difficult and most important part of generating rubrics.

SAMPLE CONTENT ASSESSMENTS

The following is a sample content assessment for a high school algebra class.

Content Assessment

Mathematics: Algebra
Grade 12
Unit: Predictions
Significant Task: Using Scatter Plots to Make Predictions
Author: Karen Dickey (2003)

Introduction: Content Assessment

The content assessment on the next few pages provides a guide for teachers to judge whether students have met the standards through performance of an important significant task. The content assessment is designed to answer the question, "How good is good enough?" The assessment also provides a framework for use by teachers to ensure equitable judgment of student work. Student performance on content assessments should be weighted heavily when determining the unit grade or report card grades.

If you have comments or suggestions on how to improve this content assessment, please go to the activity comments section on the Web site and list your suggestions there, followed by your name and school. When the curriculum is revised, your comments will help structure the revisions.

Significant Task

Students will graph data in a scatter plot, determine the equation of the regression line, and use the equation to make predictions. Once they have mastered the process by hand, they will use a TI-83 graphing calculator to plot the data and find the equation of the regression line. They will study the relationship between manatee deaths and the number of powerboats registered in Florida. Students will also collect data from the class on each person's height and forearm length, graph the data, write an equation of the regression line, and use it to make predictions for other students their age. The students will make predictions for future race times of swimmers using data provided for the number of races a person has raced compared with their times in each race. Finally, the students will demonstrate their knowledge of using scatter plots to make predictions using the number of races a person has raced in skiing to predict the person's time and using the year to predict the cost of a stamp.

Alignment Categories

By examining the activities' alignment indicated on the "Significant Task Alignments Full Text" Report from the Web site, the following areas from the state and national standards appeared to be the most important:

CT Math	
9–12 7.07	Use scatter plots and curve-fitting techniques to interpolate and predict from data.
8.02	Identify, describe, and generalize patterns from data and identify and analyze patterns of change.
9.06	Solve equations and inequalities using graphing calculators and computers as well as appropriate paper-and-pencil techniques.
NCTM	
9–12 912.02.3.00	Use mathematical models to represent and understand quantitative relationships.
9–12.02.3.0	Draw reasonable conclusions about a situation being modeled.
9–12.08.2.0	Communicate mathematical thinking coherently and clearly to peers, teachers, and others.

(Continued)

(Continued)

Directions for the Teacher to Give the Assessment

The students complete the content assessment independently.

Materials for Students

Students will need a TI-83 graphing calculator, a pencil, and a copy of the assessment.

Directions for the Teacher in Grading the Assessment

The students may earn up to 40 points on the assessment. In each section of the assessment, students can earn a designated number of points (described in the next section). The total score is computed by taking the total number of points earned, dividing by 40, and multiplying by 100.

Scatter Plot Quiz Rubric

Question 1: Each part should be graded as follows:

a. 2 points
  - 1 point for correctly identifying the dependent variable
  - 1 point for correctly identifying the independent variable

b. 3 points
  - 1 point for correctly calculating and identifying the slope of the line
  - 1 point for correctly calculating and identifying the y-intercept of the line
  - 1 point for correctly writing the equation of the line in slope-intercept form

c. 2 points
  - 1 point for correctly identifying the outlier (1, 355)
  - 1 point for explaining why the point (1, 355) is an outlier

d. 3 points
  - 3 points for correctly calculating the equation of the line of the best fit

e. 2 points
  - 1 point for explaining how the slope was affected by the outlier
  - 1 point for explaining how the y-intercept was affected by the outlier

f. 3 points
  - 1 point for correctly identifying the equation without the outlier is the best equation to use when making predictions
  - 2 points for explaining why this equation is the better choice

g., h., and i. 3 points each
  - 2 points for correctly identifying the variable to substitute for
  - 1 point for correctly solving for the unknown

j. 2 points
  - 1 point for stating the pattern cannot continue indefinitely
  - 1 point for explaining why the pattern cannot continue indefinitely

k. 3 points
  - 2 points for correctly identifying the variable to substitute for
  - 1 point for correctly solving for the unknown

Question 2: Each part should be graded as follows:

a. 2 points
  - 1 point for correctly identifying the dependent variable
  - 1 point for correctly identifying the independent variable

b. 3 points
  - 1 point for correctly calculating and identifying the slope of the line
  - 1 point for correctly calculating and identifying the y-intercept of the line
  - 1 point for correctly writing the equation of the line in slope-intercept form

c. and d. 3 points each
  - 2 points for correctly identifying the variable to substitute for
  - 1 point for correctly solving for the unknown

Algebra III: Scatter Plots Quiz Student Handout

Name: _____

Date: _____

40 total points

Show all work for full credit!

1. The following is a list of a skier's times (in seconds) for each of his first 12 races on a short course.

Race Number	Time (seconds)
1	355
2	330
3	328
4	329
5	325
6	323
7	324
8	320
9	323
10	318
11	320
12	319

a. What is the dependent variable? (1 pt.) _____

   What is the independent variable? (1 pt.) _____

b. Enter the data into your lists on the graphing calculator, and make a scatter plot of the data. Then calculate the equation of the line of best fit.

   What is the slope of the line of best fit? (1 pt.) _____

   What is the y-intercept of the line of best fit? (1 pt.) _____

   What is the equation of the line of best fit? (1 pt.) _____

c. Which point is an outlier and why do you consider it an outlier? (2 pts.)

   _____

   _____

d. Remove the outlier from your lists and make a new scatter plot of the data without the outlier. Then recalculate the equation of the line of best fit.

   What is the equation of the line of best fit? (3 pts.) _____

e. What effect did the outlier have on the line of best fit? (2 pts.)

   _____

   _____

f. Which equation is the best predictor of future race times, the one with or without the outlier? Why? (3 pts.)

   _____

   _____

(Continued)

(Continued)

g. Use your equation from part d. to predict the skier's race time on the 14th race. Show all work. (3 pts.)

_____

_____

h. Use your equation from part d. to predict the skier's race time on the 20th race. Show all work. (3 pts.)

_____

_____

i. Use your equation from part d. to predict the skier's race time on the 100th race. Show all work. (3 pts.)

_____

_____

j. Can this pattern continue indefinitely? Why or why not? (2 pts.)

_____

_____

k. Use your equation in part d. to approximate how many races it would take the skier to get a time of 311 seconds. Show all work. (3 pts.)

_____

_____

2. The table gives the price (in cents) of a first-class stamp over time where time is given as the number of years since 1970.

Year	Price
1	8
4	10
5	13
8	15
11	18
11	20
15	22
18	25
21	29
25	32
29	33

a. What is the dependent variable? (1 pt.) _____

   What is the independent variable? (1 pt.) _____

b. Enter the data into your lists on the graphing calculator and make a scatter plot of the data. Then calculate the equation of the line of best fit.

   What is the slope of the line of best fit? (1 pt.) _____

   What is the y-intercept of the line of best fit? (1 pt.) _____

   What is the equation of the line of best fit? (1 pt.) _____

c. Use your equation to predict the cost of a stamp in year 40. Show all algebraic steps for full credit. (3 pts.)

_____

_____

d. Use your equation to predict the year in which a stamp will cost 50 cents. (3 pts.)

_____

_____

Figure 15.3 gives a rubric for determining a high-quality content assessment. The rubric ensures consistency across various assessment authors at various grade levels. Districts can determine their own format for the assessments or use this one.

Figure 15.3 Rubric for assuring high-quality content assessments

Unit _____

Validator _____   Date _____

Significant Task Title _____

Check that all the components of a Format Assessment are present.

_____ **Title Page:**

_____ Format Assessment

_____ District

_____ Subject Area

_____ Grade

_____ Unit Title

_____ Significant Task Title

_____ Authors (optional):

_____ Developed: (Month/Year)

_____ **Introduction Page:**

_____ Introduction Paragraphs

_____ List the Significant Task

_____ Alignment Categories and Codes

_____ **Directions for Teacher to Give the Assessment**

_____ **Materials for Students**

_____ **Directions for the Teacher in Grading the Assessment**

Rubric for Assessing Assessment Booklets

Grade _____ Subject Area _____ Unit Title _____

Activity Title _____ Date _____

Directions: This instrument will help ensure that the assessments are of high quality. Rate the Assessment as either satisfactory or unsatisfactory in each category by circling the appropriate box. State reasons, if needed, in the Reviewer's Comments' column. High quality assessment booklets have all criteria rated satisfactory.

Criteria	Unsatisfactory	Satisfactory	Reviewer's Comments
Criteria of Judging Activities–Content Assessment	Criteria have not been identified for the completion of the significant task.	Criteria have been identified for the completion of the significant task.	
Criteria of Judging Activities–Content Assessment	The criteria focus on trivial aspects of student work.	The criteria focus on the most important aspects of student work.	
Scales for Rating Performance–Content Assessment	Scales have not been identified for rating student work.	Scales have been identified for rating students work.	
Each Category on the Scale is Described—Content Assessment	Categories have not been described or have been incompletely described.	Categories are adequately described so that with teacher discussion in grade-level or course-level groups, teachers would be able to judge the performance of an activity in similar ways.	
Checklist	One or more of the required elements from the checklist is missing.	All required elements from the checklist are present.	
Summary	Given the directions for teachers and students and the materials for students, teachers would *not* give and grade the content assessments in a similar manner.	Given the directions for teachers and students and the materials for students, teachers would give and grade the content assessments in a similar manner.	

USING THE CONTENT ASSESSMENTS

Just as teachers in every school within the district teach the significant tasks, they also use the same content assessments. What happens in most districts is that the completion of the assessments becomes a powerful incentive to teach the significant tasks. If the significant tasks are taught so that students have learned the content, then most students should do well on the significant tasks. This demonstrates that teachers are teaching a standards-based curriculum.

The content assessment should be a major grade in the grade book. When fully implemented, administrators would expect to see content assessments as part of all teachers' grading schemes. The content assessment is a way that teachers can demonstrate to parents that the students are or are not making progress on mastering the standards and preparing for high-stakes tests.

Many teachers share the rubrics for the content assessment with their students so that they know what a good performance is. Some districts have collected anchor papers that exemplify different levels of achievement. These can be loaded onto the Balanced Curriculum Web site so that all will have specific examples of work that are good, better, or best. Some teachers have used the anchor papers to assist students in setting goals for their final performances. They report that when students set goals and have performance criteria (rubrics) and sample papers, the level of the performance improves dramatically. The central office can get out of the business of publishing and warehousing tests because the tests are stored on the Web site, ready for teachers to securely download when needed. No more fussing with printing and distribution tasks. When changes to assessments are needed, they can be done easily and then downloaded to the Web site so that everyone has access to the newest and latest versions without struggling through "normal" revision, production, and distribution channels in the school district.

School-level teams teaching the same course can share samples of students' work, brainstorming about how to get work of higher quality next year. Teachers who experience success can share their strategies with their colleagues so everyone can improve.

Administrators report that students' content assessments are useful in knowing that students and teachers are making adequate progress through the curriculum. Because the content assessments are required of all who teach the course, there can now be a level of professional dialogue about how to produce even better results.

Some school districts have used a few content assessments as part of developing portfolios of sample student work. These portfolios are better than just a random collection of student work because there is a standard grading process involved. Plans are currently in the works to record students' content assessment scores on the Web site as a way to help predict results on high-stakes test. Plans are also underway to store student work in an "electronic" portfolio on the Web site.

The next chapter demonstrates how format assessments are constructed so that students have an opportunity once per unit to practice the various formats of high-stakes state and standardized tests.

16

Constructing Format Assessments

This chapter discusses constructing format assessments—assessments given at the end of each unit and designed to give students practice demonstrating their knowledge in ways that mirror the format of the high-stakes state test or standardized test.

Assessing aligned content suggests employing two strategies: format assessment and content assessment. Format assessment deals with how assessments, particularly important standardized and end-of-course tests, are structured and delivered. Students should have an opportunity to demonstrate their understanding of content using that format before the standardized test is given. For example, we know that most commercially available standardized tests have items in multiple-choice format. For students to perform their best, they need practice with all of the formats on the multiple-choice test. (However, they don't need this practice all at once—only one format assessment per unit needs to be devoted to practice with format.) Content assessments are tied to each significant task and explained in the previous chapter. This chapter discusses criteria for making sure formats are aligned between standardized tests and format assessments.

FORMAT ASSESSMENT AND STANDARDIZED TESTING

Standardized testing poses a problem for the design of format assessments. First, for most standardized testing, access to the format of questions on the standardized test is restricted. Remember in Chapter 5, part of the validity of standardized tests is predicated on restricting knowledge about the specific items and their format on the standardized test. If everyone had access to all items on a standardized test, then their formats would be known and the validity of the test would be compromised. Fortunately, most state and standardized tests do publish sample items and sample formats so that teachers will not have so much uncertainty about the format. Partial knowledge about the format of items is the best that can be expected.

Second, the format of standardized testing is primarily multiple choice (although some states are now using a variety of writing prompts and students' written answers). Students do not naturally demonstrate their learning through multiple-choice answers; most learning is more easily demonstrated in conversation with the teacher or in student products or performances. Therefore, students need to practice demonstrating their learning through multiple-choice assessments.

Teachers and administrators need to understand that there are two competing influences about what is important for the school:

- Good instruction aligned to clear subject-area standards that will produce lifelong readers, writers, and mathematical thinkers
- Standardized test results that have political and predictive implications for a school's program

In designing format assessments, these two competing worldviews of what is most important need to be taken into account. The format assessment gives students practice on standardized test formats. The content assessments give students practice using the content of the curriculum. Of the two, format assessments give students practice demonstrating their knowledge in ways tested by standardized tests but are much less important than content assessments. Content assessments are proof that students are able to demonstrate competence with the standards.

The difficulty with the current system is that standardized and state test results have high-stakes consequences for students, schools, and districts. The "reward" system emphasizes the standardized assessments as the only way the system recognizes for demonstrating competence. Therefore, attention to constructing format assessments is important so students will have familiarity with the format of the assessment. The Balanced Curriculum process does not overemphasize format assessments because this is not what is most important. We have found that reviewing the format of the standardized test once per unit is sufficient to prepare students to demonstrate their knowledge using the format of the standardized or state test. Taking a month out of the school year to practice on the format of the standardized test is educational malpractice.

USE OF WISHNICK'S (1989) RESEARCH TO PRODUCE FORMAT ASSESSMENTS

Wishnick's (1989) research on alignment between unit and standardized tests is employed to help construct format assessments. Wishnick examined the results of unit tests for all 4th-grade students at an urban elementary school. She looked for correlations between the results of the unit tests and the results for similar clusters on the standardized tests. She knew which students were receiving free or reduced lunch, which students had which teachers, and the student's gender. She developed a scale for measuring whether there was alignment between the unit tests and the standardized tests. The scale emphasized coverage and item format. From this scale, she could tell the degree of alignment between the unit assessment and the standardized assessment. Here's what she found.

1. For units that aligned with the format and content of the standardized tests, students who scored high on the unit tests tended to score high on the standardized tests. This means that unit tests, when aligned, can serve as an early confirmation that a school's curriculum and instruction are working.

2. When units are not aligned, variables normally associated with performance on standardized tests (socioeconomic status, gender, and the student's teacher) tended to have an effect. When there is alignment between the unit test and the standardized test, however, socioeconomic status, gender, and teachers have a negligible correlation with achievement on the standardized test. This is good news. This means that when there is alignment, socioeconomic status does not predict students' performance. When there is alignment, gender does not predict students' performance. When there is alignment, getting a better or worse teacher does not predict students' performance.

Wishnick, as part of her research, validated the alignment scale. This means that it is a reliable indicator and measures what it says it measures. We use this scale as part of the process of developing the format assessment to ensure that curriculum-embedded assessment is rigorously aligned to standardized or state assessments.

The alignment scale lists a series of questions grouped into six categories. In the training for the Balanced Curriculum process, participants are given training in designing format assessment so that sometime during the year, students have practice on each area, although some are practiced more than others. The categories and questions are the following:

Concepts and Skills

- Are similar concepts tested?
- Is the skill level similar?

Format

- Are the items arranged on the page in similar fashion?
- Are the lengths of the questions similar?
- Are the numbers of items similar?
- Are the mixtures of items similar?

Directions

- Are the directions delivered in the same mode?
- Are the directions formatted in similar ways?

Responses

- Are there similar types of responses?
- Are there similar hints given in the responses?

Enticers

- Are students "encouraged" or "enticed" to choose incorrect responses in similar ways?
- Are items clustered in similar ways?

Testing Conditions

- Are time limits similar?
- Is there similar importance given to both assessments?
- Are there similar response sheets?
- Are teachers allowed to assist students in similar ways within the two assessments?

Participants construct the format assessment to address the categories using 10 to 20 multiple-choice questions. The emphasis here is on giving students practice with the format. So the assessment is meant to be the beginning of a conversation between teacher and students on understanding the format of the standardized test. Some teachers give the format assessment as a quiz and then spend time talking about the structure of the questions and how to think about answering them. Others may use the format assessment like a worksheet, putting students in groups not to only determine the correct answer but to discuss how they thought about determining the correct answer. The format assessment is not meant to be a major grade in the grade book, nor is it meant to show whether students know anything about the content of the unit. The only function of the format assessment is to give students practice and allow for discussion about the format of the high-stakes test.

A sample format assessment follows. Note that the rubric used in the format assessment comes from the state (Connecticut) and is the one released to give an example of how to grade the students' answers on the state assessment. The assessment in Connecticut is not all multiple choice, so students receive practice on constructing short answers and use the rubric as their grading tool.

Format Assessment

Mathematics: Algebra I

Grade: High School

Unit: Function Junction

Developed 2003 by Gabrielle Laux (used with permission of the author)

Introduction: Format Assessment

Enclosed is the format assessment and answer page. The format assessment provides students with practice on the format used in the standardized and state assessments at this grade level. Teachers will want to use the format assessment as an opportunity to help students become "test wise."

The format assessment should be given the weight of a "quiz" in the grading scheme, not the weight of a major "test." No inference about student mastery of content should be made from the format assessment. The format assessment was not designed to cover important concepts of the unit (although many will). Teachers will want to use the format assessment as an opportunity to help students become "test wise." Teachers will want to discuss the questions with students so that students understand the format. Without the class discussions about the questions, the format assessment becomes just another worksheet.

If you have comments or suggestions on how to improve this format assessment, please go to the unit comments section on the Web site and list your suggestions under the appropriate unit followed by your name and school. When the curriculum is revised, your comments will help structure the revisions.

Additional Directions

This is the proposed format assessment for Unit 2: Function Junction for Algebra I for Mathematics.

By examining the activities' alignment indicated on the "Significant Task Alignments Full Text" report from the Web site, the following areas appeared to be the most important:

Connecticut Academic Performance Test (CAPT)	Grade 10 Mathematics
M9.4	Use the coordinate plane to represent functions
NCTM 9–12 912.02.3.00	Use mathematical models to represent and understand quantitative relationships

Directions for Teacher to Give the Assessment

The teacher needs to give out the assessment and rulers. Students should be reminded to title graphs, label axes, and indicate scales.

Materials for Students

Students need the format assessment, a ruler, and a writing utensil. Students may use a calculator if they desire.

Directions for the Teacher in Grading the Assessment

Teachers should emphasize this format assessment about as much as a quiz. This format assessment is worth 20 points broken down as follows:

- 1 point—title of graph is appropriate
- 4 points—axes are labeled correctly (x-axis is time and y-axis is temperature) (2 points each)
- 3 points—scale is appropriate and indicated
- 12 points—graph is accurate, including (2 points each):

  y-intercept is 10°

  graph declines constantly between 6:00 and 6:20

  temperature at 6:20 is 4°

  temperature is a constant 4° from 6:20 to 6:40

  temperature constantly rises from 6:40 to 7:00

  temperature at 7:00 is 10°

Teachers may want to put up sample student graphs and holistically score them with students. The CAPT scoring rubric is included for holistic scoring. This will give students an idea of how such CAPT open-ended questions are scored on the actual CAPT test.

Algebra I. Function Junction—Format Assessment for the Student

Name _____   Date_____

How the Temperature Varied

Kathy took a hot-air balloon tour of the Farmington River valley. The graph below shows how the altitude (height) of the balloon varied during the 60-minute ride.

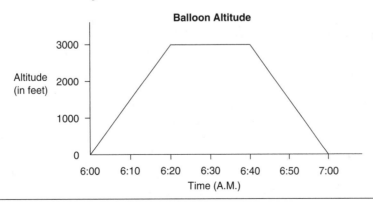

(Continued)

(Continued)

The temperature on the ground was 10°C during the entire flight. The temperature in the balloon decreased at a constant rate of 2°C for each 1,000 feet in altitude. On the grid given on the next page, make a graph showing how the temperature varied for Kathy as she rode in the balloon for 60 minutes. Remember to title the graph, label the axes, and indicate your scale.

Draw your graph for the format assessment "How the Temperature Varied" on the given grid below. Remember to title the graph, label the axes, and indicate the scale.

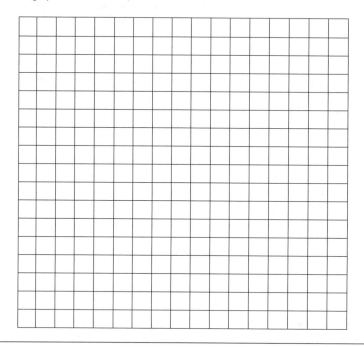

SOURCE: This format assessment is based on a CAPT Released item, courtesy of the Connecticut State Department of Education.

To ensure that the format assessments meet all of Wishnick's criteria, assessment authors complete the checklist in Figure 16.1. The goal is for each of Wishnick's categories to be addressed at least once during the year. For example, under "Testing Conditions," one of the questions is, "Are the time limits similar?" For most format assessments, the time limits would not be similar, as the format assessment is designed to be short. The assessment authors will want to provide at least one opportunity per year, however, when the format assessment's time limits are similar to the state or standardized test. This might happen during a midterm or final.

The format assessment authors check their work using the checklist and rubric in Figure 16.2 to ensure that the format assessment is complete. After the format assessment is checked for completeness, the assessment is loaded onto the Web site where all teachers can have access. Parents or visitors looking at the information on the Web site will not be able to access the assessments. Having the assessments accessible from the Web site means that the central office does not have to worry about publishing, distributing, and collecting the assessments across the district.

Figure 16.1 Format assessment checklist

Summary of Format Assessments Meeting Wishnick's Criteria

Grade _____ Course/Subject _____ Date _____

Directions: Place a Y in the grid if the format assessments meet Wishnick's criteria.

Unit Format Assessments	1	2	3	4	5	6	7	8	9	10	11	12	13	14	15	16
Concepts/ Skills Are similar concepts tested?																
Is the skill level similar?																
Format Are the items arranged on the page in similar fashion?																
Are the lengths of the questions similar?																
Is the number of items similar?																
Is the mixture of items similar?																
Directions Are the directions delivered in the same mode?																
Are the directions formatted in similar ways?																
Responses Are there similar types of responses?																
Are there similar hints given in the responses?																
Enticers Are students "encouraged" or "enticed" to choose incorrect responses in similar ways?																
Are items clustered in similar ways?																
Testing Conditions Are time limits similar?																
Is there similar importance given to both assessments?																
Are there similar response sheets?																
Are teachers allowed to assist students in similar ways within the two assessments?																

Figure 16.2 Format assessment rubric

Unit _____   Validator _____

Date _____

Check that all the components of a Format Assessment are present.

_____ **Title Page:**

_____ Format Assessment

_____ District

_____ Subject Area

_____ Grade

_____ Unit Title

_____ Authors (optional):

_____ Developed: (Month/Year)

_____ **Introduction Page:**

_____ Introduction Paragraphs

_____ List of the Grade, Subject and Unit Title

_____ Alignment Codes and What the Codes Mean

_____ **Directions for Teacher to Give the Assessment**

_____ **Materials for Students**

_____ **Directions for the Teacher in Grading the Assessment**

Rubric: Circle the boxes that apply.

Satisfactory	Unsatisfactory
All required elements from the checklist are present.	One or more of the required elements from the checklist is missing.
Given the directions for teachers and students and the materials for students, teachers would give and grade the format assessments in a similar manner.	Given the directions for teachers and students and the materials for students, teachers would *not* give and grade the format assessments in a similar manner.

SOURCE: Copyright © ABC Education Consultants, LLC.

Format assessments are structured to be the "test prep" program in the district. Purchase of test prep books with endless practice sheets is no longer necessary. Neither is closing down instruction for a month while students and teachers drill and kill for the high-stakes test. Now teachers can be confident that they have a validated way to address test readiness through the format assessments. This will leave more time for learning other important parts of the curriculum.

Section III

Staff Development for and Results of the Balanced Curriculum

D istricts that have a well-developed plan for implementing the curriculum have fewer implementation problems, but implementing the curriculum is a hurdle not all schools and districts can transcend. Chapters 17 through 19 offer suggestions gleaned from successful implementations on how to put the curriculum in place, including some advice from Superintendent Dr. Philomena Pezzano in Chapter 19, who has implemented the Balanced Curriculum in two districts over a 7-year period. Chapter 20 demonstrates the results of the Balanced Curriculum and suggests that, where implemented, the Balanced Curriculum is associated with improved student achievement.

17

Introducing the Balanced Curriculum Process in a District

I n the first years of developing and creating the Balanced Curriculum process, producing a high-quality product consumed most of the time and energy from a developer's point of view. Writing curriculum is hard; implementation is easy (or so I thought). Now I realize that implementing the curriculum is the most difficult challenge most districts face. The purpose of this chapter is to help districts address implementation issues by reviewing some implementation strategies and showing how the Balanced Curriculum Web site management tools can ensure widespread implementation.

THE ROLE OF THE PLANNING TEAM

The Balanced Curriculum process begins with planning. The district appoints a planning team to create a purpose statement to guide the project, make sure the process fits into the culture of the district, coordinate actions that will affect all students and staff, and design the authoring and implementation processes. Often included are district office personnel, such as the curriculum director, subject-area supervisors, directors of special education and bilingual education, representative building administrators, and representative teachers. The team may also be the curriculum council if the district already has one in place. It has monthly or quarterly meetings to review past and planned activities, problem solve dilemmas, provide oversight, and communicate with constituents. One of the first jobs of the planning team is to recruit authors: the best, brightest, and most caring teachers with writing skills.

SUPERINTENDENT'S ROLE

Strongest implementation occurs when the superintendent is a key player in bringing the Balanced Curriculum process to the district. Research suggests that "The greater the 'real' district-level support, the greater the degree of implementation" (Snyder, et al., 1992, p. 417). Dr. Laval Wilson, former superintendent of Newburgh, New York (now superintendent in East Orange, NJ), headed the planning team as the district leadership weighed the benefits; actions sponsored by Dr. Wilson included consultants meeting with the planning team on a regular basis, explaining the process to the school board, and meeting with principals to explain the process. Dr. Wilson clearly established curriculum writing and implementation as a district priority. Once the district reached consensus, Dr. Wilson handed over the leadership to his deputy, Dr. Philomena Pezzano (see Chapter 19 for her reflections on the process).

In another district (that shall remain nameless), the director of elementary education brought the process into the district. The planning team did not include the superintendent. Two years later, when the curriculum writing was complete and implementation began, the superintendent left the district, and curriculum implementation got lost among many competing transitional initiatives. The school board did not take the role of making sure the curriculum was implemented despite the transition. Perhaps if the superintendent took a more active role both in the curriculum development process and with the board, implementation could have been carried out during the transition.

IMPLEMENTATION STARTS WITH INITIAL PLANS FOR WRITING THE CURRICULUM: THE PLANNING TEAM'S ROLE

A planning team guides the Balanced Curriculum process and is made up of representative central office staff and select teachers and principals. This team's members need to understand that their job is twofold: get the curriculum written *and* structure implementation so the curriculum actually is taught. Here, implementation specifically refers to getting the curriculum, once written, to be taught in the district's schools and classrooms so all children have equal access to high-quality instruction. Planning teams often see only the first task of getting the curriculum written.

Choosing members of the planning team then needs to be done with one eye on curriculum writing and the other on curriculum implementation. Planning teams have brought together representatives from the central office who could impact curriculum implementation: special education, Chapter I, and bilingual education directors need to understand how the written curriculum will affect their students and teachers. These important roles should be included in the planning team, along with teacher leadership and building administrative leadership, to provide insight into problems with implementation down the road. Curriculum personnel at the central office and department chairs from secondary schools who are not leading the project may be included to familiarize them with the process so that when their turn comes to lead curriculum implementation, they can be "up and running." The planning team also needs to establish a process for recruiting curriculum authors.

Choosing staff members to write the curriculum is the beginning of implementation of the curriculum in the schools because the chosen staff members will be the personnel who most deeply understand the curriculum and will be most helpful in assisting the school to implement the curriculum. Our experience indicates that schools with more staff members participating in the curriculum writing have the fewest problems with implementation.

Early Principal Involvement

Choosing staff to write the curriculum usually involves principals. The planning team needs to meet with principals to help them understand that their job will be easier in implementation if they can recruit teachers for the writing process. In a few districts, principals attended a few days of curriculum writing to show support for their participating teachers and to learn more about curriculum writing. Savvy principals asked the curriculum authors from the school to report on progress to the school's site-based team, increasing familiarity with the process and providing context for implementation later.

Curriculum Writing

Curriculum writing can be done during the summer, during released time during the school year, or a combination of both. Summer proves to be the best option because teachers do not have to be released from classes; continuity is maintained because teachers can meet day after day, whereas during the year they may only be able to meet monthly; and camaraderie develops as the authors interact over the 2-week writing period. To complete defining, aligning, and balancing the curriculum during the summer takes 10 days of working at least 5 hours a day. Assessments can be completed during the year with released time for a pair of curriculum writers for each course, or the full author team can work the following summer. One district (Hertford County, North Carolina) used a combination of released time for authors to develop unit titles, unit introductions, and pacing guides with grade levels during the year, preparing for a summer meeting for curriculum authors to develop, align, and balance the significant tasks for the units. In another district, consultants worked over the summer with district leadership and a few teachers, developing partial courses that were completed after the district leadership trained other teachers over the next year; the courses took a year to complete using this model.

PREPARING FOR IMPLEMENTATION: UNDERSTANDING DISTRICT NORMS

Most school districts have relatively little experience doing districtwide implementation; most implementation is project-based, and schools have choices of which projects to adopt. Consequently, most districts are experienced in school-by-school implementation but have little experience in districtwide implementation. School-by-school implementation is "safer" because the district does not have to put its credibility on the line. Districtwide implementation gives a target at which to shoot for the foes of district administration. Danger lurks in such waters, which may be why a number of districts have written the curriculum but not carried through on implementation. The planning team, the implementation plan, and the curriculum authors are three resources the district needs to use to ensure successful implementation.

The Balanced Curriculum implementation is also made difficult because the process has all teachers on a grade level teaching the same course using the same significant tasks and assessing the significant tasks in the same ways. This breaks the norms of teacher autonomy, strongly held in many districts, in which teachers are left on their own to develop what is most important for students to know and be able to do, with the textbook as guide and little direction from the district or state standards. Even though district teachers developed the curriculum, the planning team needs to understand that resistance may be strong.

Not only do the norms of autonomous teachers need to be changed but also the norms of autonomous schools and principals. In many districts, there is a tacit understanding between principals and the central office that "we" won't bother each other. Site-based management has encouraged schools to be run as fiefdoms of the principal with very little central office oversight. Central office personnel may feel that it isn't their responsibility to oversee school's implementation of curriculum. Principals may feel that "big brother" from central office is, once again, putting burdensome requirements on the schools and hence on the role of the principal. Consequently, to implement a coordinated curriculum, the planning team will need to develop strategies to assist both central office personnel and principals to adapt to their new roles while lowering the risk level for early adopters.

School board members need to understand that teachers and administrators will come to them with complaints about curriculum implementation—for example, "It's too demanding of time," "There aren't enough resources," "We've never done anything like this before," and "It infringes on my professionalism." The school board members need to think through, with the superintendent, how they will respond to such complaints before the implementation process begins.

Last, but by no means least, is the superintendent and the norms associated with his or her practices. Many superintendents have not had experience with districtwide implementation. Most district projects require cooperation of "volunteers" (so schools with no interest are left out) or only affect a few schools or a range of schools—for example, an early literacy program or block scheduling in the high school. This assists superintendents to divide and conquer, accomplishing much as they work with various constituencies across a district but rarely looking toward district implementation. Superintendents instinctively understand the political risks in implementing a program or curriculum on a districtwide basis and need to develop plans to minimize the risks and the inevitable resistance.

The curriculum planning team may change composition as the task moves from writing to implementing the curriculum. Should the superintendent's cabinet take on the planning for implementation? Should the planning team be a subcommittee of the superintendent's cabinet? Should the planning team include more principals and teacher leaders?

Force Field Analysis

The committee or group in charge of thinking through and planning implementation is encouraged to do a force field analysis. A force field analysis charts those who support implementation, those on the fence, and those who don't support implementation by groups that have a stake in the decisions, such as school boards, the central office, and the schools (see Figure 17.1).

Figure 17.1 Force field analysis

The superintendent needs to fill out the sheet with the school board and the principals in mind as a way to let the planning team know what problems the superintendent might be facing. The principals need to fill out the sheets for their schools. If this can be done with a member of the planning team, it will help with implementation because the planning team will then have an understanding of the types of difficulties the principal is facing. A central office planning team member, to understand the stance of particular staff members in the central office, could visit individual members of the central office to determine where they would place themselves and their staff on the chart. This exercise can be a first attempt to move those on the fence to a supporting position and those who don't support to move to the fence. The good news is that many of the staff will support the change or are on the fence; only a few will not be supportive. This provides the data necessary to continue the planning process.

THE "DO IT ALL" STRATEGY FOR DISTRICTWIDE IMPLEMENTATION

Curriculum implementation is a complex innovation involving all the members of the organization. So some would recommend a "go slow" approach, in which the curriculum is implemented at 1st grade this year, 2nd the next, and so on. The argument goes that it could be done well at each grade level. The problem is that it would take 12 years to do the complete implementation. Research on curriculum implementation suggests another strategy. McLaughlin (1976) noted that the greater complexity in innovations with differentiated components that are incrementally introduced, the greater the degree of implementation. The Balanced Curriculum, a complex change, is incrementally introduced, implementing one significant task at a time. As a whole, however, the Balanced Curriculum should be implemented as an initiative, all at once. This means that if the curriculum was written for English and language arts, it should be implemented on a K–12 basis across the grade levels. The rule I use is, "Implement with the biggest population of teachers possible." Research suggests that this works because, among other things, large-scale implementation indicates the project is sufficiently important to allow significant organizational resources to be focused on it. When implementation is smaller (dealing with only one grade or course level), it doesn't command attention. In implementing the Balanced Curriculum, districts that implemented with large teacher populations (i.e., K–12 math) were more successful than those implementing smaller chunks (i.e., 5–8 language arts). This strategy can be effective if the district assembles its tools for implementation and develops a comprehensive plan for implementation.

Reasons for districts not implementing on a K–12 basis include the following:

- Districts aren't sure the curriculum will actually work (that is, improve achievement), so they "hedge their bets" by first implementing with a smaller grade-level span.
- Districts see implementation happening more easily with elementary schools than high schools, so the elementary schools go first. If successful at the elementary level, the district will then commit the resources (and the political capital) necessary to implement at the high school level.
- The expense of paying teachers for 2 weeks or summer work is considerable, and sometimes districts can't accumulate the funds to pay the teachers to get it all done at once.
- Districts aren't accustomed to conducting districtwide implementation. Implementing with a limited span of grade levels seems more doable and less risky. What if all the effort doesn't pay off in improved achievement? Whose fault will people perceive it to be? Limiting the number of grade levels limits the impact but also the "visibility" of the project so that district staff can limit the liability if the project doesn't go as expected.

Tools for Implementation

Any school district has a tremendous number of tools available to assist in the implementation. The first tool is the force field analysis that identifies those who are committed and those who are wavering or are not committed. Staff development resources are another tool. This includes time available, either districtwide or in the school, when staff development can take place. Some districts have staff development time at the beginning of the year, whereas others schedule staff development days occasionally throughout the year. Schools may convene grade level or department meetings that can be used for staff development. Planned well, this time can assist with implementation.

Publicity is another tool that districts can access. Newsletters, providing information to the school board, and newspaper articles are among the ways to reinforce implementation. Highlighting personnel who are following the process is another "bee-bee in the boxcar" of curriculum implementation.

Internal communication, such as memos and "doing-a-great-job" notes, provide reinforcement to those who adopt the program at the early stages. Principals will want to put this in their school plans for implementing the curriculum. Superintendents and central office staff will want to provide these kudos to principals and other supervisory staff. A note such as "Congratulations! On a recent visit I saw evidence of the curriculum posted in the halls and walls" will go a long way toward reinforcing commitment or changing a fence-sitter into a supporter.

Existing policies and procedures offer another way to reinforce curriculum implementation. Most personnel evaluation systems ask principals, teachers, central office staff, and superintendents to set goals for the year and then evaluate them on the goals that they set.

Superintendents can help set the tone by incorporating in their goals the implementation of the curriculum. To assist the superintendent, principals and teachers can also have a goal of curriculum implementation. A teacher's goal might read, "I will complete 85% of the significant tasks in the curriculum during the first year of implementation, record my completions on the Web site, and make comments on the Web site about needed improvements that could be incorporated into the curriculum." A principal's goal might read, "I will monitor teacher implementation of the curriculum by comparing their lesson plans to curriculum documents, only conducting formal evaluations when the written curriculum is being implemented, and monitoring teacher's progress by checking school-level reports from the Balanced Curriculum Web site, which aggregates completion information."

The superintendent can require principals to turn in completion reports for their schools on a monthly basis. Other central office staff members are required to tell how they assisted with implementation of the curriculum in their monthly reports. The superintendent's office then aggregates this information to pass on to the planning team.

Grade-level or department meetings are often required. These can be used to plan approaches to the next unit or significant task, debrief how the existing unit is coming along, or examine student work after the unit is completed. "How can we do this better next time?" is the question that can be answered in grade-level or departmental meetings.

Most states now require districts and schools to develop staff development plans for the year. Focusing staff development times around implementation of the curriculum will reinforce teacher's commitment. Some larger districts have staff development courses that could be centered on curriculum implementation. Schools may also be required to have a staff development plan. Depending on the sophistication of the schools, the central office could publish a process for developing a staff development plan centered on curriculum evaluation. Research suggests that "the greater the quality and quantity of sustained interactions and staff development, the greater the degree of implementation" (Snyder et al., 1992, p. 415).

Parent involvement can also spur implementation. One district published on the Balanced Curriculum Web site the units, the unit introductions, and the timeline as a way to keep parents informed about what their children were doing in school. At the first PTA meeting of the year, the school's PTA president (who had recently been trained on how to go on the Web site and obtain the information) did a presentation to parents about the new curriculum. Parents received a copy of the abbreviated curriculum and were encouraged to bring this document to parent conferences. For those who didn't attend, the document was also passed out at parent conferences with instructions on how to access the Web site.

Figure 17.2 Seven stages of concern

	Stage	Title	Main Concerns
Unrelated Concerns	0	Awareness	Little concern about or involvement with the innovation.
SELF CONCERNS	1	Informational	A general awareness of the innovation, and interest in learning more detail about it is indicated. The person seems to be unworried about himself or herself in relation to the innovation. She or he is interested in substantive aspects of the innovation in a selfless manner, such as general characteristics, effects, and requirements for use.
	2	Personal	Individual is uncertain about the demands of the innovation, his or her adequacy to meet those demands, and his or her role with the innovation. This includes analysis of the individual's role in relation to the reward structure of the organization, decision making, and consideration of potential conflicts with existing structures or personal commitment. Financial or status implications of the program for self and colleagues may also be reflected.
TASK CONCERNS	3	Management	Attention is focused on the processes and tasks of using the innovation and the best use of information and resources. Issues related to efficiency, organizing, managing, scheduling, and time demands are utmost.
IMPACT CONCERNS	4	Consequences	Attention focuses on impact of the innovation on students in the individual's immediate sphere of influence. The focus is on relevance of the innovation for students, evaluation of student outcomes including performance and competencies, and changes needed to improve student outcomes.
	5	Collaboration	The focus is on coordination and cooperation with others regarding use of the innovation.
	6	Refocusing	The focus is on exploration of more universal benefits from the innovation, including the possibility of major changes or replacement with a more powerful alternative. The individual has definite ideas about alternatives to the proposed or existing form of innovation.

SOURCE: Hall & Hord, 2001; Hall, Wallace, & Dossett, 1973.

The Concerns-Based Adoption Model (CBAM):
Knowing Where You Are in Implementing the Curriculum

The CBAM is a validated instrument used to trace the progress of the adoption of an innovation—in this case, the curriculum. It shows that individuals progress through stages of concerns: from unrelated concerns to self-concerns to task concerns to impact concerns (see Figure 17.2). "Progress through the innovation (the curriculum) depends on the appropriateness of the innovation, how facilitative line administrators were, and whether adequate time (3 to 5 years) had been given" (Snyder et al., 1992, p. 409). This allows the planning team to plan ways to take into account the levels of concern at various stages of the implementation, with the beginning stages being critical.

Hall and Loucks (1977) also proposed a validated Levels of Use (LoU) Instrument to assess the level of implementation of an innovation—for our purposes, the curriculum (see Figure 17.3). High levels of use need to be demonstrated before an innovation can claim an effect. This can also be used as a tool for tracking progress on implementing the curriculum. LoU provides for teacher interviews or questionnaires to determine the stage of use they have attained. Both instruments can be used with the Balanced Curriculum process to track the progress of implementation (see Hord et al., 1987, for sample strategies).

Figure 17.3   Levels of Use (LoU)

Level	Title	Description
0	Nonuse	The user has little of no knowledge of the innovation.
1	Orientation	The user has recently acquired or is acquiring information about the innovation or has recently explored or is exploring its value orientation and its demands on user and user system.
2	Preparation	The user is preparing for first use of the innovation.
3	Mechanical Use	The user focuses most effort on the short-term, day-to-day use of the innovation with little time for reflection. Changes in use are made to meet user needs more than client needs. The user is primarily engaged in a stepwise attempt to master the tasks required to use the innovation, often resulting in disjointed and superficial use.
4a	Routine	Use of the innovation is stabilized. Few, if any, changes are being made in ongoing use. Little preparation or thought is being given to improving innovation use or its consequences.
4b	Refinement	The user varies the use of the innovation to increase the impact on clients within immediate sphere of influence. Variations are based on knowledge of both short- and long-term consequences for clients.
5	Integration	The user combines his or her efforts to use the innovation with colleagues' related activities to achieve a collective impact on clients within their common sphere of influence.
6	Renewal	The user reevaluates the quality of use of the innovation, seeks major modifications of or alternatives to present innovation to achieve increased impact on clients; the user examines new developments in the field and explores new goals in the system.

SOURCE: Hall & Loucks, 1977.

Monitoring Curriculum and Assessment Implementation

The Balanced Curriculum Web site also contains two tools for monitoring curriculum implementation. The first involves teachers reporting completion of significant tasks. Teachers, when they have completed a significant task, log on to the Web site and indicate that they want to log their completions of significant tasks. The Web site shows them the significant tasks for the course they are teaching (see Figure 17.4).

The first significant task, "Going Batty Over Sound," was completed on February 5, 2003. The next three significant tasks from the "Famous Americans" unit are not completed because they have an incomplete message in the third column. For teachers to complete the task, they check "Completed on Default Date" (today) or can fill in another date in the "Completed On" box. Principals can get reports for their schools from the Web site (see Figure 17.5).

Figure 17.4   Teachers record significant task completions

Simply Sound 01/21/2003 To: 02/05/2003	Going Batty Over Sound	02/05/2003 00:00:00	Change to Incomplete: ☐
Famous Americans 02/06/2003 To: 02/21/2003	Who's Who	Incomplete	Completed On: ☐ Complete on Default Date: ☐
Famous Americans 02/06/2003 To: 02/21/2003	From Timeline to Report	Incomplete	Completed On: ☐ Complete on Default Date: ☐
Famous Americans 02/06/2003 To: 02/21/2003	What's My Line?	Incomplete	Completed On: ☐ Complete on Default Date: ☐

Default Date: 03/17/2003

Submit

SOURCE: Used courtesy of Hertford County Public Schools.

Figure 17.5   Significant task completion report for a principal

District/Course/Teacher
Significant Task Completion
Summary

Hertford County Public
Schools
2003-2004

Significant Tasks in Units Ending through 03/03/2004

Grade 6 Communication Skills		Completed	
Teacher A	County Middle School	78%	18 of 23
Teacher B	County Middle School	70%	16 of 23
Teacher C	County Middle School	100%	23 of 23
Teacher D	County Middle School	96%	22 of 23
Teacher E	County Middle School	100%	23 of 23
Teacher F	County Middle School	74%	17 of 23
Teacher G	County Middle School	91%	21 of 23
	County Middle School	87%	140 of 161
Total For Grade 6 Communication Skills		**87%**	**140 of 161**

SOURCE: Used courtesy of Hertford County Public Schools.

This report (Figure 17.5) shows completions for teachers teaching Grade 6 Communication Skills in Hertford County Middle School (North Carolina) for all of the significant tasks completed through March 3, 2003. For example, Teacher A completed 18 of 23 significant tasks due by March 3, 2003, for a 78% completion rate. Principals can use this information to determine teachers' progress through the curriculum. Principals will want to confer with teachers who aren't up to date with their completions to determine, with the teacher, whether they have completed the tasks and not recorded them or whether they are behind and need some assistance in catching up or leaving out a few significant tasks for the rest of the year that may not be as important as others. As part of implementation, principals receive training in getting the report from the Web site, in interpreting the report, and in conferring with teachers.

Central office staff and superintendents can get reports that summarize progress of schools across the district. The superintendent is encouraged to ask principals to submit completion reports as part of their monthly reports to the central office. In some districts, superintendents have required principals to include a goal in their yearly goals of monitoring and completing at least 95% of the curriculum with teachers in the schools. Yearly evaluations include monitoring and completing the curriculum as one of their benchmarks.

REVISING THE CURRICULUM

Instead of revising the curriculum every 5 to 7 years, the Balanced Curriculum process generates enough data so that the curriculum can be fine-tuned every year, using the data the system generates. Yearly revision ensures that the curriculum does not stagnate and is based on students improving prerequisite skills and teachers increasing comfort and sophistication in their instruction. Figure 17.6 shows four data sources for revising the curriculum: teacher completions of significant tasks, teacher comments about significant tasks and assessments, results from content assessments, and results from standardized and state tests. A small grade- or course-level committee of two or three teachers can revise the curriculum in a few days, if all the data are available.

Figure 17.6 Data sources for yearly curriculum revision

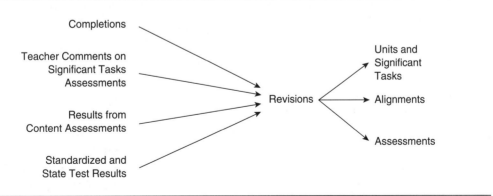

Final completion reports are used to revise the curriculum. If a large number of teachers didn't teach all of the significant tasks, then revisers will need to consider reducing the number of significant tasks or units, or the complexity of some significant tasks, to allow adequate teaching time. They might also decide to make no changes, figuring that teachers now have the experience to keep up. If the majority of teachers completed all significant tasks, then the revisers may want to consider increasing the number or complexity of the significant tasks (or both), knowing that next year's students will enter with better prerequisite skills than students did the year before.

Teacher comments about significant tasks and assessments provide another source of data. On the Web site, teachers can make comments on units, significant tasks, or assessments as these are completed. Revisers print out reports of these comments and use them to determine whether particular significant tasks or assessments need revision. Following is a sample comment report for a portion of one unit:

Significant Task Comments

Hands-on the First Day

The students will write a personal narrative describing their first day of school, including what it was like, how they felt, and what they did. They will choral read "Ann's First Day," and the class will discuss the author's use of declarative, interrogative, and exclamatory sentences. They will discuss the similarities and differences between Ann's first day and their first day. The students will compare their story and "Ann's First Day" by using illustrations of a handprint and writing characters on the thumbs, setting on the pointer finger, feelings at the beginning on the middle finger, feelings at the end of the story on the ring finger, and the best part of the story on the pinky finger. (Two handprints will be needed: one for their story, one for "Ann's First Day.")

Comments

This was a fun activity. The students were actively engaged and enjoyed the process.

I combined both hands on one piece of construction paper and called it Hand Comparisons. The children were able to see the similarities and differences between both stories at the touch of a finger!:-)

I liked using the hands to compare stories and the students enjoyed it also.

I found necessary to practice this in a whole-group setting before having individual students complete this task. Great activity! The class enjoyed it.

Fun activities for students to express themselves!

Student's liked sharing orally before writing about the story. They enjoyed drawing their own handprints, adding own personal touches.

The activity was very interesting.

Students were excited about writing on a handprint. It was a change from the ordinary and still gave them the knowledge they needed with the story elements.

Based on the comments, teachers found the significant task successful because it was fun and engaged the students but still gave them the knowledge and application they needed. This significant task looks like a keeper. The second comment about using one sheet of paper for two handprints and the fourth comment about practicing as a group before asking students to complete the task individually might be used to revise the significant task to incorporate those elements.

The revisers can also use data from the content assessments, either gathered manually or from the record-keeping system for assessments on the Web site. Figure 17.7 shows the district averages for all content assessments summarized by unit. Unit 1, 2, 4, and 5 had low averages. This may indicate that the assessment was too difficult, that the significant tasks did not prepare students well for the content assessment, or that there was a mismatch between the requirements of the significant task and the content assessment. Revisers would want to examine the significant tasks and the content assessments to determine where revision needs to be made.

Figure 17.7   Summary of curriculum-embedded assessment results used for revision

Student Results

Grade 3 Mathematics

District Summary of Content Assessments

Aggregated by Unit

Unit Average	
67.7	Unit 1
64.6	Unit 2
85.9	Unit 3
66.0	Unit 4
70.3	Unit 5
88.2	Unit 6
83.4	Unit 7
82.0	Unit 8
76.0	

Standardized and state assessments provide the last data source for revising assessments. In areas where the district did not do well, revisers examine the significant tasks aligned to that area and determine whether the significant tasks or the assessments need to be modified or strengthened (see Chapter 14).

Knowing which students did and did not do well on state assessments allows comparisons between standardized test data and the results of the content assessments. Revisers need to consider whether students who pass the state or standardized tests also pass the content assessments. If true, the curriculum is validated, and the district can have confidence that the same or better results will probably be produced in the next year. Revisers need to consider whether students who did not pass the state or standardized test also faired poorly on content assessments. If true, the curriculum is again validated. If students didn't pass the state test but passed the content assessments, then the content assessments may not be rigorous enough or the significant tasks may need to be made more challenging. Or revisers will need to decide whether students became challenged by the format of the state assessment.

If states report scores for subareas of the test, then it is possible to examine whether students who did well on the content assessments aligned with the subarea also performed well on the subareas of the state test. These data fine-tune the validation process. Revisers need to consider each data source before determining appropriate revisions.

SUMMARY

This chapter focused on strategies to implement and revise the curriculum once ithas been written. The next chapter discusses more fully the staff development opportunities that arise as the curriculum is implemented.

18

Staff Development to Promote Curriculum Implementation

This chapter focuses on staff development as the key to curriculum implementation. Well-planned staff development will encourage teachers to adopt the curriculum because the whole school system is organizing around it. The discussion centers around the overlapping roles and functions of the planning team, principals, and districtwide, building-based, and central office staff development. Building these plans into district plans for staff development or district improvement and building plans required by the state or funded programs will help to present to all a coordinated and systematic implementation process. (Thanks to Sandra Bullock, retired assistant superintendent from District 13 in New York City, for initially raising the importance of staff development.)

PLANNING TEAM

The planning team members, when designing the process for writing the curriculum, also looked toward the time when the curriculum would be implemented. They consciously planned and had a written plan for many of the following activities. They did a thorough job in recruiting teacher leaders who could assist in the curriculum implementation. Principals kept informed through updates with the superintendent and by checking on the progress of the curriculum authors as the curriculum was written. School faculty meetings reviewed the writers' progress. Writers from the school reported on their experiences. The school board received updates, along with a few presentations about the curriculum writing. District newsletters carried pictures and stories of the curriculum writers. The PTAs received updates, and administrators presented the plans at PTA meetings. These are some of the ways to let everyone know that the curriculum is in progress and nearing implementation. No one should be able to claim legitimate surprise when the implementation process starts. Given fair warning, those who might oppose a curriculum will have less impact because everyone was informed of its coming, and principals have worked with their school planning and management teams to anticipate and reduce resistance. Districts that prepare in this fashion generally find implementation easier and smoother.

Superintendents

Principals are the key to building-based implementation. Principals take their cue on how important things are from the superintendent. If the superintendent is lukewarm about the possibility of curriculum-improving outcomes, principals are likely to mirror this attitude. The planning team needs to help the superintendent structure a strong plan to influence the principals. Here are 13 things that successful superintendents do to encourage and reinforce implementation through their own leadership in staff development efforts with principals:

1. Take time in meetings to train principals so they have knowledge of the structure and function of curriculum.

2. Maintain a recurring agenda item for principal meetings in which progress on the curriculum is discussed.

3. Highlight principals who have found solid ways to support the writing and implementation of the curriculum.

4. Incorporate supporting and implementing the curriculum in principal's yearly professional improvement plans.

5. Use evaluation conferences to provide principals with feedback on how well they are doing toward their goal of curriculum implementation.

6. Visit schools and ask principals to see teachers who are doing a good job with curriculum implementation.

7. Host report sessions for the board during which principals describe how they are supporting implementation in their schools.

8. Feature high-implementing principals in the district newsletter.

9. Talk with teachers' union or association leadership about the benefits of a well-implemented curriculum to teaching staff.

10. Discuss with slow-implementing principals the need for speed in curriculum implementation. Document these conversations in a follow-up memo, focusing on agreements the principal made to move curriculum implementation forward.

11. Ensure that principals include reports of teachers' completion of the curriculum in their monthly reports. If available, principals can also report on student results from the significant tasks.

12. Name a districtwide "help" person who assists administrators and teachers in understanding and using the powerful capability of the Web site.

13. Sponsor a districtwide staff development plan that clearly demonstrates that curriculum implementation is a priority for district- and school-based staff development.

Principals

As the superintendent leads the principals, so the principals are likely to lead the schools. Most principals will act in their own best interests, and the principals need to buy in to the logic of providing all students with a high-quality curriculum that can guide and systematize instruction and assessment. Following are 10 ways to encourage staff development in learning about and implementing the Balanced Curriculum.

1. *Monitor faculty logging completions and comments on the Web site.* Follow up with those who are having difficulty. Appoint a technology coordinator in the school to assist those who are having difficulty accessing the Web site. Particularly at the beginning, survey the Web site for comments that come from the school's staff and mention to individual teachers or teacher groups that the comments were seen and were appropriate.

2. *See if lesson plans reflect the curriculum—that is, the units and significant tasks.* Keep a copy of the units and significant tasks available as a resource to use in reviewing lesson plans. Not all lesson plans will directly reference the curriculum; significant tasks are to use only 60% of instructional time. During most weeks, however, there should be at least one significant task covered in a teacher's lesson planning.

3. *Use 5-minute classroom visits as a way to survey whether the curriculum is being taught.* Once a week, visit each classroom in the school and look for evidence that the curriculum is being taught. The significant tasks often require student projects, which can be displayed around the room. Many principals drop teachers a note when they find a significant task in evidence. Keep a record and report on the percentage of classrooms with evidence of implementation during faculty meetings.

4. *Involve the school planning team or curriculum committees in problem solving around implementation.* Implementation is not just a principal's responsibility. Make addressing curriculum implementation a permanent agenda item for the school planning team meetings.

5. *Highlight progress with the parent team or PTA.* Teachers can report on successful implementation of significant tasks. Parents can comment on interesting projects their students have completed.

6. *Give parents copies of the units and significant tasks.* Have teachers report on significant tasks that have gone well. Encourage parents to ask their children about the units and significant tasks they are completing. Brainstorm ways that parents can help teachers to implement the significant tasks, including student homework.

7. *Highlight teaming in grade-level meetings around the following tasks:*
    a. Share previous units' work that students have completed. Start with examples of students who did well. Ask everyone to bring one or two examples. Discuss what helped these students do such a good job. How could the findings be extended to other students?
    b. Determine comments to be posted on the Web site. The comments suggest how to improve previous units. After a unit is over, have the group come to a consensus on how to improve the units and significant tasks for next year. One person can then place the comments on the Web site. The comments may be stronger than if everyone had to think alone and generate comments.

    c. Debrief on how the current unit and significant tasks are going. What are the problems of trying to implement the significant tasks? Has anyone found a way to address those problems in the classroom? Has anyone devised a short cut to save time to get the significant task completed in less time?

    d. Co-plan upcoming units and significant tasks. Determine various ways to organize the units and significant tasks. Which ways would work best for individuals in the group? Share the preparation so that everyone has less work.

The principal may want to meet at the beginning of the year to work with teachers of the same courses to raise the issue of sharing. Some course groups work well together. Others may need the continued presence of the principal or another support person to help reluctant groups continue the conversation.

8. *Collect and post samples of student work from the curriculum.* Encourage others to do the same. One principal reported that the healthy competition generated by displaying student projects from their significant tasks helped all the teachers produce higher-quality student work. One parent reported, "I always knew students worked in this school, but now I can see what students produced. It's really impressive."

9. *Encourage faculty to write curriculum implementation into their professional improvement plans.* Curriculum implementation does take effort, and this is a way for teachers to "get credit" for the time and effort they expend in curriculum implementation.

10. *Include implementing the Balanced Curriculum in evaluation conferences and written classroom observation reports.* Those that are doing a good job get recognition, and those who are slower to implement get a reminder that curriculum implementation is a school and district priority.

DISTRICTWIDE STAFF DEVELOPMENT

After the curriculum is written, teachers need to be introduced to the curriculum and procedures need to be put in place to encourage use of the curriculum—both staff development tasks. Districts usually introduce the curriculum during a staff development day at the beginning of the school year. If done on a districtwide basis, curriculum authors for each new course can conduct staff development for other teachers that teach that course. In large districts, 1st grade might assemble at one school, 2nd grade at another, and so on. Curriculum authors review the curriculum development process and discuss the structure of the curriculum, focusing on units, significant tasks, and assessments. Copies of the curriculum are distributed. Then school-level teams meet to convert the significant tasks into lesson plans so that everyone is ready for the first week of school. Teachers might also be taught how to use the Web site to log completions and comments.

Additional districtwide staff development can be planned from information gathered at this first meeting. A questionnaire can be distributed that asks grade-level teams from each school to list the three units and six significant tasks that they think will be most difficult to implement. This information is a needs assessment for the district to offer afterschool sessions or courses during the year that will assist teachers in understanding and implementing these difficult units or significant tasks. For example, if teachers indicate that significant tasks featuring cooperative learning groups would be most difficult, staff development sessions could be planned, either on in-service days or in after-school mini-courses that would address this need.

The planning team for the Balanced Curriculum process should continue to meet throughout the school year, perhaps on a monthly basis. The planning team may want to expand to include a representative from all the schools in the district so that the planning team can keep track of how implementation is progressing. Problem-solving sessions on overcoming individual school difficulties is a helpful way to assist implementation. If the group decides to use the Levels of Use questionnaire (see Chapter 16) as a way to track implementation, the planning team can provide the forum to share the results.

BUILDING-BASED STAFF DEVELOPMENT

Principals and school-based councils need to be active in promoting the use of the curriculum in the school. Individual grade levels or course teachers will have individual needs, and the school-based council can determine how to meet them. For example, one course had all new teachers assigned with one veteran (the department chairperson). The principal had made sure that all these teachers had a common planning period. The department chair then met with these teachers, asking them to share their approaches to each significant task, validating the many strategies that were discussed. When a significant task called for using manipulatives and the teachers had no experience with these learning tools, the department chair provided staff development on manipulative use over a couple of planning periods so that teachers would be prepared when they got to that point in the curriculum. Course- or grade-level leaders could provide the same opportunities, providing a professional role for their further development.

The point here is that the district will not be able to provide a plan to meet all of the various staff development needs of the buildings. The district can provide for general needs established by a needs assessment but will have limited time and resources to address other needs. School buildings where teachers have common planning time provide a unique opportunity to target staff development to grade- or course-level needs. Using the expertise that exists in school buildings to deliver staff development helps build the capacity of school personnel. Developing building-based staff development plans also increases the school's capacity to meet its own needs for instructional improvement. Such a building-based staff development plan can be incorporated into district, state, or federal requirements for school improvement plans.

CENTRAL OFFICE STAFF DEVELOPMENT

Before the curriculum is passed out to teachers, central office staff must meet so they understand the structure of the curriculum and how to use the curriculum's structure to serve the needs of students under their charge. Title I, special education, bilingual and English-as-a-second-language, Gifted and Talented, and special subject areas, especially in the elementary schools—such as library and media centers, physical education, art, music—need to develop scenarios so that teachers in those settings will understand how the curriculum needs to be used. For example, stakeholders in the Gifted and Talented program need to decide if they will use the newly written curriculum as a springboard to projects and explorations that are curriculum related or will they go off on their own and develop another set of units and significant tasks that is related to the curriculum but takes the ideas one step further? Will special education teachers modify the curriculum so that it is appropriate for their students and include the modifications as part of Individual Education Plans? There are no right or wrong answers to these questions, but the best approach needs to be determined for each of these important areas of schooling.

Central office staff will also need to hear from the planning committee on a quarterly basis to determine whether there are any sticking points that are causing difficulties in the schools, another staff development activity. Then they can develop strategies collaboratively to address the problems. When difficulties arose in the schools of one district, its assistant superintendent visited the schools and, with the help of the principals, encouraged group problem solving.

SUMMARY

This chapter reviewed how districts can orchestrate staff development opportunities that reinforce the implementation of the curriculum. The district planning team has a major role in seeing the implementation from a districtwide perspective and organizing district resources to meet the huge task of beginning and continuing implementation. The next chapter shares Dr. Philomena Pezzano's experience as a superintendent of two school districts, one large and one small, in which the Balanced Curriculum was implemented.

19

The Superintendent's Role

Philomena T. Pezzano

My supervisor in a previous job would start each staff meeting with a reminder that "Curriculum and instruction is the heart and soul of the school district." No truer words were ever spoken. With the recent federal legislation focusing on standards-based accountability and adequate yearly progress for all students, curriculum and instruction must become a high priority on the leadership agenda for all chief school administrators. In this chapter, I emphasize that the participation of the superintendent in curricular changes is directly related to the success of the project. First, I describe the two districts—Newburgh, New York, and Englewood Cliffs, New Jersey—and my role in implementing the Balanced Curriculum process. I then describe my perceptions of leadership aspects that led to project success. Finally, I provide leadership strategies important to the successful implementation of the Balanced Curriculum process in both of these districts.

DESCRIPTION OF DISTRICTS

The Newburgh School District in New York State is an urban–suburban district of approximately 12,500 students in 15 schools. In Newburgh, I served as the deputy

AUTHOR'S NOTE: Philomena T. Pezzano, EdD, holds a doctorate from Columbia University and is superintendent of Englewood Cliffs, New Jersey, Public Schools. She has implemented the Balanced Curriculum in two school districts, including Englewood Cliffs. Previously, she served as deputy superintendent and acting superintendent for the Newburgh Enlarged City School District in Newburgh, New York, where strong initial implementation of the Balanced Curriculum contributed to improved scores for all schools in the district after the first year.

superintendent, reporting directly to the superintendent. When I arrived in the Newburgh School District in June 1998, I had the opportunity to become involved in and assess all aspects of the school district. A new superintendent, Dr. Laval S. Wilson, had joined the district the prior July and was in the midst of a major secondary education reform initiative, the first district need identified by the superintendent.

In my role, through needs assessments, I identified the need for current, coherent curriculum, aligned to state standards and implemented districtwide. In addition, the district had recently received a large federal magnet schools grant. Curriculum development had been identified as a need to be addressed through the grant. Our magnet schools grant program evaluator emphasized that developing and implementing a new curriculum would systemically change the district and improve student performance. The superintendent determined that a curriculum needed to be coherent and aligned to standards and needed to address all curricular areas. The Balanced Curriculum process was chosen, and the project began.

My role was to lead the initiative and directly represent the superintendent; it was clear to the staff of the school district and to the community that the superintendent, through my role in the process, was leading this initiative. The superintendent actively participated in a large number of the planning meetings as well as some of the curriculum writing sessions.

Teachers developed curriculum guides for the four major subjects—English and language arts, mathematics, science, and social studies—within a 2-year period, including summers.

The Englewood Cliffs School District in New Jersey is a suburban district of approximately 450 students in two schools that followed a similar process. I serve as the superintendent in this district. During my candidacy for the position of superintendent, the Board of Education identified revision and updating of all district curriculum and technology applications as the major priority. Board members liked my prior experience in developing curriculum, especially using the Balanced Curriculum model. With the Balanced Curriculum being Web-based, implementing the Balanced Curriculum addressed both curriculum and technology. Although the curriculum coordinator (also a principal in the district) is charged with direct implementation of this project, I felt that the new superintendent should lead this initiative. In addition, having already successfully led the project in Newburgh, I brought that experience, knowledge, and success to bear.

In Englewood Cliffs, I have completed my third year as superintendent, and we are completing our second curriculum subject-area guide in social studies; our first was language arts literacy. A major difference in the development of the curriculum in this district, compared with the Newburgh District, is that the progress has been slower because fewer teachers are available to write curriculum in a small district. In the larger district, where a large number of staff members became curriculum writers, the process could move more quickly. Nonetheless, we are making steady, significant progress.

Funding for the Balanced Curriculum process was a matter that required deliberation in each of the districts because the expenditure for complete writing and implementation of the curriculum, including use of the Web site, is significant. In Newburgh, we were fortunate to have an excellent grant-writing department led by its executive director, Dr. Annette Saturnelli, who is now superintendent of the Newburgh District. When a district priority was identified, Dr. Saturnelli used the resources of the grant-writing department to find funds. In Englewood Cliffs, funding came from our general budget. In both districts, development of the curriculum was a major priority, so both boards of education supported this initiative.

LEADERSHIP FROM THE SUPERINTENDENT'S OFFICE

To implement curriculum districtwide, whether in a large or a small school district, the thrust and support for the initiative needs to come from the superintendent's office. It has been my experience in my 30-plus years of public school education that a reform of this magnitude will only succeed when supported by the superintendent. I have too often seen excellent initiatives fail to take hold when top-level administrators did not provide support.

The curriculum's success, however, is also dependent on the types of skills demonstrated by the superintendent. I would like to provide some examples of the skills I feel are required to bring the Balanced Curriculum to successful implementation and examples of how we utilized those skills in both districts.

I feel the type of leadership required for systemic reform must be collaborative and facilitative. This type of leadership builds trust between school district leaders and staff members. The superintendent encourages trust by allowing principals, other administrators, and staff members to participate in planning and developing the project.

When this project was first initiated in Newburgh, the superintendent met with all of his administrative staff to explain the process, answer questions, and make suggestions ensuring that their ideas would be incorporated as the project evolved. Of course, in Newburgh, as in most districts, we had the naysayer administrators who did not believe the process would work, thought the curriculums would never be implemented, and said teachers would not agree to write the curriculum. We knew that these same naysayers were the administrators who historically had not supported any initiatives and whose schools or programs demonstrated the least amount of improvement in student performance. In spite of their nonsupport, we assured the naysayer administrators as well as our supporters that we would take all of their thoughts and suggestions under review and consider them as we were making the decisions about the program. We also assured all administrators that we would provide feedback to the whole group at each step of the process to show that we were taking everyone's ideas into consideration. As we provided feedback, all of the administrative staff saw that their input was valued and used.

We made the decision, however, to target those administrators who supported the process to be more intimately involved in the planning and asked them to encourage and influence their colleagues to support the process. The supporters stayed the course, in part because of support from leadership during the 2 years of writing and implementation.

Many initial nonsupporters, when provided with a leadership role, led admirably. When asked what happened to spur their change of heart, they indicated that they had changed their minds about the project when they saw the improvement in student achievement that resulted from the first curriculums that were implemented. They also indicated that, throughout the process, people were heard when they made suggestions, that their ideas were valued and that the administration was willing to address concerns as they were voiced.

In Englewood Cliffs, being collaborative and facilitative was a much easier task because I did not encounter nonsupporters. In such a small district, it was much easier to garner support for new and innovative programs. In Englewood Cliffs, the two principals, the supervisor of special education, the president of the union (a special education teacher), and representatives from each grade level and subject area became members of my leadership team. Although there may have been some teachers who were somewhat reluctant to begin this process, we have been able to bring everyone on board within these last 3 years of working with the process.

Resolving conflict is another necessary skill for leaders and superintendents in this process. During any change process, especially in such wide-reaching change as curriculum reform, conflicts arise. Leaders can assure participants that they will provide a forum for conflicts to be dealt with in a professional, appropriate manner. In Newburgh, we had an example of addressing a conflict that, I believe, would have stalled the whole curriculum writing process if it had not been addressed. This conflict occurred during the writing of the first curriculum and is described below.

The writing group consisted of approximately 100 teaching staff members, along with a representative group of administrators, teamed in grade levels. We had planned for the group to write the curriculum during a 10-day period. On the third day, the group members experienced a high level of anxiety concerning their role as curriculum writers. They were unsure about how colleagues back at their schools would view them when the curriculum was introduced—Would the staff use the curriculum, or would they use only the textbooks? Would the curriculum authors be "blamed" and "castigated" for participating in the writing? Would the curriculum just sit on the shelf because no one would supervise its implementation? Would the curriculum be "flexible" enough for teachers?

Until these questions were answered, the project was at a standstill. I discussed the problem with the district leadership team, and we decided to take immediate steps to provide the teachers with answers. We decided to have anyone with a problem articulate that problem, and, using posters on an easel, we displayed the concerns to all the curriculum authors.

When the group came together after a break, we took each and every issue and addressed the concerns, then discussed how they would be resolved. Although we dealt with each concern, we also continued to support the project and communicated that we would stay the course with this project. Following that session, the group came back together and continued with their work and completed the project within the 10-day period.

It was important for me to help guide the vision and remain determined to complete the project until results were achieved. I became the expert in this process and could discuss it formally, informally, and in any venue. There was never any uncertainty about whether we would complete this project, even when uncertainties mounted.

Finally, in both projects, I served as the official "cheerleader" for the project. A major reform initiative must always have someone in a leadership role constantly supporting the effort and remaining positive about the change at all times. Whether meeting with board members, school staff, administrative staff, individual staff members, parents, or community members, I always spoke in positive terms and acknowledged the progress. The problems never overshadowed the great work the teachers were doing.

When we hit a wall in some of the schools in the Newburgh implementation process, I personally went to those schools to discuss the problems with staff members. I carefully listened to all of the concerns and provided answers to all of the questions. The bottom line, however, was that I expected the full implementation of the curriculum. While at these sessions, I took the opportunity to be a cheerleader, talking about the positive progress being made and indicating that the curriculum would be used in each class of the school. I knew that I had to remain highly optimistic at all times for staff members working on the project to believe that we would be successful in achieving our goals.

LEADERSHIP STRATEGIES

Administrators use leadership strategies every day to help achieve the goals we desire. A few were especially helpful as I implemented the Balanced Curriculum process.

Leadership Strategy 1: Communicating the Vision

The superintendent, in the role of instructional leader, must first gain the support of the board of education for this initiative to be successful. This requires fully informing the board of the process and project. The board of education needs to recognize the importance of the initiative and fully support the superintendent and staff during the implementation of the initiative. In both districts, the board of education fully supported this curricular reform, and this support contributed significantly to its success.

In addition, every member of the senior cabinet staff needs to become familiar with the process and understand his or her role in this process. For example, the business office needs to understand the scope of the Balanced Curriculum process so that budgets fully support the endeavor. The Office of Funded Programs needs to demonstrate its understanding when applying for grants.

The next step in Newburgh and Englewood Cliffs was to communicate the vision for this project, from the start, to all of the stakeholders. Any reform effort needs to enlist the support from many constituencies. Ensuring support underpinned the success of the two projects I led.

In Newburgh, we had entered into a Comprehensive District Education Planning pilot project with the state department of education, requiring the formation of a comprehensive and representative planning team comprising a broad segment of the community, including central office administrators, principals and vice principals, teachers, members of the teacher union leadership, parents, community members, and a state education department staff person. I co-chaired this team, as the superintendent's representative, providing a linkage between the planning team, the curriculum project, and the superintendent's office. In developing our Comprehensive District Education Plan, curriculum development was a clear need. The Balanced Curriculum process was introduced as a model or direction for addressing this need and was embraced by the committee. Because this group encompassed so many constituencies, the members of the planning team became our advocates for the initiative with the groups they represented, an important link when we started implementation. This comprehensive district planning team placed the Balanced Curriculum project as an agenda item each month, allowing for frequent progress reports so that the initiative could be maintained.

Finally, in our communication process in Newburgh, the superintendent and I ensured that presentations were also provided to the entire administrative staff in the district, to a larger representative group of union leaders, and to each parent group in the district. Each of these groups then understood and supported the process.

Leadership Strategy 2: Planning, Planning, Planning

The most important part of the Balanced Curriculum process is the planning for the writing and planning for implementation of the curriculum. Throughout this process in both districts, a districtwide Balanced Curriculum Planning Team was formed and met monthly to review the progress of the project and to plan continually for the next steps of the process. In Newburgh, we met monthly for the 2 years of the process. In the smaller district, because of its size and because of my experience with the process, we met monthly at the beginning of the project and then periodically afterward. I cannot stress enough the importance of planning each step of the process to ensure that when each step is being implemented, the participants know and feel that the process has been well thought out. During the planning stages, we tried to anticipate potential problems based on the culture of the district.

Leadership Strategy 3: Implementation

Once the curriculum is developed, the role of the superintendent shifts to supporting and monitoring implementation and assisting with problem resolutions. Although the principal conducts oversight of the school-level implementation, staff members need to see the superintendent continuing to have an active role in monitoring the implementation. The superintendent's first role in the implementation is to communicate the implementation strategy to all of the constituencies. In Newburgh, the superintendent used the first day of school for a districtwide roll out of this project where the Balanced Curriculum project was discussed and the writing team members recognized and thanked.

Following the districtwide meeting, each grade level from all schools met together with members of the writing team that wrote the curriculum for that grade level. They facilitated a meeting at which the content, structure, and implementation process was introduced.

Finally, on the same day, each school principal reviewed the project in their opening-day meeting and provided the opportunity for each grade level to meet and discuss the implementation in their school. This full day of learning about the new curriculum established the importance the administration put on this project.

Monthly meetings with the principals and key staff members on the schools' implementation teams kept the superintendent informed of the progress at the schools and allowed him to provide assistance with resolving difficulties or conflicts as they arose. It was also important for the superintendent to receive reports on the completion levels for each grade level at each of the schools.

In addition, during the implementation in Newburgh, we reviewed the compilations of the quarterly telephone conferences between our schools and the outside facilitators of the process. These reports would not identify individual schools but would provide a progress report for the overall district and identify problems or concerns encountered during the implementation. The teleconferences helped us as we continued to make adjustments where needed.

The superintendent also ensured that all of the groups who initially supported the initiative were provided with periodic updates on the progress of the project.

Leadership Strategy 4: Celebrating

One of the greatest lessons I learned during this project is the importance teachers place on celebrating after completing a long and arduous task. During the planning stage of the writing of the first curriculum in Newburgh, the district planning team wanted to have a celebration on the last day of curriculum writing. We decided to provide lunch and dessert and also provide each participant with a certificate and a pen to serve as a remembrance of the project. When I discussed our plan with colleagues, some doubted that the participants would appreciate them. However, on the day of the celebration, participants awaited anxiously for their names to be called to receive their certificate and pen! I also found it interesting that with each subject curriculum we developed, the participants expected their certificates and pens at the completion of their projects. We also celebrated by bringing the school district staffs together, by grade level, when the results of our posttests arrived and we had made such significant progress after only 8 months of implementation.

In closing, I want any superintendent who is considering the implementation of this type of this project to know that it is not for the faint of heart. Through all of the trials, tribulations, and celebrations, however, it has been the most rewarding and most successful project I have been involved in during my many years of public education. I would recommend it highly to any school district seeking to significantly improve their curriculum and their students' achievement.

20

The Results So Far

Fifteen Years of Data From Urban,
Suburban, and Rural Schools

This chapter summarizes the results of the Balanced Curriculum process over 15 years. The claim is that when a district or a school writes the curriculum in the format described in Chapter 7, and when the district or school takes steps to implement the curriculum and have documented its implementation across the school or district, scores have improved in every case. Some schools and district completed the writing of the curriculum but did not pursue implementation; their pre–post scores are not reported here, although, in general, there was little gain in those schools or districts. Formal studies have not yet been conducted, leaving the reader with only the anecdotal information provided in this chapter.

The first three places reported (Red Bank, Richardson Elementary, and NYC SURR Schools) that the focus was primarily on getting the curriculum written using the Balanced Curriculum model; implementation was not a focus. At this time, the Web site did not exist and the writing process was consequently more difficult. District 13 in NYC provided the first challenge with large scale implementation (over 20 schools). The research done in District 13 showed that implementation was a challenge that needed to be addressed during the time the curriculum was written, as achievement increased only in schools where the curriculum was implemented. Lessons learned in District 13 transferred to Newburgh (another large district) where implementation was addressed by monthly meetings of program specialists assigned to each school who were primarily responsible for curriculum implementation and addressed through telephone conferences with school teams conducted by Sandra Bullock (retired assistant superintendent from District 13). After Newburgh, the Web site began operations so that teachers could log their completed significant tasks on the Web site, easing the difficulty of collecting implementation data. Both Englewood Cliffs and Hertford County, NC, are districts that have written quality curriculum and provided evidence of implementation on the Web site correlated with solid gains in student achievement.

In most of these schools and districts, other efforts to improve results happened at the same time as the writing and implementing of the Balanced Curriculum. Thus, no claim is being made that the Balanced Curriculum causes student achievement to rise. Results are examined from the following:

District/Schools	Years Reported
Red Bank, New Jersey	1978–1992
Richardson Elementary School, Washington, DC	1993–1994
SURRs (Schools Under Registration Review) in New York City	1994–1997
District 13, New York City	1997–2000
Newburgh, New York	1999–2002
Mott School, Trenton, New Jersey	2000–2002
Passaic, New Jersey	2001–2003
Englewood Cliffs, New Jersey	2001–2004
Hertford County, North Carolina	2001–2004

THE RED BANK MODEL, 1978–1992

Originally developed in Red Bank, New Jersey, a school district serving a majority of poor and minority children, this evolving model increased student achievement from below to above grade level on standardized tests with concurrent improvement on state tests over 6 years (Burns & Squires, 1987). The trend continued from 1979 through 1993.

In 1979, Red Bank had adopted a Mastery Learning instructional design. Units, usually 2 to 4 weeks in length with 3 to 5 objectives for each unit, provided the curriculum structure. Within that structure, an instructional model of teaching, formative test, reteach, mastery test, was followed (Abrams, 1981; Squires & Burns, 1987) following the principles of Benjamin Bloom (1976, p. 22), which assert that entry characteristics of students need not determine instructional outcomes if the instruction is aligned to the assessments. In a school district dealing mainly with poor and minority students, this assertion had great appeal among school board members.

As a new curriculum director, I did not want to produce curriculum that was only aligned to the test; good curriculum should take into account the needs of the learner and the structure of the discipline as well. Our model involved units that were aligned to the important tests *and* to the staff's understanding of what made a good curriculum in a particular subject area, which we termed a "Curriculum Rationale" and is similar to standard statements of today (Squires, 1985, 1986, 1987). Such definitions of a good curriculum predated the current emphasis on national standards and state frameworks.

A study (Wishnick, 1989) conducted in Red Bank on 4th-grade reading and language arts reinforced this perception. Wishnick's results suggest that an aligned curriculum can overcome the usual predictors of student success (socioeconomic status, gender, teacher assignment). Wishnick concluded that

> When students were taught well enough to perform well on the unit tests, and the unit tests were aligned with the standardized test item clusters . . . not only did SES and gender, but teacher differences had little to no effect on their performance. (p. 168)

The study provides evidence that an aligned curriculum can overcome students' unearned disadvantages while refining and reinforcing Bloom's (1976) ideas. (More results from this study are described in Chapter 5.) Figure 20.1 shows Red Bank's test scores in grade equivalents from 1978 to 1992.

Figure 20.1   Red Bank test scores in grade equivalents 1978–1992

Subject/Year	K	1	2	3	4	5	6	7	8
Read 78–79		1.9	2.6	3.5	4.2	5.0	6.0	7.1	7.3
Read 79–80		1.7	2.5	3.3	4.0	5.8	7.0	7.5	8.9
Read 80–81		1.9	2.8	3.5	4.4	6.5	7.2	8.6	9.4
Read 81–82		2.1	3.2	3.4	4.3	5.5	7.8	8.1	9.6
Read 82–83		2.1	3.4	3.6	4.8	6.3	8.1	8.5	10.0
Read 83–84		2.1	3.5	4.1	5.2	6.0	7.4	8.2	10.3
Read 84–85		2.3	3.3	3.9	5.2	6.1	7.9	8.6	10.2
Read 85–86		2.2	3.5	3.6	5.9	6.1	8.3	8.2	10.2
Read 86–87	1.7	2.1	3.1	3.1	4.9	6.1	6.9	7.8	9.8
Read 87–88	1.7	2.2	2.9	2.9	4.7	5.7	7.3	7.5	8.6
Read 88–89	1.7	2.3	3.7	3.7	4.5	5.6	6.4	7.9	9.4
Read 89–90	1.7	2.3	3.3	3.3	5.0	5.7	7.0	7.2	9.5
Read 90–91	1.7	2.4	3.3	3.3	5.6	5.6	7.7	7.8	8.7
Read 91–92	1.8	2.1	3.7	3.7	5.1	6.0	6.5	7.5	9.2
LA 78–79					4.8	5.3	6.2	7.8	7.6
LA 79–80		1.6	2.9	4.0	5.2	6.1	7.1	7.6	8.9
LA 80–81		2.0	3.3	4.5	5.5	6.5	7.1	8.1	9.3
LA 81–82		2.4	3.6	4.5	5.7	6.2	8.3	7.6	9.5
LA 82–83		2.4	4.1	5.1	6.6	6.2	7.9	7.9	10.1
LA 83–84		2.7	4.4	5.7	6.9	6.4	7.9	9.8	11.0
LA 84–85		2.7	4.2	5.5	7.1	6.2	7.4	8.9	12.1
LA 85–86		2.9	4.5	5.3	6.7	7.1	7.9	9.6	10.6
LA 86–87	1.7	2.1	3.3	4.5	5.6	6.6	6.7	7.5	11.8
LA 87–88	1.7	2.2	3.3	4.9	5.7	6.3	8.4	8.0	9.2
LA 88–89	1.7	2.3	3.7	5.1	5.6	6.3	7.5	8.4	10.4
LA 89–90	1.7	2.3	3.6	7.9	6.6	5.5	8.1	8.0	10.6
LA 90–91	1.7	2.4	3.6	6.0	8.3	6.1	8.1	8.8	9.6
LA 91–92	1.8	2.1	3.9	6.7	8.0	6.7	6.5	8.6	10.4
Math 78–79		1.8	2.9	4.0	4.8	503	6.4	7.6	8.0
Math 79–80		2.0	3.2	4.5	5.5	6.1	7.4	9.2	9.0
Math 80–81		2.0	3.5	4.5	5.4	6.5	7.5	8.7	10.4
Math 81–82		2.3	3.2	5.1	5.1	6.2	8.1	7.7	9.6
Math 82–83		2.4	4.1	5.7	6.0	6.2	7.5	9.4	11.6
Math 83–84		2.5	4.2	5.5	6.2	6.4	7.5	9.3	12.2
Math 84–85		2.7	4.3	5.3	5.9	6.2	8.2	9.0	*PHS
Math 85–86		2.6	4.3	4.5	6.0	6.8	7.7	8.5	11.5
Math 86–87	1.1	2.2	3.6	4.2	5.4	6.9	7.7	8.3	11.2
Math 87–88	1.1	2.2	3.5	5.6	5.1	7.0	8.2	8.5	10.8
Math 88–89	1.2	2.1	3.8	5.2	6.3	6.3	7.2	8.2	10.0
Math 89–90	1.3	2.5	4.0	6.3	6.3	6.3	8.3	8.2	11.6
Math 90–91	1.2	2.4	4.3	6.4	7.0	6.3	8.3	9.3	9.2
Math 91–92	1.2	2.1	4.7	5.7	6.5	7.5	8.4	9.0	9.8

NOTE: PHS = Post High School

RICHARDSON ELEMENTARY SCHOOL, WASHINGTON, DC, 1993–1994

Ms. Marlene Guy, then principal of Richardson Elementary School in Washington, DC, wanted to implement the Balanced Curriculum process at her school. Richardson Elementary had successfully used the School Development Program (SDP) to improve the climate and parent involvement. Student achievement improved during initial implementation of SDP, and, despite serving students who were welfare eligible, the school had accomplished near grade-level scores on standardized tests given by the district. A series of half-day workshops conducted on a monthly basis provided the training for Richardson teaching staff. Two teachers were released on a part-time basis to assist other teachers at the school with implementation. I discussed implementation between workshops with Marlene to ensure that progress was being made and questions answered.

As implementation happened, positive results accrued. Figure 20.2 compares 1993, which was before implementation, with 1994, when the results of the first year of implementation were available. The results on the Metropolitan Achievement Tests are presented in two ways, by year and by class. The figure indicates that results were better or the same in 1994 at 1st, 2nd, 5th, and 6th grade, or four of the six grades listed. Of course, the kids attending those classes were different. Figure 20.3 shows improvements by the same class. For example, Grade 1 scored at 1.9 during 1993; the same class in 1994 in 2nd grade scored 2.7, for an improvement of .8.

Because the scores are reported in grade equivalents, we would expect a year's (1.0) growth for a year's instruction. Three class cohorts exceeded expectations. Fourth grade in 1994 was a problem. Ms. Guy indicated that the two teachers at that grade level were both novices who had difficulty controlling student behavior during the year, which may have partially accounted for the poor results.

Figure 20.2   By grade test score results: Richardson Elementary School, Washington, DC

Grade	1993–Before Implementation	1994–After Implementation
1 Reading	1.9	1.9
2 Reading	2.3	2.7
3 Reading	4.0	3.5
4 Reading	3.8	3.2
5 Reading	4.4	5.0
6 Reading	5.2	5.5

Figure 20.3   Reading scores grade to grade for Richardson Elementary School, Washington, DC

Reading Grade to Grade	Improvement
1–2	.8
2–3	1.2
3–4	−.6
4–5	1.2
5–6	1.1

NEW YORK CITY
SURR SCHOOLS, 1994–1997

During the 1994–1995 and 1995–1996 school years, workshops were held for school teams from SURR schools (Schools Under Registration and Review, identified because of declining achievement over 3 consecutive years). Concurrently, these teams also implemented the School Development Program—a school reform effort. The schools listed in Figure 20.4 improved their achievement after implementing both the School Development Program and the Balanced Curriculum process. Only schools that actually implemented the Balanced Curriculum are listed; schools not listed had little to no evidence of actual implementation.

Figure 20.4 Improving schools from New York City SURR Schools, 1994–1997

	Before Implementation		After Implementation
	1994–95	*1995–96*	*1996–97*
PS 15			
Gr 3 Reading	72.7	63.2	79.3
Gr 5 Writing	76.7	68.9	89.8
Gr 6 Reading	79.4	79.7	79.0
PS 27			
Gr 3 Reading	34.9	42.9	57.4
Gr 5 Writing	89.6	83.3	78.9
Gr 6 Reading	52.8	47.6	55.6
PS 191			
Gr 3 Reading	32.9	38.6	49.0
Gr 5 Writing	80.3	74.6	91.7
PS 165			
Gr 3 Reading	35.3	53.1	54.8
Gr 5 Writing	54.1	82.7	47.1
Gr 6 Reading	74.5	59.1	66.7
PS 156			
Gr 3 Reading	26.9	26.3	72.2
Gr 5 Writing	47.1	39.3	77.6
PS 115			
Gr 3 Reading	68.0	72.8	75.6
Gr 5 Writing	94.8	92.3	90.3
PS 43			
Gr 3 Reading	48.8	46.6	54.7
Gr 5 Writing	75.6	88.2	90.0
Gr 6 Reading	59.6	70.5	80.5
Yonkers **HostosMicros**			
Gr 3 Reading	42	45	87
Gr 6 Reading	36	42	62

NOTE: Percentage at or above state minimum levels. Gr = grade; PS = public school; SURR = Schools Under Registration and Review.

Below is a chart that summarizes the data from Figure 20.4. The schools are listed along the top of the chart. Improved achievement is indicated by a plus sign (+). The schools improved in 15 areas, declined in 4, and remained the same in one area.

Figure 20.5   Summary of NYC SURR schools achievement after writing the Balanced Curriculum

School/Grade-Subject	PS15	PS27	PS191	PS165	PS156	PS115	PS43	HostosM.
Grade 3–R	+	+	+	+	+	+	+	+
Grade 5–W	+	–	+	–	+	–	+	
Grade 6–R	0	+		–			+	+

NOTE: (+) = improved achievement; (–) = declining achievement; Blank = no data; 0 = same achievement level.

DISTRICT 13, NEW YORK CITY, 1997–2000

District 13 was the first district to complete a districtwide implementation of the Balanced Curriculum since Red Bank. District 13 is in Brooklyn, New York, with 21 schools ranging from kindergarten to 8th grade; it serves more than 20,000 poor and minority students. District 13 was also in the process of implementing the School Development Program at all its schools.

In a districtwide implementation of the Balanced Curriculum process in District 13, seven schools, all of which had implemented the process, improved. Seven percent more of the implementing schools' students were above grade level in 1997 than in 1996. This contrasts with seven other schools in the same district that did not implement, which had 6% fewer of their students score above grade level compared with the previous year. All schools continued using the School Development Program.

We examined implementation in much more depth (Squires & Bullock, 1999) and came to four conclusions:

1. *Improved student achievement is associated with implementation of a balanced and aligned curriculum.* This finding links improved achievement with curriculum development and implementation, an association not often found in the educational literature about improving schools or dealing with standards. The study clearly points out the association between curriculum implementation and student achievement. Implementation appears to be one key aspect to ensure that curriculum affects student achievement. Although staff development is important, in and of itself, it is not enough. Staff development provides the information and begins building commitment, but asking teachers to reorganize how they are using time through implementing a curriculum takes more than staff development. That's where our second major finding comes into play.

Figure 20.6   Implementing and nonimplementing schools performance, District 13, New York City

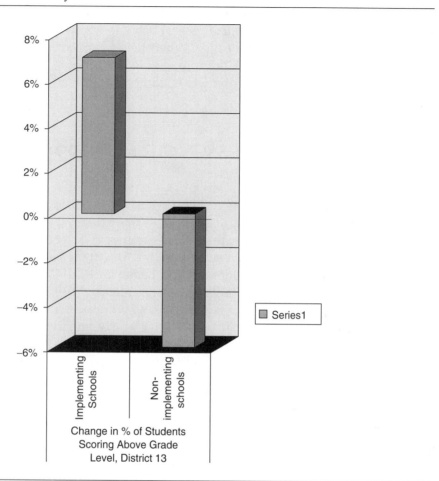

2. *Improved student achievement is associated with principals' monitoring of the implementation of the balanced and aligned curriculum.* For the top seven improving schools, all had high-monitoring principals except two who fell into the medium-monitoring category. If principals are the curriculum leaders of their schools, improved instruction is likely to follow.

3. *Curriculum implementation is more likely to happen when teams work together.* In District 13, the implementation of the School Development Program, in which teams come together, provided necessary prerequisite institutional learning for building teams to implement the balanced and aligned curriculum. Those schools who used teams succeeded more than those who did not use teams. Principals need to recognize that teams can help spread the responsibility and increase effectiveness.

4. *Initiatives from the central office can assist schools in implementing a balanced and aligned curriculum.* District 13 decided on the importance of a balanced and aligned curriculum by allocating resources for its development and for staff development that continued over the first year of implementation. District 13 provided financial resources to help schools with materials or the purchase of teacher time to implement

the curriculum. District 13 also placed schools in Tiers to help focus on achievement. Through the Tier structure, help could be obtained from the central office, and monitoring of the schools was carried out. Those on Tier IV received the most help, and most made gains. All Tier I (self-directed) schools made achievement gains with much less support from central office. When help is appropriately structured from central office to supplement existing capacity in the schools, improved results may follow. This also indicates that districts need not provide all schools with the same level of assistance.

NEWBURGH, NEW YORK, 1999–2002

Implementation in Newburgh, New York's tenth largest school district serving a multiethnic population, took place from 1999 to 2002. During that time, curriculum was written for English and language arts (summer 1999), math, science (during the 1999–2000 school year), and social studies (summer 2001). Schools were also in the process of implementing magnet school programs. After designing the English and language arts curriculum, implementation began in the fall. Implementation was monitored by one program specialist (a teacher released full time to assist with curriculum and instruction) in each school working with the principal. Principals incorporated curriculum implementation into their yearly improvement plans. Program specialists indicated implementation across schools, with elementary schools implementing at a higher level than the middle schools. The district administered the Terra Nova standardized test in the fall and again in the spring. Normal growth is .6 of one grade equivalent, because there was 6 months between the fall and spring testing dates.

As shown in Figure 20.7, for Grades 3 through 6 across the district, grade equivalent improvement ranged from a low of 1.3 (7 months more growth than expected) to 1.8 (1 year and 2 months more growth than expected). Grades 7 and 8 had growth above expectations also, scoring a grade equivalent improvement of .8 to .9 as a district.

Figure 20.7 Newburgh Enlarged School District results of fall to spring testing on the Terra Nova, 1999–2000

Grade	Reading Growth in Grade Equivalents (Expected growth = .6)	Language Arts Growth in Grade Equivalents (Expected growth = .6)
3	1.7	1.3
4	1.8	1.6
5	1.5	1.4
6	1.5	1.4
7	.8	.8
8	.9	.9

MOTT SCHOOL, TRENTON, NEW JERSEY, 2000–2002

Mott School, a K–5 school serving poor Hispanics and African-Americans, implemented the Balanced Curriculum in reading and language arts after working with the School Development Program for a year. During the 1999–2000 school year, staff wrote the curriculum and proceeded with implementation during the 2000–2001 school year. Implementation was monitored by the full-time School Development Program coordinator. Before implementation, 24% of students passed the Elementary School Proficiency Test (ESPA; the New Jersey State Test) at Grade 4. After implementation, 75% of their students passed.

PASSAIC, NEW JERSEY, 2001–2003

Passaic, New Jersey, a large district serving mainly Hispanic and African-American students, improved approximately 15% on the New Jersey ESPA (the 4th-grade state test) after implementing the Balanced Curriculum process for a year in their elementary schools in the reading and language arts program. Implementation was monitored by the reading curriculum director in conjunction with the principals. The School Development Program had been in place for 2 years in the district.

Figure 20.8 indicates that only one school met state standards of 75% proficient in 2001. By 2002, four schools met the state standard, with two additional schools missing the standard by less that 2 percentage points. School Number 6 was also implementing Success for All, another school reform program. The Learning Center was a school for gifted students.

Figure 20.8 Passaic, New Jersey, proficiency on the Elementary School Proficiency Test

	Before Implementation	After Implementation
School	Proficient 2001 (%)	Proficient 2002 (%)
No. 1, Jefferson	67.6	84.8
No. 3, Drago	69.8	91.9
No. 5	43.9	64.1
No. 6, King	73.6	73.8
No. 9, Gero	64.9	73.5
No. 10, Roosevelt	NA	57.1
No. 11, Cruise	54.3	78.2
Learning Center	94.1	95.0

ENGLEWOOD CLIFFS, NEW JERSEY, 2001–2004 (STILL ACTIVE)

Englewood Cliffs, New Jersey, a K–8 school district, is located in an upper-class suburb of New York City, near the George Washington Bridge. Dr. Philomena Pezanno, the superintendent (see Chapter 19), came to Englewood after serving as acting superintendent in Newburgh, New York, where she had charge over the Balanced Curriculum development and implementation. Planning for curriculum writing started in the spring of 2001, with curriculum in English and language arts developed during the summer 2001. The first year of implementation was 2001–2002 in Reading and language arts, with assessments developed during the summer of 2002. Results of the state tests—the ESPA for Grade 4 and the GEPPA for Grade 8 are given in Figure 20.9, with students identified as English-as-a-second-language and special education students excluded from the analysis.

For Grade 8, students in Level 3, the highest level, jumped from 5% before the project started to 29% after 3 years of implementation. For Grade 4, 16% scored in Level 3 (Advanced Proficient) before implementation. After 3 years of implementation, 80% of the students scored at Level 3. See Figure 20.9.

HERTFORD COUNTY, NORTH CAROLINA, 2001–2004 (STILL ACTIVE)

Hertford County, a rural, generally poor and minority school district, started writing the Balanced Curriculum in reading and language arts in the summer of 2001 for Grades K–8 as a part of implementing the Comer School Development Program on a districtwide basis, beginning in 1999. Implementation of the Balanced Curriculum commenced in the fall of 2001. The test results reported in Figure 20.10 show the results for the district's two elementary schools in Grades 3, 4, and 5 and the Hertford County Middle School for Grades 6, 7, and 8.

The results are displayed to show how approximately the same students (as a cohort) did on succeeding years of testing (see Figure 20.10). For example, for Grade 3 students at Ahoskie Elementary School (AES) for the 2001–2002 school year, 74.11% of students scored a three or a four on the test (which the state considered to be passing scores). Those students went on to Grade 4 in 2002–2003, and 73.4% of the students passed that year. The students neither lost nor gained significant ground, as shown by the decline of .71% (74.11–73.4 = .71%).

At Grade 4 at AES, however, 50.87% of students passed in 2001–2002; the following academic year, 75% of the students in the Grade 5 passed, for an improvement of +24.13%. Results for other grade levels showed a range of improvement from 17% to 30% more students passing over the first years of implementation. The middle school students improved almost as much as the elementary students. Riverview Elementary School was also implementing Success for All, a school reform effort aimed at improving reading achievement.

Figure 20.9 Englewood Cliffs, New Jersey. Improved scores: Percent of students at each achievement level on the state test, Grades 4 and 8.

Grade 8	Level 1 (%)	Level 2 (%)	Level 3 (%)	Mean Score	SD	Student N
Before Balanced Curriculum						
2000	5	90	5	228.6	14.62	39
2001	5	85	4	221.3	21.33	27
After Balanced Curriculum						
2002	0	81	19	233.6	20.48	31
2003	0	73	27	239.6	12.09	30
2004	0	71	29	238.4	—	28

Grade 4	Level 1 (%)	Level 2 (%)	Level 3 (%)	Mean Score	SD	Student N
Before Balanced Curriculum						
2000	13	84	3	215.1	18.8	38
2001	8	76	16	236.2	16.5	39
After Balanced Curriculum						
2002	5	79	17	231.8	16.5	42
2003	3.6	92.9	3.6	—	—	—
2002	0	20	80	244.3	—	45

NOTE: Special education and English-as-a-second-language learners are excluded from the analysis.

Figure 20.10 Hertford County, North Carolina, improved test scores

	At or Above Level 3[a] (%)		Improvement (%)	
Ahoskie Elementary School	2001–2002 (%)	2002–2003 (%)		
Grade 3		73.0		
Grade 3/Grade 4	74.11	73.4	−.71	Cohort moving from Grade 3 (01–02) to Grade 4 (02–03)
Grade 4/Grade 5	50.87	75.0	+24.13	Cohort moving from Grade 4 (01–02) to Grade 5 (02–03)
Grade 5	68.35	75.0		
Riverview Elementary School	2001–2002 (%)	2002–2003 (%)		
Grade 3		67.7		
Grade 3/Grade 4	39.02	70.0	+30.98	Cohort moving from Grade 3 (01–02) to Grade 4 (02–03)
Grade 4/Grade 5	52.81	77.0	+24.19	Cohort moving from Grade 4 (01–02) to Grade 5 (02–03)
Grade 5	65.66	77.5		
Hertford County Middle School	2001–2002 (%)	2002–2003 (%)		
Grade 6		64.5		
Grade 6/Grade 7	51.26	69.2	+17.94	Cohort moving from Grade 6 (01–02) to Grade 7 (02–03)
Grade 7/Grade 8	55.77	78.0	+22.23	Cohort moving from Grade 7 (01–02) to Grade 8 (02–03)
Grade 8	65.97	78.0		

NOTE: a. Based on a four-level scale.

SUMMARY

From the results reported here, we can claim that when the Balanced Curriculum was both written in alignment with appropriate state standards and assessments *and* documented with evidence of implementation, there was a correlation with improved scores. I do not claim that the Balanced Curriculum was the sole reason for the improvement because the Balanced Curriculum was usually one of many initiatives that the school or district was undertaking simultaneously. Interestingly, the consistency of improvement within diverse school and district settings with different student populations suggests that many schools and districts do have the expertise in-house (their teachers) to improve their results significantly by following the Balanced Curriculum model. Local teachers, who know their settings and students well, can design a curriculum that is powerful enough to be correlated with gains in student achievement after the first year of high-quality implementation. Curriculum makes a difference. This is good news for American students who can now rise to higher achievement levels through locally designed curriculum that can be implemented, managed, and changed as part of an ongoing local improvement process.

Bibliography

Abrams, J. D. (1981, November). Precise teaching is more effective teaching. *Educational Leadership, 39*, 138–140.

Alexander, A. (1960). The gray flannel cover on the American history textbook. *Social Education, 24*, 11–14.

American Association for the Advancement of Science. (2000, April 30). Algebra for All—Not With Today's Textbooks, Says AAAS [press release]. Washington, DC: Author.

American Educational Research Association, the American Psychological Association, and the National Council on Measurement in Education. (1999). *Standards for Educational and Psychological Testing.* Washington, DC: Authors.

Anderson, R. C., Osborn, J., & Tierney, R. J. (1984). *Learning to read in American schools: Basal readers and content tests.* Hillsdale, NJ: Erlbaum.

Beck I. L., & McKeown, M. G. (1994). Outcomes of history instruction: Paste-up accounts. In M. Carretero & J. F. Voss (Eds.), *Cognitive and instructional processes in history and the social sciences* (pp. 237–256). Hillsdale, NJ: Erlbaum.

Block, J. H. (Ed.). (1971). *Mastery learning.* New York: Holt, Rinehart and Winston.

Block, J. H. (1974). Mastery learning in the classroom: An overview of recent research. In J. H. Block (Ed.), *School, society and mastery learning* (pp. 28–69). New York: Holt, Rinehart and Winston.

Block, J. H., & Burns, R. B. (1976). Mastery learning. In L. S. Shulman (Ed.), *Review of research in education.* Itasca, IL: Peacock.

Bloom, B. S. (1976). *Human characteristics and school learning.* New York: McGraw-Hill.

Bracht, G. H., & Hopkins, K. D. (1972). Stability in education achievement. In G. H. Bracht, K. D. Hopkins, & J. C. Stanley (Eds.), *Perspectives in educational and psychological measurement.* Englewood Cliffs, NJ: Prentice Hall.

Brady, M. E., Clinton, D., Sweeney, J. M., Peterson, M., & Poynor, H. (1977). *Instructional dimensions study.* Washington, DC: Kerschner Associates.

Brookover, W., Beady, C., Flood, P., Schweitzer, J., & Wisenbaker, J. (1979). *School social system and student achievement: Schools can make a difference.* New York: Praeger.

Burns, R., & Squires, D. (1987, October). Curriculum organization in outcome-based education. *The OBE Bulletin, 3.* San Francisco: Far West Laboratory for Educational Research and Development.

Carnevale, A. P., Gainer, L. J., & Meltzer, A. S. (1990). *Workplace basics: The essential skills employers want.* New York: Wiley.

Carroll, J. B. (1963). A model of school learning. *Teacher's College Record, 64*, 723–733.

Cohen, S. A. (1987). Instructional alignment: Searching for a magic bullet. *Educational Researcher, 16,* 16–19.

Coleman, J. S., Campbell, E. Q., Hobson, C. J., McPartland, J., Mood, A. M., Weinfeld, F. D., & York, R. L. (1966). *Equity of educational opportunity.* Washington, DC: U.S. Government Printing Office.

Comer, J. P., Haynes, N. M., Joyner, E. T., & Ben-Avie, M. (1999). *Child by Child: The Comer Process for Change in Education.* New York: Teachers College Press.

Council of Chief Sate School Officers. (2003, January). Alignment analysis. Retrieved from http://www.ccsso.org/alignment.html.

Coyle, D. P., & Pimentel, S. (1997). *Raising the standard.* Thousand Oaks, CA: Corwin Press.

Crandall, D. (1983). The teacher's role in school improvement. *Educational Leadership, 14,* 4–9.

Crismore A. (Ed.). (1985). *Landscapes: A state-of-knowledge assessment of reading comprehension instructional research, 1974–1984* (Final Report USDE-C-300–83–0130, Vol. I). Bloomington: Indiana University, Language Education Department.

DeClements, B. (1981). *Nothing's fair in fifth grade.* New York: Viking Press.

Durkin, D. (1987). Influences on basal reading programs. *Elementary School Journal, 87,* 331–341.

English, F. W. (1992). Deciding what to teach and test: Developing, aligning, and auditing the curriculum. In F. W. English (Series Ed.), *Successful schools: Guidebooks to effective educational leadership: Vol. 4.* Newbury Park, CA: Corwin Press.

English, F. W., & Steffy, B. E. (2001). *Deep curriculum alignment: Creating a level playing field for all children on high-stakes tests of educational accountability.* Lanaham, MD: Scarecrow Press.

Farmer, R. (1988). Social studies teachers and the curriculum: A report from a national survey. *Journal of Social Studies Research, 11*(2), 24–42.

Farr, R., Tulley, M. A., & Powell, D. (1987). The evaluation and selection of basal readers. *Elementary School Journal, 87,* 267–281.

FitzGerald, F. (1979). *America revised: What history textbooks have taught our children about their country, and how and why those textbooks have changed in different decades.* New York: Vintage.

Floden, R. E., Porter, A. C., Schmidt, W. H., & Freeman, D. J. (1980). Don't they all measure the same thing? Consequences of standardized test selection. In E. L. Baker & E. S. Quellmalz (Eds.), *Educational testing and evaluation design.* Beverly Hills, CA: Sage.

Foriska, T. J. (1988). *Restructuring around standards: A practitioner's guide to design and implementation.* Thousand Oaks, CA: Corwin Press.

Freeman, D. J., & Kuhs, T. (1980). *The fourth grade mathematics curriculum as inferred from textbooks and tests.* Paper presented at the annual meeting of the American Educational Research Association, Los Angeles, CA.

Freeman, D., Kuhs, T., Porter, A., Floden, R., Schmidt, W., & Schwille, J. (1983). Do textbooks and tests define a national curriculum in elementary school mathematics? *Elementary School Journal, 83,* 501–513.

Gamoran, A., Porter, A. C., Smithson, J., White, P. A. (1997, Winter). Upgrading high school mathematics instruction: Improving learning opportunities for low-achieving, low-income youth. Educational Evaluation and Policy Analysis, *19,* 325–338.

Glatthorn, A. A. (1998). *Performance assessment and standards-based curricula: The achievement cycle.* Larchmont, NY: Eye on Education.

Goodman, K. S., Shannon, P., Freeman, Y. S., & Murphy, S. (1988). *Report card on basal readers.* Katonah, NY: Richard C. Owen.

Hahn, C. L. (1985). The status of the social students in the public schools of the United States: Another look. *Social Education, 49,* 220–223.

Hall, G., Wallace, J., & Dossett, W. (1973). *A developmental conceptualization of the adoption process within educational institutions.* Austin, TX: Research and Development Center for Teacher Education, University of Texas. (ERIC Document Reproduction Service No. ED 095 126)

Hall, G., & Loucks, S. (1977). A developmental model for determining whether the treatment is actually implemented. *American Educational Research Journal, 14,* 263–276.

Hall, G. E., & Hord, S. M. (2001). *Implementing change: Patterns, principles and potholes.* Boston: Allyn & Bacon.

Harste, J. C. (1989). *New policy guidelines for reading: Connecting research and practice.* Urbana, IL: National Council of Teachers of English.

Hertzberg, H. W. (1985). Students, methods and materials of instruction. *History in the Schools, 74,* 25–40. Washington, DC: National Council for the Social Studies.

Hord, S. M., Rutherford, W., Huling-Austin, L., & Hall, G. E. (1987). *Taking charge of change.* Alexandria, VA: Association for Supervision and Curriculum Development.

Howson, G. (1995). *Mathematics textbooks: A comparative study of grade 8 texts.* Vancouver, Canada: Pacific Education Press.

Huberman, M. A. (1983). School improvement strategies that work: Some scenarios. *Educational Leadership, 41*(3), 23–27.

Huberman, M. A., & Miles, M. B. (1984). *Innovation up close: How school improvement works.* New York: Plenum.

International Reading Association. (1984). *Responding to "A Nation at Risk": Appraisal and policy guidelines.* Newark, DE: Author.

Jacobs, H. H. (1997). Mapping the big picture: Integrating curriculum and assessment K–12. Alexandria, VA: Association of Supervision and Curriculum Development.

Kulm, G., Morris, K., & Grier, L. (1998). Middle grades mathematics textbooks: A benchmarks-based evaluation. Washington, DC: American Association for the Advancement of Science. Retrieved from http://www.project2061.org/tools/textbook/matheval/appendx/appendc.htm

Kulm, G., Roseman, J., & Treistman, M. (1999, July/August). A benchmarks-based approach to textbook evaluation. *Science Books & Films, 35,* 147–153.

Lezotte, L., & Pepperl, J. C. (1999). *The effective schools process: A proven path to learning for all.* Okemos, MI: Effective Schools.

Loewen, J. W. (1995). *Lies my teacher told me: Everything your American history textbook got wrong.* New York: New Press.

Luke, A. (1991). Basal reading textbooks and the teaching of literacy. In P. G. Altbach, G. P. Kelly, H. G. Petrie, & L. Weis (Eds.) *Textbooks in American society: Politics, policy and pedagogy.* Albany: State University of New York Press.

Madaus, G. F., & Kellaghan, T. (1992). Curriculum evaluation and assessment. In P.W. Jackson (Ed.), *Handbook of research on curriculum: A project of the American Educational Research Association* (pp. 119–156). New York: Macmillan.

Marker, G., & Mehlinger, H. (1992). Social studies. In P. W. Jackson (Ed.), *Handbook of research on curriculum: A project of the American Educational Research Association* (pp. 830–851). New York: Macmillan.

Marzano, R. J., & Kendall, J. S. (1996). *A comprehensive guide to designing standards-based districts, schools and classrooms.* Alexandria, VA: Association of Supervision and Curriculum Development.

Marzano, R. J., & Kendall, J.S. (1997). *Content knowledge: A compendium of standards and benchmarks for K–12 education.* Aurora, CO: McREL; Alexandria, VA: Association of Supervision and Curriculum Development.

McLaughlin, M. (1976). Implementation of ESEA Title I: A problem of compliance. *Teachers College Record, 80*(1), 69–94.

Merriam-Webster's collegiate dictionary (9th ed). (1986). Springfield, MA: Merriam-Webster.

Moss-Mitchell, F. (1998). *The effects of curriculum alignment on the mathematics achievement of third-grade students as measured by the Iowa Test of Basic Skills: Implication for educational administrators.* Unpublished doctoral dissertation, Clark University, Atlanta, GA.

National Council of Teachers of Mathematics. (1989). *Curriculum and evaluation standards for school mathematics.* Reston, VA: Author.

National Council of Teachers of Mathematics. (2000). *Curriculum and evaluation standards for school mathematics.* Reston, VA: Author.

National Geographic Society. (1988). *Geography: An international Gallup survey.* Washington, DC: Author.

National Geographic Society, National Council for Geographic Education, Association of American Geographers & American Geographical Society. (1994). *Geography for life: National Geography Standards.* Indiana, PA: National Council for Geographic Education.

National Science Education Standards. (1996). Washington, DC: National Academy Press.

Neidermeyer, F., & Yelon, S. (1981). Los Angeles aligns instruction with essential skills. *Educational Leadership, 38,* 618–620.

Northwest Independent School District Curriculum Management Audit. (1996). Available from Texas Audit Center, Texas Association of School Administrators, 406 East 11th Street, Austin, TX 78701.

Palmer, J. R. (1967). American history. In C. B. Cox & B. G. Massialas (Eds.), *Social studies in the United States* (pp. 131–149). New York: Harcourt Brace and World.

Popham, J. W. (2001). *The truth about testing: An educator's call to action.* Alexandria, VA: Association for Supervision and Curriculum Development.

Porter, A. C., Kirst, M.W., Osthoff, E. J., Smithson, J. L., & Schneider, S. A. (1993). *Reform up close: An analysis of high school mathematics and science classrooms* (Final report to the National Science Foundation on Grant No. SAP-8953446 to the Consortium for Policy Research in Education). Madison: Consortium for Policy Research in Education, University of Wisconsin-Madison.

Porter, A. C., Kirst, M. W., Osthoff, E. J., Smithson, J. L., & Schneider, S. A. (1994). *Reform of high school mathematics and science and opportunity to learn.* Consortium for Policy Research in Education Policy Briefs. New Brunswick, NJ: Rutgers University, Consortium for Policy Research in Education.

Porter, A. C., & Smithson J. L. (2001). *Defining, developing, and using curriculum indicators* (CPRE Research Report Series RR-048). Philadelphia: Consortium for Policy Research in Education, University of Pennsylvania.

Price-Baugh, R. (1997). *Correlation of textbook alignment with student achievement scores.* Unpublished doctoral dissertation, Baylor University, Waco, TX.

Ravitch, D. (2004, February). *Consumer's guide to high school history textbooks.* Washington, DC: Thomas B. Fordham Institute. (Also available at http://www.edexcellence.net/institute)

Ravitch, D., & Finn, C. (1987). *What do our 17-year-olds know?* New York: Harper & Row.

Reeves, D. B. (1996–1998). *Making standards work: How to implement standards-based assessments in the classroom, school, and district.* Denver, CO: Center for Performance Assessment.

Robitaille, D. F., Schmidt, W. H., Raizen, S., McKnight C., Britton, E., & Nicol, C. (1993). *Curriculum frameworks for mathematics and science* (TIMSS Monograph No. 1). Vancouver, Canada: Pacific Educational Press.

Roseman, J. E., Kulm, G., & Shuttleworth, S. (2001). Putting textbooks to the test. *ENC Focus, 8,* 56–59.

Rowe, D. W. (1985). The big picture: A quantitative meta-analysis of reading comprehension research. In A. Crismore (Ed.), *Landscapes: A state-of-knowledge assessment of reading comprehension instructional research, 1974–1984* (Final Report USDE-C-300–83–0130, Vol. I). Bloomington: Indiana University, Language Education Department.

Schmidt, W. H., McKnight, C. C., Houang, R. T., Wang, H. C., Wiley, D. E., Cogan, L. S., & Wolfe, R. G. (2001). *Why schools matter: A cross-national comparison of curriculum and learning.* San Francisco: Jossey-Bass.

Schmidt, W. H., McKnight, C. C., & Raizen, S. A. (1997a). *A splintered vision: An investigation of U.S. science and mathematics education.* Boston: Kluwer Academic.

Schmidt, W. H., McKnight, C. C., Valverde, G. A., Houang, R. T., & Wiley, D. E. (1997b). *Many visions, many aims: Volume 1: A cross-national investigation of curricular intentions in school mathematics.* Boston: Kluwer Academic.

Secretary's Commission on Achieving Necessary Skills. (1991). *What work requires of schools: A SCANS report for America 2000.* Washington, DC: Government Printing Office.

Smith, W. A., & Elley, W. B. (1994). *Learning to read in New Zealand.* Auckland, New Zealand: Longman Paul.

Snyder, J., Bolin, F., & Zumwalt, K. (1992). Curriculum implementation. In P. W. Jackson (Ed.), *Handbook of research on curriculum: A project of the American Educational Research Association* (pp. 402–435). New York: Macmillan.

Squires, D. A. (1985). The Curriculum Matrix: A management system for mastery learning. ERIC Clearinghouse on Educational Management. (ERIC Document Reproduction Service No. EA017329)

Squires, D. A. (1986, April). *Curriculum development with a mastery learning framework.* A paper presented at American Educational Research Association Annual Meeting in San Francisco, CA. (ERIC Document Reproduction Service No. ED275059)

Squires, D. A. (1987). Make curriculum decisions with student achievement in mind. *Executive Educator, 9,* 20–21.

Squires, D. A. (1999). Changing curriculum and a school's structure: Commentary on ATLAS. *Peabody Journal of Education, 74,* 154–160.

Squires, D. A., & Bullock, S. (1999, April). *A balanced and aligned curriculum implementation is associated with improved student achievement in District 13 of New York City.* Paper presented at the American Education Research Association, Montreal, Canada.

Squires, D. A., & Burns, R. (1987). Increasing test scores through whole-class mastery learning. In R. Burns (Ed.), *Models of instructional organization: A casebook on mastery learning and outcome-based education*. San Francisco: Far West Laboratory for Educational Research and Development.

Squires, D. A., Huitt, W. G., & Seagars, J. K. (1983). *Effective schools and classrooms: A research-based perspective*. Alexandria, VA: Association of Supervision and Curriculum Development.

Stake, R. E., & Easley, J. A. (1978). *Case studies in science education*. Washington, DC: National Science Foundation.

Steen, L. A. (1989). Quoted in *Everybody counts: A report to the nation on the future of mathematics education*. National Academy of Sciences: National Research Council, Washington, DC.

Stodolsky, S. S. (1988). *The subject matters: Classroom activity in math and social studies*. Chicago: University of Chicago Press.

U.S. Department of Education. (1991). *America 2000: An education strategy*. Washington, DC: U.S. Government Printing Office.

U.S. National Commission on Excellence in Education. (1983). *A nation at risk: The imperative for educational reform*. A report to the nation and the secretary of education. Washington, DC: Author.

Vanesky, R. L. (1991). Textbooks in school and society. In P. W. Jackson (Ed.), *Handbook of research on curriculum* (pp. 436–461). New York: Macmillan.

Webb, N. L. (1997). Determining alignment of expectations and assessments in mathematics and science education. *NISE Brief*, 1(2). Madison: National Institute for Science Education, University of Wisconsin.

Webb, N. L. (1999). Alignment of science and mathematics standards and assessments in four states (Research Monograph No. 18). Madison, WI: National Institute for Science Education and Council of Chief State School Officers.

White, J. J. (1988). Searching for substantial knowledge in social studies texts. *Theory and Research in Social Education, XVI*, 115–140.

Wiggins, G., & McTighe, J. (1998). *Understanding by design*. Alexandria, VA: Association of Supervision and Curriculum Development.

Wiley, K. B. (1977). *The status of pre-college science, mathematics, and social science education: 1955–1975*. Washington, DC: National Science Foundation.

Wishnick, K. T. (1989). *Relative effects on achievements scores of SES, gender, teacher effect and instructional alignment: A study of alignment's power in mastery learning*. Unpublished doctoral dissertation, University of San Francisco, CA.

Wong, K. K., & Loveless, T. (1991). The politics of textbook policy: Proposing a framework. In P. G. Altbach, G. P. Kelly, H. G. Petrie, & L. Weis (Eds.), *Textbooks in American society: Politics, policy, and pedagogy*. Albany: State University of New York Press.

Woodward, K. S. (Ed.). (1999). *Alignment of national and state standards: A report by the GED Testing Service*. Washington, DC: GED Testing Service.

Index

**CORWIN
PRESS**

The Corwin Press logo—a raven striding across an open book—represents the union of courage and learning. Corwin Press is committed to improving education for all learners by publishing books and other professional development resources for those serving the field of K–12 education. By providing practical, hands-on materials, Corwin Press continues to carry out the promise of its motto: **"Helping Educators Do Their Work Better."**